FAR AND AWAY

A. A. Gill was born in Edinburgh. He is the author of *A. A. Gill is Away, The Angry Island, Previous Convictions, Table Talk, Paper View, A. A. Gill is Further Away, The Golden Door, Lines in the Sand, The Best of A. A. Gill* and the highly acclaimed memoir *Pour Me*.

He was the TV and restaurant critic and regular features writer for the *Sunday Times*, columnist for *Esquire*, and contributor to *Australian Gourmet Traveller*. He died in 2016.

FAR AND AWAY

THE ESSENTIAL A. A. GILL

A. A. GILL

First published in Great Britain in 2020 by Weidenfeld & Nicolson
This paperback edition published in 2021 by Weidenfeld & Nicolson
an imprint of The Orion Publishing Group Ltd
Carmelite House, 50 Victoria Embankment
London EC4Y ODZ

An Hachette UK Company

1 3 5 7 9 10 8 6 4 2

A CIP catalogue record for this book
is available from the British Library.

ISBN (Mass Market Paperback) 978 1 4746 1738 3
ISBN (eBook) 978 1 4746 1739 0
ISBN (Audiobook) 978 1 4746 1740 6

Typeset at The Spartan Press Ltd,
Lymington, Hants

Printed and bound in Great Britain by Clays Ltd,
Elcograf S.p.A.

www.orionbooks.co.uk
www.weidenfeldandnicolson.co.uk

Contents

FURTHEST

THE WORLD ON A PLATE

Introduction by Flora Gill

As a child at school, a common question we'd ask one another was 'What do your parents do?' The dream answer was a job that could be found in a costume box: a doctor, a scientist, a policeman; a cool profession that appeared in Happy Families. While some parents fitted into this lucky category, the majority of my peers were left trying to explain occupations that had been simplified for children's ears and were now exaggerated for our friends. My mother, at the time, had a job that sounded very interesting at first and then immediately after, incredibly dull. She was a headhunter. 'Does that mean she puts animals' heads in frames?' a friend asked me. 'Sort of,' I replied. My father on the other hand had a job that sounded made up. 'He eats food, watches telly, travels, and then tells stories,' I bragged. 'He's a storyteller, but about real things.' 'I think I want to do that when I grow up,' a few of my classmates agreed.

Some of my favourite moments from childhood aren't mine at all, but the memories of memories. Stories I was told by Dad. They're moments that were passed through his filter, until only the most enticing, illuminating details were given to me, his words like wrapping paper enfolding the selected highlights. Dad could distil an event, focus your eyes on a single detail, and somehow give you a better understanding of the bigger picture than if you'd been there yourself.

For me, the telling of these stories was part of a routine. I would be dropped off by my mother and rush through Dad's front door to a hug that lifted me off the ground, my little legs dangling between his larger ones, kicking for the floor and not wanting to be put back down in equal measure. Then Dad would reveal the cargo I knew was hidden, and our back-and-forth dance would begin. 'I bought you a present,' he'd say. The item – usually the size of my forearm – would be wrapped in newspaper. I'd start the guessing. 'Is it a computer?' 'Could be,' he'd respond. 'Feels like a bicycle.' 'Maybe.' 'It's definitely a puppy!' 'How'd you guess?' And then I'd open it up and reveal a new doll (it was always a doll) from wherever Dad had visited, while he told me the tale behind it.

I'm writing this beneath the dolls now as they look down on me, filling the shelves in messy lines, huddled together like they're waiting patiently for a performance I'm not going to give. There are instances where your feelings towards an item change the way you view it. In another setting the dolls could make up the interior decoration of a serial killer's home: their glass eyes following you across the room before you get hacked to death by a man dressed as a limited-edition Barbie who uses your hair to make jumpers for his collection. But for me, the dolls are beautiful and calming, their eyes watching over me protectively like votive icons. Without counting them, there must be at least 300 from around the globe, made from a sprawling range of materials. There are the beaded cone-shaped women from Ethiopia, the converted water bottles from a refugee camp in Syria, the singing china doll from St Tropez, the wooden shadow puppet from Indonesia, the voodoo doll from Haiti. Each one is a story, a memory Dad shared.

Some of them I can look at and remember the details recounted as he passed me the souvenir, but some of them I've lost. Dad and I always spoke about writing their homes on their bases but we never did; he too had begun to forget the origin of each one. But luckily the stories they represent aren't lost, just separated. Instead they're captured in his writing and the events he shared with his readers.

One of the first stories in this collection is about Hyde Park. After Dad wrote the article, he went back with his photographer to get pictures to illustrate the piece. Coincidentally I was also in the park that day with some of my teenage friends. I remember seeing Dad across a patch of green next to the Serpentine Gallery, but he was too far away for me to be certain it was him. I squinted, making out his long tweed coat and the flat cap casting a shadow on his face, but I couldn't be sure. I wanted to check, to shout out his name, and maybe introduce him to my friends. But I decided against it, reaching the conclusion that yelling 'Daddy' across the park to a man that turns out to be a complete stranger would be like calling your teacher Mum, too embarrassing to risk. So I kept walking. And the moment was gone.

For some reason this image gets stuck in my head a lot these days. The picture of Dad, just too far away to see. The moment I could have called to him but chose not to. At first I thought maybe it was my brain's metaphor for how I can still feel him, even see him in a distant way, but never talk to him or get any closer. But I think in reality I just miss him so much, my mind is scolding me for the lost opportunities, the times I ignored his call, or didn't take up an offer for dinner, and squandered a potential new memory.

When I left junior school and grew up, I did as adults tend to do, and started using the correct terminology, referring to my father as a journalist and a critic. But now as I reflect on it, I think my initial description might suit him better.

Dad only wrote first-person journalism, so there's always a bit of him left in everything he writes. He never pretends to be impartial or unbiased, instead it all passed through his filter and feelings; he selected the best bits for the reader in the same way he did for his daughter. And just like in the park, while you can't talk to him or get his attention, you can see him in the distance.

So I hope you enjoy this collection and allow me to feel proud of my dad, that man with a job you can't find in a pack of cards, but who tells stories of real life.

May 2020

NEAR

Highlands

If you want an invitation for the smartest party in Europe, then you'd better hurry. In fact, you'll probably have to go on standby. Most of the tickets went months ago, although they were on the expensive side – £240. Dress is informal tweed for the men and loden for the women, with a discreet touch of muted McHarvey Nicks tartan. The venue is Dalcross.

It's not a house, hotel or hall, it's an airport. It's Inverness's airport. At 6.30 p.m. every Sunday from now until the beginning of October, the departures lounge is the place to have a dram, talk knowledgeably about the weather, lie about the fish and say 'slange-var' a lot.

Every August, for a few short weeks, Scotland becomes a foreign country. It's now that the English start talking of 'going north' and 'crossing the border'. Men in southern offices stare out at the miles of glass and concrete and see purple hills and foaming brown rivers; they dream of wet socks and oatcakes. They slip off to Hardy's or Purdey's in their lunch hours to get a last bit of unnecessary kit and tell the oily assistant that 'their heart's in the Highlands'. Their wives swing down to the Fulham Road looking for a hat with a feather, and tell the daily to clear out the freezer in readiness for the monster salmon and the plump grouse.

Scotland's brief annual independence is not gained bloodlessly. Many, many shots will be fired. There will be carnage. Next Thursday, the grouse will be driven in a Culloden-like charge over Sassenach guns (the grouse are finding it difficult to muster a decent clan this season, but then it's always a bad year for grouse). The stags, having shed the velvet from their antlers, will succumb to the sniper's shot in Glen Coe. And the salmon will be hunted by the English like elusive Bonny Prince Charlie, and with about as much success. August is when Englishmen go north to be men, and women go north to watch them.

Why the English make this annual migration back to the braes and glens is as much a mystery as why the salmon do, or the grouse don't. The obvious reason is fresh air and fun in a calendar-picture landscape. But Scotland is just as beautiful for the other eleven months, the air isn't in short supply and there are things to do that are just as entertaining as traipsing up and down a hundred yards of river watching the dead sheep float by. A week's fishing, for a single rod on a moderately good salmon river, costs about as much as a fortnight's package holiday for a family of four. A couple of days at the grouse is about the same. And that's before you take into account the rented cottage, the air fare, the kit and the tips. The truth is that most of the spawning tourists won't catch a single fish and will miss six times as many grouse as they hit.

There is a David Attenborough-ish theory that this annual pilgrimage is in fact a complex social migration, that men who are powerful in cities long to meet working men who aren't rude, threatening or ripping them off. The successful man, in other words, needs to be reassured that somewhere there is still a Sunday-evening-telly-Edwardian-style social order into which he comfortably fits. He has a desire, it is thought, to savour the 'salt of the earth'. Enter the Scots ghillie, stalker and gamekeeper.

Angus Cameron is a stalker on the ravishing Strathconon estate in Ross-shire. 'My job is as much public relations as anything else now,' he says. 'I'm on the hill with the bloke for perhaps twelve hours; I've got to keep him happy and entertained. Actually, I'm looking out for two beasts on the hill: the stag and the Englishman.' (It should be noted that in Scotland, beast isn't necessarily a term of abuse.)

The stalker is in an odd position in relation to his client: on the one hand, he is a servant paid to provide a service; on the other, he is like the captain of a ship. He's the boss on the hill and his word is law: if he says crawl through sheep shit, you crawl; if he says lie in this freezing burn, you imitate a rock. He says when you fire and what you fire at. Stalkers are almost invariably good-natured and easy-going. Fishing ghillies, on the other hand, are notoriously taciturn and bad-tempered. As one ghillie explained: 'It's all right for the stalkers, they just have to nanny their chap and watch him miss the once. I have to stand behind a tosser and watch him make a mess of it all day.' Both stalkers and ghillies have inexhaustible patience and a mind-numbing capacity to talk about rain.

Hamish Ferguson, a keeper on the Glen Ogle estate in Angus, and a third-generation stalker, says that the biggest problem these days is fitness. The soft English just don't have the stamina to walk for twelve hours a day in knee-high heather and sucking peat bog, so much more of the legwork has to be done by off-track vehicles. The quality of shooting on the grouse moor has got worse, but telescopic sights have meant that stalking game is much easier, with fewer wounded beasts.

The fishing in Scotland, of course, has always been infuriatingly hit and miss. Nobody really knows what makes a salmon go for a fly or why it particularly favours a fly cast by a woman. There are a lot of unsavoury and unprintable theories voiced in baritone brogues about that in dripping fishing huts, when the flask makes its second circuit. It's this sort of chat, the 'crack' as they call it, in gun rooms and fishing huts, that the English gent really comes to the glens for. They just love sitting around watching their socks steam in front of the peat fire, nursing a dram, smoothing out the discomfort of the day into anecdotes that will bore Fulham dinner parties all winter.

Scotland is essentially a private country. Its very lively social life goes on behind unlocked doors, down rhododendron-lined drives and up Third World tracks. The uninvited tourist often complains that only malnutrition would induce him to dine in the country's few restaurants. There are hardly any cinemas, fewer shopping malls and the television reception is crap. The Scots are both historically and temperamentally clannish. This, more than anything, is what makes August in Scotland such an exclusive venue for the English. All you need to holiday in Mustique or Verbier is money, but, for Scotland, you've got to know someone.

For resident Scots and 'white settlers' with estates, the first calls trying to wangle an invitation to fish or shoot start early in the year. These springtime invite-mes aren't Englishmen wanting free sport, they're calling to beg that they might be allowed to pay through the nose for a damp cottage and a yard or two of uninhabited river. What's in it for the women? Some of them fish (usually better than the men), a few stalk, but the atmosphere is so vigorously masculine that most stay indoors with the chalet girls peeling endless roots. Not much of a holiday, you'd think. But Scotland is never short of English women. For a start, there's hunting and there's hunting. Scotland is simply stuffed with devastatingly good-looking younger sons wasting their excess testosterone on zapping the wildlife. There may be no salmon and hardly any grouse, but there's no shortage of McChippendales and there are plenty of hostesses giving boozy dinner parties and dances where it's open season on men. The pheromone count in the Highlands reaches orgasmic proportions in August: it's an unsubtle mixture of cold houses, base hunting instinct and whisky. One young wife who bagged her husband in the Highlands said: 'I have more sex in this fortnight than in all the rest of the year. I know immediately when he's shot a stag: I get pulled into the bath. It may not be flattering, but who's complaining? Both our children were conceived in August. I just wish we had a moor in Parsons Green.' Another young wife chips in shrilly: 'I've lost two cooks to local lads in the past. This year we're employing a local woman.' The locals are amused and take full advantage of the English rutting season. Sometimes at night you don't know if it's the stags or the merchant bankers roaring away in the heather.

Dressing up is taken very seriously in Scotland. Men with good legs and men with appalling legs need no excuse to leap into frocks. The amount of chat about tweed and boots and hats that goes on in the hills would make a *Vogue* fashion stylist blush. Comely women who might feel self-conscious about strutting their stuff, or even eating breakfast, if they have to wear bikinis on holiday can look as appetising as oatcakes and honey in cashmere and sheepskin. The dressing-up gets completely out of hand at the county balls. Daggers, powder horns, eagles, feathers, knives and forks, silver buttons, furry animals, horse hair, goat skin, brooches the size of soup plates and yards and yards of tartan are worn, and that's just by the men. The balls emphasise what a small club smart Scotland really is: you have to be a laird of the county to buy tickets and most people take parties. If you're English, you have to know someone well. The dress code is strict: dresses that touch the floor for women. If you're daft enough to try and get away with an inch of ankle, you're presented with a floor-length bri-nylon shift. No high heels. Men must wear Highland dress or white tie. The behaviour code is strict as well – all violent hooliganism must be restricted to the dance floor. Reeling isn't dancing as southerners understand it, it's contact sport akin to musical sumo wrestling. Bones are broken, eyes are blacked, and more than one English lass has found that the chic frock she bought to show off her assets isn't up to containing them during the 'Duke of Perth'.

There is every chance that your fellow guests, Fulham-bound and meeting for cocktails before the return flight at Dalcross, will be exhausted, bruised, hoarse, empty-handed and probably pregnant. They will, however, have some wonderfully good gossip.

Left behind them on the estate, Hamish is about to go back out to the moor to count his grouse. His wife, Fiona, who cooks Scots clootie dumpling and cullen skink for stalking parties, is preparing a nice little Mosimann number, aubergine stuffed with polenta, for Hamish's tea. This year, when the stags are finished, they're going away for a rare holiday to the Bronx. 'Well,' says Fiona, 'Hamish will need a break after the stalking.'

August 1993

Hyde Park

Like all great journeys, trysts, campaigns and fresh starts, Hyde Park begins at dawn. It's the longest weekend of the year, and the grand and imperious gates are open to let in the sullen grey morning. Hyde is the most famous park in the world. Gethsemane may be older, the Bois de Boulogne bigger, but Hyde is the great green daddy; the space that fathered an international patchwork of geomorphic spaces. Wherever men design new cities for free and happy citizens with a sense of aspiration, leisure and culture, they plant the seed of Hyde Park. It is more than just an area without buildings, more than a bit of random green belt caught inside the intestines of concrete like trapped wind. Parks are a counterpoint to tarmac and brick, the obverse of the one-way, mind-your-step, roaringly angular, analytically civic. They are places that remind the city of what it really is, and what it actually isn't, what it grew out of, and what it aspires to be.

Hyde Park has grown to look like an imaginary land from a children's book: it has open plains and secret dells, wild places, ruins and follies, fountains and palaces. It is Britain's biggest tourist attraction – it has 5 million visitors a year. There are 600 organised events here, from political rallies and the Proms to the Tour de France and Sunday brass bands. And there are thousands and thousands of disorganised events: games of football and rounders, office parties, lonely hearts get-togethers and keep-fit runs.

I've been coming to the park since I was a child. I've lost boats, failed to fly kites, played cricket, lain in the long grass with girlfriends, walked dogs, pushed prams, taught my children to ride bikes here. If I claim to belong to any piece of country, if I feel a bond with any place, then it's with this park. This is its story for a day.

At 6.15 a.m. the Household Cavalry are up and at 'em, ready to take the horses for the watering parade. There used to be a Georgian barracks here; its classical pediments are still stuck like a bandage above the ceremonial goods entrance. Knightsbridge Barracks is probably the ugliest building in London, with the most beautiful view. It was designed by Sir Basil Spence, who managed to construct vertical bomb damage out of horizontal bomb damage. The barracks, with its timid brutalism, is the one building visible from everywhere in the park.

The troopers stamp around with that winningly martial mixture of arresting, boyish teasing and determined, robotic purpose. There is an end-of-term, exhausted euphoria about them: they've just finished their ceremonial year. The horses are being sent to Norfolk and Windsor for holidays; the relentless clip-clop, polishing and waddling is slowing down. Cavalry walk with extreme and hilarious difficulty in their great delta-winged boots, into which giggling foreign girls occasionally slip their phone numbers. If you've ever wondered what happens to the tons of horse shit produced daily by the Queen's mounted guard, it's shovelled into a clever dumb-waiter chute affair and taken away by lorry. Where to? I ask the captain in charge. He looks challenged. 'Just away.'

The guard at the goods entrance steps into the carriageway, his assault rifle at the high port: it's the best way to stop traffic. And the troop walk out, their hooves sounding brittle and beautiful in the damp early morning. We step lightly up the eastern march of the park. The great avenue of London planes flutter and syncopate, camouflaging the misty green where early-morning t'ai chi and Pilates exercises make strange hieroglyphs of bodies in the middle distance, looking like figures lost from medieval frescoes of purgatory.

If you look carefully from Park Lane, you can see the remains of the earthworks that were the Parliamentary defence of London from Royalist attack in the Civil War. This was the very edge of the city in the seventeenth century.

A hundred yards out from the barracks, the officer bellows like a man coming round from anaesthetic, and the troop smartly turn eyes left. They're passing the small box-hedged memorial to men killed by an Irish republican car bomb. They do this every time. It seems to commemorate not just the dead, but a time of quainter, home-made terrorism. Ceremony and hindsight can make anything heritage.

West Londoners occasionally wake in the early hours imagining they can hear horses' hooves, like an echo of Kipling in the dawn. Mostly they turn over and go back to sleep to dream of centaurs. Where the cavalry go is up to the officer in charge. Today's it's Notting Hill Gate. Through the northern boundary of the park they trot into a little side street, and there, in a cul-de-sac, the men dismount. The officer borrows a tenner from his sergeant and takes orders. Five coffees, three teas. He marches to a workmen's café, where the Middle Eastern owners give him a discount and beam at his boots and buttons. The troop stand around holding the horses, sucking back-handed cigarettes, and get on with the unending rounds of military teasing. The officer serves them coffee. It's just like being behind the bike sheds at school with the cool gang. Above us, a man opens his curtains and rubs his eyes and closes them again. 'Once, we were parked up,' the captain says, 'Robert De Niro came past. Didn't bat an eye. He was in London, so of course the Household Cavalry were taking tea in a mews in South Kensington at 6.30 in the morning.'

At 7.30 a.m. the Serpentine Swimming Club meets. It's not a nice morning for a dip. Even the geese have all been blown into a dirty corner by the squally weather. The Serpentine swimmers are one of those peculiar English associations that are invariably prefaced with 'intrepid' and 'eccentric'. They've been meeting here since 1864. They're a good-natured bunch who tip up in clothes bought for frugality and longevity rather than style. They clutch towels that are as thin and balding as are a good many of them.

Standing on the edge of the lake in distressingly skimpy Speedos and rubber caps, they look like shelled turtles. I can't help casting their biopic as an Ealing Comedy. They range from MPs and retired architects to hotel doormen and taxi drivers. Many of them have swum the Channel. They swim here every week, including Christmas Day. There's no mucking about, no splashing or dive bombs or lilos: today they're racing. A chap with a barrel chest, a clipboard and a stopwatch starts them in a relaxed, staggered handicap. 'Dave, where are you? Dave, get in.' They dive into the turgid, scummy water and flap their arms with a wiry purpose. After a few minutes the water looks like a war film after the torpedo. The swimming club has a small unisex changing room full of old kit and grinning photographs. It's crowded with the raucous and morbidly pale, knobbly bodies, sawing at themselves with gritty towels.

Outside, there's a little ceremony. The winner is a man called Squirrel. There's a good-natured cheer; he gets a little silver cup. A lady, presumably Mrs Squirrel, mocks him fondly. 'Happy Birthday!' someone shouts. Squirrel is eighty-four today. Swimmers depart to breakfast radiating mad, rude immortality.

The Serpentine was made by damming the Westbourne, one of the lost rivers of London. It was built by Queen Caroline. They say that, but I doubt if she lifted a finger. It is an ornamental water feature that needed an Act of Parliament and a titanic amount of money, but it set off a trend for grand, natural-looking lakes in grand, natural-looking landscapes all over the parks of England. The other stretch of water here is the Round Pond, where model-yacht clubs sail their grounds for divorce. The geese that have always been here have recently been joined by puffy, hissy flotillas of swans. There used to be only one swan, a psychotic old male who kept the others away. Now he's gone, all the riff-raff have moved in.

For most Londoners, Hyde Park and Kensington Gardens are synonymous. They flow one into the other, connected by the Serpentine. Kensington Gardens was the private backyard of Kensington Palace, and slowly grew into public use. George II was once mugged here. He asked the robber to let him keep the seal from his fob watch. The man agreed on the condition that the king promised not to tell anyone. He promised, and he never did. Rotten Row, the sandy bridle path along the south of the park, is a mispronunciation of Route du Roi. It was the other King's Road from the Palace of Kensington to the Palace of Westminster. It was the first London street to get lighting, to make sure the monarch didn't get robbed again.

Hyde Park was taken by Henry VIII from Westminster Abbey; he used it as a hunting ground. It became common ground on the edge of London, a meeting place for mobs, the illicit and the sexually commercial. The two parks have quite different atmospheres. Kensington Gardens is polite and parochial, a dog-walking, pram-pushing park. Hyde Park is more public and political; it hosted the great reforming marches, student rallies and save-the-world pop concerts. Here was the Reformers' Tree, a post office for political reform, and Tyburn. The licence given to those due to be hanged to shout a final plea, prayer or curse to the public became Speakers' Corner. Every Sunday, comfortingly like every other Sunday, the diktat of stern religion, extreme unelectable politics and bizarre dietary advice is shouted out in single-issue raps. The pre-Berlin Wall communists and pre-Darwin Christians offer a sort of puppet show of free speech – a mime with volume. The audience is mostly amused tourists. For all the blood and broken necks that bought it, you sense that this freedom of speech is not the cornerstone of a democracy. The foundation, the load-bearing beam of a free society, is not shouting: it's being able to make people listen.

In the centre of the park is a police station with an old-fashioned blue light and a red pillar box. The royal parks stand apart from the boroughs and districts that they float in: they have their own laws and customs, and the man in charge of policing them is Superintendent Simon Ovens, whose office is papered with positively enforcing aphorisms. His favourite is 'The main thing is to make the main thing the main thing.' 'I must say that a dozen times a day,' he tells me. He's very proud of the park and the policing of it. There's always a response car circling; they can be at any point within three or four minutes. There are officers on foot, on bikes and on horses. There are, on average, two reported incidents a day; there is also an astonishing 44 per cent clear-up rate, which makes the park not just the safest area of comparable size in the city but, by miles, the most efficiently and effectively policed.

What I'm surprised by is that this isn't done with zero-tolerance, obsessive zealotry. 'Look,' says the superintendent, 'with all the bylaws, it's probably technically illegal to do everything in the park, but our job is to see that the people who use it get to do what they want without interfering with the rights of others to do what they want. We have a lot of conflicting interests here, lots of different cultures.

Middle Eastern families bring picnics; they don't necessarily get on with the dog-walkers [there are a million visits by accompanied dogs a year], and the most complaints are about cyclists.' Football games have to go on beside hen parties and capoeira classes; women in burkas have to put up with girls lying in their bras and pants. But there is something about the park that seems to make people decent citizens. 'I have events with sixty thousand people here. We have to get them in and out safely with a handful of officers. If that was a football crowd, I'd need at least two thousand policemen.'

The park is innately a well-mannered, liberal, live-and-let-live place. What about sex? He leans back in his chair. 'Well, there's a lot of it. That's traditionally what a lot of people come to parks for. You've been down to the Rose Garden? It's a gay meeting place and has been for years, it's near the barracks. It's not my officers' job to go and poke around bushes to catch people doing what they're doing. We've all moved on from that. If they want to discreetly go behind an arbour, no one's going to come looking for them. If, on the other hand, you're going to have sex on a bench in front of passers-by, then you'll get nicked. But gay men are a vulnerable group – robbery, homophobic violence and blackmail. A lot of them are married, so this is clandestine and they have a right to protection. So we have a presence in the garden. Officers in high-vis jackets with torches patrol the central walk. We're there to protect gay men. They have a right to the park like everyone else.'

There is a lot of sex in the park. It is in the nature of nature to flirt and ogle and for kids to practise with their new hormones. You notice that the couples are either very young or surprisingly middle-aged. There are also a lot of mixed-race couples and a lot of discreet Asians holding hands. All the people who would get a room if they could but can't. The park exists as a great, damp, free bedsit for those who need a place to get squirmy and intense. Couples look like mating frogs washed up on riverbanks, clothes hoicked and snagged on cruxes, fingers inching the attrition of ardour across buckles and buttons and bra clasps, suckered in interminable, thoughtless, lock-jawed snogs. And on benches, the office romances and infidelities, the coy shared sandwiches, fumbled intense kisses, the stroking and clasping and the gazing.

On any summer Friday, the park pullulates with couples dry-humping before going back on commuter trains to their rightful owners in the suburbs. The Rose Garden, which at night slips into the gay rut, is by day at its most beautiful, a frothing flower garden. Tourists sit on the benches, tramps compete with the scent; families stand in front of the perilous piles of petals and grin to have their pictures taken, to be stuck in albums around the globe.

All the formal gardening in Hyde Park is meticulous, endlessly captivating. Hidden in the middle of the park is a compost heap the size of the Dome. Along with the army of gardeners, there are arboriculturists and wildlife wardens looking after sixty-two genera of trees, 130 species and 120 subspecies. On the Hyde Park side, the prominent species is the London plane. They don't just give off oxygen; their flaky bark absorbs pollution. Generations of children have known that their round seeds are fairy eggs. In Kensington Gardens, the dominant species are the chestnuts. There are walks of mulberries; a family of Cypriot women collect unripe almonds on Lovers' Walk in Hyde Park. Through the high summer, there is a fugitive, sweet smell that's like moving through the rooms of an invisible bordello – it's the flowering limes. The park has large areas of set-aside heather, wild barley and meadow grass. One woman regularly leaves death threats for the park manager on his answering machine because the seeds get caught in her dog's paws.

Over the years, Hyde Park has accumulated knick-knacks, memorials, statues, ornaments, like granny furniture. They grow to be abided and occasionally loved. There's a Wellington memorial on the south-eastern corner made out of boiled cannon, paid for by the women of Britain. It is a colossal rendering of Achilles in his rage; he's classically naked. He was the first naked man to stand in London. The mothers and the nannies of Kensington were outraged, so a fig leaf was slapped on him like a prurient parking ticket. They might have been more outraged if they had realised his fury was due to the death of his boyfriend. Now he glares in his leafy thong at Byron over in Park Lane.

There is a stone monolith to the Holocaust in Hyde Park, and a lump of granite given by the grateful people of Norway. There is the original statue that inspired part of the Rhodes Memorial in Cape Town, and the sad obelisk to Speke, who killed himself after discovering the source of the Nile. And there's Albert in his derided Gothic Revival space rocket, now gleaming gold, surrounded by more pulchritudinous allegory than even a serious German could bear. The corner groups represent the four continents; the houri from Asia on the elephant has the best pair of stone tits in London. Outside Kensington Palace, there's William of Orange – a gift from the Kaiser – and a statue of Queen Victoria, who was born and lived here in relative regal poverty. It's sculpted by her daughter. And there's a little terrier with his bottom in the air standing in a drinking fountain, in memory of Esmé Percy, an actor who died in 1957 and instantly became so utterly forgotten he might never have existed. As far as I can discover, he specialised in walk-on aristocrats and once played Ali, the grand eunuch, in the 1935 film *Abdul the Damned*.

Most magically and memorably, there is Peter Pan, the Frampton statue that is one of the most famous monuments in the world. It is certainly the most poignantly beloved and beautiful in London. It appeared overnight and was commissioned and paid for by Barrie, the author who invented him. He met the Llewelyn Davies children and their mother and their dog in the gardens and they were the inspiration for the greatest fairy story ever written. But Kensington Gardens isn't just the place where infants lost by forgetful nannies get taken to Neverland: it *is* Neverland. Every scene in the book belongs here. The weeping beech that Peter sleeps in is still living in the flower walk. The statue is on the shore of the Long Water, where he lands after his voyage in the birds' nest. Peter stands on a pixelated plinth of fairies and animals. He's hidden in an alcove of foliage, so you come upon him all of a sudden.

I sat for an hour and watched the parents bring their children, and the odd thing is that although the kids find the little mice and the rabbits in the sculpture with delight, it is the grown-ups who really get knocked back by Peter. Some to tears. This man-child playing his pipes, blowing a tune whose pitch is too high and fragile for us to hear any more, forcefully reminds them that Barrie's story is not about children but grown-ups. At the heart of the adventure, the romance and the swashbuckling is the saddest truth ever told, that we all grow up and that what we leave behind is more precious than what we gain.

And then there's Princess Diana. How naturally one follows the other. The votive cult of the dead Diana has added a million visitors to Kensington Gardens. Her pilgrimage path is marked out by the ugly goitres in the road like maudlin speed bumps. I've wandered the park for years and I still have no idea where they lead. There is the memorial children's playground with its pirate ship, a ghostly ironic nod to Pan, and there is the great, grudging, temper-filled fountain that was the lavatorial focus for so much regurgitated bile and sour resentment when it opened. Actually now, when nobody's watching, it looks rather chic and elegantly pale. The water rolls and tumbles in a pleasing way and lots of people come to dabble and just stare into the distance in a bashful, shy, enigmatic way.

I stood on the bank and the chap in a bit of a uniform came up and said: 'You can't stand on the memorial. You can sit on it, lie on it or wade in it, but you can't stand on it.' How do I get to sit on it without standing on it first? 'I don't know,' he said, and shook his head. This was the great central mystery of his calling which wasn't primarily as a vestal guard but as a contract cleaner. He works for the private company that maintains the princess's water-work. What's it like? 'Hard work, man. She needs scrubbing out every day. She grows mould and slippery.' You can see her being cleaned in the early morning as the guards go for their coffee trot.

The fountain has its own deep aquifer and uses hundreds of gallons of water that are then pumped into the Serpentine. At its conception and construction, the horizontal Diana fountain seemed like a particularly vacuous committee choice. But now, ten years later, it looks slyly appropriate, elegant, shallow and exceedingly high-maintenance, with a deep colonic most mornings, but despite everything rather winning.

Hyde Park is a polyglot pan-national place. All the tongues and customs of the world come here. A park is an internationally understandable place – streets, shops and coffee bars may seem intimidating to foreigners, but everyone speaks park. In the lunch hour, men unroll their mats and make their prayers facing Whiteleys, next to couples sharing bacon sandwiches. Filipino maids lift their faces to the sun and little gangs of Polish lads go about their laddie business. A big Ghanaian skates backwards, legs crossing and uncrossing down the boulevard, arms flailing like a man falling from a high window.

There is always a sadness to the park, an elusive atmosphere of melancholy punctuated by the squeals of pre-school games lessons and toddlers in hard hats slumped on fat, slow ponies, the parties of butt-cheeky girls with bottles of Pinot Grigio. The park is where people come to bring their sadness and loneliness. For every pair of young lovers, there is a broken heart on a solitary bench; hunched men with furrowed brows take clouds of depression to walk the aimless paths as medication. The mad and maddened come to mutter and shout at the wood nymphs and zephyrs. In the wild grass in the north of the park, a lost vicar with a suitcase and a spaniel stops and asks if we can remind him of the redeeming truth of existence. He's quietly desperate, politely overwhelmed by unhappiness.

Hyde Park, without instruction, direction, government or judiciary, has grown to be a model of a just and benign society, where people behave well not because they're made to, but because they can. Where crowds come and depart freely and in good temper. On a summer Saturday there may be 20,000 people here who will let each other be with grace and politeness. Every race, religion, age and class can play or read or eat in an egalitarian beauty and safety. You can do things here that you would never dare do anywhere else; it relieves you of embarrassment or shame; it is a small, liberal proof that if you trust people, they behave with manners and care. The park is the vindication of a quiet, levelling English anarchy. The streams of rush-hour cyclists race each other westwards like flocks of Day-Glo geese; the park grows quiet; the sun balances on top of St Mary Abbots's steeple on the southern carriageway; seven herons and a fox wait in a flowerbed to be fed by a deranged lady with an unspeakable sack.

Kensington Gardens closes at dusk. Hyde Park stays open till midnight. The darkness creeps through the trees, which become home to foxes, moths and pipistrelle bats and central European builders looking for a place to sleep. The park is lit by Victorian gaslights; they cast an ethereal pale glow, and through the avenues of planes the harsh neons of the red and white city streets glint and hiss, but here in the pearly-blue quietness the park grows bewitchingly enchanted, a hint of a parallel utopia, that other Eden.

August 2007

The Guinea Pig Club

'Have you ever met a Guinea Pig before?' asked a capable lady, as she put her hand on the door. 'No? Well, nothing to worry about. They're extremely nice, very friendly. I'm sure they'll put you completely at your ease. It's just the hands. When you shake hands . . . well, they haven't got any. Haven't got many fingers. Just be prepared. Some people find it unnerving.'

The elliptical wing of a Spitfire was unsuitable for a fuel tank, so they placed them in front of the cockpit behind the Merlin engine. The Hurricane's wings did contain fuel tanks, and they were protected, except where the root of the wing met the fuselage, under the pilot. If the tank was hit, burning aircraft fuel would be drawn into the cockpit. Within two or three seconds the plane would be virtually unflyable, the flames so intense, blown with such Bunsen force that they were invisible. Amid the struggle for control of their mortally injured machines, with the anxiety, the adrenaline, the screaming engine and the rising fear, the first moment the pilot would realise that his cockpit had become a kiln was when the dashboard melted in front of his eyes and the skin hung from his fingers like rags. Every metal object became a searing grill; bailing out a terrifying struggle to escape a medieval witch's hell. If the windscreen slid back, great gusts of flame would be flung into the pilot's face.

In 1940, there were 400 burns injuries to RAF pilots; thirty of them were fighter pilots from the Battle of Britain, which, in August, was at its pivotal, precipitous moment of indecision. The loss of aircraft was critical, the loss of pilots calamitous. The gossamer-fine net of defence of the nation was rent, the heartbreakingly young and inexperienced fliers were spun ragged by the free-ranging Luftwaffe. The engineered brilliance of the Spitfire and the Hurricane went some way to mitigate their lack of training and inexperience, but the

Hurricane in particular was prone to become a flaming meteorite. It took a great deal of courage simply to get into one. Even if the pilot survived being shot down, the chances of him flying again within months, even if his burns were minor, were slim.

Before the war, each of the services was given its own hospital. The RAF's was a small suburban one, the Queen Victoria Hospital in East Grinstead. The experience of the Great War implied that there would be few flying casualties compared to the other services. In East Grinstead, the burnt fliers found a surgeon called Archibald McIndoe. Wars are, by their tumultuous nature, times when men meet their defining moments. The point when they rise to a brilliance that in other times might have passed them by in the peaceful night. Nobody met a more admirable destiny than McIndoe did at East Grinstead.

The capable lady opened the door. The room hummed with the familiar noise of dinner. Round tables full of people in black tie and women wearing occasion hairdos. It might have been the annual general meeting of a golf club or a Rotarian dinner dance. The only thing that told that this wasn't a work do or garden society was the handful of RAF cadets, in their unimpeachably ugly uniforms and huge boots, selling raffle tickets. That and the discreet brooches bearing a small, fat, winged rodent in a flying helmet worn by many of the old men – the Guinea Pigs, as they call themselves, because they were all experiments. Nobody had ever treated burn injuries like theirs. Nobody knew where to start. There are no German Guinea Pigs because German airmen simply died of their burns. Their medicine was three decades behind ours, and they didn't know that what initially kills is dehydration. The body sends all its liquids to the burn sites, which is why they weep. They cry, and then you die.

This will be the last time the Guinea Pigs all get together. This is their final annual dinner. It is the end of a long story. After this, they'll wind up the club, have a service of remembrance with Prince Philip, and decide what to do with the current account. Now they are all in their eighties and nineties, and they'll go their own quiet ways after a lifetime of mutual support and friendship. The club has been their pride and protection, linking each of them, like the traces of a parachute, back to those desperate separate moments of destiny that threw them out to be flaming torches above the South Downs, or bright pinpricks in the explosive dark over Europe.

McIndoe was a New Zealander who had a genius for surgery. As a young man he studied surgery at the Mayo Clinic in America, and was offered a full-time position there, but he had the promise of a job in London with an eminent surgeon. When he got here, it fell through. He had an uncle who treated disfigured soldiers from the Great War, and so worked with him as a stopgap, ending up a young man with untested but extraordinary talent at a little provincial hospital, waiting for something to turn up and test him. The mighty Merlin engine and the war obliged. Nobody expected burns. The injuries of the First World War had mainly been the blast; the great, thudding blows of high explosives, the ripping iron that squashed and shattered. The treatment was little more than fleshy engineering and camouflaging prosthetics.

Since the inception of military flying, burning has always been a particular private horror of the airmen. They tend to get burnt in particular places, the exposed skin of the hands, face and neck, legs above the flying boots, and groins. Eyelids seared off, lips and noses burnt like crackling, the dreadful death of being cooked as you fall thousands of feet to the welcome oblivion of earth. Pilots have been known to fling themselves from cockpits without parachutes, preferring the silence of the wind and the unfelt impact. Being burnt alive is a horror that could debilitate aircrews, particularly in bombers, where the casualties equalled those of officers in the First World War. During the height of the bombing campaign, there was about a one in four chance of finishing your thirty tours. Would you leave the house for those odds? But you have a house because young men did. The death that waited for them was rarely quick or painless. Bomber crews had medical kits that contained tubes of cream for burns and lots of morphine. Having morphine on board was as much for the morale of the rest of the crew as for the burn victim.

McIndoe invented the modern scale of plastic surgery and reconstructive facial work. He gave young men back their eyelids and their noses, carefully grafted and replaced their faces, mended their fractured jigsaw skulls, and covered the stumps of their hands over sometimes dozens of operations – all the time working from the experience of one operation to the next. He developed the extraordinary pedicle graft – a trunk of skin that was attached from an undamaged part of the body to the injured part, such as the nose, to give the graft a healthy blood supply so that new skin could grow. He performed, if not miracles, then things that had never been done before. But he also saw that surgery was only half of it. He had to pull the young men back from the depression, self-pity and despair of nihilism. Apart from the appalling and constant pain, these young men had to look at themselves in mirrors and see all their youth melted into horror-story drawings. And they were fantastically young. It's always difficult to remember how desperately unprepared they must have been. Look at the nervous confidence, the faux-arrogant faces on *University Challenge*, and then imagine thousands of them, with fuzzy, soft moustaches and awkward pipes, and then think of taking a blowtorch to their faces and futures. McIndoe understood that the battle was to give them back hope and confidence, when the RAF thought the battle was to get them back into Lancasters. He was relentless in character-building, going to extraordinary lengths to build a sense of *esprit de corps* among the young patients, joshing and encouraging them. He employed only the best nurses, most of whom were beautiful. Sex and seduction became a large part of the recuperation at East Grinstead. Someone said, pointedly, that you could barely open a cupboard in the hospital without an airman covered in bandages and a nurse covered in very little tumbling out.

McIndoe wrote thousands of letters to fight for his patients' right to a decent life. He fought the War Office and the RAF, and, later, employers. The whole of East Grinstead became part of their reintroduction to the world. Burnt men would be taken out to pubs and shops and for walks. Nobody stared. Nobody gasped or whispered behind their backs. Many of the Guinea Pigs made their homes here, and many married their nurses. Then, after the war, McIndoe fought to give them civilian jobs. One man went to work as an engineer. 'I kept my hands in my pockets at the interview,' he said. 'I'd been there three weeks before they realised I didn't have any fingers above my second knuckle.' Of all the young men McIndoe treated, not one committed suicide.

In the ballroom I looked round the table, trying to pick out the Guinea Pigs. It's difficult – old men get old faces. But here there's a truncated ear or a taut eye. The smooth, papery skin of a burns graft looks rather becoming when it's aged. They don't look horrifying or bizarre. Each has a comfortable appearance, a sense of faces that have been lived in with a knowing ease. And because of their flying helmets, most of them kept their hair follicles, and have incredible amounts of thick hair. Even before you know who they are and why they're here, there is an aura of beauty about them. That's not wishful romance or sentimental pity, it's the simple truth. They have a look that is winning and enviable; a singular, handsome directness. And, astonishingly, they all look decades younger than their real age, as if in their final furlong God has at last given them back that portion of their youth that was stolen from them by the flames.

After the horrible hotel catering and the prosaic announcements and thanks, they mill about with the banter of men who have known each other a long time. They talk easily about the hospital and their treatments, about McIndoe and the nurses, about the war and about flying. Their stories are polished smooth with modesty, understatement and repetition. The crooked smiles and little shrugs hide crypts of pain and valour. It is as if they have made a pact to tell their lives as unremarkably as possible: 'I worked for the Electricity Board.' 'Then we moved to Bolton.' 'I was shot down over the Ruhr.' 'I watched my hand melt.' What is ultimately most moving and most valiant about all of them is this blissful ordinariness. Having been given new faces and a new start against the odds, having looked once, briefly, into the burning light of oblivion, they have made a precious, glittering ordinariness of the gift of life. They got jobs, they got married, had families and caravans. Their daughters married, their sons were a worry, they have grandchildren, they retired to gardens and charity work. They keep in touch, they look out for each other. The great victory of these men is that, with their broken hands and fractured heads and glass eyes, they fashioned for themselves the most precious, elegant object in a free society – a quiet life of small joys.

A nice man who'd crash-landed his Spitfire and lost both his legs and his face, and was so badly burnt that the man who pulled him from the cockpit got the bravery medal, who later started a limbless servicemen's charity and is now in his eighties but doesn't look a year over sixty, and whose children, it turned out, were at school with me, asked if I'd write something for him. Something about the boys who are coming back wounded from Afghanistan and Iraq. 'They have the most terrible injuries – things we would never have survived. But they don't have what we had. They don't have each other, and a dedicated hospital.' Many of the Guinea Pigs said the same thing to me. They are deeply upset at how injured servicemen are treated. To them, it's personal.

Someone began playing the piano, and they huddled round, clutching their pints, singing 'Roll Out the Barrel' like a scene from an old war movie. Their families stood back and watched them with that very English 'Oh, he's off again' pride.

Acts of bravery are generally that – an action. A moment. But the bravery of these men has been lifelong and sustained. And their great valour has been to make it look so unexceptional. They are the best of us, but only because we make sure they got the best from us. McIndoe said in 1944: 'We are the trustees of each other. We do well to remember that the privilege of dying for one's country is not equal to the privilege of living for it.'

December 2007

St Paul's Cathedral

Any city worth a flight boasts a memorable edifice: a man-made thing that is its emblem. It's a picture they will flash up on the news so you know where they're coming from. London has its clock tower, the Gothic rocket attached to the Palace of Westminster, Big Ben. But the home of an ornate grandfather clock is not how Londoners see their city.

The building that is our badge of belonging, the image we'd wear on our sleeve, is a couple of miles to the east. St Paul's Cathedral is the solemn, eternal boss and hub of our city. We look up for it, mark our bearing by it, judge our distance from the lantern on top. It is the axis of a compass. The great dome is the calm centre of the spinning city. Technically, miles from London may be measured from the cross of Charing, but we know that if we were to slog with sledge and snowshoes to reach the pole of London, St Paul's is where we'd plant our flag and grab the thumbs-up photo.

We look for St Paul's from the high places on the edge of the metropolis, from the flat marshes down the side of the river, from the Millennium Wheel, from drunken, late-night bus stops and from windy bridges. The dome glows ethereal in the night, London's own rising moon, the beacon of calm promise. And while London may be the country's capital, it has also always been its own place. A place apart, a city state within the state. St Paul's is our cathedral, London's parish church, born from London fire, risen again like the phoenix, like the resurrection.

That famous photograph of St Paul's standing like a precious egg against the flame and smoke of the Blitz remains an image of redoubtable fortitude, of London in the face of adversity, an image of grit and resistance. Three days after it was printed in Britain it appeared in German papers, billed as a city in flames, on its knees, London destroyed by the might of the Luftwaffe.

I have shared this city with St Paul's for one half of one of its three centuries. But I'd never been inside it. As far as I was concerned, it could have been filled with trampolines or angora rabbits: seeing it from the outside is enough. Because here's the thing about St Paul's: it is the most perfectly beautiful building, the greatest piece of architecture in the capital, and that's not a contentious, chin-out assertion. It's plainly, blindingly, unarguably bleeding obvious. Wren is our greatest architect, Shakespeare in stone. St Paul's is his masterpiece. It is the pre-eminent building in London – and therefore, need we add, in Britain. It is as good as we get.

You approach the west front, with its great door that is open for occasions and looks down to Trafalgar Square. You walk past a statue of a plump, crowned lady on a plinth. Most people assume it's Victoria, because it's pretty safe to assume plump ladies on plinths around these parts are Victoria. In fact it's Queen Anne, the last of the Stuarts, who suffered seventeen pregnancies that produced five living babies, only one of which made it past infancy, though the little lad died before she did. Having no heirs, she ushered in the good taste of the Georgians. She was the monarch who saw St Paul's completed.

You actually get into St Paul's through a small side door, and are immediately confronted by the sheep-pen nylon ropes, signage and desks of public manipulation. There's a queue to get a stamp, produce a photo ID, buy popcorn or a ticket. It's not a great way to enter a great building dedicated to God, and it's not cheap. I resent paying for things my ancestors have already bought for me – for more than money. But as the dean, an immensely agreeable chap, points out, you've always been charged to get into cathedrals. I expect that's what they said about burning witches. Making money seems to be part of a cathedral's point. Moneychangers and temples now happily coexist in an ecumenical, liberal understanding.

I have to shake off the irritation and the disappointment of God's turnstiles, and take a deep breath to step into the nave of the church. And there it is. A pale, clear, rhythmic, reasoned, ethereal elegance. It is one of the mysteries of human aesthetics that enclosed spaces can elicit such different and extreme feelings in us. A cell doesn't feel the same as a lift. A supermarket isn't like an opera house. We can sense minute and subtle changes in the cultural ambience of rooms. Cathedrals, temples, were specifically invented to exploit the drama of enclosed space, to make themselves huge parables, echoes of the divine. And as a rule, the inside of a cathedral will be dramatically and intentionally completely different from the outside. That is part of its magic. You walk from the secular world into the spiritual. They are Tardis buildings.

But the initial surprise and the constant shock and the overwhelming joy of St Paul's is that this inner space is the inverted image of the outer space. That sounds like a simple truism; that the inside of a box feels like the outside of a box. It's no less a revelation. The outside of the building, based on a stretched Greek cross, looks clean and clear and white. Actually, it's a carefully harmonious plainsong of decoration: ordered patterns, faces, angles, juxtapositions, interspaced with intense strata of elaborate carvings as beautifully deep, crisp and rhythmic as any in the world. It was Wren's fortune to be working when stone and woodcarving reached a pitch of excellence in England that was unsurpassed and would never be achieved again, mostly owing to the astonishing genius of the divinely named Grinling Gibbons. Wren insisted that the windows be plain glass, so inside the decoration is made by the clear light. In the autumn and spring, when the sun is low, the display of chiaroscuro around the pillars and architraves, across the memorials and the black and white tiled floor is subtle and sublime. The grades and lines of light and shadow mesmerise as they melt away like cloudfall on dappled downland. St Paul's was and is the first cathedral of English Protestantism. All the rest were reconsecrated Roman Catholic churches. But here, this room is the first attempt to build a garage, a hangar for a new religion, a new way of walking with the divine, a new spiritual democracy. Honest, egalitarian, open. Not a rich cavern of dark mysteries and unknowable miracles, but a bright, light temple to hard work, personal responsibility and the Word, bright and light enough for every man to read it.

Stand under the dome and look up. There, tastefully painted in grisaille, are the authors of the Bible. The three-second echo bounces back the word of the prophets and the apostles from heaven. The word of Wycliffe and Tyndale and Cranmer, the word of the Evangelist, of Christ, of God, of God speaking English. Wren had to encapsulate a theology, ideas and intolerances and schisms, as the country split into a desperate, piecemeal massacre of a civil war that cost a king his head and led the nation to an interregnum of grim guilt and grief. But it also left it shriven, inspired, curious, devout and energetic. And what he built to encapsulate all that was perfectly miraculous. He nailed it first time.

There is no other church in the world that so perfectly conjures the hopes, achievements and central beliefs of Episcopal Protestantism. It is named for the man who took Christianity from being a Jewish sect out to Gentiles and on to the universal. St Paul's is the hymn of England made stone. So that's the good bit. Inside the great west door are two easels supporting blown-up posters of Orthodox icon faces, those artistically Botoxed gods of the ossified ancient Church. In front of them are little metal barbecues of cheap candles, the sort you see in every Catholic church. They are the antithesis of everything this great cathedral was built to inspire – iconoclastic, superstitious bribes of grace. They are anathema and, worse, hideously ugly. The dean, bless him (because someone should), grins and says: 'Oh, they're terribly popular with the public. They really have taken to lighting candles.' Seeing that two-thirds of the visitors are tourists and a good proportion of them will have come from Catholic Europe, this is hardly a surprise. Nor is it the point, particularly in this place.

There are other design problems. A pair of vilely ugly sci-fi paperback-cover paintings of *The Agony* by a Russian artist are prominently exhibited. In the clear light of Wren's vision they jerk the head with a physical, philistine slap. Then there is the misshapen and awkward *Mother and Child* by Henry Moore, which looks like it was hacked out of feta. There is Holman Hunt's nursery painting *The Light of the World*, saccharine and sentimental and the best advertisement for atheism I know. These are all displayed with the wall-eyed ease of the Church of England doing relevant, inclusive, contemporary stop-and-think. You can feel the struggle between high and low

Church in the extraneous decoration – the distinction between liberal, Anglo-Catholic and Evangelical factions of the Church of England. This is where most of you, understandably, lose interest and start reading the inscriptions on the tombs.

But the biggest aesthetic problem is up the east end. Going past the dome to the choir, with its elaborate stall, misericords and baldachin, and the altar, behind which is a poignant but aesthetically parochial memorial to America's help in the Second World War, it's topped with a hideous stained-glass window in the apse. And then there are the mosaics. The whole eastern end of the church and the choir and north and south transepts are eczema-ed with Victorian pious pity and hyper-mannerism, turning the clear baroque vision of the cathedral into a cross between a duchess's jewellery box and the food hall at Harrods. It was Queen Victoria who thought the church too gloomy, too plain.

Despite the ceramic Episcopal graffiti, the space still soars with bright purpose. There's always been a rivalry between St Paul's and Westminster Abbey – they refer to each other sniffily as 'the other place'. The coronation, of course, happens in the minster, but the cathedral got the big fairy-tale wedding, and the churches get their precedence from the quality of their dead. The minster boasts the nation's official repository of death, Madame Tussauds in marble: the Unknown Soldier and Poets' Corner. But St Paul's had a coup by snagging Nelson and then Wellington. The Iron Duke's tomb in the crypt is surrounded by the flags of the nations that fought with him at Waterloo. There is one empty sconce – the Prussian standard was removed in 1914. Nelson is buried in the stone coffin that was carved for Cardinal Wolsey. It had been hanging around the royal family's attic.

There are a lot of military men down here: Kitchener, who wanted you, lies in his little chapel by the front door – they sing communion just for him once a year – and the generals of the American War of Independence and the wars against the French. There are memorials to brine-buried sailors, who cluster round Nelson. There's the great lachrymose Victorian gate, closed for ever on Melbourne, Victoria's favourite prime minister. Here's Howard from the Howard League for Penal Reform; here's Reynolds and, touchingly, across the south transept, just in his eyeline, is the beautiful sculpture of Turner, the Covent Garden barber's son with a Cockney accent and a miraculous eye. Here's Florence Nightingale and William Howard Russell, the first war correspondent, who made her hospitals possible. Here's Wycliffe and Philip Sidney, Alexander Fleming, T.E. Lawrence, Ivor Novello and John Donne, whose ethereal, shrouded tomb figure stands upright beside the choir. He was dean of an earlier incarnation of the cathedral and is still its presiding muse, the great poet and moral plumb line of London.

Where the abbey and the cathedral really compete is in their music. The cathedral has the better organ and usually the better organist. It also has the horrendous echo and acoustics that can kill noise before it gets to the back wall. Both churches have choir schools. I sat in as the St Paul's boys rehearsed some of their anthems for Easter week. They shove and trip into the classroom, noisy and aimless as pinballs, and take that endless laddie time to settle in the circle of chairs round the piano where their new choirmaster patiently calls for order. They flick through their books and fidget. He says something, hits a note and, without warning, the room fills like an airbag in a crash. It's replete with noise that seems to push everything to the wall, to fill every space, my ears and my head until the sound leaks down my nose and through the corners of my eyes, a noise that pumps my chest and runs round the pit of my stomach. This noise boys can make is, in the most literal, true, deific sense, miraculous. It's astonishing, not least because it comes out of the spindly, slight, grubby, slouched bodies of urchins, their faces unconcerned that when they open their mouths they can produce the closest thing a mortal can have to superpowers. The choirmaster tells me that a boy's voice becomes particularly rich and poignant the month before it breaks. There's something too touching for words in that.

There is a story that Christopher Wren sat up on Parliament Hill to watch the removal of the scaffolding around St Paul's dome – the second-largest in the world after St Peter's. If it collapsed, as many said it would, he had a carriage waiting to take him to the Channel. It didn't, but it still must have come as a surprise to the dean and chapter. They thought they were getting a spire. As he sat there and watched the egghead building emerge from the confusion of pulls and pulleys, he might have paused to think that not only was this the first Protestant cathedral of the modern age, but that he was the first architect of cathedrals in the whole history of Christianity ever to have lived to see his creation completed.

While the ashes of the Great Fire of London were still smoking, Wren, along with Evelyn and Hooke, came up with plans for the new city: rational, ordered and reasonable. It never happened because it would have taken a century to build and because Londoners wanted the footprints of their old houses back, so the medieval streets remain, but with every house rebuilt in brick and stone. The fire is the tipping point, the hinge of London's story. It cauterised the past, the civil wars, the schisms, the religious intolerance, the filth and the romance of the medieval Roman city. With it went the great St Paul's, a church bigger than the present cathedral, altered and added to, decrepit and dangerous. This was where Shakespeare was first published. By the seventeenth century it was a collapsing, venerable mess that had once boasted a spire taller than Salisbury's until it was pushed over by a bolt of lightning. Cromwell used it to stable his cavalry.

Wren's first design for the new cathedral, based on a Greek cross with a dome, was rejected by the dean and chapter – too Roman, too Catholic, too Froggy foreign. They wanted their old cathedral back, just without the brothels. So Wren, confident in Charles II's patronage, built a model of another cathedral. The Great Model cost £600, the price of a substantial real house, and it's still with us. Above the nave is the remarkable, huge and beautiful über-Airfix kit, the greatest matchstick model ever built, the St Paul's that never was. Again the Church rejected it: too Catholic, too different, domes – no English church had a dome. Steeples were English: straight up, honest, jabbing fingers to God. A cathedral needed a tower. Wren was mortified and furious, and knocked off another drawing, which is also here – a third version of the church. It looks like a hideous, misshapen Cambodian stupa or Las Vegas casino. The dean and chapter, the bishops and the aldermen, the City livery companies – they all loved it, and Wren was given the go-ahead to start building.

The official guide says he made a few alterations over the next thirty-five years. That's not quite the truth. It's a churchy porky. It's obvious he never intended to build the humpy thing. He knew that this project would last longer than most of the committee, so he never set the plans down on paper. The cathedral that we have, the one he finally built, he kept in his head.

Just stop and consider the magnitude of that for a moment. The only overall plans for St Paul's Cathedral were in Wren's head. Look at it. Imagine building it over a generation. It was an unimaginable act of bravado, genius and, some of us would say, faith. He is buried here, of course. He lived to be ninety-one, and his son, also Christopher, wrote his famous epitaph: 'Reader, if you seek his monument, look around you.'

Climb the 530 steps to the Golden Gallery on the roof, past the Whispering Gallery. You will see the astounding brilliance of this building. The simplicity is an illusion, as simplicity almost always is. The great geometric complexity of the buttresses that support the immense pressures of the roof is not on the outside of the building, but hidden in the wall. The dome that you see from outside isn't the one you see from inside when you look up. The one we see from the bus is a thin skin of wood and lead.

The really impossible part of it sits right at the top, the ball and lantern that is the cathedral's defining image. How could a dome support its weight? It should plummet the 365 feet to the cathedral floor – but it doesn't, because it's held up by God and rests on a secret A-frame that squats on the vertical wall at the base of the dome. It's a brilliant mathematical answer.

St Paul's isn't only Wren's memorial, it is the evocation of brilliant Englishmen: Evelyn and Hooke, the town planner who studied refraction and light and microscopes and made the first drawings of a flea, and Newton, the towering sociopath who said that Wren was the best mathematician of the age.

The final secret of the genius of St Paul's is that Wren wasn't originally an architect at all, but an astronomer. Together these men started the Royal Society and launched an age of inquiry into the natural world, the heavens, politics and philosophy. They were all solidly religious, and St Paul's is the perfect synthesis of the rational and the ethereal, the intuitive and the known.

A moment, a time, a dome of rounded hope and brilliance. When you reach the top of the Golden Gallery and the wind puffs your cheeks and slits your eyes, you squint out over the most spectacular view. When the first tourist stood here in 1711 he would have seen a city that had grown to be the biggest in Europe. Today you look out at what it has become, stretching away on every side, the old river curling down to the sea, and realise there's something missing. And then you remember – you're standing on it.

May 2008

Fishing

Water is the earth's most skilful designer. Water and the tidal moon are our keenest architects. Nothing that comes from the sea is ugly. Everything is sculpted and smoothed into an ergonomic, rhythmically satisfying aesthetic. Every shell, fin, stone and scale, driftwood and all the flotsam of man's manufacture are eventually whittled and worn into a pleasing aquatic beauty. And there are ships, built by men but designed by the element they live in. However meagre or humble their journeys, water makes them ultimately sublime. All of them except *Emulator*.

The first sighting of this ship-shaped thing, crouching in the bowl of Scarborough's small harbour, tugs your breath. All boats, even the most mundane plastic pedalos, have an ergonomic purpose. But not this dog of a barque, this crook-backed, axe-bowed, rusting Quasimodo decorated with the cross of St George like an ocean-going scaffolders' van. It was first light, and it hunched over the other rocking fishing boats. They were all inshore line-fishing crabbers, part-time day boats. *Emulator* is made for sterner stuff.

We'd walked the half-mile round Scarborough's long bay after a night in the Clifton Hotel. I'd lain awake in the garret tower that Wilfred Owen had slept in on his final recuperation, where he wrote some of his bleakest poetry before passing over the sea to die. Scarborough is a fine town, neat and purposeful. The penny arcades wink fitfully on the front, the fish and chip shops congeal in the chilly dawn, the cliffs hotch with seabirds. Its Victorian stucco grandeur tells of a richer past, when there were more Yorkshire tourists come for the bracing air and the sand, a break from mill and mine, when there were more ships, more sailors and fishermen, more fish.

Fish and fishing are the front line of environmental politics – an issue that stares back at you from the plate. Fish comes from that other place, the other dimension, the two-thirds of the planet that is the alien element – where we are not welcome, we can only skim and churn the surface. When you catch a fish and stare into that round, black jelly eye there is no spark of recognition, no empathy. But at least we know what to expect. The fish had not an inkling you even existed, no notion that the world wasn't endless wet.

The catching and consuming of fish is hooked to a lot of buzzy, feel-good, groovy goodery, labelled with ticks and green smiles, ports of origin – as if fish lived in fields – promises of sustainability, of fairness, of freshness. The marketing of conscience and guilt. It also comes with the bad temper of fishing limits and national waters, of quotas and trade agreements, of unions and civic decline, national pride and international obligation. Fish bring with them a lot more than omega-3.

A man loads ice through *Emulator*'s hatches, another is carrying supermarket bags. We shout hellos from the flagstones. The ice man says, 'So, you made it? Managed to get up? Step aboard.' There is no obvious way of stepping aboard – no gangplank, no break in the slim railing. You just leap nonchalantly and cling, hoping not to slither down the slick sides to be crushed between steel and stone.

Even hobbled in the harbour, it's difficult to get about. Ropes are tossed, the throb of diesel grows hectic, and *Emulator* elbows its way past the lighthouse and the edge of the still-snoring town, pointing its broken, blunt nose nor'east into the North Sea.

Why is it called *Emulator*? Who or what is it emulating? I ask Sean, the captain, a cropped, round-headed man with a gimlet stare and a pirate's earring. 'Fook knows. I think the owner likes names that begin with vowels or summat.' She's nearly thirty years old and Sean has been with her since she was launched, all his working life. He sits in the tiny wheelhouse, his feet up, a cup of coffee in the failsafe cup-of-coffee holder, in front of him what looks like an electronics repair shop: stacks of screens broadcasting streams of interference. There's radar and sonar and the local TV news. He is surrounded by a confusion of paper: lists, logs, notepads and man-muck. The grimy window grudgingly offers a thin view of the horizon, obscured by the deck, masts, derricks and strapped-on aerials, like some council house-nicking satellite. The edge of the water plays peekaboo with the wallowing bow.

There are three crew: Sean, Mark and Stephen. Mark is big, lumpy and coarse, with diligent hands and a face that looks like a frostbitten turnip. These two men are in their forties, the sea has been their life and the rest of their life has had to make way for it. And then there's Stephen, slouched and whippety, a boy in his twenties with the easy smile of a lad who's always had a lot of explaining to do. He boasts the worst set of drunken tattoos I've ever seen.

Already he has two families ashore, all girls. Women are his weakness. Women and beer. You get the sense that coming to sea is a relief. There's no beer and no women on boats. This is a very masculine place: fishing is perhaps the last occupation that has no women. I ask if there are any female fishermen. 'There's a wifey who puts the crab pots out with her husband, but lasses are bad luck on boats.'

The native wit and badinage of Yorkshire is a relentless, repetitive mockery. Every sentence begins with an ironic rhetorical question: 'You're seriously going to wear that?' 'You really think Macclesfield will win next year?' So when I ask about the diminishing fish stock, I get back the sneered 'Who do you believe? People who are out fishing all their lives, or a bunch of academic civil servants looking at computer screens? There's no shortage of fish.'

Fishing and fish stocks are one of the areas of ecology and the environment where the activists in suits are diametrically opposed to the working men who make their living from fish. As a rule, environmental campaigners support and back indigenous food producers, but not in the case of fish. And it's not just here. Around the world fishermen say there are plenty of fish, and marine experts say there aren't.

'We've always said that warming is changing where the fish go,' says Sean. 'Fishermen noticed ages before the fooking noddies. Look at sea bass. There's no quota on them at the moment because there's that many in the Channel.'

Mackerel seem to be following the colder water to the north, to Iceland and the Faroes, incensing Scandinavian and British fishermen. The land-bound experts say that fishermen have a vested interest in continuing to fish unsustainably. 'Who's got the fooking huge vested interest?' the three men bellow at once. 'Fooking ecology movement, Greenfookingpeace,' says Mark. 'That's huge business.

The environment is a fook sight bigger than fooking fishing, I'll tell you. Not one of them would work for what I take home.'

The economics of the *Emulator* aren't going to make anyone rich. Leaving aside the depreciation of the boat, diesel is the biggest expense. Agricultural diesel is 50p a litre. The engines run all day. They use about 4,000 litres a week. On top of that, they have to pay for the ice, boxes, insurance and transport on land, and the ship's owner takes 50 per cent of any profit. What's left they split between them. Last time out they fished for seven days and made nothing. They're at sea for about half a year. This week they're in debt for the fuel. They need £8,000 worth of fish to make a wage. If you tot up the hours, it's not anywhere near the minimum. But out at sea, none of those rules count.

The galley is the only place to sit. It's so cramped, if you put a stamp on it you could post it home. There are five of us on board now, but only four of us can sit at a time, which is OK because someone needs to drive and watch for tankers. There's a filthy stove and a little sink with a plastic bowl full of slopping, turgid, lumpy water. This is the only tap on the ship. There's no shower, no water you'd want to drink without boiling. They drink only tea, coffee and Tesco's cola. There are five mugs that are never washed and when you see the state of the tea towel you're grateful. We sleep in the bowels of the boat, a little dark dungeon up the sharp end with pods in the walls like Davy Jones's catacomb. The human part of this ship is made as small and claustrophobic as possible. The greatest part of it is given over to the fish, to the catch. To the cash. The engine rumbles and caws constantly, without cease.

There is a bin, a small bucket that's emptied over the side, and there's a lavatory without a seat that would be impossible to sit on because it's jammed sideways into a cupboard with a broken porthole. The thought of maybe having to sit on it – or, worse, kneel in front of it in the humping swell – is too awful to contemplate. Overall, I'd have to say that this is the most assertively filthy environment I've been in since I was a student. The boat is a Norman Wisdom assault course of pratfalls, whacked heads, lost fingers, rope burn, slicing steel, crunching blocks and grinding gears, or just simply and silently tripping and disappearing overboard.

We chug into the North Sea. It is the most beautiful day, the water gently undulating, gunmetal-blue. I spend a lot of time staring out to sea. It's better than staring at Mark in the galley. Everything land is, water isn't. It's fickle, ethereal, moody and restless, hissing and slapping, whispering and booming. Its colour changes constantly from this cold blue to salmon-silver, verdigris, golden, polished pewter, gull-grey leaden, like oil on steel. The English and Scots have fished in these cold metal waters stretching up to Iceland and Norway for 2,000 years. The sea is calm, the wind a tugging breeze. The ugly, fat boat makes the most of it and rolls and yaws like a sickening diva. I'm relieved to find that I don't seem to be prone to seasickness.

We arrive at the fishing grounds, fifty miles from the coast. We are trawling for flatfish, bottom feeders, so the bed needs to be sandy. A huge reel at the stern unravels the stinking net of blue and green nylon. It trails into the water like toilet paper caught in a fat girl's knickers. It works like a shopping bag. At its edges are a pair of heavy iron plates called the doors. They sink the net and keep its mouth open. On its bottom edge are rubber rings that churn up the sand and mud, confusing the fish, which are drawn into the back of the net, called the cod-end. *Emulator* draws for fish for four hours. The crew get some rest, drink tea, man the bridge. Seabirds follow in our wake, hanging over the boat, wings catching the stiffening breeze, like thieving gulls following a tractor as we plough the water. There are pretty and delicate kittiwakes, herring gulls and gannets, a thieving skua, but mostly they are fulmars, beautiful grey and white birds with dark eyes and strange tubular nostrils. Their name comes from the Norse for foul gull – they spit rancid oil as a defence.

The net is drawn in by a winch to a series of musical calls and instructions. Ropes hurl through tackle, hawsers sing at head height in fits of spray, chains clank and everywhere is in the way. These men's jobs are so familiar that they synchronise with a feverish elegance. The net is pulled like a purse, heavy and flickering with the pale heads of small dabs. It is lifted to the fish hopper, where Stephen crawls in and tugs a series of sodden slip knots. The cod-end mouth opens and the hundredweight of fish fall as he struggles to back out of the little hatch.

From the hopper comes a conveyor slide. The three men in yellow slick overalls stand side by side. The fish slip out in a confusion of slime and tails, gaping-mouthed. Each man has a small knife, continually stropped; with rubber gloves they grasp a fish and dig and disembowel each one. I had a go at gutting. A plaice took me two or three minutes. It was slippery and tough.

Mark holds up a leviathan the size of a four-year-old child. 'Fooking look at this. This is the fooking fish those clever fookers says doesne fooking exist any more. It's fooking extinct.' It is a beautiful, gleaming, pale-green cod. They catch quite a lot of them – not codling, but big, muscly, full-grown cod.

There are whiting and orange-spotted plaice, and little dabs and lemon sole. There are big, oval, knobbly turbot and round, smooth brill. There are enormous halibut and fearsome gape-mouthed monkfish. There are jellyfish and lumpfish, starfish and an anemone they call tits, because it looks like udders. There is an octopus they stick on the wall and watch slowly climb along the roof while asking it the football results. There is a solitary red mullet, but mostly there are haddock, thousands and thousands of them, with their great big surprised eyes, the fried fish of choice north of the border.

At my rough estimate, two-thirds of the catch goes back to the deep as corpses. Very little lives in the net. The fish are crushed and suffocated. They madly eat each other in the confusion and are drowned. Worst are the monkfish. Their wide, saw-toothed mouths gape and scoop up mud until their gills are choked solid. Morbidly, they are buried alive with earth under water. 'What do you think of this then?' says Sean.

'All this fish chucked back?' He answers his own question. 'We fooking hate it.' He searches for the word. 'It's wrong.' In front of each of the men is a wooden ruler with incised lines. This is the minimum length required for each species. Too small and they go over the side. The EU quota system means all fishing boats are catching far more than they are allowed to sell, and are then dumping much of it.

In the case of the haddock, large fish get a better price than small ones. The men know they're going to catch their quota, so they only keep the premium ones. It's the same with whiting. It's immoral, it's insane, and that's not the half of it. The quota system, which is constantly being fiddled with and fine-tuned by men who have never been to sea and probably never eat fish with a face on, ascribes quotas to boats. You can scrap your boat, turn it into a bar or brothel, but keep the quota, which you can then sell.

Sean spends hours on the radio phone to his owner, trying to buy extra quota for fish he's already caught, or is expecting to catch. So there is a secondary market in fishing quota that is traded, and the oddest people, such as investment funds, end up owning it. It's even rumoured that Manchester United owns quota.

Well-meaning environmentalists with plans and graphs and pie charts have come up with the worst possible outcome: a system, organised with a monstrous bureaucracy, where most fish are killed and thrown away for their own good. The big money is made by those who buy and sell paper quotas and never see a fish. And the cost of all this is borne by these three men and by the consumer. It is beyond the dreams of a flabbergasted Kafka, and everybody knows it is indefensible and it is sinful. And nobody knows how to stop it.

Except, of course, the Norwegians have done it. They insist that every fish caught must be landed. Instead of setting a quota for the numbers caught, they regulate the number of days boats go to sea. But what would the Norwegians know? They only have the longest coastline in Europe and are the richest people in the world.

The catch is cleaned, washed, packed into boxes with ice and stored in the refrigerated belly of the boat. We have dinner. We eat frozen burgers and chips; we have fry-ups and cold shepherd's pie. Beneath our feet are boxes of the most wonderful fresh fish from the finest cold-water fishery in the world. Finally, reluctantly, they agree to batter and fry some haddock, and I cook some gurnard fillets.

Fishermen don't eat fish, and they don't swim, and they don't drink water. If you have to stick your rubber finger up the vent of a thousand plaice, you don't necessarily want to put one in your mouth. None of them like cod. 'You should see the fooking worms they get.' We sleep for a couple of hours. My pod smells sweetly of other men's night sweats and toe jam.

The *Emulator* trawls four times a day. I try to wake up for each catch. On the second day the net catches on something on the seabed and they lose the cod-end – that's £1,000 of net. They have to stay up to sew on another one, as the boat heaves and plunges in twenty-foot waves. Then they dredge up tons of mud. It's hard and it's dispiriting. That night the moon is huge and clear, the sea platinum and jet.

On the third day there are 100 boxes of fish – monk and premium green cod, flat and haddock – and they decide to turn back to Scarborough to send them to market by road to Grimsby. It's another expense, but the prices should be better there. The fish are unloaded onto the dock. The prices are fixed. They have yet to make a profit. The *Emulator* will turn round and go back for another three days, but without me.

We are an island. That geography is our defining characteristic. Our legends and creation myths are all of seafaring people. There was saltwater in our veins, and the men who went down to the sea had a special place in our pantheon. Yet through treaties, neglect and embarrassment, through a natural desire to belong, to join in, we have relegated the sea to a damp patch. An inconvenience, an environmental black spot.

While we worry in an abstract, comfy way about the estimated, second-guessed numbers and provenance of fish, we ignore the endangered and vanishing farers who go out in boats, in the sea and the wind. Men who are formed and sculpted into a remarkable breed, whom we are conspiring to eradicate. And as we do so, we drain the salt from our veins.

For days after we left the *Emulator* I could feel the phantom sea shift under my feet, and if I closed my eyes I could see myself surrounded by the soaring fulmars, which seemed to lift the boat until it was flying with them, and I remembered Mark's farewell. 'What you going to write about us, then? You going to be nice? Actually, I don't give a fook. Write what you fooking like. We won't be fooking reading it. It'll only go to wrap fish in.'

September 2010

Shelter

'This is a perfect first date,' says an intense, pretty young volunteer with a dishcloth in her hand. Her boyfriend stands beside her, peeling apples for crumble. He smiles: 'I mean, who could say no to cooking in a homeless shelter?' Shelter from the Storm does what it says on the door: it offers a welcome to people with nowhere else to go, with no family, no mate's sofa, no safety net. A lot of couples make volunteering here once a week part of their courtship, and you can see why. It's quite the opposite of what you'd expect: it's a really good night in. Tonight, Lucas Hollweg, my editor, and I, as part of our long-term culinary courtship, have come to cook dinner for thirty-six homeless people. I say Lucas and I – Lucas has been here since 3 p.m., chopping, sautéing, running his hands through his hair and being all sorts of Fanny Cradock. I tipped up at 6 p.m. and cut the smoked salmon, a bit like Johnnie. The Blonde butters brown bread.

Outside in this dank corner of King's Cross, which is all warehouses and security lights, are lots of hunched kids. They chat and smoke into cupped hands, waiting for the doors to open. They've been out on the street since 8 a.m. 'Here, you on the telly?' asks a gimlet-eyed boy in a hoody. No, sorry. 'I know you, though. I've seen you. You sure you're not on the telly? You're on the news, aren't you?' No, really. 'Oh, well, that's good, because you look just like one of those blokes who commit fraud. You know, bankers.'

Inside the industrial space there are two dormitories, an open kitchen, some sofas, a TV, a pool table that is mostly gaffer tape and a couple of computers. It's warm, the tables are set with gingham cloths and it has one of the best atmospheres of any dining room in London. What makes Shelter from the Storm so special is the emphasis on conviviality, the safety and the good cheer, which is why dinner is so important – eating together.

At one table there is an Ethiopian girl who's a refugee. Her father is Eritrean and it isn't safe for her to stay in Addis Ababa. Beside her is a vivacious and elegant Mozambican, who found it was not safe to stay with her boyfriend. 'He is Nigerian,' she offers by way of explanation, and we laugh about the difference between West and East Africans. Now she has eyes for a young Algerian man who is in the shelter. He has a job and a room and a start, but he's come back for the company, and perhaps for this girl. 'Oh, I love him,' she whispers and giggles. Do you think he can tell? 'I think the chicken in the oven can tell,' she hoots.

Besides us is Angel, a Bulgarian who looks Romany, with masses of curly black hair and sorrowful eyes. He's writing the alphabet on a piece of paper, teaching himself English. He already speaks Bulgarian, Russian and Greek. He's a hairdresser and has spent his day at a drop-in centre, cutting tramps' hair for free: a homeless man offering charity. On the other side of me is a Polish woman in her sixties, quiet and thoughtful. She was a housekeeper. Her employers left to return to America, and she discovered that they hadn't paid her insurance or tax: a mean lie to save a meagre few quid and the consequences for her are devastating. She has no resources, no home, no benefits, and she has spent the day walking the South Bank of the Thames. 'I walk down and I walk back. It didn't rain. Things can only get better.'

The optimism from everyone is astonishing, and the willpower that you need to maintain hope is a titanic act of faith. The distinction between the deserving and the undeserving poor is a luxury of the comfortably well-off. I am struck by how many of these people are here through no fault of their own. Not drugs, not drink, not criminality. And how fragile is the hold on the lower rungs of opportunity for so many people in this huge city. One false step, one piece of foul luck and you fall straight back to the cold, hard pavement. There is a boy in the corner writing in a notebook. He is writing a book. It's not bad. 'I came down to work for the Olympics as a security man. You know, what with all that fuss and the army coming in, there wasn't a job. I spent all my money on accommodation and ended up here.' Don't you have any family back home? 'My parents were very religious, in the Salvation Army, and on their way to church there was a crash and they both died. I was sixteen. The Salvation Army took me in for a year and then said I had to make it on my own. I've always worked in security and now I've discovered I can write, so I'm writing a book.' What's it about? 'It's a ghost story.'

These are the city's ghosts. If you're reading this in your own kitchen, you might consider them. They need a little of what you have. And we all need some of what they've got.

December 2012

Frieze Art Fair

There is a woman lying on her side. She's in the corridor – naked, an odalisque, the size of a hefty hippo. She is made of fibreglass. And she's pregnant – except she's not quite pregnant. Her gravid stomach has been inverted, so instead of coming out it goes in, making a smooth white recess. People are standing and watching. Because a young woman, a fleshly, non-sculptural, real woman is gingerly getting into the tummy and curling up into the fetal position, so her boyfriend (or agent or dealer) can photograph her. People queue up to lie, sit, crouch in the pregnant woman and get Instagrammed. And as the rest of us watch for a bit, we are all struck by the great question that contemporary art invariably poses: 'Where would we put it?'

Frieze, the London art fair, has grown so much that it obliterates the small, fastidious magazine that started it and gave it its name. It's put on every autumn in Regent's Park, the large green space given to the people by George IV while he was prince regent. Stucco cliffs of near-classical good taste surround it. This address has always been smart, but never fashionable.

Frieze week is the biggest week in the year for London taxis. My cab driver tells me it's bigger than Christmas. It books out every restaurant and club and every hotel room; invitations to dozens of dinners and cocktail parties and smartly casual breakfasts ping into the in-boxes of anyone who has ever signed a gallery's visitors' book. The streets are clogged with branded courtesy limos. This thing, this art, this stuff, has grown huge, overflowing like a great popcorn machine.

And when you get into it, to one of the half-dozen special privileged-preview VIP days, you walk for an hour and think: Really? *Really?* Did this stuff really pay for all that? For all the hotels, all the dinners, all the taxis, all the airfares, all those hairdos, and all that cashmere, and the waft of Fracas? Did it really pay for all this? Yes, it really did. And not only that, but it has spawned a dozen other, similar plastic art fairs around the globe.

A major contemporary-art gallerist, who wished to remain anonymous, said that art fairs are where his business has now gone. The gallery itself is useful as somewhere to keep the stock and the staff out of the rain, but it doesn't make money any more. Another dealer told me that I should stop thinking about it as art in the 'old museum, twentieth-century, harsh reverential sense. What it is is fashion, dear.' It's an international business, with catwalks in different cities. It sells old-money cultural security to emerging-nation new-money insecurity.

The fair is split into two halves, Frieze London, which features contemporary art, and Frieze Masters: like the before-and-after shot in a beauty ad. The Masters lives in a tent that has no visible means of support: pale, minimal, elegant. Inside it is light and calm. The gallery booths are spacious and full of the sort of art that made us fall for art in the first place, a compilation album of all the best bits. Sing-along anthems from a $10 million Brueghel to delicate and poignant American Indian ledger drawings. All this is so easy on the eyes – so effortlessly seductive and such a relief that this is a sure thing. This is art that guarantees you a happy ending.

Frieze London, on the other hand, is a big, awkward, pile-'em-high contemporary warehouse, wall-to-Walmart. The cacophony of the avant-garde: messy, smudgy, bad breath, raw and loud. The walls shout at your eyes till they just go blurry. The problem with art is that the bad obscures the good. It's like a choir where only one person can sing in tune and everyone else bawls. Altogether, it looks like an early round of a TV talent show for painting. Part defiant posturing, part insecure overstatement and part immature enthusiasm – with a modicum of talent. In the middle, Larry Gagosian tries to put on a grown-up show. A series of Jeff Koons sculptures pang with a glossy insouciance above the art world's dirty laundry in the surrounding quarters. Each polished shiny object has a large, black-suited, wired-up security guard standing beside it: art bouncers. They're a look that just screams new money. A dealer close to Gagosian, who insists on remaining unidentified, says these bouncers are a necessity: 'Do you know how difficult it is to get the fingerprints off of a Jeff Koons?' Easier than getting your fingerprints on him, I should think.

Frieze is a shuttle of the international art crowd: smug, bored, knowing. There are a lot of brand-new collectors here – they say Chinese is the new Russian. And thousands of art middlemen and women, ready to explain and stroke and reassure. Because contemporary art isn't easy. It's not obvious. You need to be told. This stuff has to be – simply *has* to be! – better than it looks. The question that Frieze Masters poses to Frieze London is: 'Now, why are you so ugly?' But the really tough question is: *What is an artist?* And if you mention this to any of the actual moderators and mullahs in the contemporary tent, they roll their eyes and sigh. But still the question hangs like a terrible family secret. Because in the Masters tent the answer is obvious: an artist is a person who makes art. And you know he or she's an artist because you can see the art. So the art validates the artist and the artist the art. But in the contemporary tent it's not that simple, because it's mostly conceptual. This isn't about skill, or application, or craft, or ability. It's about the concept, stupid. An artist is someone who thinks about art.

Put this another way: is a baker still a baker if he gets someone else to make his bread? If an artist can be someone who collects a lot of objects that someone else made for another purpose, and puts them all together in a room, how do you know he's an artist and not just a janitor? Well, you need an art moderator – an explainer, a guide, a mentor – to tell you. And Frieze is replete with art Sherpas who will take you up the magic mountain of contemporary culture. They hold the collectors by the hand and convince them that the piece of stuff, devoid of skill or craft but full of concept, is art. They explain what it means and why it speaks to other bits of art conceived by other people. And, together, that this will make a market you can invest in. The market works only if all of the Sherpas are moving in the same direction, at the same time, at the same speed.

It's a tricky and rather impressive business to watch. The most impressive concept in all of art is the market itself. Someone thinks of art and sells a token of that thought to someone else – guaranteed by the word of a third party – who will then sell it at a profit. A contemporary-art dealer, someone who acquires for some of the most bullish and acquisitive collectors in the world, met me between steepling cliffs of childishly drawn, scribbled and dribbled abstracts, nailed-up bits of plastic, taxidermied animals, T-shirts printed with arty slogans and a small bronze sculpture of someone taking a dump, and said – unattributably, of course – 'You know, no one enjoys this. No one in the business likes doing business this way. It is the worst possible way to see art, but it is what the market wants. And, you know, when you leave here, you will remember nothing. Nothing will stick.' The concepts evaporate, to be reassembled the next month in Basel or Venice or Miami or New York.

I look at the pregnant woman, and there is a child in her cave womb now. And a market-motivator father is taking a picture. Is the child the art? Is the photograph the art? Is the statue the art? Is the child the artist? Is the father the artist? Or is it really just all a piece of furniture?

Outside, in the drizzle, the snaking line waits for its courtesy car or its special bus to take it to the next room full of big ideas. I meet an old artist with the collar of his coat up, looking for a pub. 'Do you see it?' he asks with a sense of excitement. 'No, not really.' 'Oh, it's definitely there. Something's happening. The art is rebelling. You can't keep taking inspiration and beauty for granted. You can't cynically lock it away. It will break out and overwhelm us. It always does. Whenever there are moments like this – dull, cynical hiatuses of too many excuses and too much bollocks – art bounds ahead, pushes through with something amazing, and I can feel it. Let me tell you, it'll make this lot feel pretty foolish.' Not all the hired muscle in the city will keep the fingerprints off art.

Maybe something is biding its time over the horizon. Something that's more than an empty womb.

December 2013

Goodwood

I had a dream. I'm in a car. It's a Maserati. I'm in the passenger seat. The engine makes a noise like Johnny Cash picking up the soap in Folsom Prison. We're on a country lane. It's narrow, with twists and turns. There are people on both sides screaming at me and waving. They look frightened, but I can't hear what they're saying. We're going far, far too fast. And then suddenly ahead of me there's a white brick wall – it charges at the car. In a panic I look at the driver, and it's a member of Pink Floyd. Panic goes into sixth gear – it's the drummer from Pink Floyd. Fuck, I'm just another brick in the wall. But when I open my eyes I'm not safe, home in bed. I'm still in the Maserati with Nick Mason, who is the drummer from Pink Floyd, and here is the smile of a man who thrives on this kind of own adrenaline.

'Well, that was fun,' Mason says as we unstrap and get out of the Maserati. Around us, and beneath us, stretches Goodwood, the seat of the Dukes of Richmond, a 12,000-acre estate that lies sixty miles south of London and is famous for the motor-racing track, the world-class horse-racing track, the organic farm, the golf course and its club, the fantastic pheasant shoot, the hotel and the stately home with the art and the naturally sublime views. Oh, and the Second World War airfield, where, even as we look, the helicopters of those who simply can't face a three-hour traffic jam from London are landing. What could be more agreeable than Goodwood? Grandiloquent Goodwood and its two annual motoring events, the Festival of Speed and the Revival. A big boy's vision of a patrician heaven. A great, green toy box that surpasses the dreams of oligarchs.

Nick and I and the Maserati have just completed the Hill Climb, a race up a wholly improbable course, and one of the main events during the four-day Festival of Speed. It's the sort of thing aristocrats come up with instead of completing full-time education, learning to read without moving their lips, or working. They invent dangerous dares and limb-snapping games to weed out the weaker heirs. Goodwood is a paragon of toff derring-do. There is barely an inch of this blamelessly pretty estate where you can't be rendered a bruised black-and-blueblood. The motor-racing track was built by the current duke's father in 1948 but was mothballed after he became disillusioned with the sport. Now Goodwood's Festival of Speed and the Revival have become two of the most popular four-wheeled events in Europe, attracting more than 300,000 people each year as well as sponsorship from an elbowing scrum of elite and desirable luxury-goods brands. Belstaff has just launched a line of clothing called Goodwood Sports & Racing.

How did all this happen? How did Goodwood become the posh daddy of corporate entertainment and the mass-market pleb's day out? This is the story of aristocratic folk. Bear with me. Bring your best doffing cap. We're going back into black and white and the impermeable permafrost of the English class system.

The British aristocracy, for the most part, has been strangled by its own articulacy, drowned in the mass of the middle class. The only real trace of it is a few sepia-toned photographs ironically hung in five-star-hotel bathrooms. What is left of the old aristocracy is sorry, lost and irredeemably stupid. Refugees in their own houses, living in corners, cutting out coupons, eating from cans, complaining to the postman about the state of the nation and the hell of modernity. But if you had to save one, just for breeding purposes, as an ideal specimen, it would have to be fifty-eight-year-old Charles Henry Gordon Lennox, Earl of March, heir to the Duke of Richmond, Gordon and Aubigny, and the man behind Goodwood.

Within a minute of meeting Lord March you will be aware that he is warm, charming, amused, interested and self-deprecating about his deftness in a very British way. He's also easy on the eye. He works far more diligently and longer than he would like you to notice. He is not the man he would have chosen to be, but then that's the toll that heredity demands. He wears his titles and history with a fatalistic shrug, like a birthmark, or a limb. He would have been, if all things had been egalitarian, a successful photographer, which he was, for years, in London. But that wasn't his fate. The luck of the Gordon

Lennoxes is that they have bred themselves better than anyone else. (When you consider that breeding is the only thing aristocrats have to do, it's astonishing they've produced so many human mules.)

Gordon Lennox is the family name. The double-barrel usually means an injection of mercantile cash somewhere back down the line from a fortuitous marriage. 'March' is a courtesy title for the heir to the dukedom. Charles's father, eighty-three, is the current duke. None of the ten Dukes of Richmond have been mouth-breathing window lickers. All have served their nation and managed to stay away from packs of cards and showgirls. The fourth duke fought two duels, winning both, built Lord's Cricket Ground, and died of rabies in 1819 after being bitten by a fox in Canada.

The titles originate from the seventeenth century and one of Charles II's mistresses, a French lady whose talents were admirably suited to her calling. She was a goddess on her back but a spy on the side. The French king paid her a fortune to share the English king's pillow talk; the English king paid her a fortune to keep the pillow under her bottom. She was possibly the most publicly loathed woman in all of Merry England's history. One day, what was believed to be her carriage was stoned by a furious mob incensed by her Catholicism. The window was pulled down and Nell Gwyn, the king's other mistress, pushed out her famously beautiful embonpoint and shouted, 'Pray good people. I am the Protestant whore.'

King Charles's illegitimate son was made the first Duke of Richmond, and, not to be outdone, the French king made him the Duke of Aubigny. With this auspicious start, the Richmonds amassed wealth, art and position, all of which is expensive to maintain, and by the time Charles got to the big house, something middle-class needed to be done to keep the spoons polished. He was and still is a very good photographer – that was the life and vocation that he loved and might have continued but for the ancestors frowning down from their draughty walls, stonily calling him to his birthright. So he set about preserving the estate and the house and his grandfather's racetrack. He reinstated it for the Festival of Speed in 1993 with a smart counter-intuition that is rare for his class. Charles celebrated the motorcar when everyone else was saying that it was utilitarian and pointless. He insisted that there was a great romance in cars and that there was nowhere to go if you felt romantic about them. He understood that a lot of people would pay to spend a lot of hours just watching cars do what they were made to do, which is make a lot of noise and go very fast. He also knew that a lot of very famous people would turn up to drive them. And that nearly every retired racecar driver with all his limbs would love to take a spin around the track. Film stars, pop stars and aristocrats don't have to be asked twice to come to Goodwood to show off their vintage Morgans and Ferraris. There is a *concours d'élégance*, a beauty parade, of which I am occasionally an inexpert judge. We walk around looking at polished curves and chrome back ends, staring in the way that you're not allowed to look at women but with a similar yearning.

There are hospitality tents and shops and restaurants and dim sum as far as the eye can see, and there is music and promenading and buckets of champagne, and it's all wrung with a silky confidence that comes with a certain British *élan*. The festival has grown and grown until it's like Woodstock for highly tuned combustion engines that howl protest songs against the dullness and boredom and risk-filtered tedium of modern motoring.

Lord March does have a real love for cars. He likes to drive fast. He once crashed into a tree and damaged his leg and back, but he doesn't complain. I ask him what he drives, and he has to think, like trying to remember the names of your cousins. He has the prototype of an AC 16/80 and a 'March'-bodied Riley from the 1930s. He likes bikes too. He has an R5 BMW from 1934 – he makes sure I write that down – as well as a Ducati. He doesn't mention the sit-upon lawn mowers, but I've seen an awful lot of them because there's an awful lot of lawn.

Then there is the Revival, every September, which is the same thing all over again though in fancy dress. This is fantastically barmy but winning entertainment. The British are very partial to dressing up in what Americans call 'costume'. They used to stipulate an era for everyone to come dressed up in, but then they gave up because the public's grasp of history wasn't as keen as their need to come as a First World War fighter pilot or a cancan dancer. So now everyone comes as whatever or whoever they like. And thousands a year do, and it is a spectacular and otherworldly vision. A milling horde that looks like extras from every British film ever made, particularly war films. And to make it all matter, Lord March runs an organisation called Goodwood Actors Guild, with more than two hundred thespians who mingle with the crowd and have impromptu dramatic moments, like nostalgic theatre. So you might come across Lawrence of Arabia on his camel or Charlie Chaplin having a quiet moment or an Andrews Sister broken down at the side of the road. Seen from a distance in the summer light it could also all be a Day of Judgement, the rising of ghosts. Goodwood's Revival is a little like passport control to heaven.

The last time I was there Charles asked if I'd like to go round the track with a man dressed as J. R. Ewing driving me in a large American car with fins that rocked through the corners, while beside us the twentieth century rolled past. Wars and politics, weddings and parties, entertainments and vanished jobs all swam into the distance. Above us a flight of Spitfires and Hurricanes rose from the airfield in tight formation with the unmistakable fruity sound of the Merlin engine. They banked and climbed in the blue sky where seventy years earlier the Battle of Britain had been fought on days exactly like this one. Even the weather had come in fancy dress.

On the last evening of the Revival, Charles hosts a grand costume ball. And a ball is what his family is most famous for. The Duchess of Richmond gave a ball in Brussels in 1815 on the night that Napoleon marched his army into the Battle of Waterloo, in Belgium. The young British officers had to hurry to their regiments still in their dress uniforms to fight. Byron wrote of it in *Childe Harold's Pilgrimage*, the poem that made him the first celebrity:

> Ah! then and there was hurrying to and fro,
> And gathering tears, and tremblings of distress,
> And cheeks all pale, which but an hour ago
> Blushed at the praise of their own loveliness.

That could also be the epitaph of the British aristocracy. Two years from now will be the 200th anniversary of the ball. I expect Charles is coming up with something spectacular.

I sit in London's Wolseley restaurant at lunchtime waiting for Lord March. He bustles in, as hurried as a man who fills his days with the eternally optimistic expectation that an extra hour will be produced from some ethereal clock by some accomplished flunky. He walks through the room. Businessmen reach out to greet him. Lunching women beam. He knows everyone, and I've yet to find one among them who has a critical word to say about him. He talks candidly but guardedly about his life and achievement of securing the great pile of responsibility passed to him without choice, making it not just solvent but hugely successful and an enviable brand that grows year by year without desecrating or cheapening the estate. He takes it seriously, but he's not serious about it. Given another life, given the choice, he might have remained in the terraced house in London and taken pictures. He's done his duty, done what the silent ancestors with the eyes that follow you around the room have demanded of him. He has secured the land and the heritage for generations of Lord Marches. But he's also something even more impressive, something they never were – he has managed that aristocratic oxymoron: he is a self-made man.

September 2013

The Shipping Forecast

An old expat who'd lived for thirty years in the unflinching sunlight of Malta said that over the years the things he missed about England had fallen away. First the clothes, then the attitudes, then the yearning for Blighty news and culture. He said it's like sloughing off skin, and I wondered what he'd turned into. Did he emerge as some new Maltese butterfly? No, he said, it was as if he was the same but lighter, unencumbered by the received and unwanted assumptions and dispositions of inherited location, excused the prejudices of birth. What was left behind, he said, was just him, but less certain of things, slower to take offence, with fewer table-thumping opinions.

The bits of England that clung to him most stubbornly were food; and the preferences that had seemed unimportant back in Sussex became sentimental cravings abroad – the junkie's fear of running out of marmalade, the hoarding of fruit-and-nut chocolate, the dreaming of Marmite and sausages, the need to make shepherd's pie and drink warm gin. There were phantom yearnings, too, for stuff he'd rarely ever eaten and never missed when it was available: crumpets, meat pies, Tunnock's teacakes. But slowly these too faded from appetite. Last of all, he said, was breakfast. The first meal was the last to vanish. How difficult it is to give up the comforting morning; we will happily eat the same breakfast all our lives. But eventually that too went. Was there anything of his old home that he still missed? 'Well, oddly, there's a voice,' he said. 'I still sometimes listen to the Shipping Forecast.'

A really odd, arcane public-service radio broadcast made late at night and early in the morning giving detailed weather forecasts to the fishermen that circle Britain with a shorthand series of directions that are meaningless to landlubbers, the Shipping Forecast is always exactly 370 words long, and it comes attached to names that are the fishing areas and marine districts. They form a litany, a catechism, a sort of blank verse of evocative names. Not one person in a hundred would be able to point to them on a map. They start in the north-east with Viking and work down the east coast along the Channel and around Land's End, up the west coast, past Ireland and the Hebrides and up to Iceland.

We usually hear the Shipping Forecast in bed, in the dark. It's like the technical instructions to a prayer for the nation, a shanty for the sea that has protected Britain for ever. It conjures pictures of the grey and severe ocean, stern and implacable, the lighthouses that prick the darkness, the ships ploughing the fields of water. Calling the names is like a child's nursery rhyme or a counting game. It is absurdly and yet profoundly comforting. It is our secret. You could live as an arriviste, a refugee, a migrant in Britain for a lifetime, marry a native and have children who thought of themselves as English as rain, but you might never know about the Shipping Forecast. We don't talk about it. Not to strangers. Not to each other. There's nothing to say. It's a collective saga of Britishness. It is mundane in its primary intent and deeply spiritual, profound in its metaphysical meaning. It has, though, occasionally crept into culture – both popular and highbrow. Radiohead and Blur have used it as lyrics, as did Jethro Tull. Seamus Heaney wrote it a sonnet, and Carol Ann Duffy a poem. Comedians have traduced it.

The fact that the Shipping Forecast is not written by anyone, has no author, and that it changes and remains the same somehow adds to its effect. It isn't a stirringly patriotic verse or an anthem to be usurped by politicians or regiments; it's just about the weather, and we're all about the weather, and it's written every day by nature – our nature. Good, moderate and poor. Gusting, veering and backing. We can never go to the named places. No one has ever been drunk there or went to university there. No one got married there, no one has an aunt that lives there. They are mystical names, like the knights of the Round Table. The ingredients in a spell. And the sea has always been a protective moat, the salty disinfectant that saved us from foreign contagion. It has also been the tide that has carried us away. The sea is our escape from this wet, claustrophobic, angry little island. We listen to the names on the Shipping Forecast in the dark. They are the stations on the route to freedom.

Most people travel to find something – something new, something exciting, something hot, surprising, inventive. Travellers, people who make going their business, or do their business to finance the going, are often trying to escape as much as to discover. We – I count myself among them – are trying to lighten the load of our inherited national character, to be rid of the natal mud. But we are part-time refugees, always returning, hoping that we may have dumped and discarded some of the stifling jingoism in the Channel or the Bay of Biscay or the Atlantic; that we manage to return to be in Britain without having to be too insufferably British. We don't want a life sentence on a hot island as remittance men, banished slowly to go naked or troppo.

I don't look forward to a day when I can get over the withdrawal symptoms and cravings for cucumber sandwiches and the smell of wet cut grass. There is nowhere and no one I want to be more than the person I am right now. I just want to empty my pockets and travel lighter and fleeter. I want to be less shocked and more surprised. The Shipping Forecast is a verse of both longing and leaving. The push and the pull of the tide. If you were never British it will mean little to you, a random list, but if you were ever one of us, it'll stab to the pit of your suntanned stomach. You will taste the salt of the cold, grey seas. And now, here's the Shipping Forecast, the hymn of the British: Viking, North Utsire, South Utsire, Forties, Cromarty, Forth, Tyne, Dogger, Fisher, German Bight, Humber, Thames, Dover, Wight, Portland, Plymouth, Biscay, Trafalgar, FitzRoy, Sole, Lundy, Fastnet, Irish Sea, Shannon, Rockall, Malin, Hebrides, Bailey, Fair Isle, Faeroes, Southeast Iceland. Goodnight, and God bless.

August 2013

Humberside

I'm Adrian, I'm an alcoholic. I haven't drunk alcohol since I was thirty – twenty-eight years ago. Drunks court trouble: social, financial, physical, emotional and magistrate.

I was arrested just the once. I was stopped lots of times, shouted at, moved on, warned, searched on sus, pockets checked – 'I'm not going to find anything sharp in here, am I, sonny?' 'Only my wit, constable.' I was nicked for being drunk in public, which was bad luck because I hadn't been sober in public for a decade. I'd called the police, that's how drunk I was; or rather, I told the barman to call them on my behalf – either that or unlock the door – so I was arrested for being drunk. Actually, I think I was really arrested for calling a policeman 'darling'. They did the bar for having drinks on the table after hours and me for drinking too many.

The constable walked me down Earl's Court Road to the police station. I asked if he was going to handcuff me. 'No. You're not a runner.' I was pushed into a cell that was already full. We were an Ealing Comedy cast of drunks: a tramp, a businessman who'd passed out on the Tube, a Scotsman off the oil rig who'd been on a three-day bender and a hippie who said he was actually stoned, but couldn't tell the police that.

I lay on the floor with my coat as a pillow. The light stayed on all night. In the morning, a piece of toast was thrown at my head. The sergeant said I could have a drink from the standpipe. We were taken to the Magistrates' Court, where we waited in a small Victorian cell for them to deal with the night's prostitutes. Even moral turpitude has manners: ladies first. As I waited to go into the dock, the policeman who'd arrested me whispered: 'Say you're sorry. They like that.' So I said I was sorry and unused to strong drink, and was fined £15. We were all stamped with justice in half an hour.

I was impressed at how the magistrate arranged the fine to suit our circumstances: the businessman got the most, the Scotsman, then me, then the stoned lad got a tenner and the tramp wasn't fined but held for a medical check-up. It was the class system at work, when any Englishman can glance at his countrymen and know what they should be fined.

We were tipped out into the street at opening time and, naturally, made for the nearest pub for a breakfast pint. At the other end of the bar were the policemen who'd arrested us. There was a curt raising of glasses and a nod. Now when I fill in forms that inquire about criminal records, I say 'yes'. It was a very Anglo-Saxon experience: none of us complained that it was unfair or a waste of time; it was simply part of the warp and weft of our island life. A night in the cells seemed a sort of birthright, part musical joke, part Rotary Club morality. We were, in that peculiarly circular English expression, no better than we should be. I only tell you this to show I am not a disinterested party in this story of drunk England.

Drink is a problem, it is our problem, the lubrication of our national character, and it appears to be getting worse. The after-dark centres of market towns and cities are given over to avid drunkenness, a zombie invasion, and drink is taking a greater toll on our health – particularly that of the young and, of them, particularly women. Liver damage is rising exponentially among the under-thirties, the price of alcohol has never been lower, and the amount of time you have to work to afford a bottle of vodka is shorter than it's ever been. Sober voices are calling for something to be done, among them the Association of Chief Police Officers and the prime minister, who say we need a return to drunk tanks – not that anyone can remember what a drunk tank is. So, I spend a night out in the north-east to see what they are talking about.

Matthew Grove, the Commissioner for Humberside Police, is another of these voices, on his patch, Grimsby: not as nice as it sounds. From London it takes longer to get there than to fly to Moscow. Somewhere north of Doncaster, everything turns to black and white and fades to mono. Grimsby is on the road to nowhere. If you have ever wondered who lost the cod wars with Iceland, the answer is Grimsby. It didn't just lose, it was routed. This was once the liveliest, gutsiest fishing port in Europe. Now it does a bit of processing when the Icelanders pass on stuff they're too busy to handle. It suffers all the dull litany of deprivation: high youth unemployment, lack of investment, worn-out infrastructure, underachievement, bad education, and is one of the least diverse and most pasty-white pockets of England. There is plenty of grubby petty crime and domestic abuse, but apart from that it's lovely, as is Cleethorpes next door.

Cleethorpes: that isn't as nice as it sounds, either. A chilly holiday resort – the tourists have all gone the same way as the fish. Grove meets me off the train with his press secretary. They're firm-handshake men. Famously, Grove defeated John Prescott on his home ground to get the Commissioner job. He is a man I expect would describe himself as direct, no-nonsense, a people person. He thinks he's a leader of men, a natural doer. Every sentence comes with an implied exclamation and a smiley face. He is the sort of man perennially drawn to local politics, a civic bull in search of municipal china shops.

He drives us through the dark and silent streets of Cleethorpes early in the evening. They're horror-film empty, nothing stirs in hunched and grubby semi-detached streets that emanate a forbidding depression. Grove talks in capital letters about the need to claim back the night, how decent people are scared to go out after dark. He resents the squalor, mess, rudeness and implicit violence of the drinking culture. It's an insult to a decent community! Far too much police time and effort are being put into cleaning up after people who can't hold their drink. So he's posited the idea of a drunk tank, which sounds solid and exclamatory.

What actually is a drunk tank? The details are still sketchy: a place, perhaps a converted container, where the inebriated, the hopeless, could be taken to sober up, possibly copulate and then be fined, as with a traffic offence, without taking up magistrates' time or causing trouble. Who would do the locking-up? I ask. G4S can't arrest people; the police would still have to do the detaining, and the drunks have got to be offered some sort of medical help.

'Well, all that can be worked out,' he says with the airy dismissiveness of the big blue-sky thinker. 'It's just a suggestion. But something must be done!' We get to the police station, a forbidding compound surrounded by a tall fence and electric gates and arc lights and clusters of CCTV. There's no blue light or obvious public entrance. 'If I want to report my cat's missing, where do I go?' I ask. 'Oh, I think there is a public entrance somewhere, but it's probably not open now. This isn't a very nice area, you know.' So they had to lock up the cops in case they get robbed? Inside I'm shown a call centre, which is not as exciting as it sounds, and have a briefing with the Police and Associated Forces Outreach Organising Public Safety Confederation, or something or other, that comprises real cops, auxiliary hobby cops, the fire brigade, the drug squad (but they've lost their dog) and the council licensing authority.

We're briefed by a lady who addresses us all as 'people' and apparently learnt her public-speaking skills from watching American police dramas. Everyone looks bored and shifty. A girl from the council winks at me, not because she wants to check my basement access, but because she wants me to know that this is being concocted for my benefit. The Commissioner looks pleased and motivated, the police watch him with weary stone faces – the way circus animals watch the man holding a chair. So we walk out into the chilly sodium night. A policeman looks up and says: 'Full moon. It's going to be a rough night. It's always worse when it's a full moon, coppers know that. And the last Friday of the month: payday. That's bad. And heat: you don't want it to be too hot.' Then it begins to drizzle. 'Ah, that's better. Rain, it's like having an extra policeman on the beat, is rain. The copper's friend.' I had no idea policing was so like gardening: rain at night, copper's delight; full moon in sight, Old Bill's blight.

Cleethorpes' strip of bacchanalian sin is a sorry and insipid little thing. It's not Las Vegas, it's not even lost property: a meagre high street that is, like most high streets in provincial towns, gasping for trade. The shops are given over for charity and hairdressing. (Why are there so many hairdressers in the world?) There are payday-loan shops and dozens of fast-food caffs, pubs and cavernous clubs. At 10 p.m. the streets are busy with men who have plainly been drinking since knocking off work. It doesn't kick off until about 12. The young stay at home, preloading on cheap supermarket beer and own-brand vodka, telling stories, watching telly, Facebooking, texting, orchestrating the night. They turn up lively, with the edges sanded off.

We're joined by Martin Vickers MP, a local man and a Tory. I ask what he thinks of drunk tanks. 'It's an interesting idea,' he says, in the way politicians do when people suggest funding research into extraterrestrial rectal probes. We stand outside a club, looking like a Victorian Methodist fact-finding tour. A policeman with a lot of braid asks if we'd like a uniformed escort. We all say 'No', emphatically and too quickly. The youth begin to fill the high street: loud, bouncy and effortfully up for it, or for something. The girls are in tiny frocks with plunging cleavages and gaping backs, chubby carmine toes squashed into perpendicular platforms. The shoes are enormous, vertiginous plinths of self-proclamation. Tattoos dodge down spines, across builders' buttocks, and slide off cleavages. The girls tug at themselves, pulling down hems, cantilevering bras. They're loud and confident and brilliantly vital. The MP regards them askance, not in shock or surprise, but with a sort of paternal concern. They frighten me.

The boys have all made an inverse effort: they wear jeans, T-shirts and trainers, the uniform of active insouciance. Only the carefully gelled hair gives away some personal insecurity. Everyone is pissed, stoned or both. I've been led to expect a Hogarthian melee of violence and vomit: girls squatting in gutters, lads jumping on heads, comatose sex against wheelie bins, screaming rows, hair-pulling, bottling, blood and puke. Actually, it's all rather good-natured. Every bar and club has three or four bouncers: tough, calm ex-servicemen, mostly, all licensed, all wearing badges of office, implacable as they go through the dull ticket collection of checking fake IDs.

A boy hasn't got his. He feebly exhorts, wheedles, then begs. It would be easier for a camel to get through the eye of a needle. He nods in surrender and trudges away. His mates call blessings after him. Head down, he is the saddest kid in town. One of the few obviously foreign men, in a suit, comes up and asks who I am. I tell him I'm a journalist.

'Oh, that explains it. This is my club,' he says as girls say hello and boys pat his shoulder. He is clearly the man to know. 'I wondered why the extra police were out. It's not normally like this. I wish you were here every week. My staff have to take care of the street, look after the incapable ones, break up squabbles. It shouldn't be their job. You write that.'

'How's business?' I ask.

'OK, up and down. It's quiet tonight. My margins are down to the bone. We're being killed by supermarket booze.'

His drinks are a couple of quid a shot for some childish-looking coloured cocktail or £6 for a bucket and half a dozen straws. Inside the music is thuddy and ear-splitting, primary-coloured lights streak and syncopate. There's not much sophistication or glamour here. It's a functional space for the kids to make their own, like a school dance. They show off their bedroom-mirror moves in little votive coveys, as if imploring a good harvest, or a boyfriend, or an end to world hunger.

Anthems bang out of the speakers and suddenly the whole room is miming the same words, with exaggerated operatic movements. Confessing love to each other histrionically, couples fall onto each other's faces with sweaty, open-mouthed snogs. They touch all the time, like bees communicating simple pheromone truths: I'm here, you're here, we've known each other all our lives, we grew up here, we belong here, this is our Saturday night.

As the night tips over into the next day, the dancing becomes more incoherent, the snogs reduced to general face-licking. Outside the police arrest a drug dealer, a sorry-looking boy who's staring down a whole new life path. There is a fight between two girls and a chorus of supporters. It's broken up by bouncers, who hug the combatants like amorous bears, while the mascara-striped faces screech invective and vicious promises. Kids mill in the streets, smoking and telling stories of the evening: who with whom? Where? Who knew? Who's going to tell? Who cares? It's the elaborate narrative web of belonging and community that weaves the tapestry of your life from nappy to shroud. Most people are now really, really drunk: glassy-eyed, staggering, lamp-post-butting, hedge-vomiting drunk. The kebab, pizza and chicken shops are rammed with children shovelling glistening, greasy gobbets of meat and bread into their mouths. Chewing and laughing and shouting and singing and smoking, like a great choir of the orally juggling.

A girl comes up and hugs me because she says I look sad. I do look sad. Then an excited lad points and shouts: 'A scientist. Look! A scientist. Are you a scientist? Are you Doctor Who?'

The last nightclub on the strip is by the sea. It has a licence until 5 a.m. The manager worries. Nobody's in good shape now. We, three old men, stand and watch. I feel awkward, uncomfortable, I radiate a parsimonious sobriety. Grove asks rhetorically: 'Where's the sense of shame in society? No one feels guilt or responsibility. When we were young, if we were caught like that' – he points – 'we'd be ashamed. Your dad would make you ashamed. I want to bring back the sense of shame in our communities.'

We pack up and go back to the police station. The desk is quiet, the cells hold the drug dealer and a sorry boy who's been brought in for a domestic. He thumped his girlfriend. He doesn't look ashamed, he looks stoned and resigned and unsurprised.

At 5 a.m. the emergency ward at the hospital is calm and efficient. There's only one person in the waiting room and the doctor says it's been a relatively normal night. Perhaps a third of the cubicles are occupied by drink-related injuries. 'We don't distinguish between causes,' he says. 'The only thing with drunks is, if they're passed out they have to be supervised. They can die. It's rare, but you lose the swallowing reflex and can inhale vomit, so they are put near the nurses' station. We stick a drip in them to rehydrate them, and they wake up without a hangover.' He smiles. 'All part of the service.' You couldn't do that in a drunk tank.

As the Commissioner drives me back to the train station in the dawn, he asks why we can't drink like the Continentals: a glass of wine with some tapas in a café, all ages together; a glass of beer, an aperitif, then the *passeggiata*, dressing up smartly. Why can't we change the culture? I look at him and keep my mouth shut. At the station a fox trots down the line, a drunk is sprawled over a bench. 'Why don't we drink like the Greeks or the Italians?'

Really? Because we have a choice, that's why. Because we're from the north, from the cold, from the drizzle, from the place where the moon drives us nuts. Who would want to drink like an Italian granny? Sip wine with a raised pinky, chew a carrot, when you could be out there with all your mates, people you fancy, people you don't, people you shag, people you wanted to. You can go mad, get totally munted. You can let go. Why have a polite chat when you can have a legend? When you can weave a myth that will last you all week, that will stay with you for ever? Why would you want to ponce about in the grottoes of Dionysus when you can get trollied in the mead halls of Valhalla? This is who we are, this is what we do – or what I did.

I don't miss drink, ever. Being an alcoholic is not the same as being drunk. But I look at these kids in this thin, worn-out, under-privileged, unlovable corner of England and I think: how brilliant that they can still get out and manufacture this much enthusiasm, fun and mad entertainment, this much togetherness and community and hope out of so little, such meagre education, so few jobs and prospects. The drink, drugs and music are not just their culture, they're their achievement. I mention to the Commissioner that if he wanted to stop this carnage every weekend, all he needed to do was pull the licences and make the pubs and clubs close at 11 p.m., like when we were teenagers. 'Ah, well, yes, of course, but it isn't quite that simple,' he says. 'Why not?'

Well, I'll tell you why not. Because it's the kids' nights out that are keeping this town above water, solvent. Grimsby and Cleethorpes are living off the money the kids scrounge, earn, get given: the taxis, the fast-food joints, the watching police and the tooth-sucking, finger-wagging, slut-shaming Commissioner are all serviced and paid for by these inventive, funny children. If you want to shame someone, try pointing in the mirror. You should buy them all a drink, put up a statue to the inebriated kid, Cleethorpes' biggest benefactor.

December 2013

FURTHER

Bethlehem

A cold coming we had of it. It started with the Mossad grilling from two twelve-year-old immigration girls at Ben Gurion airport. Almost everyone in Israel who exerts any street-level power turns out to be an improbably young woman with a face and figure out of the Song of Solomon and a manner that implies she would happily drive a tent peg through your sleeping philistine head. 'Why exactly don't you want an Israeli stamp in your passport?' Well, personally, you know, I'd adore one, but a lot of other countries might not appreciate it. 'You are a journalist?' Sorry. 'Who are you planning on talking to?' Baby Jesus.

And then there was no room at the inn. Baby Jesus has a sense of humour. You mean you have no rooms at all? 'None. We have no confirmation of you. And you know what time of year it is?' Don't tell me, there's a census. It's the perfect start to a story about Bethlehem and the real heart and soul of the millennium. Forget your domes and Ferris wheels and all-inclusive tropical luxury breaks seeing in the sunrise twenty minutes early. Bethlehem is the hub – the *raison d'être* of it all. If this was just another two-camel sheep station in the desert, then all we'd be celebrating on 1 January would be computers that can't count. I'm here to spend one day in the life of God. Sunday. God's day. I finally get a room at the Hyatt. 'I'm sorry, you can't check in until 7.30. Sabbath, you know.' Of course, God's dad's day. The Hyatt is a tour-guided pilgrims' hotel of irredeemable ghastliness. It's full of money-belted Southern Baptists in baseball caps with peaky inspirational messages. At breakfast I hear a shingled pensioner in complete Christian combat gear ask: 'If you see any Jews, can you bring one over to me?' 'Sure, honey. What do you want? Orange Jews or grapefruit Jews?'

No corner of the earth has been gilded with as many great

expectations as the Holy Land. It is the crucible of the two greatest stories ever told, the Bible and the long homeward journey of the Jewish Diaspora. In terms of tears and blood, and inspiration and hope, nowhere else can begin to compete. What I expected, what I wanted, was some sort of visible exclamation of it all: steeples and spires, gilded domes and Roman pillars, mixed with a pre-war Yiddish sophistication, cafés with chess players, violin music wafting from upper windows, carpets and diamonds, all that old dusty, winey, velvet sentimental richness. I wanted hand-waving and philosophy and cheesecake and chicken soup and Barbra Streisand. It's not here. Not remotely. Not any of it. And it was foolish to imagine it would be.

Israel is a half-century-old Middle Eastern country built in a hurry on the horns of a dilemma. It's low-rise breeze block with limestone cladding. It's dust and rubbish. Cacophonous neon, fraying tempers and suicidal driving, all strung about with barbed wire and observation towers and concrete security chicanes and a sense of extemporary make-do-and-mend. Israel is a work in progress where the architects' plans were written after the foundations were laid. The other thing is size. Size shouldn't count, but Israel is very small, and the Bible implies that it's vast, all those journeys, all that old age and those wanderings. Forty days in the wilderness and you could wander round the place twice.

Early on Sunday morning I set out for Bethlehem, which is virtually just a suburb of Jerusalem. 'Would you like to go to the Mount of Olives first?' asked my Palestinian driver, who started pounding his horn under the British mandate. Sunrise on the Mount of Olives, that would be wonderful. Up to a point. The Mount of Olives is a car park. More precisely, a bus park and turnaround roundabout. May all your beatitudes be platitudes. But it's not finished yet. Piles of rubble and extruded steel macramé for reinforced concrete fray around its edges. The bulldozers and trucks are already kicking up the dust. An early Arab sits with a sad donkey beside a Portakabin waiting for the stream of photo opportunities, more Kismet-me-quick than hosanna. Beneath us, in the hazy grey morning light, lies unprepossessing Jerusalem. Only the golden Dome of the Rock catches early rays and glitters a counterpoint to the dun city that crawls up the dun, sparse hills. The mosque is the third-holiest site in Islam, and it only just avoided being blown to somebody's kingdom come by furious Israeli sappers after the Six-Day War. Somewhere on the slope beneath us, in the stepped cemetery, Robert Maxwell awaits the Day of Judgement. Two minutes is more than enough. The garden of Gethsemane is just around the corner. It's also tiny. An amenity area of gnarly olives and municipal scrub planting, about as spiritual and contemplative as a Little Chef playground.

You approach Bethlehem through Israeli security barriers, where nervous, sullen, clean-shaven young soldiers in green fatigues smoke cigarettes and heft their combi rifles-cum-rubber-bullet launchers. A few yards away there's another checkpoint. This time the young men are in black uniforms with moustaches. They smoke and cradle Kalashnikovs and are the Palestinian police. Their shoulder flashes say Tourist Police, which could mean they are there for us, or that they are just visiting themselves.

Bethlehem is an Arab town, part of the disparate segregated ghettos of the proto-Palestinian state. I walk up to Manger Square in the centre of town. This is Bethlehem's moment, and it knows it. Moments like this only come along every 1,000 years, and they're going to make the best of it. The place is one huge, confused building site, getting ready for the prayed-for influx of millennial tourists. They are building a multi-storey car park and bus station, an Arab heritage centre. The streets are being repaved. The gift shops and falafel shops are being scrimmed. Hoardings explain that the money for this development has been given by the Swedes and the Norwegians, the Japanese and the European Union. Palestine is a *Big Issue* state: it only exists on the philanthropy of strangers. But then again, so does Israel.

'O little town of Bethlehem, How still we see thee lie' is pounded away in a reggae timpani of hammers and grinding gears. I'll never sing carols again without the ferrous taste of irony and cement dust. The Church of the Nativity, which covers the actual spot where Christ was born, is the oldest place of pilgrimage in Christendom, invested first by the Emperor Constantine's mum, who came here and built the original chapel, which was later shrouded in a second, bigger church. Although most of the religious buildings in this part of the world have been flattened by the ebb and flow of competing dogmas, Bethlehem has remained remarkably untouched. However, the church is not a pretty building: it is a lumpy block with haphazard additions and three tackily illuminated crosses on the roof. The doorway has been reduced to a serving hatch that a single person has to double up to pass through. How they are going to get a million pilgrims in and out is a mystery, but then so much about this place is a mystery. Inside, I was underwhelmed by the grandeur and venerability of the place – a timeworn barn with fat pillars and coarse tiles, and bituminous Eastern votive paintings of boneless, agonised saints daubed onto fraying alligator skin by nameless jobbing artists. Very ornate beaten-silver, icon-encrusted altar screen and hundreds of kebab-restaurant lamps, electric and oil, that trail a contradictory confusion of wires and ropes.

The reason for the contradiction in design, and indeed lighting, is that the church is held by three competing sects: the Greek Orthodox, the Armenians and the Roman Catholics. Welcome to God's car-boot sale. They have spent the past 2,000 years tit-for-tatting each other into an uneasy non-speak. At this point, I should admit that I am a believing (as opposed to a practising) Christian, but of the Protestant and low-Church variety. We don't go in for this sort of thing, this fixation on lumps of rock and pilgrimage and the argy-bargy of sites. Any smugness on my part, though, must be tempered by the admission that if it were the Bible that you were talking about, then we'd be in there swinging to get hold of Ezekiel before the Methodists or the born-agains.

There is a strict rotation in services, each ancient Church's monks waiting in the wings to clear the airwaves to God after the last heretic lot. Each has their own changing room and kit locker. This is made all the more complicated because the real holy of holies is not in the church but in the cellar. Downstairs, in a dank dungeon the size of a coal hole, is the exact spot (honest) where Christ was born, marked by a fourteen-point star to represent each generation back to King David. Next to it is the place (honest to God) where the manger stood. In this Stygian blackness everyone has their own set of lamps that hang like a thirteenth-century Transylvanian interior decorator's showroom and have to be blown out and relit for each service. Ah, but that's not all. The Armenians and the Greeks share the altar and its painting. But the Catholics have their own, so the canvas has to be removed and replaced with something equally tatty and glaucous. The Catholics also have the exclusive right to the manger – an area the size of a small lift – where the priest and his helpers all cling together chanting, waiting to be transported. As the Armenian bishop, who actually turned out to be Australian, set up his stall for early Communion, I sat on a low stone bench trying to summon up some sense of spiritual peace and awe, a sense of place. A troop of Ukrainian pilgrims shuffled their way downstairs and then crawled between the bishop's skirts to get under the altar and kiss the star. They came up crossing like tic-tac men. A scowling cowled monk hissed at me. I looked blank. 'Your legs! Uncross your legs! Don't you know you're in church!' Leg-crossing is obviously some ancient Eastern mortal sin. Defeated, I escaped back up into the crepuscular fug where the Romans were grouping in their 4 – 2 – 4 formation, chanting their Tridentine *haka*. The Greek Orthodox priests, big lads with full beards and stiff black chefs' hats, bided their time by barking at tourists, harrying them, keeping them moving. If the Lord's my shepherd, then these blokes are his huge sheepdogs.

The one thing all the chanting prelates are united by is a fierce, barely contained irritation with the pilgrims. There's no congregation for any of these endless rounds of services, and loitering is firmly discouraged, with flapping hands and a shove in the back. Run-of-the-mill vanilla Christians are an irrelevance or a sacrilege, flies in the Communion wine. I watched an American pilgrim hold a towel round his waist because he'd come all this way without realising that entering an Orthodox church in shorts was likely to upset people.

Just down the newly paved Norwegian road, but away from the general tourist beat, is the Milk Chapel. I must admit, I'd never heard of it. But then veneration of Mary doesn't come with my lot's hassocks. The Milk Chapel is supposed to be where Mary went to lactate before the flight to Egypt. It's a cave built into chalk. Which came first? The milk or the chalk? Only a Catholic could tell you.

Inside is an illuminated case showing mum with her *tsitskeh* out for baby Jesus, surrounded by roses and fairy lights. It is of a transcendent level of kitsch, unsurpassed in any votive shrine I've ever seen. The crumbly white walls have been blackened by oil lamps and candles, but holes have been scooped out all over it by desperate women who believe that to eat this holy rock will bring nourishment to their barren breasts. The monk in charge sternly discourages this practice. Of course, that sort of animistic superstition is hardly in keeping with a modern Church. Oh, silly me. I've misunderstood. He has a supply of chalk out the back that he'd rather sell to the women. A group of Irish ladies kneel in the pews chanting an endless round of 'Hail Mary, full of grace... Pray for us sinners now and at the hour of our death', over and over and over, as if God were hard of hearing. I escape again, into the hot, mechanical sunlight. I don't want to piss on anyone's candles, and there's quite enough competitive religion here, but frankly, selling blessed chalk as ex-vitro fertilisation to despairing women is beyond me.

Bethlehem is a place that attracts extremists. The government has just cleared out a number of the more frothing millennial revelationists. But in the desert hereabouts there are still pockets of fundamental Americans in beards and loincloths begging a little honey to go with their locusts, smiley in the knowledge that they only have a couple of weeks to go. And the local overworked psychiatrist specialises in come-again Christs. In fact, there's rumoured to be a special ward for them in the hospital: 'I am the second coming.' 'No, love, you're the thirteenth this month.' And John the Baptists waiting in outpatients for their medication: 'You think I'm mad, you should see he who comes after me.'

Back to Jerusalem, and the Church of the Holy Sepulchre. Birth to death in a single day. The old town of Jerusalem is quite picturesque, huddled behind Suleiman's curtain wall, built to keep Christians out. It has eight gates, from the evocative Dung to the bricked-up Golden Gate that will only open for the true second coming. And the Damascus Gate, famous as a home pitch for Palestinian–Israeli needle matches. Inside, the old town wiggles and winds in on itself, a labyrinth of narrow alleys and high walls, hiding dark courtyards.

It's segregated into four quarters: the Jewish, Christian, Arab and Armenian. The Jewish quarter has had a lot of money spent on it. It's neat and rather soulless. A small boy stops me in the street and says: 'Welcome to Israel.' The Armenian quarter is perhaps the saddest, containing the prettiest church in Jerusalem. The Armenians have had a miserable time of it. They are the oldest Christian Church in the world and they've needed to be. Set in a particularly volatile march between East and West, they've been roundly slaughtered by absolutely everyone. A menu in an Armenian restaurant gives a potted history of the troubles they've seen. It's unremitting and quite puts me off dinner, almost as much as dinner puts me off dinner. I really expected it to end up with: 'But we had a good day in June 1370. The sun shone and we went on a picnic.' The walls of the Armenian quarter are plastered with gruesome photographs and explanatory maps mourning their genocide. It's a measure of their continuing bad luck that they are forced to do this in Jerusalem, not a place to try to elicit sympathy for your pogroms. 'Holocaust? Don't talk to us about Holocaust.'

The Arab quarter is the liveliest: a huggermugger market of fruit and meat and clothes and cupboard shops selling videos and plastic toys and garish sweets, blaring with Arab pop music and dodgy archaeological coins, the widow's mite pendant or thirty pieces of silver as a necklace. The little bureaux de change, with a nice biblical turn, call themselves moneychangers. And there's a bric-a-brac of religion. Everyone is catered for here. Crucifixes hang happily with Stars of David and Fatima's Hand. Dimpled pink baby Jesuses lie among the worry beads and rosaries. Fezzes steeple the side piles of yarmulkes, mezuzahs nestle in checked Palestinian headscarves, T-shirts crawl up the wall, Yasser Arafat's face overlapping a picture of a machine pistol with the embarrassing slogan, 'Uzi Does It'. And it strikes me that, for all its crassness and exploitation, you can't deny that the free market succeeds where ages of argument and bullets have failed. It makes short work of theological and political differences. You may struggle for 1,000, 2,000 years over the minutiae of dogma, but here business makes all religions one big, dollar-friendly, happy family. I toy with the idea of buying a crown of thorns. There are dozens in various sizes at very reasonable prices. But I can't decide who to give it to. Maybe they only seem funnily ironic here.

The Via Dolorosa, Christ's last trip as a mortal, is, like everything else, not what I expected. A narrow, circuitous route, it starts outside the city wall by Golgotha and then traipses past the Arab souvenir shops, with the Stations of the Cross marked obscurely on the wall, competing with adverts for barbers and pirated videos. There used to be eight Stations of the Cross, but in the Middle Ages they became so popular in Europe that market forces added a few more. Now there are fourteen. Christ fell here for the first time, here for the second time, and way over here for the third. You can hire a lightweight, half-size cross from the Holy Sepulchre and do it yourself, like hiring a scooter in Skiathos, or a bicycle in Penrith. It's a novel way to get around, by crucifix. I get caught behind a confused group of Filipino Catholics who swapped over at each station. 'I'm No. 8, the woman wiping the brow,' 'No, you're No. 9, falling for the third time.' Anyway, they were going backwards. I noticed that nobody had volunteered to be the two thieves. That would be real humility.

You come to the Church of the Holy Sepulchre almost by accident. It has no vista. It's almost swallowed up by the Arab warren and, again, it's not a beautiful building. Big and bulbous and cavernous. 'In my father's house there are many rooms' has been taken literally. Chapels and altars burrow into the darkness. The fractious bad temper of the Church of the Nativity is multiplied. Here, six, or is it eight, separate pre-Reformation sects vie for supremacy over the holy of holies. A platoon of ancient Egyptian Christians are actually squatting on the roof. Nobody agrees on anything. The brass lamps proliferate like an arms race, spreading ever more gloom. And it's here that I realise what these churches, and indeed Israel, remind me of: it's the way-out-there, end-of-the-universe, lawless, freebooters' planet from *Star Wars*, a votive frontier town mining spiritual gold from dross, a federation of disparate and weird aliens in funny hats and exotic robes, with obscure and ancient ceremonies, tortuous languages and bizarre habits. Here, along with the Orthodoxies of Rome and Greece and Russia, Armenia and Serbia, the ancient Copts and Ethiopians, the Falashas, Black Christians from Zanzibar and Angola, there are wimpled Carmelites, cassocked Cistercians, Franciscans, Benedictines and free-range, born-again ecstatics. Outside there are Ashkenazi Jews, Sephardic Jews, the Chassidim, Hezbollah, the PLO, and there are migrants from Hungary, Russia and Poland, from Morocco, Alexandria, Slovenia and Slovakia, the Carpathians. There are Baptists from Alabama and Methodists from Michigan. There are Catholics from Macao and Hyderabad, and everybody, everybody, is drawn to this barren lump of sun-cracked rock that produces nothing more than avocados, miniature machine pistols and olive-wood salad servers. But in this dusty rock is the world's largest deposit of crude religion and the natural gas of intolerance. It's in the air. In the dust. You can feel it prickle your skin in the heat.

The first thing you see in the Church of the Holy Sepulchre is Christ's morgue slab, a polished piece of marble on the floor, guarded by the inevitable squadron of hanging lamps. It's kept wet. Pilgrims prostrate themselves like flocks of thirsty sheep to kiss it, dipping their fingers to genuflect. Next to it is Golgotha. The sights in the Holy Sepulchre come like rides in some ethereal Disneyland. Golgotha, the Hill of Skulls, is up a windy staircase, a small room packed with various denominations of professional and amateur pilgrims, gunning their Instamatics at a large, cut-out Christ. Like the hero in a Pollock's theatre, it syncopates in the stuttering flash. Again the X that marks the spot of the cross is under the altar, so they crawl between legs to get a snog. And it was here that I saw the only example of real ecstasy. A nun from some exotic denomination, with a pointy hat and a medieval wraparound headscarf affair that looked like a linen wetsuit, was transported; her pretty, virginal face a Flemish picture of pity and pain and adoration. It was a fleeting glimpse as the crowd of collected supplicants with their umbrella-waving guides pressed us on to the very heart of the Christian faith – the resurrection.

Without a resurrection, there is no Christianity. Everything else we can and do argue about, but this is the peg on which all the rest hangs, the central, death-defying act of faith. The tomb is housed in yet another marble Wendy chapel. It's falling down and is supported by RSJs as an unfortunate metaphor for the state of organised religion. The room itself can hold perhaps a dozen people, so the pilgrims queue four-deep for hours to get a look in where they can click a shot to ascertain that, phew, indeed, there isn't a body. The line is hot and bothered. It sways and bulges. A lot of people have come from cultures where orderly queuing is not in their natures. There's a babble of bad-tempered muttering. Monks harry and shoo and elbow the crowd. This being Sunday afternoon, it's time for evensong. A flying picket of Roman Catholic brothers, fit lads, start to manhandle the crowd without explanation. The volume of complaint rises in a dozen languages. The queue dissolves into a pushing, shoving throng. Those at the front have been waiting for hours to look in at an empty room, and they're not taking this on the other cheek. They're probably not even Catholic. The brothers get stuck in. Old American women begin spinning into the outer darkness. A Spanish tour group starts shoving back. The monks call up reinforcements. A flying wedge splits the pilgrims in half with some premier-division high-elbow work. In the distant gloom, a choir starts chanting Latin, the monks redouble their efforts and are joined by a Palestinian guard. Everyone's shouting now. The guard gets to the door of the tomb and I notice he is wearing a revolver. I can't imagine any other holy place in the world where it would be acceptable to allow a man with a gun. And certainly not here, where the Prince of Peace passively accepted crucifixion. The choir enter the fray, fronted by a chap swinging a censer like a teargas canister. The pilgrims retreat, an angry, confused mob. The monks face them like riot police. A bishop arrives, looks in at the tomb – phew, still no body – and chants evensong. The organ pipes up.

Offstage, another choir starts. That sonorous, sad, dusty descant that is Russian, or perhaps Serbian, or Armenian. For a few minutes the two sects compete in a discordant counterpoint. Then the Romans retreat to a side chapel and the Eastern Orthodoxes, led by an imposing bloke in a duvet beard and a hat that looks like Darth Vader's bed cap, takes his place at the tomb and has a look inside – phew. He does his thing. The Catholics may have retreated, but they've regrouped and they're not giving up; they've still got control of the organ. An Orthodox monk produces a mobile phone from his sleeve and has a muttered conversation – probably with the archangel

Gabriel. Snatch squads of prelates manhandle stray lambs. This is a schoolboy vision of the Middle Ages, and it makes *Life of Brian* look like a documentary.

The most poignant and distressing thing about all of this is that there's no congregation. Nobody's listening. Visitors are disinvited. This is between God and the professionals, as opposed to the merely faithful. Faith is a fugitive and difficult thing. One moment you're full of it. The next you can barely find a vestige. If you look for it straight on, it vanishes. You only glimpse it out of the corner of your eye. However annoying and bovine and crass the tour groups of retired American born-agains and Irish single mothers' clubs are, they have been brought here by faith. They haven't come to Israel for the view, or the relaxing luxury, or the food, or that famous Israeli hospitality. They've come to a troubled, dangerous corner of the world because this is where faith began. They've come with their own troubles to allay, with terrible sadnesses, with guilt and with fear and with hope, often at the end of their lives, on pilgrimages they have promised themselves and saved for over years. They don't have the luxury of a monk's vocation, the glorious lack of responsibility that a life in holy orders gives you. And, at the one place where they should find solace and conviction, they are treated like idiotic cattle, as an irrelevance and a nuisance. But still, they leave, not just with their olive-wood nativity sets and their rosaries, but with their faith. And that's nothing short of miraculous. God works in mysterious ways.

Here at the spiritual meridian of the millennium, like everything else, nobody can agree what day of the month it is. There's the Roman calendar, the Julian and the Gregorian. The Muslims think it's the fifteenth century. So the great irony is that there's going to be hardly anyone here celebrating the millennium anyway – and oh, 1 January is a Saturday, so the Jews can't make it either.

December 1999

St Tropez

It's fireworks, not cigarettes, that are the perfect pleasure. Cigarettes are close, they come after sex. Fireworks are sex. I've never seen a firework that I didn't want to see again, never seen a display that wasn't over way too soon. 'A million pounds,' said a girl sitting beside me. I could feel her expertly enhanced breasts press into my arm. I would have liked to pin a catherine wheel to each of them. 'A million pounds, the fireworks.' Of course, I thought she might have been making the opening bid of a proposition. We watched the pyrotechnics over the bay in silence. St Tropez is the best place to see fireworks: only here are they a mirror of the audience – all flash and noise, signifying nothing.

A million pounds is this year's St Tropez catchphrase. Last year it was half a mill – that's inflation for you. Everything is a million: what he spent on soft furnishings, what she's wearing in jewellery, her monthly alimony. Everyone's got a million on the tip of their tongue or up their nose. The girl takes one of my cigarettes and smiles and goes. I've had my million and my fireworks. After these there are balletic dancing fountains in the swimming pool, gyrating to Offenbach's cancan; syncopated spigots are a bit of an anticlimax, but then the band starts on the Perry Como medley. If they cost a million, he was deeply ripped off, whoever he is.

This party is an outdoor, sit-down dinner affair for 1,500 of someone's closest friends. Nobody I've asked has any idea who. There are rumours, of course. He's the sprightly chap with the badly squiffy wig over there. No, he's the bloke in the pink safari suit, or perhaps he's upstairs in bed, never attending his own parties, just listening through the shutters with his hand down his trousers. He made a fortune out of servicing fire extinguishers, or selling mirages, or the white slave trade, bauxite, olives, golf umbrellas. Anyway, whoever he is, I'd like to take this opportunity to say thank you, it was a splendid party.

I came in the train of a star – a real star, not a St Tropez light-the-blue-touchpaper-then-you-retire star – and as such we've been given the treatment. A motorbike outrider, valet parking and a hurried entrance surrounded by bouncers through the kitchen. It's an odd thing about celebrity: the higher you are up the *Hello!*-ometer, the more meagre the entrance you get. The back door is the stars' door. Only very famous people get to use the tradesmen's entrance; we emerge into the throng through a serving hatch. If I'd been travelling with royalty, I expect we would have had to go through the first-floor lavatory window. The Pope probably has to use the catflap, which would explain why he's always crawling on the tarmac.

On the dancefloor, girls of an exquisite beauty and gaseous sensuality, a species that denies origin or Darwin, sway and cantilever like ecstatic giraffes with men. Small, bandy, floppy-limbed, furry men whose lineage could only be the first act of a Wagner opera or a Grimms' fairy tale. The men are as hideous as the women are beautiful. They bury their sweaty, chewed-gum faces into honey-coloured tummies and the girls pat their heads and look at them with beatific smiles of divine pity.

Anywhere else, this nudely comical clinch would be ridiculous, look repellent, but here it's the right and natural order of things. St Tropez is time out on taste, half-time for morality. Some French celebrities recently complained in a magazine that St Tropez is becoming impossible, overrun with arriviste nobodies who gawp at each other and clog up everything. Well I'm sorry, but how can they tell? How could you know who was this year's arriviste hoi polloi as opposed to the indigenous arriviste hoi polloi or last year's arriviste hoi polloi? St Tropez is a square-mile traffic jam of frauds, leerers, liars, frotteurs, provocateurs, wannabes, has-beens, never-wasers, chancers, crooks, conmen, hopers, no-hopers, dreamers, nightmares, drifters, seekers, movers and shakers, both vertical and horizontal. In short, it's a sticky nougat of all the failings, vanitas, insecurities and exhibitionism that make being human such fun. Although it's constructed on the rigorous hierarchy of money and sex, it's a bizarrely egalitarian place.

The men rolling off the £20,000-a-day yachts are as desperate to be thought of as being as amusing and attractive and exciting as the hitchhiking Czech hookers who endlessly stroll up and down the dock. The stalled Porsche driver could be a grommet manufacturer from Trondheim or an Algerian thief. The girl on the bicycle might be a Hollywood movie star or she might just be a girl on a bicycle.

At lunch on the beach, where a tender picks up customers from the rented yachts and the bankrupt Bentleys doze in shady stables, everyone is familiar, everyone like a regular customer. We sit and swivel as the thonged buttocks brush the Perrier bottles. This isn't a restaurant so much as a daily dating game, a slowly gyrating tease.

In the evening, everyone flocks to the same nightclub. It has an enviably democratic door policy that has nothing to do with position or fashion or who you know or who you are, it's simply money. You bribe your way in. The palmed £1,000 is your entrée at this carnival of coupling. Sex is a gamble and this is its premier casino. Like all gambling, it's a game of chance, and the odds are stacked against you.

Every evening for a week I watched two young men with surnames that would have opened any door in the world and marked them as multimillionaires eat a late supper and then go ever-hopefully to the nightclub, only to return every breakfast unsnogged, ungroped, still fizzing with hopeful urges. All that effort, all that money, and a solitary bed. Even though St Tropez's *raison d'être*, its oily, provocative mission statement, is fornication, it's probably the hardest place in the world actually to get laid. I think the only people who have sex here are those who brought a bedtime snack with them. This place is all gong and no dinner.

St Tropez is one long stretch of the imagination. If you fly in a helicopter down the coast from Nice, there's no hint or sign as to why this place is as peerlessly wonderful and moreishly awful as it is. The architecture is crass, the geography is dull, the waters poisonous and fetid, and the weather is the same as most of the rest of the world. Yet here, on this thin promenade, celebrity was invented. Out of the sluggish surf arose the twentieth century's great, useless invention: undeserved, unearned, transient fame. God created woman, and then bikinis, and immediately afterwards playboys, coke dealers, PR agents, freelance photographers, valet parkers, gigolos, pimps, lounge lizards and a lot more women.

This is the place that gave us the jet set and the paparazzi and mass gossip and lies with six noughts. When you get back home with your mixed-grill tan and your untapped libido and say, 'Yeah, St Tropez, actually', the name all on its own gives you a little ersatz, tacky cachet. You've been through the tradesman's entrance of celebrity, the catflap of fame.

August 1999

Mykonos

Let's get one thing straight. Jeremy Clarkson. Clarkson is very straight. He's so straight you could grow soft fruit up him. If you put oil in his belly button you could use him as a spirit level. There isn't a kink, a curve or a rococo gesture about him. Clarkson likes to define himself by what he's not. And what he's principally not is bent. He's so unbent that there are those who might say he was actively homophobic.

But they'd be wrong. He's not homophobic in the way some are, say, arachnophobic. If Jeremy came across a homosexual in his bath, he wouldn't jump on the loo seat holding his nightshirt tightly at the knees and call in a desperate falsetto for his wife to come and deal with the huge, hairy thing. No, Jeremy feels about homosexuality rather what Neville Chamberlain felt about Czechoslovakia: a far and distant place of which he knows nothing; and, frankly, he doesn't care who buggers about with it, just as long as he's not expected to lend a hand. Though it must be said there is a sweaty whiff of the lower fourth about him. A touch of the schoolboy sniggers when it comes to queers.

When we first planned this article, he wanted to take me to Norway for the World Powerboat Championship. Well, you can imagine: all Heineken, herring and handbrake turns. No, I said firmly, you really don't need to get in touch with more high-octane petrol heads and their interminable back problems. You need to get in touch with some sexuality. Not yours; yours is best left sleeping under its rock. You need to reach out for someone else's. And so it was. We landed on sunny Mykonos. My own relationship with homosexuality is perhaps no less irrational than Jeremy's for a heterosexual man. I love it. Having been brought up in a theatrical family, I spoke Polari (gay slang) as soon as I could speak English. I'm drawn to camp humour, bitchiness and gay culture. I feel at home with everything except their genitals. My hard-and-fast rule has always been one willy in bed at a time. 'You know what you are?' a gay friend told me. 'You're a stray – a straight gay man. But there's still time.'

I haven't been to the Greek islands for a decade. Christ, make that two decades. But I have happy, sybaritic memories of them, and as we stepped off our little jet it all came back to me. The memories were despite the geography, rather than because of it. The Greek islands must have been made when God was going through his brief minimal, brutalist period. Mykonos is a sparse, crumbling, camel-coloured lump. There are features, but none of them are interesting. The building material of choice, which the Greeks use with chaotic abandon, is concrete and breeze block. But then this is the only landscape on earth where it looks organic and harmonious.

Despite being mentioned in the *Odyssey* and Herodotus, and therefore possibly the oldest tourist destination in the world, Mykonos is principally famous for its very modern homosexuality. Since the 1960s it has been a Mecca (probably not the right word) for young gays in search of a bit of the other, or rather a bit of the same. Mykonos means 'island of wind', which you, like Jeremy, may find a sniggeringly funny joke for a gay resort.

The first surprise is that not everyone is homosexual. I don't know exactly what we were expecting. *La Cage aux Folks* meets Gay Pride week, I suppose. But as well as being slippery heaven, Mykonos is also Hellenic St Tropez. Athenian families weekend here and pay monumental sums for whitewashed Portakabins and rock gardens. They do that paternal promenading thing of getting all dressed up and strolling purposefully around town in the early evening. But whereas in Italy or Spain this would be a jolly occasion, a chance for young people to meet and possibly mate, here the families march in descending size, led by fathers who have the mien of minotaurs and glare at any male under fifty. They're followed by daughters who sulk behind thick fringes, their eyes streaming from the fumes of their moustache peroxide. Mykonos is obviously a place for dressing up. Not fashionably. This is Greece, after all. But making an effort.

And plainly, oh, you can't imagine how plainly, Jeremy needs some holiday clothes.

I can't think where he thought he was going when he packed. A weekend's go-karting in Lincolnshire, perhaps? After an enormous amount of coaxing I manage to get him into a beach-front boutique run by a mere slip of a chap who immediately confirms all Clarkson's worst fears by asking him his star sign. Getting Jeremy to try anything on is more effort than getting Naomi Campbell to choose a wedding dress. Finding something he *could* try on is even harder. The small Asians who stitched this stuff can't have imagined anything his size outside of a Hindu temple. The waif-like shop boy regards Clarkson's stomach the way a plumber regards a blocked septic tank. Then, with a little squeak, Clarkson dives into a corner and pulls out a pair of culottes. They fit. After a fashion. A long way after any known fashion. They are, without qualification or demur, the most appalling item of holiday clothing ever made. They can only have been designed for a bet. They're a patchwork of garish, oriental offcuts that look like a mental hospital's sewing bee's quilt turned into po'boy's clam-diggers. They come from the Waltons' cruise-wear collection, and Clarkson adores them. He does little mewing pirouettes in front of the mirror. Out in the unforgiving sunlight, Jeremy saunters. I follow at an anonymous distance and watch as sensitive gay boys press themselves against walls to let this taste-apocalypse pass, just in case he's contagious. It's time to meet gay guys, and they come out at night.

Pierro's is, they say, the oldest and most popular gay disco bar in the Aegean. It's a two-storey town house, set on a tiny square. We arrive fashionably early. I've managed to convince Jeremy to leave the Tennessee troll kecks in his room. And he's relaxed and ready for a night on the town. Except he's not. He's about as relaxed as a greyhound in the soft-toy department of Hamleys. He sits stiffly on a bar stool, clutching a beer, imagining he's insouciantly invisible in the way only a six-foot-four, pubic-headed, Spacehopper-gutted, hulking heterosexual in mail-order chinos and docksiders can.

After five minutes he hisses: 'Psst . . . I've been picked up.' Where, how, who, why? 'That man over there. Don't look.' He shrugs at a gaspingly beautiful, olive-skinned, long-lashed twenty-year-old Greek boy with black curls falling over his shoulders, and a thin singlet barely covering a body that would keep a girls' school dormitory panting for a fortnight. 'He fancies me.' No, he doesn't. 'Yes, he does.' No, he's having a thing with the transvestite barman who's standing behind you. 'How do you know?' I just know. Gaydar. Gaydar is a queer sixth sense. 'But you promised, swore you were straight.' I am. I just inherited gaydar from my mother's side, and anyway I saw them kissing two minutes ago. Jeremy is not convinced. The only thing he is convinced of is that every homosexual on the planet is yearning to do the love that dare not speak its name (unless you hit your thumb with a hammer) to him. This, you will have noticed, is a common delusion among stridently heterosexual men. What makes you think gay men want to worship at the temple of your body, Jeremy? 'Well, they do. It's obvious. they're homos. I'm a man. I'm virgin meat for them. It's well known that what homos really fancy are straight, married blokes. I thought you were supposed to know about these things.'

Jeremy, let me say this with utter conviction. Trust me. Relax. Nobody here fancies you. Not on drugs, not for money, not remotely. Virginal and married as you are, you really aren't God's gift to gay men. You're not God's gift to straight women, either. In fact, you're not God's gift to anyone, except perhaps Colonel Sanders. The only thing that's remotely, attractively gay about you is your name. 'What, Jeremy?' No, Motormouth.

The bar begins to fill up. By 2 a.m. it's a hog-throbbing, bouncy, smiley pick-up joint. Jeremy and I might as well be fire extinguishers. Apart from all the other stuff, we're just way too old. The age limit is severe – young men between eighteen and thirty who look like footballers. The street outside could be a Manchester United summer school. There are one or two overtly camp queens, but in general the desired effect is sporty and butch.

On a balcony next door, three taut Hinge and Bracket trannies strike Dietrich poses. They look as coyly old-fashioned as black and white movies. I get caught in a corner by a nice Spanish architect who intensely explains the gay blitzkrieg theory of culture. Apparently, all culture is trailblazed by gay men. They're followed by straight women, who in turn attract straight men, who make the scene passé and mainstream, so the gays move on and invent something else. I nod and smile and apologise for being here and messing the place up.

Jeremy has managed to find a pair of organically grown real women. They've just been married to each other in Vermont and are on their honeymoon. He gives me a wink. By 4 a.m. I'm exhausted by the relentless fitness and exuberance. I don't think I can stand another bump-and-grind conga in a miasma of Égoïste and Le Bleu.

We walk back to our hotel through the wide-awake town. I pass on the gay theory of culture to Jeremy. 'Well, they didn't make any Ferraris or the Mustang or the Blackbird Stealth Interceptor, did they?' No, I don't think gay culture stretches to engineering. Though they might have done the Teasmade and the trouser press.

'Have you noticed anything strange about this place, apart from all the puffs?' he asks. 'There are no drunks. No vomit in the streets, no fights, no screaming gangs. If this were northern Europe, the place would be awash with blood, piss and sirens by now.' And it's true. A recent US study found that gays were the least violent and aggressive men on earth (beating Tibetan monks on a technical knockout). There must be more muscle and testosterone in Mykonos tonight than in a season of rugby league. But there's no trouble. In fact, gay men as a demographic are more law-abiding than the rest of us. More civic-minded, socially concerned. They vote more, earn more, clean up more. They read more. Go to more theatres. Consume more. Have better jobs. Better health. Pay more taxes. And are better-educated. In fact, gay men are model citizens. On paper we should all be aspiring to be gay men. By rights, logically, we should hope all our sons were gay. There's just that one little thing. 'It's not a little thing,' splutters Jeremy. 'It's a bloody big thing. A huge, hideous, humiliating, hurting thing. And I'd rather live on a sink estate in Cardiff and ride a bike without a saddle.'

Next morning, Jeremy comes down for breakfast. So how did he enjoy his first gay nightclub? 'It was surprisingly good fun. Those two I was talking to.' The Velcro Sisters? 'Yes, the fuzz-bumpers. I was in there.' No, you weren't. 'I was, I could have pulled.' Jeremy, they were lesbians, on their honeymoon. 'Exactly. What's a girl need on her honeymoon?' Oh, good grief.

Today we're going to the beach. Now, how many beaches are advertised as being paradise? Plenty. All over the world, paradise is offered as standard. But here on Mykonos they've improved it. Here they've got Super Paradise. Super Paradise Beach is a long strand of grey gravel that swelters under an unrelenting sun. It's a bit like walking on the bottom of a goldfish bowl. At one end there's a bar that has a throbbing techno-house, garage, conservatory, granny-flat disco pumping continuously. The beach is gay-graded. It starts off as Greek hetero couples, drifts into international hetero singles, then Euro singles peeping out of the closet onto vanilla gays with fag hags, then very gay gays, and finally, up at the far end, very stern, serious, professional, alpha-male gays.

Jeremy leads the way until we're sitting pressed up against the far cliff in the middle of a seal colony of vast, oily, naked, predatory homosexuals. You'll have to imagine this. These men don't just have honed, chiselled bodies: they have the sort of bodies that no sport, exercise or a lifetime with Twyla Tharp can contrive. These muscles are solely for the purpose of display, and they are staggering. Entirely hairless and greased up to shine like a motor show. Every time they move, a new bit of body pops up. These guys are human advent calendars. The comparison with Jeremy's body is as astonishing as it is hilarious. It certainly seems to astonish the rest of the beach. Only David Attenborough could swear that Jeremy and the gay men were from the same species.

Clarkson is Day-Glo white. Yorkshire white, with a tinge of blue. He looks like a collapsed wedding cake displayed in a mixed grill. The alpha gays don't do much except smoke and rearrange their muscles. Occasionally they saunter to the water until it laps their groins provocatively. Now, I haven't had the pleasure of seeing a lot of willies all together since school. My, they've changed, and I must say I was astonished at the sheer variety.

Pubic hair is not completely depilated. It's tonsured into amusing little penile moustaches which, seen together, rather resemble a group photograph of pre-1914 Austrian hussars. The penis is the one muscle that really doesn't improve with exercise or working out. I mean, there are some organs here that are frankly distressing. Bent, humpy-backed, varicosed, spavined, goitred, gimpy bits of chewed gristle. They've been so abused, they should be made wards of court and given their own social workers. The owners never leave the poor things alone, they are endlessly tweaking and arranging and straightening and fluffing up. Actually, it's quite funny. Like a lot of obsessive, surface-wiping suburban housewives rearranging the front-room cushions. All keeping up with the Joneses.

Do you know the difference between a heterosexual man on the beach and a homosexual man on the beach? Well, apart from the body and the back, sack and crack wax, obviously. A straight bloke walks into the sea and looks at the horizon. A gay man faces the beach. It's all about front. There is a constant scanning here. Everyone's staring and sizing up. Every time you look up, you make eye contact. 'I am an insecurity camera.' The gaydar is jammed with traffic. Even the gently frotting men in the surf look over each other's shoulders, sending out intense sonar messages. There's not much noise here. There's no laughter. Just a bit of low muttering. It's not remotely relaxed. It's not a holiday. This is a naked sales convention. Pure erotic capitalism.

After an hour, Jeremy's bored. He's exhausted his game of seeing how many euphemisms for back-to-front sex he can come up with. He points up a concrete hill. 'They keep going up there in ones and twos. Why?' Well, why do you think? 'Let's go and see.' This is it. For him, this is confronting the great fear. The peek into the heart of *Boy's Own* darkness. This is what he came for.

So we trudge up the hill. Very separately. It's uncomfortably hot. The light is neon-bright and along the cliff there are men standing or lying. Entirely on their own, like dropped bits of gay litter, waiting to be picked up. It's Hampstead Heath without the trees and wet knees.

I get to the edge of a cliff and lie down. In the pale-blue sea below, naked men swim lazily, looking perversely like they're in old Hitler Youth movies. About twenty feet away on a flat rock, a man with a body apparently made out of knotted brown pipe cleaners and bacon rind has laid out his towel. He's wearing nothing but black leather biker boots. Now, who gets up and thinks: 'Nice day for the beach – towel, suntan cream, condom, biker boots'? He hasn't even got a book. He's here all alone like some Greek-myth punishment, marooned on this rock, chained by his libido. He stares at me, then slowly turns round and bends over; sporting a pendulous scrotum, he looks like a malnourished, shaved bulldog. I look away, then glance back. He's gently masturbating at me. More for effect than intent. I can't say I'm not flattered, but then I can't say that I'm interested either.

Jeremy, sweaty and puffing, stumbles up. 'Have you seen . . . I mean, have you seen . . . ?' He's Bill Oddie after sighting a dodo. Yes, I've seen. You need a beer. So we go back down to a little hilltop bar above the beach where a waiter in a cerise mini-sarong, matching cut-off singlet and alice band serves lager and fried octopus. I look down at the supine, oily gravel and admit that I don't like it here. I find the constant appraisal, the naked audition, the mime propositions wearying and uncomfortable. And the pitiless eugenics of homosexual coupling are depressing and sad. There is no space here for the old, the fat, the ugly or the shy. The emphasis is on a particular style of physical beauty to the complete exclusion of imperfection, intelligence, humour, flirtation or courtship. Not that these things aren't valued by gays per se: they're just not packed, along with the condoms and biker boots, and brought here.

It's this little matter of zipless sex where gays and I part company. 'It's quite good here,' says Jeremy. 'I'm glad we came.' Well, that's him all over. The great contrarian. Never happier than when he's next to something he can tease and have a bit of a cathartic rant at. As I said, Jeremy's defined by what he's not. Here he's successfully confronted that last frontier – the pubescent boy's fear of homosexuality – and it's not that bad. He's not been gang-banged by the Village People. He hasn't caught a falsetto laugh or a burning desire to collect Lalique or an ear for show tunes. Best of all, they haven't asked for his autograph. He's finally found some butch blokes who blissfully couldn't care less about cars.

December 2002

Moscow

All things considered, it had been a long and contradictory day. I was still sitting in the grey suit I'd stepped into twenty-four hours ago in a grey London dawn, and here we were, the suit and me – two airports, two dinners, two parties, three time zones, four traffic jams, three bodyguards and approximately thirty-six small, perfectly perky breasts later – clutching the international hospitality of a warm Coke, slouched on the sofa with a troika of new Russian friends, a photographer and a translator, and Clarkson.

In a gents' club in downtown Moscow somewhere, Jeremy is keeling over like a stricken junk. He is still wearing most of his London suit, but he's also casually thrown on a virtually naked Ukrainian lady with legs longer than the Trans-Siberian railway and a smile that could melt buttons. She's not wholly naked, she's still wearing the merest thong... Oh no, that's come off, revealing a pubic tonsure as slim as a gulag snout. Though I expect it looks like a mohair beanie from where Jeremy's sitting.

'My, these are very attractive lap-dancers,' he shouts by way of polite conversation to our host, a charming and taste-free Russian plutocrat who guffaws with the insistent *joie de vivre* of a man giving final directions to a squadron of nuclear bombers.

'No,' he shouts above the 1990s Yankee disco rap. 'No, no, not lap-dancer – prostitute!' And then he turns to me and asks: 'Which one you like to make fuck with? One fuck, two, how many? Have here or take away, my present.'

You know, terribly kind and generous and all, but I just couldn't, I waffle in a grisly, Terry-Thomas voice that only comes out when talking about sex to foreigners. 'What, you homosexual?' he asks with inquisitive pity. No, no, well, not so far. 'Why, then just take a little one, you don't do nothing. She do everything. Have two. Watch. Do yourself.'

Well, er, actually, you see, I'm sober and I'm embarrassed. Sober embarrassment is the great British prophylactic. He looks confused, but then sober embarrassment is not an emotion that clouds the Russian psyche often, if at all.

What I really like about this wonderful brothel, not that I'm much of an expert, is the private room with shower and toothpaste and the two-way mirror wall, which is like a cross between a KGB interrogation room and a Travelodge. And I like the catwalk stage, where the girls do burlesque numbers, including a Scottish parody to piped bagpipes. It is more St Trinian's than de Sade. The girls all have a ferocious, chiselled beauty: no slatterns or jades, no pneumatic implants or cosy, slappable cellulite. They scowl and smoulder with a lean and hungry look, the thousand-dollar stare of ambition. Finally, what I like most about the brothel is its name: Secret Service, written in English rather than Cyrillic, presumably because here in Moscow, retirement home of Philby, Burgess and Maclean, the English Secret Service are famous for being always availably shagged for money.

So we leave empty-handed. The owner gives us two consolation T-shirts and has his picture taken with Jeremy. I must be one of the few visitors to a Russian brothel whose only physical encounter is a hug from a short, hideous central Asian pimp.

We came to Moscow because neither of us had been before and because it's getting ever more difficult to find corners of the world where they don't get *Top Gear*. Moscow turns out not to be one of them.

They start asking for autographs at the luggage carousel. 'Is that man from *Top Gearski*?' a wizened old peasant asks me brightly. No, *nyet*, sorry. His face subsides into its default setting of eternal Slavic disappointment.

Jeremy and I always have a little competition to see who can come up with the best local contacts. This time I'd got a fixer, a photographer hot from Chechnya and Beslan, the editor of Russian *Vogue* and Gwyneth Paltrow. Clarkson only managed the editor of Russian *Top Gear*. He turned up at the airport with a posse of Spetsnaz bodyguards in blue camouflage with machine pistols. My fixer turned out to be Ivana Golightly, madder than mushrooms by moonlight and more intense than Tiger Balm on the testicles.

Dima, the photographer, was a modern miserablist whose cynicisms were as flat and unrelenting as the great ineffable steppe. At one point he asked me: 'Is this evening going to be another meal in an absurdly expensive and glossy restaurant with grotesquely rich and powerful men and incredibly beautiful and sophisticated society bitches without morals?' Well, yes, I suppose it might. 'Pah, then I'll go home and sit in the dark with a Pot Noodle.'

The road into a city from its airport is always like the trailer advertising coming attractions. The one into Moscow is longer than Tolstoy and makes you realise how Napoleon lost his flight. Cars are the promise and the curse of new capitalism, the first stop of entrepreneurial freedom and the jam of competition. Russians drive with a terrifyingly self-destructive attrition. All motors are the same colour, sprayed with a cementy-grey, grimy antifreeze road filth, as if the dirt were still recalcitrantly communist, painting Mercedes, Ladas, Skodas and Range Rovers the same militant colour-of-Mother-Russia muck.

Through the electrically curtained windows and the drifting exhaust fumes we pass acres of tower blocks, monolithic hives for workers. Marching in a flattened and beaten landscape, even a decade dead, the weight and purposeful hideosity of the grand socialist experiment leaches the humanity out of you. The buildings are more despairing than any Third World slum because they were created with a steely focus to blot out the horizon of singular happiness.

A ceiling of thick curdled cloud hangs over the city like the state's dirty laundry. Occasional stands of scrawny silver birch add to the feeling of a world without colour sketched in charcoal. You believe that in Moscow even the rainbows would be grey. That's if they ever get enough sunlight to make one. The air is sulphurous, thick and metallic. It pricks the eye and sours your throat. This is not a pretty place, but it hums and mutters with an awful power. Like a monstrous turbine, Moscow is magnetic, mesmerising.

After a long silence, Jeremy looks away from his window and says,

'I already love this place', and beams. I know what he means. The city squats like a weightlifter over the flat iron bar of the Moscow River. It's built on a series of concentric ring roads. The garden ring carved by Stalin marks the inner city, where the government buildings, the grand monuments and temples to the collective will and grand design live. People move about on the broad streets wholly out of scale, frail and tiny, cogs that have fallen out of the building. We look like ghosts in the machine.

Red Square comes as a bit of a bright surprise. In front is Lenin's mausoleum, on top of which Party leaders reviewed the cold, priapic rumbling rockets of May Day MADness (mutually assured destruction), and where a soldier still stands guard in front of the waxy corpse of Vladimir Ilyich Ulyanov. He marches over to us and asks with a guilty glance if he might have a photo with Clarkson on his mobile phone. Some images are simply beyond irony or explanation.

There is a big party, a launch for Martini. All of smart Moscow is here in a barn of a nightclub that was once a factory. Outside, the limousines are jammed five-deep, chugging into the night air. Inside, Gwyneth Paltrow has been flown in for international glamour. She stands in a party frock in a small wooden box with her bodyguards, like a little Punch and Judy show. Photographers and film crews jostle as smart hostesses and the wives of the new rich are bundled in to shake hands. Finally, Jeremy and Gwyneth meet and stare at each other, blinking in the continuous flash like a pair of giant pandas brought together in a distant foreign zoo. It was, Gwyneth told me later, the weirdest experience of her life. Whether she meant Moscow or Clarkson, I didn't ask.

Restaurants in Moscow are hysterically, emphatically, purposefully expensive and gaudy. They're more gaudy, camp and flash than the Bolshoi Christmas Special. Turandot – named after a mad Chinese bint who had her boyfriends executed – is a so-so Chinese–Japanese fusion restaurant that has hand-painted, gold chinoiserie walls and dishes that start at about $50. The restaurant itself cost hopeless millions, and the handful of women lunching here have had no less expensive work. I've not seen so much radical cosmetic surgery as in Moscow. It's not just a little tasteful tweaking and augmentation, a sly cheat of nature. It's the complete hot-rod rebuilding. Even their mothers wouldn't recognise them.

I went to another, designed by Philippe Starck, which had gold Kalashnikov lampstands. If you want the Christmas-cracker wisdom of what the difference is between America and Russia, it's that America is wholly without irony and Russia is wholly without anything that isn't an irony. I sat at a table with new Moscow entrepreneurs, the Boss-suited, Swiss-wristed, soft-English-speaking hewers and carvers of the new Russian economy. They talk all the consumer stuff, the cars, suits, houses and holidays, but it's just a veneer. Underneath they are the children of the revolution – you know, 'I'm told that the European Community was created to do to Russia what the West couldn't do with bombs.' No, it wasn't. I'm a member, I voted for it. 'Ha!' they give a little tragic laugh. 'You know nothing.' But I live in a society with a free press and access to information. 'Ha!' More tragic smirks. There is no conspiracy theory too convoluted or improbable for the Russian psyche, and all plots lead to Moscow. They are rigorously, collectively paranoid and vain. The only obvious face-value truth is that nothing is what it seems and everything's worse.

They believe in Russia's might and Russia's right. They see nothing untoward in using gas and oil and power as a carrot and stick. 'What's that mean, carrot stick?' It's an expression. 'Like a Kalashnikov and a cabbage?' Yes, I expect so. 'It's our gas. Why shouldn't we use it as a knife?' shrugs an international tax lawyer and mining investor. Handing me the caviar, he says: 'We're the most well-read country in the world. All Russians read classics.' 'Mostly tragedies,' adds Dima.

Russia's great natural resource isn't subterranean melting fossils; it's suffering. They have the world's largest deposits of suffering. They cherish their ability to suffer and take grim pleasure in handing it out by the ladleful to others. The rigour of eighty years of communism has made them demon capitalists. It turned out to be the best training for the free market. There are no fences, no lines in the snow, no limits. Free market means that everything is for sale. You want a policeman, a judge, a politician, a censored press? You pay for it. It's all open, universally understood. It's not corruption, they shrug. It's just pure reductive capitalism.

It's almost irresistible to compare Russian society to the dolls-within-dolls, the tourist's gift. In fact there are now only two dolls, a fat, rich doll and a poor, thin doll. Perhaps a third one: the rich doll's bodyguard. The amount of cash washing round Moscow is astronomical, inconceivable. It's divvied out among a tiny sliver of the population whose poor taste and eye for the surreally expensive are turning the city into Dubaiski. Women clear out entire shops; men decide they want to collect and buy everything at once.

Sovietologists say this is simply the excitement and childish extravagance of the new. Soon it'll calm down, they'll grow manners and taste and become biddable. But why the hell should they? Have you ever seen a glutton who says: 'That's it. I've had enough of greed'? That's not how the market works. Outside the garden circle Russia lies flat, skinny, endless. There's precious little trickle-down, no sweetener for the ugly hardship of the masses. They are still out in the cold, rubbing their hands over their suffering. 'It's just Russia reverting to type,' said one of my businessmen.

Beside Gorky Park there is a little wind-whipped desert of green on which they've dumped all the old communist-era statues. Brezhnev, Khrushchev, Lenin, Stalin, the symbols of international workers' solidarity and the memorials of heroic soldiers, combine drivers and motherhood. They look both absurd and sad. Nostalgia can give anything an aesthetic makeover, even Soviet realism. However clunky and misbegotten these angular and operatic posed figures are, they have an integrity that is utterly absent from the expensive international magpie tat of the new Russia. On this grotty green, with its babushka selling tickets, its shivering drunk and its chipped and mildewed statuary, is the collective memorial to a thudding, single, awe-inspiring idea. While it is a received Western wisdom that the collapse of communism was a good thing and a triumph for us, this is a reminder that the towering twin tragedies of the twentieth century were that communism didn't work and capitalism did.

Moscow doesn't look like a city returning to its tsarist roots. Rather, this must be what Rome was like a decade after it fell to the vandals and barbarians. People move through its heroic avenues and its underground people's temples, and they don't belong any more.

This is a city from another era, a place of giants. If you want to know what eye-bulging, hideous whimsy contemporary Moscow can aspire to, let me tell you: I only saw one black man while we were there, now that Tanzania and Ethiopia no longer send their brightest to be indoctrinated in collectivism. This one black man was in our hotel, where diplomats and pop stars and Gwyneth stay. He'd been imported as a Yankee shoeshine. Nothing is without irony.

January 2007

Sicilian Mummies

Palermo's airport is named Falcone-Borsellino. It sounds like a 1970s American cop show, and you'd be forgiven for not knowing who either of the names belongs to. They were a pair of mortally brave magistrates who tried to finally break the ancient grip of organised crime in Sicily. Both were assassinated.

They don't like to talk about the Mafia to strangers here: it's an embarrassing family concern, none of our business, a private tragedy. Sicily is a secretive place. You can sense it in the blackened, baroque streets of Palermo, the capital, where the bomb damage from the 1943 Allied landings still hasn't quite been cleaned up and where the tenement palaces are inhabited by North African refugees. It's a watchful and masculine place, beautiful and thwarted.

Sicily's history is as mordant and miserable a romance as any in Europe – well into the 1950s these were among the poorest peasants in the Western world. For centuries they eked out a meagre life, suffering constant vendettas and feuds, injustice, exploitation, honour killings and murderous codes, all surrounded by the smell of mandarin blossom and incense. In Sicily, blood called to blood for blood down the ages.

The Capuchin monastery in Palermo is a discreetly blank building. It sits in a quiet square beside a graveyard, across town from where, in 1992, the Mafia settled its account with Magistrate Borsellino. Outside the door, tucked into a corner, are a couple of hawkers peddling postcards and guidebooks; inside, a friar sits behind a table selling tickets and more postcards and votive trinkets. It's a slow day; he reads the paper.

Down a flight of stairs, past a wooden statue of Our Lady of Sorrows, is the door to the catacomb, the waiting room of the dead. Surprisingly large, with high, vaulted ceilings and long corridors stretching away at right angles, it's cool and dank and smells of sour, spiced dust and rotting cloth. The windows are high and diffuse the sunlight into a pale glow. Fluorescent bulbs vibrate, adding a medically forensic, anaemic brightness. Hanging from the walls, propped on benches, resting in their decrepit boxes, are nearly two thousand dead. They're dressed in their living best, the uniforms of their earthly calling. There's no one else down here.

In Europe the desiccation and preservation of corpses is a particularly Sicilian affair. There are other examples in Italy, but the great majority are in Sicily, where the relationship between the living and the dead is especially strong. Nobody knows how many there really are, or how many have since been removed from catacombs and buried in cemeteries by priests uneasy with the theology of keeping votive corpses. The phenomenon provokes an instant question: why would anyone do this? Why would you exhibit decaying bodies?

I walk down their ranks with that awkward confusion of trying to make sense of what it is I'm actually feeling. In the West we don't often see dead bodies – the absence of life is shrouded and hidden. These dead have a mystique; they come with an attitude and previous convictions. Examining the corpses with a morbid interest – so this is what death looks like – I realise that the big difference between the living and the dead is that you can stare at the dead with an intense, close-up curiosity that the living would never tolerate. And then I think they really ought to be playing Michael Jackson's 'Thriller' as background music, given how like prosthetic, schlock-horror-effect zombies these bodies look, how comically and pathetically the great denouement of nature mimics not just art but cheap art. Their jaws hang open in silent yowls, rotting teeth grin with menace, eye sockets stare bleakly, shreds of hard skin cling to shrunken cheeks and arthritic knuckles. These people are mostly small, their arms crossed as they sag against the wire and nails that hold them upright, their heads lolling on shoulders, bodies slowly collapsing with the effort of imitating a past life.

The corridors are segregated into religious folk and professional, meaning doctors and lawyers and a couple of vaudeville grand soldiers in their *carabinieri* uniforms. There's a women's corridor where, the guide points out, we can admire the fashion of the past. The skeletons stand in shredded rags, grimed and bleached a murky grey. There is little to admire. A side chapel is devoted to those who died virgins, especially poignant and by contemporary mores a pathetically cruel appellation to carry into eternity. When they were interred here, they must have appeared as symbols of purity among the decay.

And then there is a small chapel for infants. The children are dressed in their party frocks, propped up like living-dead dolls. One sits on a nursery chair with a little skeleton on her lap, perhaps a younger sibling, unbearably pitiful and simultaneously laughably grotesque.

This isn't like the catacombs of Rome, an archaeological excavation of tombs. Here the bodies were always meant to be seen, and they charge you a small fee for the pleasure. There are signs to remind you to be respectful and not take photographs, but they sell them. It's not clear if this is a religious experience or a cultural one, but it is a tourist attraction.

The first and oldest mummy is a friar: Silvestro da Gubbio, standing in his niche since 1599. (The word 'mummy' is from an Arabic word for bitumen, which resembled the blackened resin the ancient Egyptians used as a preservative.) Most of the bodies are from the nineteenth century. To begin with, they were exclusively friars and priests attached to the monastery. As time went on, the religious men were joined by benefactors and dignitaries and notables.

No one knows exactly what started the mummification; probably by chance it was discovered that a body left in a crypt with a particular atmosphere of coolness and porous limestone would actually dry out rather than rot. Then a system was devised. The newly dead were laid in chambers, called strainers, on terracotta slats over drains, where their body fluids could seep away and the corpses slowly desiccate, like prosciutto. After eight months to a year they'd be washed with vinegar, put back in their best clothes, and either placed in coffins or hung on the walls.

Preserving ancestral bodies is done in any number of places, but they're rarely displayed like this. Sicily has so many cultures, so many people came here with their practices and beliefs and were assimilated, that little bits now and again rise to the surface, their origins long forgotten. It has been suggested that perhaps the practice is the residual echo of a much older, pre-Christian rite – belief in the shamanistic power of corpses. Not every corpse would have dried out; some must have rotted, and so the preservation of others might have been an intimation of God's will, a divine hand keeping certain individuals as they were as a mark of a particular worldly goodness. As saints' relics are used to aid prayer and belief, maybe these bodies were thought to have been preserved by God to reinforce faith. Or perhaps the catacombs were made as a great vanitas, a memento mori, an illustration of the passing of all worldly ambition and the inevitability of death and the vanity and foolishness of storing up wealth on earth.

In later years some of the bodies were more elaborately preserved by means of chemical injections, taking the responsibility out of the hands of God and leaving it to undertakers and science. In one of the chapels a little girl, Rosalia Lombardo, lies in her coffin. She appears to be sleeping under a filthy brown sheet. Unlike many of the other strained and dried mummies, she has her own hair, which hangs in doll-like curls over her yellow forehead, tied up with a big yellow silk bow. Her eyes are closed, the eyelashes perfectly preserved. If she weren't surrounded by the grinning skulls and rot of this place, she could be just a child dozing on the way home from a party. The naturalism and the beauty are arresting; the implication that life is a mere breath away, disturbing and spooky. Rosalia was two when she got pneumonia and died. Crazy with grief, her father asked Alfredo Salafia, a noted embalmer, to preserve her. The effect is dreadfully, tragically vital, and the grief still seems to hang over this little blonde head. (Salafia sold his mummification fluid – keeping the formula secret – to funeral homes in the United States, as the fashion for embalming spread after the slaughter of the Civil War.) In Palermo, Rosalia is mentioned as a sort of semi-deity, a magical little angel. The taxi drivers say, 'Did you see Rosalia? *Bella*.'

Savoca is a silent village that crawls up the side of a hill until it reaches a view across the eastern end of the island to the sea. A tightly wound place that corkscrews back on itself. This is where Francis

Ford Coppola filmed *The Godfather*. The bar where Michael and his tragic wife had their wedding reception sits on the tiny square looking exactly as it did thirty-seven years ago on-screen. There's no obvious sign mentioning the movie. They don't like the association; most Sicilians I ask profess never to have seen it.

At the top of the hill is a convent, a place that looks more like a youth hostel than a Gothic medieval institution. There are only two nuns here, both Indians from Jharkhand. They wear woollies and jackets over their saris. In a side room, laid out in temporary plywood packing cases, are a couple of dozen cadavers that are being studied by a trio of scientists.

They're an unlikely team: Arthur Aufderheide, an octogenarian American from Minnesota who started as a pathologist and moved on to become one of the world's top mummy experts; Albert Zink, a big German who is the director of the Institute for Mummies and the Iceman in northern Italy; and a young Sicilian, Dario Piombino-Mascali – excitable and nervous, constantly worried, enthused and driven and possibly brilliant – who has a bolt through his eyebrow and a jacket that has 'Boxfresh' written on the back, apparently without irony.

I find him leaning over a very un-fresh box and delicately lifting the surplice of a nineteenth-century priest. He is looking for an unobtrusive piece of organic material for Professor Zink to do tests on. 'Ooh, is this what I think it is?' We all poke our heads up the vicar's frock and concur that it probably is. A thin pouch of powdery dry skin comes away in his hand. A half-centimetre sample is labelled and packaged. He's not going to miss his scrotum now.

An enormous amount can be gleaned from dead bodies about the day-to-day lives of the past – diet, illnesses and life expectancy. Knowing more about diseases like syphilis, malaria, cholera and tuberculosis centuries ago can help us get the better of them today. The scientists move methodically, checking the corpses' heights and ages, examining skulls and teeth, looking for the ridges interrupting the enamel that signify years of malnutrition. Two mummies are gouty. Five show signs of degenerative arthritis. Almost all these people suffered horribly from dental conditions – tartar build-up, receding gums, caries and abscesses.

Abdomens are checked for missing organs. One of the bodies has had its soft tissue removed, and others have been stuffed with rags and leaves, including bay leaves, perhaps to mitigate the smell, or because they were supposed to have some preservative value. Filling out the shrunken forms would have made them more lifelike. The skin has the waxy quality of parchment, the clothes feel sticky and damp, the faces bloat and yawn, mouths give up wizened larynxes and shrivelled tongues for examination.

The scientists are respectful of the bodies, never losing touch with the fact that they were human – they were like us – but still they refer to each one as 'it', to keep a distance, a dispassion, when they're pulling out a molar.

A few years back these bodies were vandalised in their crypt. People broke in and poured green paint over them. Lurid and humiliating, it spatters and dribbles across their faces and coats and shoes, making them look even more like characters from a funfair ghost train. The nuns who are keepers of this strange congregation look on with pity and distaste. They tell me the bodies should be decently buried, allowed to return to dust. One says there's nothing spiritual or uplifting to be learnt from all this.

The paint-spattered, rag-filled bodies will soon be returned to their empty niches. At the moment the arched alcoves along the wall hold nothing but hundreds of dried, dead centipedes. A number of bodies are still kept in their elaborate coffins. Gingerly, I lift a heavy lid that may not have been moved for over a century and peer inside. The air seems to escape with a thick sigh, and the smell grabs the back of my throat – not a rotten smell but the odour of beef tea and the clogging aroma of dry mould and fine, powdery layers of human dust. It's a smell that is dramatically unforgettable, the tincture of silence and sadness, the scent of repeated prayer heard in the distance, or of remorse and regret, a smell that's both repellent and intimately familiar. Something sensed for the first time, but also with a strange and compelling sense of déjà vu.

We will never know for sure what these corpses meant to the

congregations who laid them out and dressed them. They remain one of Sicily's many mysteries. We are left with our own concerns, thoughts and doubts when confronted by these comic and tragic visions of death. It is difficult to untangle the feelings aroused by the bodies, frozen on the journey between nothing and nothing – the mysteries, fears and hopes, the contradictions of life and loss, that are eternal and universal.

The beautiful town of Novara di Sicilia has a large and piously decorated church. In front of the altar is a secret door to the crypt, and at the press of a hidden button the floor opens electronically, just as in a James Bond film. Down a flight of steps is a room with carved stone niches containing the variously and now familiarly sagging bodies of six more prelates. On a high shelf stacked with skulls is a box containing two cats, naturally mummified, like a faint shadow of ancient Egypt. They got trapped in the crypt, a reminder that, even with nine lives, there's only one end.

February 2009

Puglia

There is another Italy, an Italy native Italians never see. It exists in parallel with the country they tread, separated by a gossamer curtain of artful romance, public-school poetry and Merchant Ivory moments. A place of fine-art postcards, plonk sipped under inky cypresses to the sound of cicadas and a distant bell. It is a nation elegantly arranged around cobbled streets and boys on Lambrettas, designed by Ruskin and Fellini. A place of sentiment and hot pathos, starry with wishful thinking. Italians know it's there: they can hear the carousing. They often get asked for directions to it in loud, slow English voices with added 'o's on the nouns.

This other Italy is a seasonal nation that springs up fresh every May and sinks back into the earth come the autumn term in September. It is the English fantasy of Italy, a place that is carefully and lovingly guarded against the fantasies of other tourists and the reality of Italians. Its heart is English Tuscany and bits of Umbria – all those places that look like the background for early Florentine martyrdoms.

Italians, it must be said, are endlessly astonished by the English worship of Tuscany. They stare into our faces, trying to see what it is we're seeing. A Milanese friend told me that the motorway from Vespucci airport in Florence becomes the road to Damascus for the English. They have instant conversions, see God and go blind. And the Italians really don't understand our fashionable obsession with Tuscan food. It's fine, unsophisticated peasant grub, big plates of stuff for men who harvest corn and sunflowers, and pick grapes. What do the English imagine is in Tuscan olive oil? I've been asked. Well, certainly not the Tunisian or Algerian olive oil that is almost certainly in it. Tuscany produces far more oil than the trees of Tuscany could possibly supply.

The English have been slow to move away from their beloved

Chiantishire, but some intrepid, panama'd Livingstones have wandered into bits of Lombardy and the northern lakes, Portofino and the Ligurian coast, to find they already belong to others – too Euro, too Hollywood, too yachty, too Russian. Recently, a new frontier has opened up. A new bit of Italy has been offered for colonisation by holiday: fashionable Puglia. The glossy magazines are full of it. Could this, the editorials sigh, be the new Tuscany? The new destination for the grand tour of the English in beige linen? I went mob-handed, with the twins, nanny, another family, more twins, my mother. I realised guiltily that I hadn't been on holiday with my mother since I was fifteen.

Puglia is the stiletto heel of Italy, facing the Adriatic and the coast of Albania. There are few good hotels here, few of the sort offering a room with a view that would have the English venturing out of Tuscany, so we took a house. One of the things Puglia is famous for is its *trulli*, small, round, stone-built hovels with conical black roofs. They cluster in fields looking like the search for a Hobbit sequel. It wasn't one of them. We rented a villa – always exciting. The Blonde trawled the web like a CIA counter-intelligence hit man to discover what lurked behind the travel agents' jaunty prose. It was the family home of an Italian television personality. If you've ever seen Italian television, that's not necessarily promising. We got there in the dark, so it wasn't until the first morning that we saw how very beautiful it was, sparsely and chicly uncomfortable, but with a vain atmosphere of decaying grandeur and touches of childishly Italian kitsch. There were plenty of beds in eccentric places, and nearly enough bathrooms with nearly enough water. There was a cinema. The whole place had the faded-in-the-wash look, with a tidemark of family memorabilia, like clues in a detective story: a restaurant bill in a drawer, family photos, an African dictator. From some angles it was an elegant palazzo, from others a Victorian borstal surrounded by a breeze-block wall.

The garden was full of fruit trees and crickets, with a venerable, heavy white mulberry tree where my mother would sit in the morning, sipping tea and eating berries. It had a pool and huge, sun-baked lizards for the amusement of the children, chickens for breakfast eggs and, cantering across the trellis above the dining table, a scuttle of rats that would leap through the candlelight and scamper into the darkness. I couldn't quite work out whether the rats counted as local rustic charm or an insanitary plague that demanded threatening letters to the agent. I felt rather the same about the ad hoc demands to pay a supplement of €20 to have someone fill the dishwasher or serve dinner. It's the sort of thing you don't really want to consider on holiday, but it's indicative of the truth of Puglia – its defining truth.

This is a very, very poor place. It has always been poor, since the Greeks got there, then the Romans and the Goths, the Normans and the Spanish, the Neapolitans, and finally the republic. Under each new ruler there was the same constant: poverty. Most of them never bothered to turn up: absentee landlords demanding a pitiful tithe of cheap labour, some fruit. So the Church looked after Puglia – actually, the Church looked after the Church – and assured the Pugliese that they would be rich enough when it mattered: when they were dead.

Since the unification of Italy, Puglia has mostly been run by communists, plundered by army recruiters, patronised by politicians and plagued with a particularly efficient and vicious version of the Mafia. It gets money from Rome and from Brussels, and communist mayors order up spaghetti factories, cheap public housing, business parks, access roads and electricity pylons, then the Mafia arranges to build them. Or, at least, start building them. Building things is what communists do – they believe in concrete and blocks of things, and the Mafia believes in half-doing them as cheaply and as badly as possible.

So, Puglia is a rubble of ground plans, boarded factories, empty warehouses. There are dirty roads that lead to pointless roundabouts, and lots and lots of stained, grotty high-rise flats in clusters, in a landscape of dumped rubbish, discarded white goods and collapsed cars. It looks poor. It is poor. All the money, the socialism, the crime and Catholicism have conspired to keep it the way it's always been. The ports of Bari and Brindisi are rife with corruption and smuggling and streams of illegal Albanians and desperate West Africans who've risked their lives for the whiff of a better life in Europe. You see them looking picturesque on street corners, selling fake Ray-Bans and Rolexes.

All this, the English can ignore. They can see round it, over it. They have a remarkable selective vision that simply wishes away the ugly and the callous. They can see round corners into beautiful olive groves and fruit orchards. They sigh over Greek ruins in the middle of 1970s cut-price civic hideousness. The magazines have carefully cropped photographs of sun loungers and pools and sky with bits of beach. I saw one headline that promised Gallipoli (not that Gallipoli) would be the new Positano, which must have given some PR a spontaneous orgasm. Italian Gallipoli is a working-man's exhausted holiday resort. It could possibly, at a pinch, be the new Margate – a dirty, grey beach with cheap, temporary caffs and Benidorm-style hotels set against the scrub and blown rubbish of a motorway hard shoulder.

There is one spectacular, unmissable gem in Puglia: Lecce, the finest complete baroque town in southern Europe. You have to drive through twenty minutes of suburb first – lumps of dystopian, crusty apartment block and gap-toothed shopping arcades – but, if you're English, you won't notice any of that, and finally you'll find somewhere to park and walk into this miraculous town, with its Roman amphitheatre and interlocking cobbled streets of energetically decorated houses and shops, its squares with astonishing cathedrals and palaces, town halls and hospitals. This isn't the romantic baroque of northern Italy, or the histrionic baroque of Austria, or the clear, aesthetic baroque of Germany. It is the touchingly gaudy, excessive baroque of the very poor, very hot, very bright south. The façades appear to have been designed by a race of giant patissiers. The decor isn't so much carved as piped. Surfaces burst and sprout with mythological faces, grotesque gargoyles, pneumatically naked dryads, mythical animals and all the vivid bestiary of fairy tales and peasant romps. It is votive, bucolic craft, and it elevates you with its passion and the intimacy of its conception, and it beggars you with the breadth of its achievement. This was all paid for by the poorest people in Europe. The façades of these buildings both mock the grandees who would use them and demand them, and elevate the sweat, the humour and the energy of those who made and paid for them.

Lecce is a miraculous and beautiful place, not despite its surroundings but because of them. Is Puglia this year's smart Italy? God knows it needs the tourism, but not as a delusional annexe to Tuscany. It's ugly, it's rough and it's underdeveloped. It's full of the poor, the illegal and the lost. It's dirty and it's despondent. And if you want to know what peasants eat, go to Aldi and see what's in their shopping trollies.

Puglia is run by socialist bureaucracy and criminals, along with the innate Italian corruption and nepotism. The English ability to see selectively over all that, simply to filter out the reality of daily life from a place for the sake of some higher holiday calling, is depressing, patronising and belittling, for both them and, ultimately, us. Puglia deserves and needs investment and infrastructure and services, and friends who visit. It doesn't deserve a lot of English fantasists in panama hats, braying at the architecture, pretending this is some sort of undiscovered riot of deliciously secret Italy.

September 2010

Canal du Midi

Of all of Jeremy Clarkson's ruddy, intransigently stubborn, pouty, Yorkshire-contrarian beliefs, hunches and prejudices, perhaps the most obtuse and unbelievably counter-intuitive is his deep, soulful love for the French.

You would lay good money on the fact that Jeremy would be an arch frog-botherer, that he'd have a Falstaffian loathing for the cringing, beret-wearing, philosophy-spouting, bike-pedalling, arrogant French. He'd be mocking their Napoleon complexes and flicking Agincourt V-signs from the Eurostar. But *non, mon brave*. He admires the French above all of God's creation. He says he likes their attitude, their style of life, their priorities, their dress sense, their undress sense, their flirtatious insouciance, the way they smell, the way they eat small birds under napkins, and the way they drink their wine. But mostly what he adores about the French is that they have never heard of Jeremy Clarkson. Jeremy's love of the French is unrequited. And that's the way he likes it. He can wander around without people stopping him to share a photo, or ask why he doesn't like Peugeots, or just to shout: '*Mon dieu, mon dieu, zut alors, c'est motorbouche!*'

He is explaining all this to me in the garden of a restaurant in Carcassonne, while we're having our photograph taken. 'Look around you and sigh,' he says expansively, waving his glass at the fig trees, the battlements and the remains of the cassoulet. A passing Frenchman pauses to watch and asks if this is someone famous. He looks again and suddenly recognises the big fella. '*Mais bien sûr!* Eet ees Tom Jones.'

I, on the other hand, take a more orthodox view of the French. Like you, I think they are ridiculous, self-absorbed, cultural prigs who are breathtakingly selfish and dismissive, and suffer an inferiority complex that they cover up with bombast, boasting, Olympic sulking and baroque mendacity. In France, telling the truth is the sign of a boorish lack of intelligence and imagination.

So, here we are in the Midi. Jeremy – or Tom, as I shall now always know him – has come to show me why I should love them, while I trust that a weekend will convince him they are as adorable as their pop music. Carcassonne is a good place to start. Jeremy points to its ancient beauty: the old roses draped across pale stone, the gravel, that particular hoity *élan* with which the French move through the world, the over-coiffed ladies with too many rings on their lardy fingers, the young lovers with their wandering hands. The sky is pale-blue, there are sparrows, and it's beguiling. But it's French, so not what it appears.

There is, as they say, beneath the paint and the perfume the scent of *merde*. This crenellated hill town where they shot the film *Robin Hood* is a lie. It's a modern tourist's recreation. The French destroyed the original themselves. This bit of the country was host to one of the worst pogroms in Europe – one of the few times a power has managed to exterminate an entire religion. The Cathars were a Christian sect notable for their pacifism and abstinence. French Catholics saw this as an unforgivable heresy, and set about killing all of them. The cardinal in charge of the cleansing was asked how the besieging soldiers should tell the difference between a heretic and a Catholic. He replied: 'Kill them all. God will know his own.' The French are surprisingly bad at history, although it's perhaps not so surprising when you consider how often they come second in it. Unable to beat anyone else in Europe, the French regularly turn round to beat each other. The Cathars, the Huguenots, the Terror, Vichy, Algeria. There is a torture museum in Carcassonne, a lot of tableaux of nylon-wigged shop dummies being eviscerated, hanged, stretched and intimately ravaged, in a display that manages to be tackily sadistic and embarrassingly erotic.

We are to take a boat down the Canal du Midi. Tom says he's wanted to do this all his life. I will, he says, 'be rendered speechless by the unfolding diorama of bosky French perfection'. Or words to that effect. We tip up at a hot marina, full of white-plastic pleasure boats that look like bathroom fittings on steroids. We are shown the ropes by a friendly and efficient Cornishman, who sailed through here and decided to stay. Tom tells him to ignore me, because I won't understand anything, and then says he doesn't need to be told anything because he already understands everything, but is there a TV for the Grand Prix? There is.

We cast off, or slip anchor, or whatever the nautical term for 'mirror, indicate, manoeuvre' is. The boat is really an idiot-proof wet dodgem with two cabins, dodgy plumbing and lots of rope. We fill the fridge with rosé and salami and olives, and Tom Pugwash gets in the captain's chair with a pint of wine, forty tabs, a plate of sausage, and open water ahead of him. I must say, I've never seen him so happy. I suggest he puts on suncream, because his bald patch is turning the colour of a Zouave's trousers. 'Do I look like a homosexual?' he shouts gaily. No, not even a Frenchman could mistake Clarkson for a practitioner of *le vice anglais*.

The boat is very slow. But, too soon, we approach a series of locks and a happily lethargic Pugwash turns into Captain Bligh, bellowing at me to do things with ropes and bollards while explaining the principles of lockishness. I'm not comfortable doing *matelot* stuff, I come over all Nelson when confronted with knots. But Tom howls and gesticulates, the boat jostles and butts the groin. Locks may be triumphs of Archimedean engineering, but they're a terrible bore. Why can't there be a ramp, or a lift? The French lock-keepers all have jobs for life, and behave like it. They also have pleasant cottages and little businesses on the side, selling gardening gloves to soft-handed English people with third-degree rope burns. They take an hour and a half for lunch every day, from 12.30. It would be entirely possible to come on holiday to the Canal du Midi and spend all of it bobbing in a queue waiting for a Frenchman to finish his baguette and tup his neighbour's wife.

We stop off for lunch in tastefully picturesque little towns. French public holidays are arriving like locks at this time of year, and your froggy workman takes what they call *le pont*, 'the bridge': that is, they make an extra holiday out of the loose days between holidays. So pretty much the only people who are open for business are English. And jolly good they are at it too; the best food we ate here was made by a couple from the Midlands. The excellence of French bourgeois cooking is now as rare as Cathars.

One evening we sat outside a café in a typically French square, where a French pop group was tuning up. At the other tables, families drank wine and ate a late dinner of steak and *frites*. 'Look at this, just look at this,' says Tom. 'You can't pretend you don't want to live here for ever and ever.' We'd already been beaten to it. The locals all turned out to be from Rotherham, and waved at Jeremy and took pictures and asked what he thought of Peugeots. Apparently, most of the town is now owned by expats, happy to exploit the locals' sophisticated reluctance to work. The band struck up 'Smoke on the Water'. Tom beamed and played air guitar.

There is no denying the canal is beautiful. Now bereft of practical purpose, it has settled into being a metaphor, a parable. Pootling down it past the arching beams of the plane trees is possibly the most relaxing thing I've ever done. There is something about the glossy water, the slow perambulation, the rhythm of the passing trees, the birds singing, the dappling, piebald light. You could feel the care fall away, your shoulders slump, the brain cease to race. It is, I expect, what dying's like. When you hear the faint voices calling, 'Go towards the light, granddad, don't fight it,' I expect this is what you'll see. I hope death comes to us like floating down the Canal du Midi. Through the tree trunks you could see the fields, running to the hills in the distance. They are thistle-bound and choked with weed. It looks so peaceful because it's moribund, comatose. France, with its huge state, its insincere smile, its polished manners, is rotting like a pear from the inside out.

There is one more thing we have to do. Jeremy wants to play a game of *pétanque*. We find a gravel pitch and he says: 'Now, I've got to tell you, I'm very good at this.' Jeremy is very, very competitive. Over the years, he and I have played golf in Cheshire, raced Ski-Doos in Iceland, jet skis in Barbados, fired Kalashnikovs in Basra and raced battle tanks in Baghdad. I've won every time. Except for golf, which was abandoned due to helpless laughter. *Boules* was Jeremy's game, on his adopted home pitch, and despite appalling gamesmanship and outright fouling, it was Agincourt and Waterloo all over again. Tom Jones, *nul points.*

July 2012

Beirut

As you drive the Corniche in from the Bekaa, the city appears with a gasp, or rather a sigh, from between the trees, like an image from an old oscilloscope, pincered between snow-dusted mountains, cosseted by the pale Mediterranean. Beirut reclines as if it's just swum ashore and couldn't be bothered to climb off the beach. It settled into its plain like glittering mercury. It is not made of the same stuff as the rest of the country, either corporeally or metaphorically.

No capital city I know is as divorced from its surroundings as bold Beirut. Lebanon is a china ornament that has been dropped and won't know how many pieces it has broken into until someone tries to pick it up. Everybody agrees it is broken, but no one agrees where. At the moment, it is best left lying there, pretending to be just resting.

Beirut remains not exactly oblivious, so much as studiedly nonchalant. In the 1970s it was riven by a civil war of desperate theocratic antipathy and certainty. The old colonial city was blown apart and a more functional one has risen in its place. There are still corners chopped with bullets, still there are blackened shells of public buildings. As you walk, people will point out that that street was once the border between murderous factions, a front line as implacable as any trench. But now it's just a road.

'And here, just here where I'm standing,' my local guide says as we're looking for a pastry shop, 'here is the Shatila refugee camp.' You've heard of the Shatila refugee camp: 1982, a massacre of Palestinian refugees and Shiites by a Phalangist Christian gang under the tacit auspices and connivance of the occupying Israelis. The UN called it a genocide. It was before I became a journalist, but I remember it as an example of some of the most vivid front-line reporting, and retrospectively one of the things that made me think this job might be worth doing. And this is here, where I am standing now, this is the camp? 'Yes,' says my companion, surprised that I sound so surprised. But there's nothing here, no sign, no huge weeping statue, no garden of remembrance, no here, here. 'Well, we all know it's here,' he says.

It's a run-down, busy series of apartment blocks and gritty, sclerotic streets. You'd never know, unless you knew. That is the remarkable truth of Beirut: it is a city that has decided not to forget, but just not to mention the difficult bits. It's as if collectively they've come to the conclusion it's best if they don't ask and don't tell. For everyone's sake, there is a mutual amnesia. This is not the modern way for national psychosis. We tend to recommend truth and reconciliation commissions, inquiries, probing judges, revealing books, but the Lebanese think they'll just make things worse by talking about them. As a journalist, I find this goes against the grain, whereas the investigative reporting that I've read all my life about Northern Ireland, it must be said, hasn't made anything better. And privately, as a member of a family, I can understand the reality of not going there; of least said, soonest mended. Where sometimes just buttoning your lip and sighing theatrically is the best option.

Whether this will work in the long run is, I suppose, questionable; perhaps it will lead to worse neuroses in years to come. But you can look at the history of all cities as being lairs of buried crimes and injustice, the shades of the millions of unresolved and unjust lives that are drowned out by the hustle and the bustle, and the need to get on with contemporary life. But all history is as much a result of selective forgetting as memorialising.

Beirut is the sophisticated older woman who fell on hard times. The city hums with an elegant, hectic life. It feels natural and unselfconscious. It glides past the increasing number of old Syrian women begging outside boutiques and the dozens of small refugee children selling back biscuits at traffic lights. The cafés are full of young people of a prestigious beauty, flirting, writing theses, smoking hubbly-bubblies, having dinner with groups of mates.

While this may look like any francophone post-colonial city, it is also an insouciant public defiance. The café is not a French invention, or even a Western one; it comes from here or hereabouts, the troubled, forgetful, hot and furious further shore of the Mediterranean. And generally, what is called Arab or Levantine food was first made for public consumption in the company of strangers in Beirut. So when you drink the thick, intense coffee and eat the small pastries – or, my new favourite discovery, a flatbread rolled and stuffed with *labne* and honey – you are taking part in something that was invented here, not imported.

This is the ancient land of the Phoenicians, a shadowy people overshadowed as ever by more bellicose and destructive neighbours. The Phoenicians are memorable as traders; they dominated the commerce of the Mediterranean, invented the alphabet and the two-tiered bireme. Romantically, they were known by the Greeks as the 'dealers in purple'. Phoenicia means 'land of purple' because they had discovered the natural dye made from the small murex snail, possibly as early as 1500 BC. Purple became so valuable that it was worth more than its weight in silver and led to the first sumptuary laws that in turn led to one of the most useless but marvellous words: *porphyrogennetos*, which means 'born to wear the purple', born to greatness. In Rome, only aristocrats could wear togas dyed with Phoenician purple. It had a miraculous property. Not only was the colour rare and beautiful, ranging from an effete mauve to the hue of dried blood, but it would actually become more radiant and lustrous with washing and sunlight. So the older and more used it was, the finer it looked, which naturally reflected the grand accomplishments of the dictator who wore it.

The Lebanese cornered trade around the world. There are now 10 million of them running businesses in every city and town with a port, a river or a crossroads, and they have been doing it longer than anyone else. The purple of the achievement seems to grow brighter and richer with age and use. If any city were *porphyrogennetos*, it's brave Beirut.

This is all the sort of stuff you think about sitting in cafés, watching the wilfully bright and busy and beautiful Lebanese saunter on the broken parapet of history, understanding, hoping that in the end it will all fade, like everything else.

March 2015

Syrian Refugees

Brigadier-General Hussein Zyoud settles himself into a chair. Fretting and plaiting his fingers, he needs a smoke. The lugubrious face sags around a drooping military moustache, the go-get-'em camouflage stands out incongruously in his large office with new multiple flat screens for PowerPoint presentations and CCTV. There are a lot of chairs: for his photographer, who records his every handshake, for my photographer, for his translator and my translator and various aides and minders and staff officers.

The general is the custodian of Jordan's borders, and the responsibility of standing on the edge of chaos without a cigarette weighs on his broad epaulettes. He does this a lot – meeting people. He's a popular man with factfinders and international committees. There are hotel-reception flower arrangements and bright flags of the sort young men are supposed to die for. One boasts a large peregrine's head with a map of Jordan in its eye. The kingdom's awkward outline is the reason we all come here: this semi-detached nation is surrounded by the neighbours from half a dozen heretical hells: Israel, Syria, Iraq, Saudi Arabia and a watery sliver of Egypt. A waiter serves cups of coffee; the general capitulates, and fires up a ciggie.

Jordan's borders leak refugees. Throughout the nation's short history after its duplicitous colonial creation in 1946, it has taken in next door's unwanted cast-offs: millions of Palestinians in the 1950s, 60s and 70s, then Iraqis, and now Syrians, who are, even by this 'hood's high standards, fleeing a peerlessly vicious and indiscriminately vile war. As I write, more than a million of them have left the country to claim thin and desperate sanctuary.

I ask the general why he has kept the border open. He shrugs. 'It is our history, we take in refugees. It's what we do. I will show you. I will show you everything. You can go wherever you like, to understand.'

Not only has Jordan kept its border open, but its army actively helps refugees. No other state's armed forces do what the Jordanians are now doing for their neighbours – and nobody dares calculate how much they might be risking by being the Middle East's Good Samaritan. As we leave the office for his 4×4 with a flag on the front, the general pauses: 'We had your Prime Minister Cameron here, you know? I have a photograph.' And there's the PM sporting his best jut-jawed Dave of Arabia face.

Jordan is an arid country, but as we drive north it turns into beautiful rolling green farmland, olive groves and grazing. In the late-afternoon light it looks like a Victorian academy painting of an idyllic Holy Land, with the addition of countless black plastic bags. An oily pall of smoke smudges the horizon. We stop to admire a tourist's view of the border, and the general points out that we can see three countries from here: Syria, Israel and Lebanon; over there is the Golan Heights. It's tranquil, but the hot air carries low thuds, like heads hitting carpet. Mortars. 'They are coming. They are beginning to cross,' says the general. 'Do you want to see? Perhaps it's more dangerous.'

The United Nations High Commission for Refugees has warned us that the official danger level for the border has risen to five. Tom, the photographer, points out that this doesn't mean much unless you know what it can go up to: is it like Spinal Tap and goes up to eleven? 'No, it's five out of five,' says the UN official with a tightly thin smile, and: 'Could you please sign these waivers?' It is, just for this moment, the most hazardous border in the world.

As the light dies we turn onto a rocky track through olive trees and halt in a narrow valley: on one side a sloping hill, on the other broken land. The car lights are extinguished and we stand in the blue shadows and cooling dust. 'That is the border,' says the general. I stare at the distance. 'No, no, here. Here in front of you.' The track peters out and half a dozen steps away is Syria: dirt, rock and shrubs that crumple into night.

And then, as I watch, figures appear out of the darkness. It's a shock, I hadn't believed we'd see anything, but, bent double under sacks and stumbling across the uneven ground, men and women clutching small children and the flotsam of their lives heave with the scuff and grunt and sighs of folk who are trying to hurry silently in fear. Families hold hands, they move past us like heavy ghosts, not looking to the left or right. Among them now are Jordanian soldiers in full combat gear, helmets and body armour strapped tight, with automatic weapons. In front of them is a long, steep hill; on the far side, in its protective lee, is a makeshift reception centre. This is the last leg of one of the most dangerous journeys on earth. The bare slope faces Syria: it has no cover, just pale scree. At the summit there are already silhouettes on the skyline, moving like a drunken conga, a dance of death against the star-bright sky. I watch for an astonished minute as the flow of refugees rising out of the night increases from a trickle to a migration – they'll have waited for the veil of darkness to make for this invisible line in the sand.

The sound of not-so-distant artillery goads them forward. A woman struggles past me tugging a child – a girl in sandals, little more than a toddler. The mother wrestles a suitcase that swings like a pendulum, and in her other hand she has a large bag. I take the bag from her; she lets go without a murmur or a glance. The soldiers all carry luggage or a child, everybody shares the weight – the general, the translators, Tom, the fixers, the minders and the staff officers, we all grab something and together we struggle up the moonlit hill. This bag is heavier than any case I've packed since my school trunk. The handles cut my hand, the weight wrenches my shoulder. The summit recedes, the ground is uneven and rolls under foot. I can't possibly put the bag down or hand it back. This woman has carried it for so long, along with the weight of her responsibility and circumstances. So I crab behind her, arms numb. The skyline remains stubbornly distant, the back of my neck prickles as the ordnance rumbles, and then finally, finally, we're there.

I look back down at Syria, malevolent in the moonlight. On the other side, below us, is a hurried and huddled collection of Portakabins and tents, and the hum of a generator. I drop the bag beside the exhausted mother and her hollow-eyed child and attempt an insouciant smile. She nods. Hala, my interpreter, passes, hugging a suitcase. 'Can you ask this lady what she's got in the bag?' There's a short exchange. 'Oil, cooking oil.' She's lugged a gallon of olive oil from Syria to Jordan, the world's thirteenth-biggest olive producer. I don't say that aloud, I just wish her and her daughter luck: '*Inshallah*.'

We have all wondered what we would rescue from the burning house. Photo albums, the jewellery box, a Damien Hirst drawing. What people whose houses really are on fire or blown up take are blankets and shoes and cooking pots and radios and the tools of their trade and their papers – deeds, licences, the proof of who they are or were – and mobile phones. Nobody trains you to be a refugee, there are no helpful government pamphlets.

These newborn refugees are learning as they go; as they sit in family groups there is no sense of joy or even relief, just an exhausted, subdued misery. Tolstoy pointed out that all happy families are alike, but every unhappy family is unhappy in its own way. He was wrong. There is a terrible, bland sameness in despair. Their stories are told in a repetitive monotone, almost banal in their sadness. 'My grocery shop was crushed by a tank. We have nowhere to live. Our house was blown up by a bomb. My family's in prison. My husband is dead. I don't know where my brothers are. We were forced to leave. We have nothing. Everything is lost. There is no water. There is no food. There is no help. There is no hope.'

There are a few tears, no histrionics, precious little anger, and there's no 'making the best of it', no community singing – this is way, way beyond any Blitz spirit – just a blinking, passive capitulation as the tireless Jordanian soldiers move among them handing out clean water, cartons of juice for children, and biscuits, and their own rations – the officers have trouble getting their men to eat. And there's no gratitude. This isn't a salvation, it's not a new start, it's not a lucky escape when a man, a widow, a family, a village are forced to make the choice to be refugees. It is an unconditional surrender, not just of the house you live in or your profession, but of your security, community, your web of friendships, your dignity, your respect, your history and your future – not just yours, your children's future. The middle-aged man is never going to get his grocery shop back; the mechanic is never going to return to servicing Mercedes.

A bowed gent stands exhausted with three daughters in the queue to register. How old are they? 'This one is four, this one twelve and this one six.' In a whisper, he adds the school years they were in. Earlier, a Palestinian told me that the refugees may think they'll go back in six months, or a year or two. They all bring their house keys. He added: 'I still have the keys my parents brought from Palestine. There are no more doors left to open.' An ancient woman bent almost in half and shrouded in black is helped by two boys, her grand-children. They forced her to leave their house. She fought them, she wanted to die where she'd lived, but she was the last person left in the village. They say she is 100 years old, older than the country she's been forced to flee.

At the edge of the little reception camp is a hut on stilts, the size of a potting shed, decorated incongruously with peeling wallpaper patterned with butterflies. A soldier in helmet and flak jacket looks at a black and white television screen plugged into a geeky box. He has a little joystick and a series of buttons. Behind him is a rough, hand-drawn map of the border. This is the night-sight camera post, panning over Syria. As clear as day we can see an army camp, men walking about, a road with cars, a tank emplacement – and here are refugees dodging down the last track. 'Look,' says the soldier as he zooms in on a small hill. At its crest there are two dark dots. 'Ambush.' A pair of snipers. How far away? I ask. 'Close,' he replies matter-of-factly.

This night there are a handful who have made it across with bullet wounds; they are taken away by ambulance. The rest of the refugees are put on buses that glow magically in the desert like mystery tours. They should be used by the army to take soldiers on leave, but every day the military gives up 450 vehicles to the refugees. On board, the passengers sit in an exhausted stupor, children flop across adults, nobody asks if we're nearly there yet. It's getting late and cold as the dusty luggage is stuffed on board. Something is pushed into my hand. A child has given me a wilting posy of white wildflowers; her mother beside her is the woman whose oil I carried. She says, 'For you, a piece of Syria,' and they get on the bus that bumps its way down the track back into the night.

The refugees don't think the Zaatari camp is in Jordan at all; they talk about Jordan as out there somewhere. This is a limbo, an unplace, as detailed an image of purgatory as you are likely to find on this earth. It has about it an ethereal whiteness: the UN tents and prefab huts are white, the sky is white and the ground it all sits on is white. The Jordanian government offered a lump of desert to keep the refugees, but it was so dusty that it posed a serious respiratory-health risk, so the UNHCR imported tons and tons of white gravel to lay on the sand. People are reduced to ants on this vast, pale sheet, a dystopian science-fiction set holding more than 100,000 souls – the population of Blackburn or Exeter – 70 per cent of them women and children. The logistics of building it in a number of weeks are numbing, and there is no water – Jordan is chronically parched. Imagine the sanitary needs of 100,000 people. Try to imagine the condition of the Portaloos – they make Glastonbury look like The Ritz. The Jordanian police won't patrol the camps, it's too dangerous. Military gendarmes lounge at the perimeter in armoured cars in case of serious trouble – there are sporadic riots. People can't come and go; there is a perimeter fence and security supplied, worryingly, by G4S. It isn't a prison as such, but desperation, utter poverty and powerlessness make de facto prisoners of the refugees, particularly the women.

The cost so far for Jordan is over £465 million; contributions from other countries amount to £140 million. The UNHCR calculates that it needs half a billion dollars to run the camp and look after the Syrian refugees, and that will have to come from donations. But the half-billion will only keep the camp going until June. This is a Herculean undertaking, like a space programme in the desert, and there are 14,000 new arrivals every week. The UNHCR offices are a series of Portakabins cordoned off at the edge of the camp, surrounded by an angry clamour of supplicants. A woman presses against the wire gate. Two small children cling to her chador, and she is alternately begging and demanding from the G4S guard. Finally, someone pulls her inside, the children like limpets. She's taken to an office where veiled women interview her. She arrived three days ago with four children under twelve, she has no husband, she has no extended family, and here she begins to weep. They are alone; the children press against her like bookends, and she says she is also six months pregnant and doesn't want to have her baby here, in the white desert. She draws a deep breath, angrily wipes her eyes and whispers: 'I am humiliated.'

Anger blooms in the camp, domestic violence rages as men bereft of respect take it out on their wives and children. A man came into the UNHCR demanding that they do something for his wife – make-up, hair, better clothes – because she was becoming unattractive and he didn't want to have to divorce her. The staff gave him short shrift. Others have asked for another tent so they can have a sex life away from their children. The staff say there are more important things to be concerned with, but privately they agree that, if it is your sex life, there probably isn't. There are also reports of daughters being married off to men who have money or access to outside, who might be guides for the family to a new life. If they're married, they're somebody else's responsibility, and it is also protection against the stigma of rape. There are short-term marriage contracts, a sort of Madam Butterfly prostitution, usually involving older women or desperate widows. The camp is prey to gangs, to politics and vendetta. It feeds liverishly on boredom. Children go feral: there is nothing for them to do, no trees to climb.

A refugee camp is a community with everything good and hopeful and comforting about community taken out. There is precious little peace, no belonging, no civic pride. There is, though, still the gossamer web of human kindness. Villagers who left Syria together collect together to form protective huddles; in one kitchen block, a group of women who have known each other all their lives cook rice, aubergine and a little fried chicken. The smell is wonderful after the camp. They tease me, confident in their togetherness.

Outside, a man beckons me to his tent. He has a generator and is charging mobile phones; it is a little business. He asks me in. He's a big man in a cloth cap and he pushes me hard. I fall through the door and his wife laughs. He says he's a communist and 'in our village we buried the last illiterate person in 1974. Now, look,' his voice rises. 'These children. Will they ever read and write? We are going backwards.' He offers me coffee, insists with anger, insists. To him, hospitality is more than a politeness, it is a hold on the last threads of dignity and self-respect. It is important to accept it from people who have nothing. People give us things all the time, sweets, advice, good wishes, smiles, lectures. There are street stalls where you can buy expensive smuggled goods, from underpants to microwaves – Syrians are famous entrepreneurs – and even somebody making vivid-pink candyfloss in this desperate desert.

We watch a boy shimmy up an electricity pylon and gingerly attach wires to steal power. Men gather and wave their arms and look at the white sky. They want Scuds to come and kill Assad. 'Where is NATO?' someone shouts in my face. 'Where is your NATO? It is because we are Muslim they don't come. In Europe you treat animals better than we are treated here.'

Refugees are the collateral damage of wars, they are the pieces that have been taken off the board. The hot news story is the conflict itself; this intransigent, complex headache of unwanted, awkward, lumpen people doesn't have the dynamic interest of global politics or the screen-grab of smoke and bodies and Kalashnikovs. Whatever the outcome in Syria, these people have already lost, lost everything but despair and a gut-churning sense of injustice that will fester. Lacking power or influence, swept aside by events that were not of their making, they will slowly turn to dust, go from unconsidered to unremembered, their grief evaporating in a region where every handful of dirt is someone else's calamity.

In Amman, Jordan's capital, old Iraqi men smoke hubble-bubbles and play cards. They were much younger men, with futures and hopes and aspirations, when they dealt the first hands here. They are served by Palestinian waiters who have never seen their homeland. In the camp, a small boy in a red tracksuit is trying to find medical help; he needs a shot for his asthma. His father comes over and says he saw us last night on the border. He starts to tell the story of his village, Deir Ba'alba. 'It was surrounded, burnt and shelled for months. The people couldn't escape and it was destroyed and everyone was killed. The whole village.'

He comes to a ragged stop as he tries not to weep in front of foreigners and his surviving child and his dignity. 'Remember Deir Ba'alba. Please, it's important. Remember Deir Ba'alba.'

A refugee camp reminds you, if you need reminding, that you are your brother's keeper, but he is heavy. So perhaps you might remember Deir Ba'alba. I only wrote it down phonetically, so say it out loud to someone else.

March 2013

FURTHEST

Ethiopia

First the good news. The long rains have finished and they were long enough, deep, thick and wet enough. Ethiopia is expecting a beneficent harvest, so that's a relief, or an absence of relief. You won't have to wear the T-shirt, listen to the bald rockers or be distressed by the news this year. Whoever thought you'd read: 'No famine in Ethiopia'? Now the bad news. That doesn't mean they're not starving. Hardly anyone's got the cash for a mouldy banana. If you look at early maps of Africa, below the Sahara is a big, dark blank inscribed with just one name: Ethiopia. It floats in ignorance, stretching from the Horn to the Niger. The one African name known to Europe since the Middle Ages; the land of Prester John, the legendary Christian king who stood outside the Western world. Ethiopia claims it was the first Christian country. Ethiopians say they have been Christians for 3,000 years, 1,000 with the Old Testament and 2,000 with the New. They also say they are one of the lost tribes of Israel, belonging to neither black nor Arab Africa, existing in Africa but not of it.

The name itself was given by the Greeks and means 'sunburnt people'. Abyssinia, its other name, is Arabic and means 'mixed people'. Ethiopia is a loose, conflicting collection of shifting tribes and cities half as old as time. There are Christians who circumcise their children, and animist tribes who castrate other people. In the north there are hermits who spend decades living alone in caves, in the south there are sun worshippers who wear metal wigs and terracotta plates in their lips. It has some of the oldest churches carved out of solid stone and the third-holiest city of Islam. It has more than 64 million people, eighty-six distinct languages, and hundreds of dialects. The official lingo is Amharic, one of the earliest written languages and the only phonetic one that reads from left to right, though it started from right to left, then, bizarrely, went both right and left in a zigzag like a man ploughing a field.

In Ethiopia, nothing is quite what it seems. You only believe half of what you hear, and it's usually the other half that's true. Ethiopia is a country that elides fact and myth, where everything seems to come as part of an illusion. It's the alleged home of the Ark of the Covenant and the true cross. There are thirteen months in its year, so a lucky few have no star sign. Its twelve-hour clock begins at dawn, so world-time seven o'clock is Ethiopian-time one o'clock. When people make appointments they rarely stipulate which watch they're using, so they are regularly six hours late, which is nothing to the rest of us, being three years early. Ethiopia still uses the Julian calendar. They haven't even begun to think about building their millennium dome yet. They've barely thought about building the twentieth century. Ethiopia is the home of coffee. The Blue Nile rises here. Ethiopia grows *teff*, a grass eaten nowhere else, which makes a soggy, fermented bread that looks like a cross between grey foam rubber and tripe. It is rolled up in the manner of airline face flannels.

But, singularly and importantly, Ethiopia is the only African country that was never a European colony. Its borders were not drawn with a lazy arbitration in the Foreign Offices of London, Paris or Brussels, but were carved out by fearsome warriors with spear and serpentine sword. Central to Ethiopia's pride, and indeed Africa's, is the fact that it boasts the only African army that ever decisively beat a European one, at the Battle of Adwa in 1896. Not quite the only one, but the first since Hannibal. Coincidentally, also against the Italians. Finally, and most opaquely, it has an extraordinary number of people with little wads of tissue paper shoved up one nostril.

Addis Ababa (which means 'new flower') lounges like a rotten wreath over a series of hills, in turn surrounded by the impressive curve of the Entoto Mountains. It's a relatively modern city, just over a hundred years old, built round hot springs. It's also 8,000 feet above sea level, so every flight of stairs is a consultation with a breathless amateur cardiologist, and every Ethiopian is a middle-distance runner. The city is generously, panoramically free of any smidgen of beauty, but not without a fearsome charm and noisome excitement.

It's a black-rap Dickensian stew. The indigenous juniper forests that once shaded it were cut down for firewood generations ago, and replaced with antipodean eucalyptus trees that drink like Australians and are good for nothing much more than admiring and burning. Every night, straggling lines of folded old ladies carry vast bundles of firewood down from the hills. The women carry them because they're just too big and heavy for the donkeys.

Addis is 70 per cent slum, a lurching, teetering stack of shanties – rusty corrugated iron, slimy plastic sheeting, mud reeking of eucalyptus gum, dung and smoke, rather like a long-haul economy toilet. They creep and elbow amid the crumbling, cheap concrete buildings like live Polyfilla. Addis boasts Africa's largest market, the Mercato, a sprawling dark compost of rickety shops, stalls and livid life. There are streets of tailors sewing rags on ancient Singers, alleys of people weaving sweet-smelling grass, making traditional dining plates with coned covers. There's a labyrinthine spice market with precipitous, bright peaks of turmeric and chilli, cumin, coriander and poppy seeds and ground roots with only indigenous names, whose scents are mysteriously, tantalisingly divorced from any Western flavour. There are tiny tables selling handmade newspaper pokes of incense for the elaborate coffee ceremony that all families have once a week; steeples of gauzy wool and cotton shawls with delicate silk borders. Lorries deliver man-sized bound sheaves of *chat*, the mildly speedy drug that many poor chew as an escape, a solace and a hunger depressant. Addicts roam the streets with bloodshot eyes, wild hair and cupped palms. What you rarely see is anyone buying anything. No bag-laden women arguing over fruit or veg. Just thousands of young men loitering and waiting.

Even by African standards, the bothering and begging are exhaustive and unremitting, and the beggars world-beating in their decrepitude and infirmity. Here are the legless, armless, eyeless and toothless; the polio-crippled, the mine-maimed, the buboed and leprous, the self-mutilated and the plain mad. And the pickpockets. In one morning I was dipped three times, and marvelled at their consummate, prestidigital professionalism. Addis is potless poor, too poor even for advertising. None of the painted walls flogging Coca-Cola and

Sportsman cigarettes that decorate the rest of Africa. You want to know how broke it is? It's too broke to even afford rubbish. The meagrest scrap has a value until it vanishes. But it does have filth, gratis from Dame Nature.

With an unbelievable collective self-restraint, it's safe, probably safer than most European capitals, but there is a prickling sense of tension, a muttered, in-your-face, eyeballing exasperation. Some of the most bellicose tribes who ever lived came from hereabouts. A chap couldn't get married until he was a proven, motiveless murderer. Addis feels like the squall before the storm, like it's waiting for something. A spark, an excuse. What it and I are also waiting for is the funeral of Haile Selassie. Like most things here, it's late – twenty-five years, two regimes, three wars and a pair of famines late. To finally lay to rest the conquering lion of the tribe of Judah, the king of kings, the direct descendant of Solomon and the Queen of Sheba, the only new god of the modern era, will be to finally tie up one of the last loose ends of the twentieth century.

While history is written by Western white men, its chief protagonists will always be Western white men. Selassie drifts through the convulsive modern age like a small, dark, topied ghost. He was the twentieth century's Zelig. Most people only know of him as the faintly ridiculous deity of the Rastafarians, seen in the yellow, red and green of the Ethiopian flag on T-shirts with Bob Marley and a joint. Yet if you shift the eyeline of history from its well-oiled western axis and look up from the hot, ancient south, Selassie is a monumental, titanic figure, a catalyst and central protagonist in the story not just of Africa, but of the entire modern world order. He came to power in a confusing internecine struggle in the century's first decades and was murdered by communist revolutionaries known as the Derg. His forty-four-year reign descended into a static feudal mire of oligarchic intrigue, corruption and fear. So powerful were his image and aura that they physically, as well as symbolically, had to smother him to death. The king of kings was secretly interred under President Mengistu's personal lavatory. Even as a corpse he could frighten the pants off his subjects. Look at photographs. All his life he seems to have had only one impervious sarcophagal expression, a granite stare that glares at posterity with all the regal confidence of a heritage that disappears back into the mist of fairy tales. He was the head of the only independent African country. He led Ethiopia into the League of Nations, and witnessed its demise. In Geneva he made a speech that echoed round the world in defence of the independence of small countries. It is one of the great pieces of twentieth-century oratory, and as relevant today as it was then. It could have been said of Kuwait or Kosovo or East Timor.

The Italian invasion turned Ethiopia into the Spain of the Third World. The old colonial powers' shameful self-interest, the demeaning, secret Hoare–Laval pact between French and British foreign ministers, tacitly allowed Mussolini to carve up a new Roman empire, proving that, for all its brave words and olive-branch ambitions, the League would never confront a Western power. The dates for the start of the Second World War tend to be arbitrary, dependent on individual countries' experiences. Actually it began in Ethiopia in 1935, with mustard gas dropped on a lion-maned army armed with spears and leather shields. The appeasement of France and Britain, and Mussolini's trumped-up border incidents, were the green light for Hitler's piecemeal annexations. Selassie's Ethiopia was the first country to fall to fascism and the first to be liberated.

The British intelligence officer Orde Charles Wingate and a messianic collection of repressed homosexuals, tortured explorers, noble-savage worshippers and eccentric misfits, along with guerrilla patriots, brilliantly outmanoeuvred the Italians and restored the emperor to his throne in 1941. Post-war Ethiopia under Selassie was one of the founding countries of the United Nations. He was a prime instigator of the Organisation of African Unity, which still has its headquarters in Addis. At home he was Victorianly enthusiastic for selective modernism, particularly in education, though anyone who had read a book or gained a degree was likely to find themselves a political prisoner. His predecessor, Menelik, sent his army officers to be trained in imperial Russia. Foolishly, Selassie continued the practice *après Lenin* and found himself a medieval ruler with a nascent, educated middle class frustrated by no prospects, an officer class who were hard-line communists, and a pampered, venal family who intrigued at every opportunity. And a country that was slipping into famine. Selassie was caught on film feeding fresh meat to his Abyssinian lions (now extinct) as his nation starved. It was all bound to end in tears.

Today you can reach the royals on their website, www.ethiopiancrown.org. His Imperial Highness Prince Ermias Sahle-Selassie Haile-Selassie is president of the Crown Council. Through the miracle of email, I have arranged to have dinner with him. Ironically, in Addis's best Italian restaurant (established 1946). It's to be a small, informal briefing, so I've also invited Dr Richard Pankhurst, the grandson of the suffragette and a world expert on Ethiopia. To actually break bread with a direct descendant of Solomon will be quite something. It makes our own dear royal family's lumpen Kraut origins seem rather dowdy. Regally an hour and a half late, Ermias arrives with a train of twenty family members, bodyguards and aides. I suddenly feel that I'm hosting royal Band Aid. It's an embarrassment of seeds of Solomon. So embarrassing that I haven't enough cash to pay for them all and have to make arrangements with the jolly Italian owner, who waves his hands and invites me back for dinner on the house. Ermias is a one-man charm offensive. All Ethiopians have infinite reserves of charm. Talking to them is like having your secret places softly massaged with warm butter. He says he's nervous. Indeed, his weakly handsome eyes look frankly terrified, and with good reason. This is the first time in twenty-six years that all Selassie's descendants have returned after fleeing the Derg, with its self-named Red Terror and its Cambodian-style mass murders, including asking schoolchildren where they lived, taking them home, then shooting them in front of their parents. The regime lasted seventeen years, until overthrown by the slightly rosier-red Tigray People's Liberation Front, part of the regime that is still in power. Nobody knows why they've allowed this burial to take place, how they will react, or indeed if anyone will turn up. Will it be tens, or tens of thousands? Selassie's name has been expunged from school books and public life for a generation. Will they remember? His grandchildren are dotted around the world – England, Canada, Greece, Italy, the United States. They are Italian businessmen, Midwestern social workers, Greek hairdressers.

Ermias lives in Washington DC. He does a little bit of this and a bit of that and a lot of philanthropy. The American capital boasts a large Ethiopian refugee community, mostly taxi drivers. In his Italian suit, with his seamless small talk, Ermias seems further from Ethiopia than even Washington. Yes, of course, he'll give an interview and pose for a picture, though he must be discreet, you understand. Would he mind if I joined the family the next morning in the church service to mark the start of three days of mourning and celebrate the seventieth anniversary of Selassie's coronation? Of course, I'd be very welcome. A waiter leans purposefully across the table. Ermias's eyes blink with fear. The man jabs a finger and talks rapid, emphatic Amharic. He will be at the funeral. The late emperor was a great man. Ermias shows me his best Washington politician's face: 'I'm very touched by the reverence of the common people.'

Six o'clock in the morning, and there's still a chill in the air as dawn breaks over Selassie's square, domed cathedral. We take off our shoes and carry them with us inside. They are too valuable to be left at the door. Priests, acolytes and choirboys pad round a central tent that represents the holy of holies, the spiritual home of the Ark. Leaning against it are sacred paintings done in the Ethiopian manner, with their pale skin and mournful wide brown eyes. The women stand on one side, then men on the other. Young servants in white cassocks and broad shawls pile carpets on top of carpets for our comfort. The priests process round the church, swinging clouds of incense, carrying their elaborate silver Ethiopian crosses and richly bound Bibles. There's much genuflecting and kissing and we are given T-shaped croziers to lean on. The congregation looks like an ethnic heat for *One Man and His Dog*. We are an odd bunch. The royal family confused and nervous in black, some of the granddaughters sobbing behind their veils. A couple of big-haired and elaborately shrouded Rastafarians, including Bob Marley's widow, the very laid-back Rita. And then, beside me, a porcine pink gent in a pin-stripe suit with polished socks and a large signet ring who could only be English and turns out to be Sir Conrad Swan, KCVO, PhD, FSA, Garter Principal, King of Arms Emeritus. What on earth is he doing here? The service is long, over three hours, delivered in monotonous Amharic and an older ecclesiastical language like Latin called Ge'ez. It makes the hair on your neck stand up and dries the mouth. When they start singing, the bishop intones a Gregorian-style chant that sounds both Orthodox and Arab and the choir provides a deep rhythmic descant that is unmistakably African. A sonorous, liquid-black, speechlessly sad rise and fall. This is perhaps the oldest Christian service in the world, largely unchanged for 1,700 years. It's as close as any of us will come this side of the grave to knowing how the apostles prayed. Halfway through, Selassie's throne is produced from behind a screen.

The priests step forward and usher a prince to sit in it. The Abun, the patriarch of the Ethiopian Church, is a kingmaker. A pivotal politician. His blessing is essential to any pretender, and the man he's placed on the throne is not Ermias. It's a tall, bald someone else. My prince is three down the pecking order, looking characteristically worried. Damn, I fed the wrong royal. As the service finishes, the carpets are rolled back and a trap door is opened. We all squeeze into the crypt and there, finally, he is. The last of the line of Judah. Behind a glass partition like a sweet-shop window. His coffin is draped in a white and silver net curtain with a photograph propped on it. It looks like a small piano. In two days a procession will move him from here to the cathedral, and there lower him into a marble sarcophagus beside the altar. We all stare at the little box, not really knowing what to think.

The Sheraton Hotel rises out of the shanty slum like a huge taupe palace. It is by some way the grandest building in Addis. I wouldn't normally mention it, except it's without doubt also the grandest hotel in Africa. Every capital has its hubristic, tourist-enticing, foreign-built splendido, but none come close to the magnificence of this place. For a start, everything works. The fax in your room, the ranks of fountains, the staff, your own butler, drinks come when you order them. The numerous restaurants serve decent imported food and the clean pool has underwater muzak. This would be a very grand hotel in Hollywood. In Africa it's unimaginable. I also mention it because for a brief time it becomes the royal court. A huge *Gormenghast* of intrigue, rumours and factions. The royal family effortlessly pick up where they left off and, as a confused foreign observer, I find myself the recipient of a steady stream of off-the-record briefings, debriefings, unbriefings, points of order and just straightforward lies. The players stalk the bars and lounges, knots of retainers huddle and whisper with slidy eyes. All is not well in the court of Selassie. The first thing that happens is that my blessed prince disappears. I call to confirm my interview and he's gone. Where? His aide, an implausibly smooth chap who probably has a double first in the novels of John Grisham and Raymond Chandler, says he's hiding and asks me to come to his suite. The phones are not safe. He tells me the prince was being followed, they'd had to change cars. The government's putting out aggressive signals (an article in the English-language paper written in 1970s Cold-Warese; fraternal, peace-loving people, feudal capitalist stooges, etc., accusing Haile Selassie of funnelling wealth abroad, which is unlikely as he was famously ascetic except when it came to uniforms).

While we're talking, another man enters the room and silently loiters. Let's talk in here, says the aide, and opens a door. It's a closet. He ushers me in among the swinging coat hangers, he tells me that if I'm inclined to mention a split in the royal family I'll just make a fool of myself, and he can tell I'm no fool because I ask such naive questions, pretending to be stupid. I'm obviously a very clever journalist, he chuckles conspiratorially. No, no, I really do know nothing. I really am a very stupid journalist. For instance, I'm pressed up against a svelte Ethiopian whispering in a cupboard. Back in the bar, where the piano player tinkles out golden movie moments, I try to make some sense out of the royal family, but it's like juggling mud. Yet another prince shimmies over and French-polishes my bottom. Then, in an aside, mentions that of course I know there's a man pretending to be me in the Hilton Hotel. 'He says he's a reporter from *The Sunday Times.*' Oh, good grief. I can't work out who any of you are. Now I have to find out who I am. And here he, or I, is. Across the lobby rolls one plump young Englishman, dressed in thick bird's-eye worsted. To an Ethiopian eye he is the epitome of a Brit gent abroad, but to me he looks utterly fictional. The plummy voice has just a hint of suburban cul-de-sac. The coolness a sheen of cold sweat. He hands me a card. Anthony Bailey, MIPR, MIPRA, managing director, Eligo

International Ltd Berlin, Brussels, London, Lugano, Madrid, Milan, Paris, Sofia. 'I am', he says, dropping heavily into a chair, 'the press secretary to His Majesty, the Crown Prince Zara Yaqov.' The man in the throne? 'Yes.' Can we talk to him? 'Ah now, that may be difficult. He's not very well. You could put some questions through me and I'll give you written answers.'

'We have just received a letter from Her Majesty the Queen.' Of the United Kingdom? 'Of course.' Sorry, it's just that there are so many monarchs about. 'You know you once stitched me up over the King of Greece.' No, I didn't. I've never met the King of Greece. 'Oh yes you did.' I'm pretty sure I didn't. 'Maybe it was A.N. Wilson, then.' I'm not him either. It turns out that Crown Prince Zara lives in straitened circumstances in Manchester and is looked after by Rastafarians who are trying to get him interested in breeding another heir (as if there weren't enough already). Among all the subterfuge and rumour I'm pretty sure that's a fact, because frankly you just couldn't make it up. The next morning Bailey slips the text of Her Majesty's letter (our one) under my door. She is very pleased 'that at long last, Emperor Haile Selassie the First is being accorded a proper burial'. Which is nice.

Crown Prince Zara's question-and-answer is a double dose of Mogadon. With it comes a tart note: 'As I have not heard from you as we agreed, I have cancelled today's appointment with Empress Work and the crown prince.' But we never agreed. There never was a meeting. And who is this Empress Work?

'You weren't supposed to be told that His Royal Highness was unwell,' yet another prince tells me in the corridor. This is getting like a pantomime audition. Why, what's the matter with him? 'I can't tell you. But you should find out.' Thanks. The closet aide asks me to go to a safe phone in the lobby and dial a number. It's my prince. He's fearful for his life. It's terribly sad. He doesn't want to be the cause of any danger for his people. He's in Rome.

When power and prestige slip down the plughole, this black farce is what you're left with. The conquering lions of Judah are just the scum line left on the bathtub of history. It's funny, but it's not as funny as it's pathetic.

The funeral starts early, at 4 a.m. I get to the cathedral an hour after dawn. It's already hot. It's going to be scorching. The coffin, draped in the Ethiopian flag, rests on the steps, surrounded by a patriotic guard of old warriors in baboon-fur Alice bands and long, bright tabards with a lion embroidered on the back. They carry boiled-leather shields and blackened spears. On one side of the bier sits the royal family and on the other the Abun, priests, and monks of the church, dressed in the rich panoply of their calling. Bright togas and robes, coruscating coronets and mitres all thickly encrusted and decorated.

Their croziers and huge silver crosses are garlanded with ribbons; acolytes hold aloft velvet and silk sunshades intricately embroidered with stars and suns and images of Christ, like the serried domes of a visionary city. Stretching along each side are lines of choirboys and girls in bright surplices, holding flags and honey-scented tapers. They sing Latin dirges and sway like a gentle ocean. On a gold throne is the patriarch, swathed in burgundy velvet, barnacled and filigreed with gold, wearing a multi-storey crown. This steepling tableau is like something dreamt by a black Velázquez. It beggars anything contrived by the Vatican. Here in scabrous Africa it's truly a vision of unimaginable splendour, dignity and ancient pomp.

Slightly apart stand a line of khaki-clad men, ancients with grizzled beards and yellow, rheumy eyes, dressed in tattered uniforms and battered sola topis. They are survivors of the war against the Italians. Their medals, paid for with the philanthropy of blood, droop on thin chests. Some carry faded photographs of Selassie or themselves in their martial prime. One stands stiffly erect in worn rubber flip-flops.

The coffin is lifted onto a flat-bed truck swathed in the flag. The guards surround it, spears at attention. The procession, slowly and with much confusion, makes its way through the slums, to Revolution Square, a flat, featureless area that recently held a million people to welcome home Ethiopia's Olympic runners. Now the ranks of waiting metal chairs are mostly empty. A few dozen officials and Anthony Bailey sit pucely steaming in the sun. There are perhaps 3,000 or 4,000 Ethiopians watching with a sullen, nothing-better-to-do interest.

Over a crackling loudspeaker there are ponderous speeches. The sun and the boredom climb. The coffin is manhandled back on the truck and heads off through the otherwise engaged streets towards the cathedral graveyard, where, three hours later, the crowd has grown dense and patient. Perched on gravestones and monuments, it's mostly old men and women who must remember Selassie and his empire with fondness. For all his stiffness and faults, his people were materially a lot better off then than they are now; it's the price of bread that matters most. But the government can relax. This is not a popular demonstration of dissent. It's all about the past, not the future. There will be no trouble. Another service, more tapers and hymns, more speeches and, in front of the coffin, white-robed choristers chant and rhythmically shake silver rattles. Then the great Ethiopian war drum is banged, beaten to send Selassie to his marble grave. A voice behind me says: 'The last time I heard that drum was in 1935.' It's Bill Deedes – Lord Deedes – the most venerable of all correspondents, who was here with Evelyn Waugh and is the model for Boot, the hero of *Scoop*, the funniest book ever written about journalism, one I feel I have been unintentionally plagiarising. His presence somehow closes the circle, and he's about to have his pockets picked and his camera nicked.

Surprisingly few Rastafarians have come to bury their god, but then I hear one say: 'I-and-I know he still lives.' Of course: he's immortal. This is not his funeral. Selassie is alive somewhere in the vastness to the south, preparing a land for his chosen people. In the West we tend to sneer and snigger at the Rastas with their drugs and knitwear and belief that a small black Third World dictator could possibly be a deity. But Jamaicans saw the only black man from Africa who had ever defeated the whites; who stood in solitary, righteous splendour in an otherwise enslaved continent. An emperor obliquely mentioned in the Bible, a black man whose status didn't derive from running faster or punching other black men harder. And who is to say that the conquering lion of the tribe of Judah, the descendant of Solomon, is any sillier an object of worship than a carpenter from Nazareth? Only time can give religion dignity.

He stands unhelpfully behind the coffin as it see-saws up the steps, carried by the royal family, in a confusion of priests and cameramen.

Slowly it makes its way from the sunlight into the cool, dark shadows; the heavy iron doors clang shut. The last emperor has made his final journey from lavatory to cathedral.

Later I ask yet another royal how he liked the service. 'It was terrible, the family was distraught. The crowd should have been prostrate, the women ululating. It wasn't fitting. It was so sad.' Perhaps, but nothing like as profoundly sad as the lives eked out on every street corner. I'm told, in strict confidence, naturally, that the coffin didn't fit its grave, but is propped up in a corner. In death as in life, Haile Selassie was a bigger man than he appeared.

December 2000

Japan

On the face of it, the Japanese are very like us. We are both island nations, about the same size, both mongrel populations with constitutional monarchies; it rains a lot, they drink tea, we drink tea. We're both obscurely addicted to odd sports (cricket, sumo), both had empires, are bellicose, mistrustful of foreigners and are passionate gardeners. Neither of us is particularly good-looking, we are both repressed, both suffer a class system, drive on the left, and only in Britain or Japan is having a stiff upper lip explicable as a compliment. But that's just on the face of it. Underneath, we're chalk and tofu.

You don't have to go to Japan to have an inkling that the Japanese are not as the rest of us are. In fact, they're decidedly weird. If you take the conventional gamut of human possibility as running, say, from Canadians to Brazilians, after ten minutes in the land of the rising sun you realise the Japs are off the map, out of the game, on another planet. It's not that they're aliens, but they are the people that aliens might be if they'd learnt Human by correspondence course and wanted to slip in unnoticed. It's the little things, like the food. They make the most elegant, delicate food in the world and then make it in plastic for every restaurant window. Only a Japanese person could see a plate of propylene curry and say: 'Yum, I'll have that.' And the loos. Heated loo seats are slightly worrying the first time you encounter them, but after that they're a comfy idea; and there are buttons for jets of variable power, warm water, one for back bottom, one for front, with pictures to tell you which is which, and hot air to help you drip-dry. All of which is strangely addictive and makes you question your sexual orientation, or at least wish for diarrhoea.

But it's not that which gets the canary of weird coughing, it's the lavatory paper: it's like rice paper. They have twenty-first-century bogs and thirteenth-century bog roll. Your bum's clean enough to eat sushi off, but you need to scrub your fingernails with a boot scraper. This is a country where the men pee in the street but it's the height of bad manners to blow your nose, and they wear woolly gloves on their feet.

Hiroshima is shockingly empty of grave resonance. You feel next to nothing. There's a memorial garden in the bland civic style, a hectoring museum and the peace dome – one of the few brick-and-concrete buildings in old Hiroshima whose skeletal rubble has been preserved as a symbol. It was built by a Swede.

The atomic bomb that wiped out Hiroshima, killing 140,000 people and reducing a wooden city to ash and black rain, was, if you ask me, with the benefit of hindsight, all things considered, a good thing. As a direct result of Hiroshima, the war ended. The emperor overrode his military, who wanted a banzai suicide last battle, and broadcast their unconditional surrender.

The only vibration left in the place is a saccharine sentimentality and a trite, injured morality. Hiroshima wears its unique, nuclear-age victimhood with the simpering pride of a geisha's wig. The quiescent kids in quasi-naval uniforms line up for peace studies and group shots; all make peace signs, or maybe they're victory signs, because if anyone won the peace, Japan did. Any sense of sympathy for this place is snuffed out by the petition I'm asked to sign insisting that the Americans apologise for dropping the bomb.

Well, hold on, Tojo. When it comes to apologies, Japan's silence is cacophonous. What about your treatment of prisoners of war? 'Oh, they were soldiers,' I'm told with a quiet, slow patronage. What about the Chinese massacres? 'Exaggerated.' The Korean comfort women, don't they deserve apologies? 'Oh, they're just making a fuss because Japan is rich and they want money. And 20,000 Koreans were killed in Hiroshima.' True, they were slaves, and when they asked if there could be a memorial for Koreans in this peace garden, the Japanese said no.

Let's get the Japanese as victims into perspective. During the war in the East, half a million Allied soldiers died. Three million Japanese died and 20 million other Asians perished under Japan's brief expansion into an empire. That's 20 million we in the West rarely remember. As I stand here, the newspapers are full of Koreans and Chinese bitterly denouncing Japan's new school history books, which deny any culpability. The Japanese don't think they're worth a sorry. The detonation of an atomic bomb above Hiroshima was the starting gun for modern Japan. It blew away not just the most deeply cruel military government but a 1,000-year-old political and social system – the most inhuman and exploitative ever designed. The violent burst of the nuclear age was the best thing that ever happened to Japan. It didn't destroy anything like as much as it created.

What's extraordinary about Hiroshima is how fast it has grown back into a huge neon and concrete city that looks as if it's been here for ever. Before the war, Japan had an economy that was a small fraction of America's. A wood-and-rice peasant place, its main exports were textiles and soldiers. Today, even in the slough of a prolonged depression, it's still the second-biggest economy in the world, with a GDP as large as Britain's, France's and Germany's combined. That's astonishing, not least because Japan is about one and a half times the size of the UK, with twice as many people and only a third of its land habitable, yet it has no natural resources to speak of. So where did it all go wrong? How come Japan has such commercial success but still manages to be a socially weird disaster? Because, have no doubts, they're not happy.

Kyoto is Japan's old imperial capital, and escaped being Hiroshima by the whim of an American diplomat who once visited it. Kyoto boasts more heritage sites than you can shake a fan at. And you get there by a bullet train that looks like God's suppository and is twice as fast. The bullet trains run like clockwork, as if there were anything as techno-regressive as clockwork in Japan. The ticket collectors bow when they enter carriages, and there are little girls in pink cheerleaders' uniforms who collect rubbish. It's the symbol of modern, efficient Japan. But, and I'm not obsessed, the lavatories are pee-in-your-socks squat jobs. It's very odd.

Kyoto is a disappointment: an ugly sprawl of low-rise confusion. The streets are a tangle of stunted electricity pylons and cat's-cradle power lines. Hidden among it are thousands of shrines and temples, which are beautiful, up to a point. There's an anaemic, minutely obsessive quality to them and they're very repetitive. I did rather love the gardens, though: vegetative taxidermy. Everything is tied down, wired up, splinted, truncated and pruned. In the pools, albino carp slip and twist with a ghostly boredom.

Religion is one of the reasons Japan is so socially crippled. In the beginning they had Shinto. Now, if religions were cars, Shinto would be a wheelbarrow. It's your basic animism: ancestor worship, goblins and ghosts, tree and rock spirits. It lacks the most rudimentary theology. It made the emperor into a god descended from the sun. Onto that was grafted Buddhism – the wrong sort. Not the happy Dalai Lama stuff, but Zen Buddhism via China. Zen is so desiccatedly aesthetic that nobody knows what it means. On top of all that, the Japanese chose to add Confucianism. Now, it has been said there's no such thing as bad philosophy and that below a certain level it simply stops being philosophy at all. Confucianism is the exception that proves the rule. It's unpleasant and lowbrow. Confucius and Taoism were the excuse-all, get-out-of-work-and-responsibility for the samurai. Modern Japanese people get born Shinto, married Christian, buried Buddhist and work Mazda. Consequently they believe everything and nothing. There is no solace in Japanese religion, no salvation or redemption, hope, encouragement, and, most importantly, no concept of individuality, which is why you always see them mob-handed. A Japanese man on his own doesn't think he exists. It's just a static, miserable round of corporate responsibility and filial duty. I've never come across a place whose spiritual options were so barren. This pick-and-mix theology has stunted Japan like a tonsured, root-bound pine tree.

Kyoto has the most famous rock garden in the world: the ultimate Zen experience, fifteen stones set in raked white gravel. You're supposed to sit and ponder. Nobody knows who made it or why, but it's deeply aesthetic, and fundamentally risible. Look, I'm sorry, but this is the emperor's new garden, an impractical joke. It's medieval builders' rubbish. Oh, but then, silly me, of course I don't understand. I'm constantly being patronised for my coarse sensibilities and told that naturally I couldn't comprehend the subtlety, the aesthetic bat-squeak of Japanese culture. No country hides itself behind the paper screen of cultural elitism like Japan, which, considering they've bought their entire civilisation from other people's hand-me-downs, is a bit of a liberty. When it comes to Japanese civilisation, it's mostly eyewash. Kabuki theatre is only just preferable to amateur root-canal work. The three-stringed guitar is a sad waste of cat. Japanese flower-arranging is just arranging flowers. Their architecture is Chinese, as are their clothes, chopsticks, writing, etc. The samurai were thugs in frocks with stupid haircuts, and haiku poems are limericks that don't make you laugh. Indeed, they are so aesthetically difficult that one haiku master managed to compose only 23,000 in twenty-four hours, including gems like: 'The ancient pond, / A frog leaps, / The sound of the water.' Marvellous.

And then there are geishas. In Kyoto's wooden old town, hundreds of Japanese tourists loiter, cameras at the ready. Nothing happens in Japan unless it happens at 400 ASA. Kyoto has 7 million tourists a year, 90 per cent of them indigenous. It's a pleasure to see that even at home they travel in gawky, bovine groups. They're waiting for a glimpse of a geisha slipping into a teahouse. There used to be 20,000 geishas in Kyoto; now there are fewer than 200. They hobble out of their limousines, bowing in all their pristine, extravagant absurdity. Geishas are trained to devote their lives to rich, drunk men.

Only the very, very rich can afford geishas. The salarymen dream of them. The trainee geishas, the backs of whose heads are dressed to represent vaginas, clip-clop down the road, their smiling white faces making their teeth look like little yellow cherry stones. A geisha's *raison d'être* is to pour drinks, giggle behind her hand, tell men they are handsome, strong and amusing, listen to boastful lies and never show any emotion except bliss. Occasionally, for a great deal of cash, some will allow men to copulate with them. We, of course, have geishas back in Blighty: we call them barmaids.

Then there's the traffic, the fabled stasis of millions of drivers Zenishly not going anywhere. Naturally the cars are all Japanese, though not models you'll ever see in the West. Strange, clunky, mis-shapen things in tinny, bright colours, with antimacassars. Dozens of men lurk around car parks in white gloves and the uniforms of Ruritanian admirals, waving batons. They look like retired chief executives, and many of them are. Japan has a bonsai social security system, relying on businesses to over-employ on minuscule wages as a way of hiding unemployment. After schoolkids, retired men have the highest hara-kiri rate. In a country with no sense of individual value, belonging to a job is their only source of self-worth. A Japanese man tells me that the key to understanding Japan is to grasp that it is a shame-based culture. In the West, success is the carrot. In Japan, fear of failure and ostracism is the stick. This isn't merely a semantic difference, it's a basic mindset. Westerners trying to do business here complain that it's impossible to get decisions made. The Japanese negotiate for months without saying yes or no. Nobody wants to lay their face on the line; there is no comeback from failure. Decisions emerge out of group inertia. Japan manages to be both rigidly hierarchical and enigmatically lateral. It's no accident that alcoholism is endemic: drunkenness is not a social problem, it's social cohesion for a depressed and confused male society.

The thing Westerners worry about before getting to Tokyo is that all the signs are pictograms. Well, being constantly lost is as close as you're going to get to knowing what it's like to be Japanese. Most of the shop signs, though, are in English, but written by people who don't speak or understand it. So they're a continual source of amusement. Japan actually has two written languages: borrowed Chinese characters and a phonetic squiggle alphabet. Usefully, there is no word for claustrophobia and, more disturbingly, I'm told, no indigenous one for the female orgasm.

Sex is where the weirdness of the Japanese peaks. I should start by saying that the widely held belief that you can buy soiled schoolgirls' knickers from vending machines is apocryphal, but it certainly could be true. It would hardly be out of character.

The area around Shinjuku station is the Japanese red-light district. There is the better-known Roppongi, which is distressingly reminiscent of Bangkok, but Shinjuku is the real local thing, and foreigners are not encouraged. I was told that the station has more people going through it in a day than go through Grand Central in a month, and it's only the second-largest in Tokyo. Salarymen stop off at one of the many bars, get tanked on beer and sake and perhaps slurp a bowl of noodles before staggering off to a girlie bar. In the streets girls ply their wares, and gangs of lost boys, all sporting the same long-fringed peroxide hair and mod suits, try to recruit schoolgirls for Tokyo's latest sex craze, telephone dating. Men go to booths, pick up a phone and chat up a girl. If they hit it off, they go to a bar and reach an arrangement. This is not seen as prostitution because the girls audition the men and they do it on a part-time basis. The latest, hottest variation is bored married women, called literally 'someone else's wife'.

Yakuza gangsters slip past in blacked-out BMWs or saunter round the streets, conspicuous in shiny suits, permed hair and laughable socks and sandals. Japan's Mafia, they invest every facet of life with a dull, unsophisticated violence. They're universally seen as modern samurai and folk heroes.

Every street has seven or eight storeys of girlie bars and sex clubs. What do you get inside? Well, what do you want? If you're Japanese, you probably want pole-dancing crossed with amateur gynaecology. You can rip the knickers off a teenager and, for a bit extra, keep the knickers and a souvenir photograph. Underpants do seem to loom large in Japanese sexual fantasies. You could catch a massage with a happy ending, or go to a fetid little room, stick your willy through a hole in the wall and be manually relieved by an old lady sitting knee-deep in Kleenex, wearing a cyclist's anti-pollution mask.

And then there's the weird stuff.

If you do pull a prostitute, there are the 'love hotels': themed, by-the-hour rooms where you get sex toys in the minibar. Although used mainly by the sex industry, their original purpose was more prosaic. Traditionally, the Japanese live with their in-laws, and, in a cramped apartment with paper walls, marital harmony can be strained. So harassed couples, carrying the shopping, sidle in for half an hour's conjugal bliss. It takes the spontaneity out of sex, but then, if you asked a Japanese man to do something spontaneous, he'd have to check his PalmPilot first. To say that they appear dysfunctional when it comes to fun is missing the point.

Japanese men must be the vainest, with the least justification, on the planet. Hairdressing, waxing, face-packing, ear-grouting and general pandering and pampering to aesthetic hypochondria are multi million-yen businesses. My favourite bit of male kit was an electric razor specifically for thinning body hair. The reason for their *X-Files* sexuality is again said to be down to religion. They don't consider sex as something that demands a system of morals. This is a country where eating etiquette is more complex than the instruction manual for a Sony video, but with your clothes off, anything goes. There are no rules, not even handy hints on sex. Anyone who thinks that ethics are best kept out of sexual politics ought to go to Japan and see where it ends up. And there's another reason for male sexual dysfunction: Japanese boys' relationships with their mothers. Worshipped is not too strong a word. Mothers are adoring handmaidens to their sons, often literally.

Worst of all – by far, far and away worst of all – is the Japanese males' view of women. Historically, women were next to worthless: peasant daughters were regularly sold into prostitution. In the nineteenth century, most of the brothels of the East were staffed by Japanese girls, or they were sold to factories as indentured textile workers. Today, women rarely make it above the non-commissioned ranks of business, which is still the preserve of very, very old men. In offices they are ornamental secretaries, encouraged to wear short skirts and have harassing lunches and drinks with their bosses.

Women are either silent housework drudges or sex toys. You see this dehumanising view of women in *manga*. *Manga* are those ubiquitous pornographic comic books. Men read them openly on the trains and buses. You can buy them anywhere. But the motherlode of *manga* is a massive basement bookshop in Tokyo with staff dressed like fantasy cartoon characters. Pick up almost any book at random and be prepared for a sharp intake of breath. The stories, such as they are, generally involve schoolgirls being attacked and raped; the scenarios are inventive in their nastiness. Children are abducted, gagged in their beds, dragged up dark alleys. The victims are small and defenceless, with unfeasibly large breasts and round, tearful eyes. They are regularly killed or commit suicide. I kept thinking that the last pages must be missing, the ones with the comeuppance, but there are none. And, to add a peculiarly Japanese weirdness, the drawings are delicately censored. Minute slivers of genitalia are Tipp-Exed out.

Nothing is as unnervingly sordid as *manga*, and nothing would so distress the European parents of a daughter. And the Japanese think less than nothing of it.

How young girls react to the violent sexualising of their youth is equally depressing. They consume; they shop with a myopic concentration. You stand at a crossroads in the shopping district of Tokyo, with video screens flashing out Western ads and pop videos, and when the traffic lights go green, which they do to the sound of cuckoos, 1,500 people cross the road. That's 1,500 every three minutes, all day, every day; and most of them are little girls.

For a nation that puts such a high premium on elegance, Japanese girls walk incredibly badly. They slouch and yaw on foot-high platforms, dye their hair a sort of gingery blonde and look as sullen as four-foot-high Japanese teenagers can, which isn't very. Their parents despair of this generation, calling them bean-sprout children because they lack the backbone and single-mindedness that forged Japan's economic ascendancy. They're giving up on the exam-passing, company-cog work ethic and exchanging it for a Western girl-band fanzine mindlessness. This teenage rebellion isn't political or social or even sexual, it's a plastic copy. It's not even active, it's passive and pouting and decorative. These kids are turning themselves into the living embodiment of the *manga* comic victims: pigeon-toed, mini-kilted, white-socked sex dolls. They are a generation of social anorexics who want to remain provocatively pre-pubescent.

This was a culture that forged a minimal aesthetic of tatami mats and single twigs in vases. But now it's drowning in puerile, syrupy decoration. Even police notices come with cartoons of Disney coppers. These teenagers are running from the heartless culture of guilt and blame, to hide in a fairy-tale nursery.

I started off this journey by saying the Japanese were weird. Well, weird is an observation, not an explanation. By the end, I was absolutely convinced that the explanation is that they are not eccentric, not just different, but certifiably bonkers. Japan is a lunatic asylum built on a hideous history, vile philosophy and straitjacket culture.

If Freud had lived in Tokyo, we'd never have got analysis. He wouldn't have known where to start. It's not that we can't understand the subtlety of Japan. It's that we've been looking at it from the wrong angle. When you stop reading the signs as cultural and see them as symptoms, it all makes a sad, shuddery sense; the national depression, the social Tourette's, the vanity with its twisted, eye-enlarging, nose-straightening, blonde-adoring self-loathing. The psychopathic sexuality and the obsessive, repressing etiquette.

For 300 years, Japan committed itself to an isolation ward. It tried to self-medicate by uninventing and forgetting things. When it finally let in the rest of the world, its fragile arrogance couldn't cope with the deluge of information from a far more robust Western civilisation. Its plan had been to take the technology and medicine and turn its back on the rest, but it can't be done; you can't put on the suit and not the beliefs that went into tailoring it.

Japan has become the West's stalker, a country of Elvis imitators. To walk among them is like being in a voyeur's bedroom. They loathe the objects of their obsession. An English banker who has lived there for over a decade, speaks the language, married a Japanese girl and takes his shoes off in his own home, told me: 'You have no idea how much, how deeply, they despise us. Don't be fooled by the politeness; it's mockery. They are very good at passive aggression; it's the only type they're allowed.'

He went on: 'You must have noticed they're obsessed with perfection: a perfect blossom, an ideally harmonious landscape. They can't abide a chipped cup. We're imperfect, coarse, smelly, loud.' Japan has taken the worst of the West and discarded the best. So it has a democracy without individualism. It has freedom of speech but is too frightened to say anything. It makes without creating. And, saddest and most telling, it has emotion without love. You never feel love here. They have obsession, yearning and cold observation – even beauty and devotion – but nothing is done or said with the spontaneous exuberance of love, and I have never been anywhere else in the whole wide world where you could say that.

I want to finish back in Hiroshima. After the war, the survivors of the atomic bomb were ostracised. People would hire private detectives to ensure that prospective spouses weren't from Hiroshima. So the survivors lied and hid their guilty secret and trauma. Imperfect, embarrassing and tainted, they should have died. It's the absence of the Western idea of love – of brotherly, charitable love or sensual love – that finally explains Japan's appalling, lunatic cruelty.

In the market of Kyoto I saw something that was so madly bizarre, yet so unremarkably mundane, it summed up something of Japan. A very old woman, bent in half and tottering on crippled legs, slowly and painfully pushed her own empty wheelchair.

September 2001

Islamabad

Can anyone explain why it is that poor people always travel with exponentially more stuff than rich people? Islamabad airport's single luggage carousel is a stuttering Himalaya of cheap suitcases, sadomasochistically trussed cardboard boxes, bicycles, cooking pots, nests of occasional tables, cuddly toys and those one-time voluminous tartan plastic sacks that are such a feature of Third World airports.

Worn seams and zips give up under pressure and eviscerate yards of bright nylon, wholesale tea sets, packets of biscuits, make-up, sweaty meat and the scented dandruff of spice. Waiting noisily to claim this detritus is a stasis of passengers, their extended families and airport workers all packed in by a jam of trolleys. Tiny women struggle with screaming toddlers, sliding veils and suitcases that are twice their own body weight.

As always when dropped into the developing world, I'm staggered by just how many are they who are waiting – good-naturedly – to be developed. That and the awesome variety and profligacy of their hot smells.

The only people who pack more luggage than the indigenous have-nots are the visiting know-alls. The news media's chaos-proof priority metallic boxes that so consciously mimic the military 62.627mm hardware they've come to witness are a suitably hermetic, hard-edged symbol of the gap between them and us. They pile up in the executive lounge. It takes a mind-numbing, hernia-inducing amount of ordnance to project the blonde, Botoxed face of a perkily serious disaster weather girl from Wichita back to Wichita. This is the biggest story in the world. The hugest events saga for a generation. It's an unmissable hack's hot ticket. There are reputations to be made, prizes to be won. The sound-bite, one-shot grab of the news has landed. A thousand satellites beam their unblinking inquisition down on Islamabad.

Islamabad is not a pretty place. An extended heartless suburb; a modern capital built next to the politically comforting garrison in Rawalpindi. It's an anaemic mixture of ersatz Western aspiration and cruddy Eastern decay. Its barely beating pulse is the Marriott Hotel. Not a place you'd choose to spend a honeymoon, but a perfectly adequate, internationally anonymous businessman's stop-off that has now been taken over by events and the minders of events. 'The War Against Terrorism', 'America Strikes Back', or, in Fox's case, 'Nuke The Tal Heads, Let Allah Sort Them Out' all comes to you from here.

Outside, policemen with pistol-grip shotguns and mirrors on sticks hang around the emetic fountains and dusty office plants. 'All for guarding Christiane Amanpour,' my driver tells me. In the lobby, where Amanpour mimes from silent screens, the journalists' soundmen, cameramen, producers, runners, fixers and clipboard-carriers lounge in the coffee shop trying to look cool and alert, searching the multiple pockets of their khaki vests for mobile phones. These converted fishermen's waistcoats are the risible bibs of first-time-away-from-home greenhorn. A refugees' collective is already selling cheap knock-offs in the foyer.

The size of the news teams is awesome. CNN is reported to have taken thirty rooms on the day after the New York and Pentagon attacks. NBC has a reputed sixty people here, including a lawyer. The gym and conference rooms have been taken over as dormitories, news agencies are pleading and begging for room to lay a sleeping-bag. Before the war, a bed went for £55. Now they're £180. The hotel has put in fifty extra phone lines, and even though Pakistan is ostensibly a dry country, the media's collective dusty tongue has persuaded them to turn the sarcophagal basement disco into a bar. With unconscious ironic perception, the sign on the door advertises: 'Happy Hour For Non-Muslims Only'. It's lunchtime and the hacks pick over the Western-style menu. The most dangerous thing they'll ever do here is eat the food.

It's time for today's riot, which is scheduled to take place in Rawalpindi, twenty minutes away. The crews hit the road in a long, bored convoy. The demonstration is a well-rehearsed affair. It starts under a kerb-side awning, mullahs and Taliban supporters taking turns to yell into a squeaky public-address system. Dodging the traffic, a sparse crowd gathers slowly in the afternoon heat and dust, small boys hawk 'Osama Is The Great Majid' T-shirts. Barrows sell slices of cold coconut and squeezed sugar cane and lime juice. A pile of grubby bank notes is collected on a table.

This media-sponsored event is being held next door to a police barracks for convenience, so that no one has to go too far if they're arrested, and the riot cops won't have to walk miles in their home-made body armour, carrying cut-up oil-drum shields and lathis (heavy wooden sticks). A truck arrives and hands out Pakistani white-and-green flags. The fearsome, radical, anti-Western militants politely help the cameramen up onto the lorry and carry their equipment. They smile and say please and thank you and move out of the way so we can all get a better look. Little groups of young men race up and down screaming themselves hoarse.

The cameramen mingle, picking out suitably contorted faces, asking them to do it again. After an hour, with much yelling, the stuffed effigies arrive by motor scooter. President George W. Bush and Pakistan's General Pervez Musharraf ride pillion. 'Ah, at last, now we can start,' sighs a German cameraman, shouldering his equipment. The media converge and jostle for the shot of mad militants that will solidify stereotypes back home. An old man tries to whack Bush in the nuts with a stick, young martyrs hold him back – he might do some premature damage and anyway, Bush hasn't got any, he's a dummy. They all laugh.

This march isn't going anywhere. It doesn't have to. The cameras will take it all over the Western world. We all just jostle up and down in a chaotic open casting for a drama that's being produced 10,000 miles away. The shouting and anger is all in Urdu but, cannily, most of the blood-curdling banners are in English. The ratings-friendly girlie presenters are each given a quiet space to do their 'Today, opposition anger erupted again onto the streets' speeches to camera.

They have a problem. What does a spunky career girl wear in a Muslim country, surrounded by death-loving fanatics? For most of these women, the vast, elaborate mystery of Islam is reduced to an entirely feminist couture issue. What's the point of the £200-a-pop tint job and the professional-but-fun bob if you've got to cover it up with a veil and look like some welfare peasant? You can wave goodbye to the audience. But then again, they do want to be culturally sensitive. So they've agreed to come up with a cute Disney-approximation of local dress – a thin shawl worn casually and loosely over the head in the manner of Benazir Bhutto.

In the early-morning kitchens of Des Moines it may look rather chic, a bit *Arabian Nights*, a bit of glam Eastern mystery, but here on the hot street it's sniggerably ridiculous. Bhutto is not a great role model. The corruption charges against her are longer than her sari, and anyway, Islamabad is a cosmopolitan city by regional standards, and, within reason, a non-Muslim Western woman can look like a non-Muslim Western woman. There have been some salutary style disasters, though. Presenters dyeing their hair black to fit in, and one donning the local salwar-kameez, but in a silk that was so thin it showed off her underwear. But then, what do these Bhutto Babes know? What have they ever known?

The riot settles into interminable speeches, the police lean on their shields, the cameramen look at the light and hump their stuff back to the Marriott in time for the morning news back home.

In the hotel, the action is all up on the roof. It's surprisingly difficult to get onto the roof. I go into CNN's large suite of offices, along a corridor stacked with priority boxes and room-service trays, where the station manager, a sort of Mary Poppins with rabies, is talking on three phones. She says they'll have to clear my access with their PR in London, and introduces me to a sandy, unsmiling, forgettable Rick, or Mick or Dick, 'Whom you'll probably recognise.' I don't. It's mutual.

The male staff huddle over a computer screen glowing with a piece of avian Armageddon kit. They talk technical knowingly. TV hacks love military hardware. Among the world-time clocks, the pinboard notices and staff rotas on the wall there's a large reminder that your per diem is $55, not the advertised $65. Damn, only a month's salary in Pakistan.

The PR back in London asks who exactly my story is for and what exactly it'll be about? I lie. I get permission.

Fortuitously, the Marriott's roof has been built in undulating concrete waves like shallow, slope-sided graves. Each dent is inhabited by a news gatherer. They've hurriedly built nests, platforms and sunshades with crooked lights and miles of tangled cable. The whole place looks like it's held together with gaffer tape. Satellite dishes mushroom. The hotel is charging £350 a day for every slice of room. The electric parasols cost well over £700 a week to insure. War-zone rates. The insurance industry has had a bad couple of months. It needs to recoup.

On the hour, every hour, this precipitous shanty town of speculation hums in a dozen languages, beaming the rumours of war around the world real-time. Everyone pretending they're up here on their own. There are stampy-foot tantrums if someone gets too excited and bleats into the microphone next door, giving the game away. In the morning the CNN guy, in regulation blue shirt and chinos, points this way to get the uninspiring backdrop of Islamabad, and in the evening he points this way to get the setting sun and the hazy mountains. 'You know, they actually burn all the city's rubbish right there. It's a big problem,' Tom Badman tells me, saddened but not shocked by the city's lack of dramatic professionalism. 'Hi, just ask for the Badman.' The Badman is CNN's satellite engineer. 'This is my place.' He takes me to a canvas lean-to. Inside there are banks of pop-concert boxes with buttons and dials, 'We built all this ourselves, here's my Tieman encoder. That's the Advent, your Miteq Upconverters, and the Zircon HPA.' He loves his kit. 'We were up and running in twelve hours.' Tom's a can-do kind of guy. Secretly, I suspect he thinks he's Radar from *M*A*S*H*. 'I learnt my business in Vietnam. Most of the engineers here were in Vietnam.' And there it is. Out in the open. Vietnam.

Nam is the unsaid, heart-wished whispered prayer of broadcast news. Everyone devoutly yearns that this will be their Vietnam. The story that'll make them a veteran, one of the few. An old Asia bore with a book of memoirs and an arm-in-arm photograph with guys who didn't make it on the desk in the den.

A young reporter from ITN bounds up. This is his first job abroad, he's as happy and keen as a Labrador puppy. In fact, he looks a bit like a blond dog who needs walkies. He came out here lugging a complete anti-contamination suit with gas mask and he couldn't be happier. Well, he could be – if they let him wear his flak jacket on the roof, he'd be happier. So what's happening? He doesn't know. 'Yesterday, the news agencies said there was a breakthrough of refugees on the border. Well, we hadn't heard anything here, so the studio read me the front page of the *London Evening Standard*, and I went live and repeated it back to them.' He giggles conspiratorially at this subterfuge.

And here's the thing. Nobody knows anything. There is precious little news, just speculation and reaction to reaction. A sedate game of pass the microphone round the videophones and roofs of Asia. 'Back to you in the studio, Tracey.' Islamabad is about as dangerous and exciting as Cincinnati. The 'America Fights Back', 'Strike Against Terrorism' stuff is all coming from New York or Atlanta or London. Out here, they get told what the agenda is and the crews go and find confirming footage to be mulled over by Stateside boffins with competitive tie knots. Occasionally, they'll put a bland question to a passing politician who's so jet-lagged he doesn't know if it's breakfast or the table decoration.

There's precious little journalism being done out here. Most of these Bhutto Babes and Dicks in blue shirts are only used to putting subtitles to pictures. They couldn't find a story if it were printed on the English-language menu in the coffee shop. And anyway, how do you go about finding the news when a month ago you didn't know Pakistan from pick'n'mix? What you do is hire a local who does.

There are some things you should understand about Pakistan. According to the United Nations, it's the second-most corrupt country in the world. Personally, I think it only avoided the number-one spot by bribing someone. It is also deeply, deeply politicised. Pakistanis talk politics endlessly, and with a sophistication that would beggar most Westerners. In its short life, this place has had more politics than most countries would think either decorous or polite in a couple of centuries. And they are the world's greatest conspiracy theorists. Nothing is obvious. And Pakistan has a vivid and cacophonous free press in both English and Urdu. It covers the political spectrum from really, really hating America to just being a little peeved with it.

Where do the vast majority of Pakistanis stand on the War Against Terrorism? Well, let's put it this way – the most popular boys' name for babies born recently is Osama. And although the press is free, the journalists aren't. They're just cheap. And they're being bought up wholesale by Western news teams. Almost anyone who can speak passable English is now a guide and expert. The going rate set by CNN is $100 per day for everyone. That's a vast amount. In fact, there are so many Yankee greenbacks being pumped into this economy that it's dropped the local exchange rate by about five cents. A bright English-educated Pakistani journalist who specialises in Third World industrial ecology, and who has been hired as a researcher by an American rolling-news team, tells me he is never asked for advice, just told what to go and fetch. 'They're missing so much and getting such a biased picture, but they get this shopping-list from America every morning. For instance, I was asked to find some people for the "Why do they all hate us?" story. So I went and got a selection of academics, politicians and high-profile commentators. The sort of people you'd expect if you were doing it in America. And they said, "No, no, no. What we want is a really angry mullah with a turban and beard who looks like he hates us."' Anyone here a frothing xenophobe who speaks English?

The cascade of cash has had more serious effects. Journalists are poaching relief workers from aid agencies. In the north, they're paying so much for transport and bribes at border crossings that charities trying to deliver aid can't compete. It hasn't helped that President Bush threw away a line implying that NGOs might be front agencies for terrorism. The director of Médecins Sans Frontières in Islamabad tells me he's been called in the middle of the night by a journalist who asked him for a refugee's phone number. He laughed as he told me, but without much humour.

Peshawar is one of the most romantic cities on earth. The city of Alexander and Rudyard Kipling's Kim. It sits on the Grand Trunk Road, a fork of the ancient silk route, and is guarded by a great dun fortress. Here you can buy a Kalashnikov for a pricey £350 (there's been a run on them). Or your own weight in hashish, or the sweetest pomegranates or the most delicately embroidered silks. Peshawar teams with rumour, disease, feuds, sewerage, exotic smells, a ferocious beauty and vibrant life. It's also simmering with anger.

Twenty years ago, there were 40,000 people here. Today there are more than 4.5 million. But most people have given up counting. At this moment, Peshawar is the most exciting place in the world. The eye of the storm of events. There are also 1,500 journalists here, all of them hanging out in the Pearl Continental Hotel, owned, incidentally, by the same chap who has the Marriott in Islamabad. They get up on the roof every hour, moan about the food and the plumbing and the lack of news.

The food on the North-West Frontier, by the way, is famously sublime. I walk round the storytellers' market, the smugglers' market, the refugee camps and the twisty dark alleys of Peshawar for a week and never see another Western face, except at press calls or for the Friday-after-mosque pretend riot. Of the many, many stories, rumours and half-truths that infest these crowded streets, my favourite is the one about the food parcels.

The food aid dropped by the US Air Force, besides being vegetarian in strict accordance with Muslim dietary law (actually, the Afghans eat virtually nothing but meat; it's the Hindus who are vegetarian), comes with plastic cutlery – presumably so that the recipients can't use it to hijack a plane afterwards – but everyone here eats with their fingers. So much for cultural sangfroid and intelligence in depth. But wait, that's not the joke. They've been gathered up and smuggled back over the border, and the peanut butter and jam are being sold to ravenous, homesick Americans desperate for some taste of the Midwest.

On my first night in Peshawar, a man sidles into my room and asks, in the manner of Peter Lorre in *Casablanca*, if I'd like to meet a mujahideen colonel, a veteran of the Russian war who has access to 'many things and people'. Many things and people? I say, 'That might be nice.' And an hour later a car arrives. It will take me to Zareef Khan. But we must leave instantly.

Now, as a general rule of cowardice, I don't get into cars with a pair of strange Pathans in the middle of the night in a beguilingly enigmatic law-lite city full of hungry, impoverished folk whose relatives my country is bombing. Especially as kidnapping is, by tradition and convention, one of the border's chief money-earners. But a story's a story. And so I find ERIC. I'm not making this unfortunate acronym up. It stands for Educational Resources and Information Centre. They have headed paper to prove it.

Colonel Khan turns out to be an urbane, garrulous charmer with a mobile phone and computers and an office not unlike CNN's. He's the sort of bloke who defies trust by his strenuous attempts to impart it. He has the conman's fault of giving you just too much information. 'In view of present circumstances, ERIC provides travel, transportation, makes appointments and will discuss news analysis,' says his press release.

'So, what can I do for you?' Zareef Khan asks with the sincere grin of a Californian cosmetic surgeon. 'Would you like freshly wounded? Old wounded? Limbless? Recent refugees? Or long-term? I can arrange extreme Taliban mullahs or very extreme Taliban mullahs. Or just Taliban. We have gun factories and heroin. You tell me?' Well, how about a morning with recent refugees, and perhaps an extreme mullah after lunch? See how we're feeling? He speaks to a driver. 'Take them to the place we took the Belgians and the Japanese and that American crew. Good. Now our rates are $150 a day, and please, would you give something to the refugees for photographs? A hundred, 200 rupees [£3] will be fine. No more. You'll spoil the market.' So this, then, is what you find at the border of darkness: disaster tourism, package-tour war. The horror, the horror.

I go in search of the media. They are in a municipal hall to witness the convocation of the much-heralded, US-inspired, moderate government-in-waiting. The ranks of potential potentate politikers look absurdly like a big-hat competition. A collection of overdressed extras for *Indiana Jones and the Turbans of Doom.* I just know that they just know, as they stroke their beards and try to look enigmatic, that this is a farce. A non-starter. A remote-control propaganda photo call. In a city with upwards of 4 million refugees, most of whom have plenty of good reasons to hate the Taliban, not a single Afghan turns up to show support. While down the road, in the press club, there is a packed public meeting for the hastily convened Movement to Oppose an Imposed Government on Afghanistan. Imran Khan is the key speaker. It is an intelligent, emotional and wide-ranging political meeting, and I am the only Western journalist present.

Watching the news channels each evening, the speculative reports and brief clips seem to become more and more unreal, spinning out of context, relevant only to themselves, and it strikes me that our precious and protected freedom of speech has become a sycophant. When the Bhutto Babes and Dicks in blue shirts keep their jobs through ratings popularity, none of them wants to say the hard, contrary, unpopular stuff, and advertisers won't be seen dead endorsing uncomfortable news. The competitive nature of rolling coverage makes broadcasters look to the channel next door for the agenda. They outbid each other to pander to a public mood. Our great Western free press has collided with our great Western free market and is giving the punters what they want.

To say that truth is the first casualty of war is a cliché. But in this case, the victimisation is self-inflicted. This conflict is posturing on the edge of a precipice and no one is shining a light into the abyss.

In another part of town, the Jamiat Ulema-e-Islam (JUI), the most radical and potentially violent of Pakistan's Islamic parties, is holding yet another rally. On a fountain, standing above the throng, is a pert little girlie presenter doing her 'Behind me, anger erupted...' stich for the camera. She's wearing jeans and a tight white T-shirt that shows off her excited, perky little nipples. It is about as deeply insensitive an act of provocation you could wish to see, and the fundamentalists are all seeing and all winding up for a bit of an alfresco fatwa.

Good, I think, they're going to drown the dumb bimbo, I'll get a story and she'll be dead. A mullah spitting Koranic tin tacks rushes into a doorway, presumably for his Kalashnikov, and then runs back and gives her the shawl and skirt he's just bought.

It's not the reaction we've been led to expect.

February 2002

Kalahari Bushmen

The desert doesn't hoard the sun: it is generous with it, profligate. But it keeps nothing in store for the darkness: the nights are cold, often bitter. The desert lives in the moment. It is opportunistic, it has no plans, no expectations. Drink when you can, eat when you can. Follow the sundial of shade, and then shiver in the monochrome night.

The desert isn't for everyone: for a creature with a memory and the ability to plan ahead, it can be a deeply worrying place. The desert is amoral. It doesn't care: you're as useful dead as you are alive. Your position at the top of the evolutionary tree, your money, your cultured good taste, your hopes and expectations mean nothing here; you're just another roll of the dice, a stumble and a sting away from being a mass of skull minerals.

Part of the Kalahari was once a primeval lake fed by four rivers. The whole place is now a flat, pristine jumble of sand and thorn that has a beauty that beggars the four walls of language. It is the birthplace of the super-mammal and possibly – probably – man. As a species, we grew up and moved on, and if your particular adaptation is to be able to plan the future and remember the past, then getting out of the Kalahari will be something of a priority. Run, don't walk. In a blink of 10,000 years, you can be in downtown Manhattan with air conditioning and internet pizza delivery. Phew!

But some people stayed behind. My first introduction to the Bushmen of Botswana comes just before dawn. It is still cold, and the light is a clear rose-grey. There are no circling kites or eagles yet, but the thorn trees are already alive with finches and pied crows. The camp is a collection of small, beehive-shaped huts woven out of twigs and thatched with grass. Around the embers of last night's fires lie the sleepy, wriggling forms of children. Dogs stretch and scratch under a spiky acacia tree.

Around one of the fires, recently kicked into life, a group of men stand warming themselves. They are the hunters, and they're expecting us. However quiet you are, the Bushmen are always expecting you. These are the people who call themselves, without hyperbole or bragging, the First People. They are short, with amazingly wrinkled baggy skins. Bushmen are said to have loose skins so that they can stuff themselves in rare times of glut. Their faces are vaguely Mongolian, flat with high cheekbones; they have sparse, tightly curled hair and they smile with smoky, tea-coloured, almond eyes. A lot of things have been said about the Bushmen: that they are a separate species (no human could live here); that they can channel themselves into animals; that they have extrasensory perception; that the men have permanent erections, and the women have labial aprons that hang to their knees. Most of this is the kind of hokum that allows more advanced, aggressive tribes first to distance themselves from the Bushmen, then to exterminate them. This little gaggle of ragged-looking chaps dressed in fifth-generation Oxfam rags – including one tweed suit, a Surrey cardigan and a collection of skiing hats – is the very end of an unbroken line that stretches back 30,000 years.

They are, like their forebears, hunter-gatherers. Men hunt, women gather. By the end of an exhausting day we've got a collection of roots, some salad and nuts, and I've got a pocketful of huge yellow-and-black jewel beetles. These things fly like barely aerodynamic Liquorice Allsorts, and when the women catch them they pull their legs off, which they don't like, but which stops them going anywhere. I learn that breaking legs off things is a Bushman trait. The first rule in the Kalahari cookbook is: 'Don't catch anything twice.' I also learn that the beetles can give you a nasty nip with the joint between their head and their thorax carapace.

I'm interested in what, and how, the Bushmen eat, because therein lies the link between us and our past. The bit of our brain that deals with taste is the oldest part of our cerebral cortex. Bushman societies are a loose collective, and work like a pyramid of cards: everyone relies on everyone else, and the structure only stands with everyone bearing the weight of the whole. All food is collected individually, but it is owned and consumed collectively. The communal sharing of food is the only way a clan can survive intact: it eats as a unit or it dies as competing individuals. The Bushmen are endlessly tolerant of each other and strangers; they rarely argue or fight; their children are never punished. In fact, childhood is a special time: children are adored and marvelled at, they are a constant source of joy and concern, which is made all the more achingly poignant when you know that the infant mortality rate can be as high as 40 per cent.

At the end of the day, we make a fire under a thorn tree and prepare dinner, sitting in a circle and stripping the leaves. The women hull nuts with their teeth, making fearsome cracking sounds, and spit the kernels into a hardwood mortar. Teeth are used as scissors, tin-openers, Magimixes. To the nuts are added salad greens that taste like spinach. These are pounded together, and then my beetles are raked into the fire.

Now, I have no particular rules about beetles. In general, I will eat anything that anyone else will put in their mouth – as long as it doesn't involve a bet. The beetles are baked for two minutes in medium-hot sand (that's gas mark 6, or 200°C), then the hard wing-cases are pulled off and you pop one in your mouth, just like that. How to describe my first taste of beetle? They're gooey, a bit like meatier soft-shell crab, and utterly delicious. I'm not just saying that: they're really, really good, with a big, fresh flavour. I asked for more, but they were for the salad, and were pounded with the nuts and spinach and, finally, a touch of seasoning. Salt is rare in this part of the Kalahari, but there are quite a lot of ants that taste very salty, so if someone asks for the salt you can say, 'There's some crawling up your leg.' The salad was fabulous: sophisticated, fresh, moreish. If you were served this in Harry's Bar you'd want to know the recipe. But then you'd wish you hadn't asked.

Hunting with the men was altogether different. After four fruitless days out with the boys, I realised why there isn't a Garrick Club in the Kalahari: if they didn't let women in, the men would starve. Hunting is man's work. It's also the measure of Bushman social structure – a good hunter is a Kalahari tycoon. The chaps set off early in the morning, led by Albert (not his real name), a wiry, nicotine-coloured man who looks as if he's well into his second century. He's probably about forty. He's wearing a pair of baggy chef's trousers. 'I've got a pair of those at home,' I say through the interpreter. 'Oh, are you a hunter too?' he replies, and beams with camaraderie.

The Bushmen's ability to track even small insects is remarkable; their ability actually to catch anything isn't. As Americans say, they have problems closing the deal. Bushmen hunt by stealth; they get very, very close to their prey and then shoot it with tiny poisoned arrows. They hunt antelope like this, and they can crawl right up to a sleeping animal, but more often than not it gets away.

In the end, our bag was one bullfrog with teeth that could shear through steel bolts and eyes out of *The Omen*, which I had to carry in my pocket, and something called a spring hare, which is the most risibly pathetic excuse for an animal I've ever seen: legs like a small kangaroo, the body of a guinea pig, the face of a gremlin and ears like babies' bootees. We cooked it in the ashes, and it actually tasted like a cross between chicken and rabbit. The bullfrog was so wholly disgusting, I've never been so pleased to see something beaten over the head and buried in red-hot coals. Bullfrog, if you're thinking of trying it, tastes of old newspaper soaked in a hot gutter.

What the chaps really like doing is sitting and smoking. Smoking is the great national pastime, and they all carry pipes made from bone, which they fill with ferocious tobacco. They don't play football, go to the pub, play dominoes, make matchstick models of the *Golden Hind* or visit prostitutes, they just sit in any bit of available shade and do real, grown-up, Olympic smoking, which I reckon is deeply civilised. We have a thing or two to learn from this ancient culture.

The central mystery of Bushman life is the trance dance. This is part religious ceremony, part party, part outpatients' clinic – it can go on all night, and few people outside the loose-knit groups of the Kalahari have seen it. As the sun goes down, the women sit round one end of a fire and sing rhythmically as the men move about, chat, prepare skins, then sit opposite them. Some men wear rattles made of moths' pupa casings, and they slowly start circling the fire. As the chanting becomes hypnotic, sparks gust into the purple sky like swarms of iridescent insects and the circling and stamping becomes more frenetic, you notice that one man is losing control, like a drunk or a sleepwalker. He's slipping into the trance. When this happens, another man will stay close. Anything can happen: the dancer can dance into the fire, run into the bush, fall into a thorn tree. During trance dances, the Bushmen believe that they become imbued with animal potency and enter a spiritual realm where they can contact God, fight evil spirits, gain healing powers and see visions. The trance is dangerous and exhausting. One Bushman I spoke to said it was so frightening he couldn't do it any more.

The clapping and chanting sounds like the song and heartbeat of the desert. In the black night the fire casts long, flickering shadows, the moon is so huge you see every dry seabed and mountain range on it. A trance dancer grabs a woman. He's seen she's sick, and as he holds her his body goes into terrible spasm. He's taking her illness and her pain into himself, and it makes the hair on the back of your neck prickle. Hour after hour, it goes on. Eventually, on the edges of the fire's halo, I fall into a fitful sleep and wake in the chilly morning, the pink light, the twittering finches, the children snuffling under blankets, dogs stretching. The fire is a white pile of smoking ash and weary tongues of flame. The women are still chanting, and a trance dancer still circles, feet numbly stamping the sand, rattle crackling out its rhythm. His eyes are glassy, his limbs rubber. He's been dancing for nine hours. The ceremony is older than bricks and mortar, older than handprints on walls, older than memory; it has in it the seeds of all future religion and belief.

Walking with the Bushmen isn't just another safari, with wild people instead of wild animals. This isn't some sort of reverse anthropomorphism. The Kalahari Bushmen are our oldest relatives, the people who stayed behind. Visiting them is coming home.

April 2002

Vietnam

All countries are two places, the country in the atlas and the place in your head. Vietnam suffers from the cartography of the collective imagination. We know Vietnam from dozens of movies and from shelves of books. Anyone over forty knows it as the leitmotif of their youth, the rhythm section for the middle-aged. What we know of it, though, is its reflection in the mirror of America's angst. A country that lost two syllables became atrophied simply as Nam.

The first thing you realise on arriving is that it doesn't look like Nam at all. And the reason is simple: Nam movies aren't shot here; they're filmed in the Philippines and Thailand and California, which is a bit like making a film about the English Civil War and filming it in Spain.

Saigon is now officially named Ho Chi Minh City, but universally still called Saigon. A bustling, modern, haphazard Asian town, its centre is a couple of broad French boulevards, a cathedral and an opera house. Most of what we associate it with is gone or never existed. The gum-chewing prostitutes in pedal-pushers and wrap-around shades that so inflamed the Western imagination, white-mice military policemen, the palls of smoke on the horizon, the sound of helicopters and Texan accents: none of it's here.

What's most conspicuous by its absence is the soundtrack. Saigon should be set to music. The Doors, Jimi Hendrix, Country Joe and the Fish, at the very least Jonathan Pryce. Real-time Saigon's signature tune is the hysterical whinny of thousands of two-stroke engines. Saigon has got on its bike and gone to work. Here they drive on the right, and on the left, and on the pavement. In the morning the boulevards are a torrent of little engines going this way, and in the evenings they go that way. There's no point waiting for a gap to cross: you have to trust, take a deep breath and step into what seems like certain death. But the river eddies dexterously round you. It's as close as I'm ever going to get to being Moses.

The other thing movies don't prepare you for is how elegant and poised the Vietnamese are. Women ride their bikes wearing long, pastel-coloured opera gloves. The national costume, the *ao dai*, is a high-necked silk dress worn to the calf but slit up both sides over baggy silk trousers, revealing a tantalising triangle of skin at the waist. Vietnamese men never weary of pointing out that it reveals nothing and hides nothing.

I've come here to find the war, what's left of it, what's made of it. War tourism sounds ghoulish, a sort of panoramic rubbernecking, but then millions of people visit Flanders Fields, and when you dig a bit, it's difficult to be a tourist in any city that's innocent of battle. Venice is sunk in plunder, as is London. Istanbul, Athens, Paris, Florence and Siena are all places where yesterday's *bellum* becomes today's brochure. So perhaps it's just a matter of time, and Vietnam has reached the moment when current affairs drift into the nostalgia that is history's waiting room. And as new wars are queuing up, champing to get started, it seemed a good time to look at what happened to this one.

Well, there's precious little to tell you there was ever a battle for Saigon. Uniquely for a communist country, there are hardly any monumental memorials; generally, they'll put up statues to heroic postmen and martyred librarians, but not here. The landmarks of war have been obliterated or papered over. The Caravelle Hotel, famous for a million dispatches, is just another comfy, hideous, international bed-and-continental-breakfast. The American embassy, the fulcrum of such despair and ignominy, has been flattened for more prosaic offices and apartments. The corner where the Buddhist monk poured petrol over himself, assumed the lotus position and combusted has a bright little shrine, and with fine, inscrutable irony they've built a much larger gas station opposite. The president's palace is now a half-hearted museum, kept as it was left – a perfect example not just of the banality of despotism but of the political law that military dictators have taste in inverse proportion to their power.

The one stop all war tourists make is the War Remnants Museum, known colloquially as 'the babies-in-the-bottles museum'. Here the clunky tat of murder and mayhem is lined up. Bits of defunct ordnance detumesce in a junkyard of impotence. It's strange how old-fashioned the rusting kit looks; the accessories of war date just as fast as handbags and hats. The babies in the bottles are a pair of distressing infants, stillborn with defects caused by Agent Orange, the carcinogenic defoliant sprayed over half of Vietnam. It doesn't figure large in American war movies. Nobody says: 'I love the smell of Agent Orange in the morning; it smells like babies born without faces or genitals.'

And there's an army-surplus market, an unloved warren of drab, mouldering stalls. Most of the stuff here is modern or fake. There are enough Zippo lighters with obscene exclamations of proud despair stamped on them to make you imagine the entire army dropped them down the back of the sofa before running home; and thousands of dog tags – little tin labels written in the truncated language of the lonely-hearts ad. Who'd want to buy one of these things? If it's real, how could you live with it, and if it's fake, why would you want the notice of the pretend death of a fabricated life?

A couple of hours outside Saigon are the Cu Chi tunnels, one of the great engineering feats of the twentieth century built with the equipment of the tenth. An entire underground city on three floors that stretched for miles, with hospitals, dormitories, operating theatres, magazines, armouries, factories, canteens, kitchens and booby traps – much of it underneath a US Army base. The hellish ingenuity is staggering. Throughout the war, 16,000 people went through these tunnels, and 12,000 were casualties. Only a few hundred yards are still open; the rest have been closed like a dangerous pit. Even though they've widened them to accommodate round-eyes, they're still not for the claustrophobic or those with dark nightmares. You're shown around by old North Vietnamese Army officers in their green uniforms, who giggle when you trip the home-made landmines with a childish pop, and show you with relish the groin-tightening ingenuity of the spiked deadfall traps. In a clearing in the wood, my little guerrilla asked me to find the door; it is, he says, three yards from where I'm standing. I search fruitlessly; he's happy and pulls up a trap the size of a laptop from under the leaves. I can just drop through if I curl my shoulders. The Vietcong used their size against the Americans: a well-fed Midwestern boy would stick like a cork. My guide scuttles as I crawl along the slimy, dank burrow, which smells of the Earth's knickers. The torchlight makes the shadows dance; it's like an oven; I drop sweat, panic simmers. We drop to another level and he flicks his torch. 'Hats', he whispers. Hats? He points. There, above my head – *bats*.

At the end of the tour, I'm asked what sort of gun I'd like. There's a range. You can have your own little firelight at a dollar a bullet, which is probably a lot less than they cost the Americans, all things considered. The cut-out target GIs have been replaced with tourist-friendly animals. I nail a badly drawn elephant with an M-16 and, just to be impartial, a Kalashnikov. It is a strangely unevocative experience. Beside me is a Vietnamese sporting a Vietcong bush hat. 'Hi there,' he says in a broad American accent. 'I just love a gun.' I ask where he's from. 'Here – well, actually, from Atlanta, Georgia.' A child of the thousands of South Vietnamese who became wrong-side rich refugees. He theatrically mounts his M-16, empties a clip and misses a tiger. He's too fat to get down the tunnels.

Going north, we travel to the old heart of the war. The names hark back to copies of *Life* and *Time* and the six o'clock news; Da Nang, Hue, the Perfume River and Khe Sanh. We stop briefly at My Son, the ancient towers built by the Cham people, who were Hindus and ruled parts of central and southern Vietnam for a while. Stuck in the jungle like the temples of doom. This should be the Vietnamese Angkor Wat: about seventy intricately decorated, astonishing, vast and beautiful tombs. They got B-52'd and only a fraction remain, surrounded by sodden craters; they're eerie, a collateral civilisation. Hue, on the Perfume River, was once the imperial capital of Vietnam. Its forbidden city rivalled Peking's, an enclosed royal town of thirty-two palaces that's down to four now. The rest are pulverised, rubble. Here I meet a group of American military padres, middle-aged men with their wives who have come to relive their boy-scout war. They're open and instantly warm in the way Americans are, but also infuriatingly closed to insight or profundity. It's nice, all of it. They've had a nice time, the food's nice, the people are nice. The war wasn't nice but what can you say? Back home, these vicars counsel other veterans caught in a loop. The repeat play of horror. When diplomatic relations between the two countries were reinstated, old soldiers began to trickle back to lay ghosts, search for themselves, find a closure. What they found was more shocking than anything they'd imagined. A universal, heartfelt kindness. The Vietnamese were honestly touched that they'd bothered to come back in peace to share the memory and the mourning.

The infamous Route 9 points toward Laos through the demilitarised zone (DMZ) and the beginning of the Ho Chi Minh trail, the secret supply route that led to the delta in the south. At the beginning of the war it took six months to walk with mortar rounds on your back. By the end it was a motorway with service stations and barracks. At a strategic position overlooking the trail is Khe Sanh, the airstrip and fortress that saw the bloodiest battle of the war. Billed in the press as President Johnson's Dien Bien Phu, the surrounding precipitous hills and gorges have more familiar names, like Hamburger. Only now are they growing a first layer of spindly scrub and eucalyptus to replace the three-tiered rainforest that once lived here. More ordnance and chemicals were dropped on these mountains than in the whole of the Second World War.

A damp, hot fog has descended, stifling even the coffee plantation that grows here over the landmines, and it raises a question: 'What did I expect to find on this battlefield?' By their nature, battles go. There's only ever what you bring to them, a later personal history. The clipped Sunday magazine photograph for my school dormitory wall, the marches in Grosvenor Square to pick up girls, the late-night arguments with grown-ups, and the music that was the ambience for my youth. Still, there's an atmosphere: a deadened, mordant, sad echo. I find a verdigrised bullet and yearn for the hectic jazz of scooters going somewhere.

Hanoi is a beautiful city, a Frenchified place of lakes and an ancient warren of hawkers and food stalls. You can visit the Hanoi Hilton, the POW jail, though the Vietnamese naturally remember it as where they were interned, tortured and guillotined by the French. But I've lost my appetite for memorabilia. I've been cured of what I came to indulge. There's a new Hanoi Hilton, a real one with room service. The Vietnamese economy is booming, as fast as 10 per cent a year over the last ten years. If the opposite of love isn't hate but indifference, the opposite of war isn't peace: it's prosperity. Vietnam hasn't turned its back on Nam, but it's moved on. It's America that still picks at the scab that needs the catharsis of celluloid and paper, and looks for other people and places in which to dump its frustration and vengeance.

There's a great war cemetery in the DMZ. A silent, empty place, with over 10,000 graves laid neatly in the jungle. Incense smoke curls in the evening light. The guardian holds his squirming daughter and tells me that 50,000 Vietnamese visit every year. They must come secretly, like guerrillas. An underground remembrance. Three million Vietnamese died in the war, 4 million were wounded, children are yet born victims. In one of the museums is a case of medals donated by an American sergeant. Embossed in plastic is the stark message: 'I was wrong, I am sorry.'

January 2003

Las Vegas

There's one of those plastic laminated non-biodegradable notes in my hotel bathroom. It's headed 'PRESERVE OUR FUTURE': 'Preserving the earth's vital resources is something we can all take part in. In an effort to save water and energy and to minimise the release of harsh biodegradable [*sic*] detergents . . . please leave this card on your pillow and we will remake your bed with existing linens.'

I read it twice.

I'm in a hotel that has built a replica of Venice's Grand Canal – on the second floor, so that it won't wash away the crap tables downstairs. This is a city that blows up the hotels when they're slightly soiled, that sweats neon, that sprays ice water from the lamp posts and puts dancing fountains in the desert. This is a place that, when they started nuclear testing next door, sold picnics for those who wanted to get a closer look – and held Miss Atomic Bomb contests with bikinis shaped like mushroom clouds. These are the people who are wagging a finger at me and asking me to be parsimonious with the laundry.

Well, welcome to Las Vegas – where irony just curls up and dies.

There are no clocks in Las Vegas. Time is as welcome as a temperance band. And they don't like windows much, either. Sunlight is a nag. The oxygen-enhanced, mortician's chilled air pumps sprightly through the perma-dusk, rolling over acres of slot machines numberless to man. They in turn chunter and twitter, halloo and burp with a replete mechanical joy. A syncopated cacophony that sounds like a goblin's stockyard, it goes on ceaselessly, twenty-four unmeasured hours a day, seven nameless days a week. It is the song of Vegas, a tuneless choir, a turbine, a great bulimic consuming engine.

But if you really want to see what makes Las Vegas hum, where the juice actually comes from, then you need to get into your gold stretch limo and motor into the desert, where the temperature's touching

120 and the wind's fresh-baked from Death Valley. Out here it's hot enough to melt silicone implants.

Go on until you get to Black Canyon. Stretched across it like concrete biceps is the Hoover Dam, holding back the mighty Colorado fresh from carving the Grand Canyon. It takes your breath away. In its time, the Hoover Dam was a lexicon of superlatives and a directory of statistics. Longest. Deepest. Highest. Strongest. Farthest. But now what it most is is beautiful. Beautiful and moving. It's a staggeringly elegant, emphatically muscular paragon of form following function. It's one of the great engineering achievements of a mightily engineered nation. Amid its restrained dabs of Deco decoration is a plaque that proudly proclaims that the Hoover Dam was built 'to make the desert bloom'. And then you turn around and look and consider what the desert actually grew.

From here, Vegas looks like the cover of a schlock science-fiction novel – you can just make out the Great Pyramid and the Eiffel Tower, the Doge's Palace and the New York skyline, all set in a desert. It's like a parallel universe. Here's Earth's doppelgänger. It exists almost lifelike – like life, but not quite.

If you're in the market for metaphors, the Hoover Dam and Las Vegas represent the contradiction, the dichotomy, the yin and yang, the Cain and Abel of America. On the one hand its amazing can-do energy, the guts and the belief in the ability to build your way out of depression, to conquer the West, the vision to weld, blast and rivet a modern Promised Land out of hot air and rock; and on the other, that glittering Shangri-La of cynical exploitation. A place conjured not out of hard work but from luck, whose foundation is the fortuitous fact that, given a chance, pretty much everyone's guaranteed to be a loser.

In Spanish, Las Vegas means 'the meadows'. Within living memory there was grass here. But the water table has dropped. It's all dust now. Yet this is the fastest-growing area in America – 6,000 people move here every month. It fills two new phone books and a new street map every year. Suburbs sprawl over one another and down the valley; unnaturally emerald-green golf courses and gated hacienda-style communities with orange terracotta-style roofs sit box-fresh and spookily silent.

Many of the people moving here are old – they huddle in the

icy shade. But why shouldn't the American Dream end up in an air-conditioned desert with golf courses and Krispy Kreme doughnuts and Celine Dion? Celine lives here. In a high-end, lockdown community guarded by a squad of 'men in black', who are the only visible living things. There's an Italianate-ish hotel and a shopping mall, pristine in pastel shades that vibrate with a lonely boredom. The man-made lake and the putting greens are empty; not even a shadow would venture out into this heat.

Celine Dion, the woman made mega-global by an iceberg, has famously signed the biggest, fattest contract known to belted ballads to perform at Caesars Palace: a rumoured $100 million for three years and 50 per cent of the profits. It cost another $95 million to build her the Colosseum, a 4,000-seat circular state-of-the-artless auditorium. The acoustics are so amazing you could hear a tear drop. Its pride and joy is a new sort of smart rear projection that has the clarity and brilliance of a TV screen. It's very impressive, and as we wait for Celine to come on, they project a picture of the audience back at itself. We're entranced. We can't get enough of ourselves. Waving and grinning. Applauding our own wonder, breaking out into helpless, self-gratified giggles. You can tell we're going to be a hard act to follow.

However elaborate, grandiose and monumentally tasteless Vegas becomes, it is never going to be anything as astonishingly and monumentally tasteless as the people who come to visit it. For starters, it's the sheer size of them. These are the fattest people on the planet. Vast, lardy, adipose flesh, ladled into sweatpants and sports shirts; grotesquely ripe girls add cartoon plastic breasts as a moment of firm bas-relief between their gobble-gobble triple chins and the rolling savanna of their stomachs.

As a visiting foreigner, I understand that fat is a measure of class here. But, oddly and unexpectedly, so is hair. The confections of intricate macramé, the weaving, haymaking, clipping, twisting, tying, fretting, teasing, lassoing, gluing and dyeing that go into these coiffures are remarkable, and it's all apparently extempore, amateur, home-made, created with the verve of frontier embroidery and done without mirrors. Hair lives aloof and apart. And for the men, their facial hair is an equally exuberant vernacular that bears scant regard for the formal function of the features it swags.

Anyway, Celine finally comes on, and the audience drags itself away from itself and claps as best it can, with its hands full of napkins nestling pints of sticky cocktails and boxes of snacks to ward off the ninety minutes of rumbly pangs.

My guess is that most in this audience don't get out to live shows much. Just being here seems to be a jewel in some sort of bigger experience. Certainly, Celine doesn't have to work hard to win them over. They're a sure thing. Not that that stops her – she doesn't so much project songs as implore them to leave her body. Those huge, over-produced, emotionally incontinent power ballads sound like the forced exorcism of goody-goody ghosts. You half expect – half wish – her head would swivel 360 degrees as that ungodly French-Canadian glottal accent sobs, 'Could taste your sweet kisses, your arms open wide'. For all her gym-tuned, dance-coached stagecraft, Celine still manages to look like the fat kid who won Weight Watcher of the Year. Her body is corded and knotted with self-restraint. Her movements are over-rehearsed and picky-precise – more Prussian cheerleader than Martha Graham. She looks good for an age she won't actually reach for a decade and does that Vegas thing – begs. She begs the audience to love her with a naked, generalised, 'I'm everybody's' sycophancy. There's more than a hint of bunny boiler, a manic desire to please and a smiley-implied nameless threat if we're not appreciative enough. In fact, her stage presence is a weird hybrid of Pinocchio and Buffy the Vampire Slayer. The show finally sinks beneath the applause during an encore of Celine, alone, howling on the deck of the *Titanic*. The audience troops out, stuffed but underwhelmed. Still grazing from tubs, hungry for the next gobbet of experience.

Next door, the dedicated merchandise shop will sell you any amount of Celine-ish memorabilia – books, calendars, coffee cups. Oddly, they all seem to have someone else's picture on them. Mostly a chubby, plain, brown-haired girl. Only a forensic scientist could make the connection between this Celine and the wind-tunnel face and tortured blonde hair of the woman we've just seen. Celine has succumbed to the Vegas makeover.

It happens to all acts that end up on the Strip. They lose kitsch control. There is some style gland that goes malignant in Nevada. The most famous example is how Rock'n'Roll Elvis morphed into Vegas Elvis. It happened to Sinatra and Noël Coward. There is a museum here dedicated to Liberace, where you can look at his wilting and dusty capes and flares, marvel at his mirrored Rolls-Royce, peek between your fingers at his bedroom and wonder how this man successfully sued a newspaper for suggesting he was gay. And then, of course, there are Siegfried and Roy. Celine, incidentally, is beginning to bear a distinct resemblance to Roy – or perhaps it's Siegfried. Siegfried and Roy put on, without hesitation, the very worst speciality show I've ever seen. They do tricks so ancient and so bad that they must think we were all born yesterday. But then, compared to them, we pretty much were.

Visitors to Vegas adore Siegfried and Roy. They're an institution. They're like folk dancers. Or folk art. And you have to be one of the folk to get the point. What else could explain adults watching a nonagenarian in a leather codpiece whipping a giant puppet dragon for no apparent reason?

But everyone's really here to see the white carnivores, hoping against hope that just maybe, just once, the tables will turn and Siegfried and/or Roy will get to see the inside of a big pussy. Sadly, not this time. Siegfried – or maybe Roy – stands up, his voice syrupy with that authentic Vegas-style emotion, and says that their life's work is to breed these rare species that have already become extinct in the wild. Well, without going into the whole Germanic, eugenic, white-power-subtext thing here, do you think they really believe this? These sad animals are mutants; how long would a white lion last trying inconspicuously to blend into the Technicolor Serengeti? A white python looks like nothing so much as an elephant's tampon, but then you realise . . . well, of course! Las Vegas is their natural habitat. Where else in the world would be the environment for a Liberace tiger?

Celine's show is directed by a former member of the creative team of Cirque du Soleil. At the moment, there are three Cirque du Soleil shows in Vegas, and there are plans for more. One of them is O, at the Bellagio. The title is enigmatic. It could mean naught, nothing, zero. It's spectacular. It cleverly steals images from surrealism and children's-book illustration and mixes them with elegant and simple acrobatics and dance that rely heavily on costume and props. It is unencumbered by plot, character or narrative. It makes absolutely no intellectual demands on the audience whatsoever. It's a perfect Vegas commodity and the ideal evolution of the big lounge act. There are no stars. All the performers are immediately replaceable. The production can be edited without anyone noticing. It's Lego theatre. You add bits, take bits away, make it taller, shorter, longer, cheaper, more elaborate. There is no end to the fun you can have with this circus.

In one of the Bellagio's fine restaurants, the dining room is unnaturally quiet; high rollers and their bored by-the-hour dates eat in comped formal silence. You can't help but notice that gamblers have very small stacks of words – and they don't like risking them.

I'm gripped by a party at a centre table: rough-looking men in matching goatees and Hawaiian shirts; women with exuberant hair and cantilevered chests. They're all solidly drunk. The man who is apparently the host rolls in his seat and shouts over and over, 'Porterhouse and Roquefort, honey... porterhouse and Roquefort... That's all the words you need to know tonight, honey, only the best tonight, only the best, porterhouse and Roquefort.' The other diners shoot daggers from under their brows. These trailer-gawky hoi polloi don't belong. They have their burger bars and fist food. Waiters hover with intent. But they *do* belong. More than the rest of us. This is who Vegas is for. The glitzy, fleeting imitation of high life and good luck for the habitually, congenitally luckless.

Outside on the steaming Strip, little Artful Dodger pimps hand out business cards for prostitutes. 'Nature of business will not be shown on credit card statement.' They offer two-for-one deals. I haven't the nerve to ask if this means you get an extra girl thrown in or you can bring a friend.

Downtown, away from the Strip, lie the low, sagging, aluminium-and-cinder-block bungalows of Vegas's poor. 'Slums', the limo driver calls them. They wouldn't count as slums anywhere else in the world, but they're a definite contrast to the imported-marble-and-fibreglass wonders of the world up the road. Here, the time that's been banished from the casinos sits heavy and ticks away slowly. Store fronts are boarded up. In a pawnbroker's window the trays of chunky, 'lucky' diamond rings sit unredeemed, and unredeeming.

The wedding chapels advertise their past nuptials – Michael Jordan and Joan Collins (not to each other, as far as I remember) – and their special deals. The runaway brides hover in their tulle or Guinevere outfits. Best men and ushers sit in air-conditioned waiting rooms like extras from *Blue Hawaii*, *The Godfather* and *Cleopatra*. The limo drivers lounge, smoke and flick through pornography. There are stuffed white horses, chariots, thrones, slaves, coffins and sequinned, bewigged and smoky-glazed Elvises. Across the road a porn shop advertises for dancers. No experience necessary.

If you want to love Las Vegas, if you want to imagine it as an egalitarian, glittering, high-kicking good time that can be had by all, then you have to pay it off. You need protection. You need to keep feeding it from a very deep cup of irony quarters, because the moment you lose the knowing irony, it's pretty rough.

This railway stop in the desert turns everything it grasps – energy, water, civilisation, art, marriage, talent, hard work – into dross and kitsch and sad, temporary, tacky junk. And it manages to do it without any *élan*, sophistication or sincerity. The longer you stay here, the harder it is to keep the smile pinned to your face. This isn't quite the banality of evil; it's just the cheapness of avarice.

In a neglected corner of town, where pick-ups slump in front yards and the air is thick with sunburn, there's an empty lot which collects the shards and fragments of old hotels and casinos, bars and restaurants. It's a cemetery, a boneyard of electric signs and neon, and there's something very peaceful about it. The billboards rest in the sunlight. The extinguished cowboys, giant cocktails, lucky clovers and cartoon mice all recline with an unexpected final dignity. A man apparently short on luck, holding a bottle in a brown bag, scoots through a hole in the chain-link fence and slides into the shadow of his lean-to home. It's a name: Debbie, written in script. It rests against a wall. 'I remember that,' the limo driver says. 'That was from the Debbie Reynolds Hotel – didn't work out.'

October 2003

Sudan

There are rumours of war, of genocide, of ethnic cleansing; they are whispered on the gritty, boiling wind that blows across the border from Sudan. In ones and twos and tens and hundreds, refugees struggle into Chad with stories of systematic murder, rape, slavery and scorched earth. I've been down this mine-sown track before: five years ago I covered the man-made famine that was an attrition against the Dinka in the south. That twenty-year conflict has finally been settled with a peace deal brokered by the Americans and paid for by oil; now the murderous bullying has moved up into the large western province of Darfur, where the irregular bandit cavalry, the Janjaweed, are wiping out black farming communities. The Arab-Islamic government of Khartoum denies any culpability and says with a shrug that this is a little local conflict between farmers and nomadic herdsmen.

Meanwhile, the UN steeples its fingers, sucks its teeth and equivocates, hinting that perhaps maybe this might be the worst humanitarian crisis in the world at the moment. Maybe perhaps 100,000 people are dead, and perhaps maybe a million more are on the pending list, waiting to get across the border before the rains come.

Our own US Security Council and the G8 have decided they don't have any immediate plans to intervene in Darfur, so the voiceless and unheeded continue to stagger through the desert into Chad, a diplomatically dumb country spectacularly unprepared for guests. The accusations of ethnic cleansing and genocide hang in the air, but few with the power to do anything about them want to say the words on record. It's like casting a spell to summon the apocalypse. Once said out loud, the world is a step closer to having to confront another Rwanda, another Kosovo. But there is a selective deafness abroad brought about by conflict in the Middle East, Iraq and the constant sirens of global terrorism, and unstated but ever present is the real-world wisdom that this, after all, is just another Africa story from the continent that brought you all the defining examples of horror; where the usual calibrations of misery don't apply.

I have no doubt there are dozens of marvellous and edifying things about Chad: being here is not one of them. Chad, or Tchad as they call it locally, as if named by some passing Yorkshireman, is really no more than a cartographer's patch. The French left it here as somewhere to keep the bottom of the Sahara in, and for those platoons of Foreign Legionnaires who had the most to forget. It's about the size of Germany, with a population of just 9 million. I remember it from my school atlas – it had the lowest per-capita income in the world. It isn't quite the poorest country on earth any more, but it is way, way down there: 80 per cent of the population live below the poverty line, 80 per cent work the sand. Its primary exports are a handkerchief of cotton, a few cattle and a near-monopoly of the world's gum arabic needs. Gum arabic is essential in the manufacture of good-quality watercolours. Not a lot of people know that; in fact, not a lot of people know anything about landlocked Chad. It has no airline, no railways; it has 21,000 miles of road, but only 165 miles of them are tarmacked. Life expectancy is forty-eight years, and only if you don't expect much. It does, though, have a glut of human diversity: 200 ethnic groups. In the north, the Goran, Zaghawa, Kanembu, Ouaddai, Baguirmi, Hadjerai, Fulbe, Kotoko, Hausa, Boulala and Maba – all Arab and Muslim. In the south are the Moundang, Moussei and Massa, who are for the most part Christian, which in Africa always comes hyphenated with animist, and they're black. They are the blackest black, blue-black, matt-black black you've ever seen.

Chad, along with Sudan, is hung across one of the least-reported, potentially most volatile cultural fault lines in the world: the border between black and Arab Africa. Before the Europeans ever arrived there was a history of exploitation, slavery and massacre. Here, the appellation Muslim or Christian comes with baggage and chains. Chad isn't one of those failed states we hear so much about from smug, over-achieving nations; rather it's a stalled state, one that never really made it off the starting blocks of independence. It goes through the stately motions, and boasts plenty of initials after its name from international organisations.

It has ambassadors and a billion dollars of debt, it signs international treaties (though I notice it hasn't ratified the international law of the sea yet), but it isn't defined by the niceties of statesmanship. Like Sudan, Chad is a slave to the land on which it precariously squats, earth blasted and dominated by the sun. This is the hottest place I've ever been. Temperatures are regularly in the fifties; they have climbed the thirties before sunrise. This isn't just weather, something mundane to be endured: it's a godlike thing, a shimmering, psychotic, physical presence. It's like living with a bright murderer. Achievement is not measured here, as it is in the damp, green First World, by invention and energy, but by the ability to do as little as possible, for as long as possible, in as much shade as possible.

Chad has three pressing problems. It has the black curse of Africa: unexploited oil. It has the same flag as Romania, and it has between 100,000 and 200,000 refugees. It has gone to the UN to protest about the flag business. To get about, you either hitch a lift on a lorry, hire a four-wheel-drive and stutter across the desert, or beg a seat on one of the small humanitarian flights that sustain a skeletal relief effort. After a couple of days hanging out in the two-storey breeze-block and barbed-wire boredom of N'Djamena, we managed to get a flight into the east. At the airport the top-secret French Mirage fighters screamed secretly into the shimmering morning air to spy on North Africa. The French can never actually leave their old colonies. They hang around like gun-toting divorced husbands. We fly to Abéché, which puts up with another French base; legionnaires lounging in the shadow of their jeeps, sporting nut-hugging camouflage shorts and coquettish little berets. For all their surly *élan*, they always look like the backing group for the Village People.

We drive on to Iriba, a town made of mud that rises out of the desert like geometric worm casts. The deafening silence is broken only by the morning throb of the baker's generator and the occasional call of a lovesick donkey. There is nothing to see here, nothing to play at, nothing to talk about, nothing to do except squat in the shade and throw stones at meagre chickens. You can't help but wonder at the terrifying boredom threshold you'd need to call this place home.

Iriba has the only hospital for the thousands of refugees stretched across hundreds of miles of border. It's a brick building of three or four little wards and a room that makes do as an operating theatre. In the compound are some sagging, dusty tents for the therapeutic feeding of malnourished children, and there is some shade for their mothers and those who have no bed. The hospital is run by Médecins Sans Frontières – Chad has few doctors, and they all work in the capital or for the UN.

There is only one doctor-surgeon, a Belgian girl who looks like she has stepped from a Frans Hals painting; bosomy and blonde, she's like a ghost among her black patients. She dreams Belgium dreams, of dairy products, yoghurt, cheese, fountains of milk. She makes her rounds with professional cheerfulness. The sick regard her with that stoic fatalism that is the small dignity of African hospitals. Just having made it here is staggering good fortune.

She stops at the bed of a woman who has given birth to tiny twin boys. They lie like little plucked birds, their bodies flickering with breath. Their mother arranges her shawl to give them shade, gently flicks away the flies – but she won't feed them. She is lactating but she won't feed them. And the hospital won't give them powdered milk because they can't guarantee its supply for the whole of their infancy. It's a stand-off. The mother won't or can't say why, one remorseless hour at a time, she can starve her sons to death. She lies apart with an impassive, locked-away beauty, like an odalisque, watching her boys eke out their tiny reserves of existence. The doctor is frustrated. The mother stares, speechlessly daring judgement. The universal blessing of children is for the refugee a curse. How could a lonely girl without a husband or family welcome another pair of mouths, two widow's mites, into this stark, hopeless life? I can only guess at the monstrous ill fortune and misery that led her to this hopeless impasse. She can't kill her babies, as women sometimes do out here *in extremis,* but she can't help them into her world either, so she lies here silently jammed between the intolerable and the unbearable.

Outside, a thirteen-year-old boy takes painful little steps, helped by an orderly. His brother stepped on the mine that killed him and took this boy's foot, and doctors had to remove one of his testicles. A group of men sitting in the shade give him a little clap. They may be guerrillas: they have bullet and shrapnel wounds; one is paralysed. Nobody asks.

I stand in on an operation in the little theatre. It's hardly sterile. There are sheets over the windows to keep out the desert, but it becomes stifling. Flies hopscotch over the sixteen-year-old girl lying on the table. She has been hit by a truck. They use ketamine as an anaesthetic. In the West it is only used as a veterinary drug; here it's a godsend. But while the bone-deep lacerations in the leg are being disinfected, the girl comes round. Her eyes roll with terror, hands jerk, a soft mewing grows to wails, then screams. The nurse reaches for another hypodermic cosh. 'I think she'll probably lose this leg,' says the doctor.

In the therapeutic feeding centre, children are given high-protein porridge; mothers and grandmothers finger-feed tiny mouthfuls into slowly ruminating mouths. These children, with their stretched-parchment faces, sparse hair and huge, sorrowful eyes, are always shocking, and I am aware of the irony of how ancient, wise and calm starving children always look. A woman rocks a spindly, floppy toddler. He is dying, she says. And closes his eyes. 'No,' explains a nurse through an interpreter. 'He's very dehydrated. He will die if they don't get fluids into him.' She adds that the mother shouldn't have taken out the saline drip they put into his arm. She tries to fit another, but the mother pushes it away; no, she insists, her child is dead. The nurses, though compassionate in a matter-of-fact way, get grittily frustrated at the lack of understanding in these mothers. Medicine is so second-nature to us, yet so mythical to them.

There is a little albino lad about two years old who is everyone's favourite. They call him Petit Blanc. He is responding well to the therapeutic feeding, the wrinkled skin filling out and dimpling. 'He won't last long,' she says. 'They never do, albinos. Skin cancer.' Does his mother know? 'She does now. I told her.' Can't she do anything? The doctor shrugs: 'Keep him out of the sun.' But all this woman has between her and the blistering, baby-murderous sky is a thin veil. 'You see, already he has the melanomas.'

About an hour away from the hospital, past dead tanks, relics of a defunct civil war, is the desert refugee camp of Iridimi. Built for 6,000, it sags under the needs of 14,000 souls who live beneath plastic sheets and rags stretched over thorn trees. Each day brings more lorries laden with Sudanese blacks and their bright bundles of belongings. They trundle in from the border, herding skeletal donkeys and matted goats, moving further inland as the Sudanese Arab militia cross the border to rob the last vestiges of property and livestock. The gunships that make up the Sudanese Air Force drop handmade bombs on border towns. The war in Darfur is being pursued by the last irregular cavalry still plying their trade: the Janjaweed. On horses and camels, they surround black villages. They are supported by regular army troops. The Sudanese government denies involvement, claiming they are local groups. The Janjaweed live by looting cattle, grain, small amounts of cash and slaves.

The government's reason for not intervening is clear: it's ethnic cleansing and genocide. There is meant to be a UN-monitored ceasefire, but the casualties, terrified women and starving children still stream across the border. The refugees' stories have a metronomic repetition: their villages are shelled or bombed, the Janjaweed surround them and kill all the men and boys old enough to be remotely threatening. They systematically rape the women, taking some as slaves; they then burn the villages and the crops they can't steal, and ride off with the livestock. And still the government claims the Janjaweed have nothing to do with them.

Khartoum offers access to the international community to check these calumnies, these accusations. Anyone can come to see that really Sudan is lovely – a hot Switzerland with mosques – but, invariably, the promised visas for observers and NGOs never materialise. If they do manage to get one, access to the worst area is limited. There are 500 applications from humanitarian agencies alone gathering diplomatic dust. This pattern of denial and opaque promises of transparency is familiar after twenty years of war in the south. Who is going to do anything about it? Who will stand up to the Janjaweed? They are among the most feared, sadistically ruthless, irregular thugs in a continent glutted with military horror. The refugees joke about them with terrified black humour: they all wear leather necklaces of little bound spells that are meant to protect them from bullets or knives, landmines and violent death. Little Dark Age incantations against the ordnance of modern war.

Anyone who doubts that this conflict is either genocidal or ethnically motivated only has to visit these camps. All the refugees are black; there are no Arabs here. And, even more shocking, 90 per cent of them are women and children. The children up to the age of five are about 50-50 girls and boys, as you'd expect. From five to fifteen they are 70 per cent girls. Some of the men would have stayed to fight or hide with their livestock but, as Sherlock Holmes used to say, 'when you have eliminated the impossible, whatever remains ... must be the truth'. It is impossible to imagine any other explanation for this disappeared generation of men than systematic murder. The women tell of deaths, terrified flight, lost children, missing husbands. 'We will never go back,' says one. 'Unless the UN have soldiers, and only if they are white soldiers,' adds another.

The refugees are related linguistically and tribally to the Chadians on this side of the border; they have moved and traded together for hundreds of years, and are now welcomed. It is humbling to see with what good grace the people with the least offer shelter and succour to those with nothing. The majority of refugees are not in the rich First World, but in the poorest bits of the Third World, where they and their hosts grow poorer.

The greatest problem after safety is water. From sunrise to sunset in the camp, a long line of women wait under the deathly sun to fill containers from a couple of standpipes that are fed by large plastic bladders, which in turn are filled by lorries. I have to drink at least six litres of soupy water a day to stop my tongue cracking and my throat closing up. But I never see these women drink. Their bright cotton shawls flap in the wind, revealing a little arm or resting head tied to a back. In the white light, the rivers of cloth look like spinnakers of saturated colour, printed with the repeated pictures of other people's good fortune. You see Mercedes badges and BMW signs, footballs, mobile phones, aeroplanes, the faces of politicians who've promised prosperity, cities of skyscrapers – the ragged incantations for an unavailable life, and the shaming irony of a desperate African version of designer labels. Here is a picture of a house you would be happy in, a diploma you could get if there was a school, a car, a comfy chair. Impossible, ridiculous cotton dreams of a fantasy luxury.

A mile or so outside the camp, in a stand of knotted acacias, is an ancient stone-lined well, one of the Sahara's fabled oases. It doesn't look like the painting. A dirty, shit-strewn muddy quag, where herdsmen sweat and slither at the heavy job of tending their xylophone-ribbed flocks. They perch precariously on the edge of the well; the thick water at the bottom is only a few feet deep. In the bed of the wadi there is a stinking, half-burnt pyre of donkey and goat corpses. The desert is littered with animal cadavers; elsewhere, parched livestock stand in little bits of filigreed shade and wait to die. The sun desiccates their bodies to tough bags, leather and bones that grin at the sky. For some reason there are no carrion eaters, no vultures, so the dead lie around like old teabags. When the rains do come, they'll become slimy and get washed into the wells and wadis, and leach into the water table. The risk of a cholera epidemic is just one runny, squatting child away.

The desert and the water won't support the Chadians and the Sudanese refugees, and there are signs that the welcome is growing thin. Charities drilling in search of new wells for permanent camps have been angrily stopped by farmers.

We drive on a spine-fusing, hip-dislocating, brain-poaching journey to Tiné, a market town that crosses the border. It sits on one of the skeletal lines of trade and communication that bleach into the Sahara. The route down from Libya meets a crossroads from Sudan into Central Africa here. The border itself is no more than a dry wadi and some trees, under which sit a squad of Chadian soldiers. There are a couple of impressive mosques and a large covered market. Prices are astronomic for the bits and boxes of white goods that made the Homeric saga through the desert to end up here.

Across the dry river and the shade trees you see the other half of town, the Sudanese half, a mirror image of mud-brick and minaret, utterly deserted, where not a soul, not a donkey exists. It's a town that's suffered a stroke: one half paralysed, the other bereft and staggering. The Janjaweed came, murdered and expelled the left-hand population. People ask, how could the Sudanese do this to their own people? I've heard Sudanese spokesmen with honey voices rhetorically ask the same thing: 'Why would we do these things to our own people?' The answer would seem to be that the Arab-Muslim regime in Khartoum doesn't consider the black inhabitants of their southern and eastern regions as their people, their kin, at all.

With its rigid, prescriptive interpretation of sharia, Khartoum attempted to develop chemical and nuclear weapons. It was Khartoum that sheltered Osama Bin Laden and Al-Qaeda while they planned the embassy bombings in Nairobi and Dar es Salaam. Khartoum pursued a civil war in the south for twenty years, engineering famine as a weapon of mass murder. And it still accepts the oldest, most inhuman of mass crimes: slavery. Blacks are captured, kept, bred and ransomed as slaves. This is a blatantly racist, genocidal regime. The UN has called the catastrophe in Darfur the worst humanitarian disaster in the world, but that's a euphemism. It describes a consequence, not the cause. This is a calculated crime. The greatest inhumanitarian disaster in the world.

In another refugee camp, at Touloum, a boy, perhaps twenty, approaches me. He is wearing a once-smart sports jacket and trousers and – a rare thing – spectacles. 'You speak English?' he asks. 'I was a student of English in Darfur at the university. I was in my second year.' He looks round the ragged shelters. 'This is a bad place, very bad. We need two things: water and an English department.'

I think he means it as a joke; it's a bleakly funny line. But he is absolutely serious. He is close to tears and I understand what a struggle it must have been to get to university at all, what a monumental investment, not just for him but his family, his village; this slightly bookish boy in his Western charity clothes and wise glasses, already approaching statistical middle age, cast out as homeless, begging flotsam among a diaspora of grieving women. It is such a pitiful waste. A damnable squandering of this heroic spark.

On the long, dry road home, I stop off at the hospital in Iriba.

The woman who had pronounced her son dead has had her prophecy fulfilled. The war-wounded men come and bury the little bundle in the graveyard behind the latrines. She sits hunched, facing the wall. She doesn't cry. I haven't seen one of these women cry. Inside, the mother has begun feeding her twin boys, her reasons for offering them life as secretly implacable as had been her decision to withhold it.

July 2004

Gold Mine

Above the Kloof mine, a white man sits all alone in a hut. The hut is hidden in a two-storey hangar and the hangar is built over some heavy-duty muscle machinery. Engineered in England when engineers weren't just youths who mended radiators, it's caged in and hung with clanging stairways. The man sits in front of a console of buttons and switches; he stares out of a window at a large calibrated circle with a moving pointer like the wheel of fortune. Nobody's allowed to enter the hut. There must be no distractions. He notices me out of the corner of his eye and cups a surreptitious fag. Another man hangs around the landing; perhaps he's here in case his mate needs a pee; perhaps he's here to kill him if he goes *tonto.*

The lives of thousands of men hang on this bloke's attention span and his reactions to a complex series of Morse whistles that come from deep under ground. He is the winch man, the winder. He plummets the double-decker wire cages packed with men down into the earth, so that they can mine gold.

The lift doors clang shut. Daylight slides up the cage; we start to fall. It feels like someone losing their grip over a cliff. The lift vibrates and judders, down, down, gathering speed. After mere seconds we're in the Cenozoic era, past the Holocene epoch; instantly past the time of the first whites in South Africa; past the first black tribes to migrate from the north's steamy forests; past the Pleistocene, Pliocene, Oligocene, Eocene and Palaeocene epochs. Down, down past the time of the super-mammals; down past the first hominoid; down past the Sahara as a jungle; into the Mesozoic era, past the Cretaceous, Jurassic and Triassic periods. Down past the first dinosaurs, the reptiles and amphibians, the land plants, down past the continental separation; down into the Palaeozoic era, the Permian period, past the Carboniferous epoch, past the Devonian and Silurian periods;

down to Proterozoic rock that is two and three-quarter billion years old, one and a quarter miles beneath today's sunlight.

High above, the man in the hut watching fortune's needle fall pulls a switch. The lift jars to a halt. The door shudders open, and I step out into the hot, damp air that doesn't belong down here any more than I do.

South African gold mines are not at all what I expected. I was looking for some approximation of a northern English pit village with better weather. But they sit alone in the beautiful country of the rolling high veld. Their headgear stands like castle keeps or *campanili.* The mines look a bit like futuristic Tuscan hill towns; there are no shanties, no bustling camps of shebeens, markets and brothels, just suburban back roads with municipal flowerbeds and alleys of trees punctuating miles of discreet razor-wire fence.

The gold mines might almost be deserted; only the arc lights and complex security at the gate betray their importance in the land. Gold mines, like icebergs, hide their power beneath the surface. The reason for South Africa is the cold comfort of gold. This reef of ore was discovered in the 1880s on farmland in the Boer homeland of the Transvaal. The area, Witwatersrand, gave its name to the currency. The discovery started a rush of prospectors, first from the Cape and then from all over the globe. Out of the mining camp grew Johannesburg – a city the Zulus call Egoli, the place of gold. And out of the ground came money. Inconceivable amounts of cash, to pay for the most successful country in the world's most unsuccessful continent. The gold was formed by a great inland sea, washed up on its tideline. As the sea dried up, the gold was covered by new formations of sediment and rock, and then the old seabed was tilted sideways – one edge touching the surface, the rest falling away in a great arc under ground. It was, and is, by far and away the largest deposit of gold ever discovered.

But gold has its curse. It paid for the apartheid regime. It brought injustice and torture, it paid for clandestine wars in at least three neighbouring countries, and it financed the Southern Hemisphere's first and only nuclear bomb (in 1993, South Africa abandoned its secret nuclear-weapons programme). This gold should now be making amends and helping pay for a new rainbow South Africa, but just when it's needed the most, mining gold has faltered. It is, they say, a sunset industry. It may only last another fifteen years, perhaps another fifty.

Having once accounted for half of South Africa's economy, it's now down to 12 per cent. And the mines are prone to strikes. Their history and ownership make them unpopular with the ruling ANC government. Gold Fields, which owns the Kloof mine I'm going down, is at the moment resisting tooth and nail an asset-lipo-sucking, hostile bid from the ironically named Harmony Gold Mining Company – a smaller, loss-making outfit. It's an expensive and desperate raid to dig the deepest grave in Africa for one or other of them. Troubled Harmony needs a rich seam of gold to mine, or else its future looks bleak; Gold Fields would be devalued by association.

The high value of the rand against the weaker dollar makes deep mining an unprofitable business at the moment. Gold stands at 2,633 rand ($427.70) an ounce, but only needs to go to 2,643.80 rand for it to be very profitable; at 2,799.31 rand, they are drowning in money. Mining is cyclical, but the cycle is emotional, not economic. There's nothing rational about the value of gold – a war, a disaster, a dramatic shift in geopolitics, a frisson of unease and the world runs to the security of gold as it always has. They're planning even deeper mines, perhaps four miles deep. The technical problem is the lift rope. It becomes too heavy to support its own weight. But they're working on it. No, it's not what I'm thinking about as I start to walk down the tunnel towards the stope, the gold face. What I'm thinking of are earthquakes. This part of Africa is low-risk for tremors, but the constant blasting deep under ground slaps the face of Hades; it teases and irritates the silent, blind rock, which twitches and shudders. Two days ago a quake that broke windows on the surface trapped forty-two miners. The last I heard, they were still down there in the fetid blackness. Do you worry about quakes? I ask the guy next to me. 'Ach, they happen most days.' Aren't you frightened? He looks at me sideways. 'Yes, very, but what can you do? Where can you go?'

And I'm thinking about my outfit. A one-piece cotton overall that was laid out in the VIP changing room, along with a pair of woolly socks and Wellington boots. Rubber knee and elbow pads (made by crippled miners), a white-plastic hard hat, a pair of rubber gloves – one red, one green – and some second-hand red pants. I draw the line at the pants. If I'm going to be buried for ever, or brought back up in a bag, I'm not meeting my maker, or the surgeon, in a pair of someone else's puce Y-fronts.

At the mine head I'm given a belt with a heavy battery pack, a lamp that clips to the helmet and a silver box with breathing apparatus in case we hit methane or CO_2. 'It'll give you half an hour's breathable air, as long as you stroll and don't panic,' says the cheery miner who offers the unnervingly sketchy health-and-safety talk, which mostly boils down to: 'No worries, trust us and look where you're going.' Smilingly, they make me sign in triplicate fifteen pages of medical legalese that indemnifies them from having to have the remotest concern for my well-being.

To all intents and purposes, I'm now the mine bitch – don't panic, stroll. Up above, everywhere you look there are safety posters, imploring care and attention the way communists used to demand sacrifice and patriotism. One billboard points out that there have been almost a million shifts without a fatality, which sounds encouraging until you realise that each miner counts as a shift, so it's only about four months. Nine people die down the Kloof mine most years, usually from what they literally and amusingly call 'ground falls'. That's the mine ceiling hitting you on the head, crushing your organs, snapping your spine and mushing your pelvis to dog food. Occasionally they just get hit by a train.

The mine tunnel starts off high and broad, like an underpass or a Tube platform. There are lights bolted to the roof, and along the walls run tubes and hoses carrying water and compressed air. The ground is flat and even; there are narrow-gauge rails set into the rock. Every so often a right angle of timber is placed across them; if one of the locos goes loco, then this is meant to derail it. The trains pull the rocks and, as the tunnels get narrower and the ceiling lower, when they pass you have to push yourself against a wall. There are holes in the floor that drop down to other levels, the engines dump their rock down them, and from there they are humped to the surface. The railway line stops and the tunnels become rougher, bored-out holes in the rock. The floor falls away, we have to scrabble in single file down hastily hacked stairs, in corners there are piles of pit props and metal jacks. The air smells acrid and mineral; it seems to rise and fall. Pumped in, it gusts through defiles like the breath of a sleeping dragon. Slick with sweat, I stumble and reach for a guardrail. Something brown darts over my hand. A cockroach. Astonishing, this little creature, our most faithful companion, like a loathed ex stalked us here to the centre of the earth. This brazen, admirable, wavy-feelered meaty pebble skitters through the hot dark, feeding on sweat and skin flakes, and drill grease.

The tunnel loses coherence and direction. We stumble and graze on the rock. The ceiling crawls down the walls, the floor crawls up to meet it and I stoop in between. Up and down and around, I lose all track. The path is like a slow, sharp, awkward switchback. I've no idea where I've come from, or which direction is back. The lights have run out. There is only the lamp on my head to keep back the darkest, matt-blackest blackness on earth. It's an absence of seeing. I'm bent double, my hard hat jarring the jutting cliff, my belt catching and the battery jamming on the shale. Now I'm wriggling, scuttling and crabbing in the loose, sharp gravel. I feel so soft and squidgy and alien, blind and maggoty in this emphatic mineral world.

Up over a trench wall of rock and I'm there, dripping, panting. This is the end of the tunnel, where there is no light. Here is what it was all for, a slanting reef of gold-bearing rock. It's a yard of pebble-dash that is dun and coarse. There is no gleam, no vein of bright fire: that's just Old Testament stone that hasn't felt air or seen light, undisturbed for more than 2 billion years. This is as close to the centre of the earth as we can get. The rocks down here can reach forty degrees. The piles of wood buttressing the ceiling, stuffed with metal bags, inflated with water to jam them tight, lean at mad angles. The stout, wound jacks, their metal elbows aching, strain against the ceiling. Within a day the earth's pressure will compress them, inch by solid inch.

This face is blasted new every morning, the supports are ad hoc, the mine chases the shoreline of this ancient beach. The miners work along the slanting slope of ore, the lights on their helmets make the shadows dance and stutter, eyes and teeth and black sweat gleam. It's a scene of theatrical chaos, medieval illustration, biblical, mythical. It's a devil's cathedral. If the root of all evil is the love of money, then this hole is where they planted the taproot. This is the bargain basement of sin, the adoration of all lucre, the well of avarice; this anaerobic blackness harbours the metallic seeds of progress and civilisation and the wide-eyed yearning that still sends men billions of years back under ground.

I'm in a space that's a yard high and drops or climbs out of sight after about thirty feet. I look up and the oven rock touches my nose. A black miner, naked to the waist except for a string of good-luck charms, taps my shoulder and I take up a drill like a Lewis gun with a ten-foot bit attached to the barrel. It's driven by compressed air and cooled by water. A man behind me supports the snaking power lines. I push the trigger; it howls and spits with a horrific torment. The noise careers around this slit in the rock, looking for somewhere to escape. Slowly it spins a hole in the reef. We drill a hole every yard; I ask the gang boss what they put in them. He throws a foot of plastic-bagged grey sausage of sticky putty at me. This is the explosive. Is it fired electrically? 'No, we have a half-hour fuse.' Do you use a warning whistle or horn? 'No, it's done at a specific time.' So you make sure everyone has a watch? 'No, the team leaders make sure everyone's out.'

Although all I can see around us is a team of ten or twenty miners, actually down here, above us and below, in front and behind, burrowing along a myriad of wynds, there are 10,300 souls, working on faces stretching miles from the main shaft. Every day they blast new faces; every afternoon the next shift collects the rubble. There is an unmappable filigree of years of tunnel, blocked and collapsed, healed and gaping under ground.

An engineer back in London described deep mining to me as being like that game where you stretch a tissue over a glass and place a coin in the centre, and then burn the tissue with a cigarette, trying not to make the coin fall. Every blast alters the geophysics of every bit of the mine. The tensions holding up the ground are constantly readjusted in a way that is impossible to measure or predict. Down here you think that perhaps the only thing that keeps it from crushing out the light and the air is the vanity, the sheer, naked desire of the mystical power of gold.

We walk back to the main tunnel and wait for the lift. The miners are mostly black, but not necessarily South African: they're drawn here from Mozambique, Botswana, Zimbabwe, Lesotho and Swaziland. There are eleven official languages in South Africa, and under ground they speak a twelfth: Fanagalo, a made-up tongue broadly based on Zulu. The white mine executives are shifty about it – embarrassed. Fanagalo is old South Africa, the racist sound of apartheid. It's the voice of orders, masters and servants. Officially the miners speak English, but Fanagalo is what they call out down here in the dark. The white miners are mostly specialists and officers: big Afrikaners with unconsciously gay moustaches. They tower over the small black Africans. The relationship between them is both touching and strained. The body language of each group is defensive; there are patronising smiles and an exaggerated courtesy, but little eye contact. Even their handshakes are different. The Afrikaners squeeze your knuckles so you'll never play rugby again; the black Africans shake your hand and then grip your thumb, a gesture of welcome and solidarity.

The lift has got lost, so I sit and talk to some of the miners. Crespo, forty-four, from Mozambique, starts teaching me Fanagalo. *Molo* (hello), *sphoku sphoku* (stupid), *hamba kahle* (go well). He speaks good English as well as Portuguese, Afrikaans, Sesotho, Shangaan, Tswana, Inhambane, Ndau, Swazi, Zulu and Xhosa. 'You say you speak twelve languages?' a white miner interrupts. Crespo looks away and shrugs. 'Really?' The white man raises his eyebrows, juts his chin. His look says: 'You can lie to this soft, liberal English journalist, but don't think I don't know you.' Have you ever been abroad? I ask him, to cut the atmosphere. 'Oh yeah,' he says, misunderstanding. 'I've travelled all over this country. I've been everywhere.'

The friction wasn't just between whites and blacks in the mines: there were vicious, bloody inter-tribal wars. The men's dormitories were segregated by allegiance and there were battles under ground, gangs waving crowbars like assegais, chasing each other like moles.

The lift finally arrives and there are a hundred or so miners waiting to go up. A delicate, smiling black man in the huddle says he's a trained geologist, but he can't tell anyone here because they're only hiring unskilled miners. 'It's no good in this country, no good with my skin,' he whispers. But then everyone in South Africa with a skin could say that. The wire door clangs open and I'm pushed by helpful hands into the back of the cage. And silently, as if by convention and ancient habit, all the white miners rise to the front of the crowd and squeeze in. As the door closes, one black chap in a hurry pushes in; a fat, aggressive Boer shoves his sweaty-bearded face up close and screams questions and abuse. It's pointless and unprovoked bullying, perhaps for my benefit, probably just for fun. It gets no response, so he turns to teasing a mate who is phobic about the lift. Finally we step out into the bright, clear, warm sunlight of the high veld in autumn, and the world seethes with colour. I hadn't realised how muted and monotone Hades below is, nor noticed how gloriously blue and domed the sky is. The miners stream past as I look up and slowly spin like Julie Andrews.

At the Kloof mine they get nine grams of gold per tonne of rock, and they extract 34,000 kilos of gold a year. That's a lot of rock. Much of refining is about reducing that volume. The ore-bearing reef is brought up from the face and tipped onto a conveyor and fed into huge silos. From the silos, it's moved to spinning drums like tumble-dryers the size of Bovis homes. Inside there are rods or steel balls; water is pumped in and slides out as a thin slurry, which is then treated in great vats with cyanide and carbolic. This is filthy and dangerous. I walked on a gantry round the top of one of these vats at night. It was ten storeys up. A soup of rock and poisonous water was bubbled with compressed air. It was very scary.

The gold is then transferred to carbon, in the shape of burnt coconut husks from Sri Lanka, and baked in ovens. The resulting grey ash is taken to a hangar that's half demolished, with ecclesiastical light streaming through the holes in its ceiling. In the middle of this huge room is a smelting pan, and dropped into it are three white-hot elements that turn the metal to liquid. The pan steams and glows white. This is the central mystery of gold. Very few miners ever see this, the final act, the consummation of the drama. The heating elements withdraw, and slowly the pot is tipped sideways. Over its pouting lip trickles the neon-white-and-yellow ore. It smokes and bubbles and moves like live eels. It slips into moulds on steps; the molten metal falls from one to the next. This is the dance of gold, and it's as mesmerising as it's been for 7,000 years.

Gold-mining was the first industrial job. Men were watching the magic of the bright, molten gold before they'd learnt to write. Gold is bewitched and murderous and exciting – it's the antidote of divinity and holiness and selflessness – but gold gets things done. It's the measure of achievement, it's the spur and the reward, and it's been the answer to the meaning of existence since men first asked the question.

The ore cools in the brick mould, then is tipped out with a dull thud. A miner in rubber gloves picks it up, puts it in an incongruous kitchen sink and starts to scrub. A shell of base dross falls away; the bar shines, yellow, golden. It's fascinating. Out of that black, hard rock emerges this stuff that never tarnishes, never rots, never rusts, that glows for ever. All the gold ever dug still exists, except for a couple of ounces burnt off the nose of the space shuttle. It's all still here, the riches of Troy and Egypt and Babylon, the jewellery of Rome, the vast treasure of the Andes and Central America; pirates' doubloons and empires' sovereigns; wedding rings, the regalia of kings and the teeth of pimps; the wealth of nations and the confidence of currencies.

It's in vaults, in mouths, on fingers, in ears, in gardens, in secret crevices, under the mattress or the floorboards. We dig it up and polish it and hide it again. And if that's not madness, then it's golden. And of all the gold that was ever mined, 40 per cent of it has come from here, out of the Rand on the high veld. Since the 1880s, South Africa has smelted 1.6 billion ounces of gold, and you know what? There's the same again still down there, under ground, in the blackness, waiting.

April 2005

Tasmania

Along the road out of Marrawah there are seventy-seven pademelon wallabies, forty-two Bennett's wallabies, thirty-five Tasmanian devils, eight wombats, six spotted quolls and six brush-tailed possums all flat on the tarmac in various stages of decomposition. Native crows sit corpulently on fence posts like the queue at a butcher's. Tasmanian roads are the best way to get up close to the island's secretive and weird wildlife. There aren't many cars here but they're driven with lethal abandon. The wildlife ranges from the singular to the frankly bizarre: an antipodean collection of concept creatures with spare pockets, scales, beaks, spikes, flippers, pogo-legs and a genetic inability to recognise a pick-up coming the other way.

We are driving out to the tip of the north-west coast, and on the way we've picked up a possum. We pull off the road and tie it to the back of the truck like a bunch of good ol' Mississippi boys on a Saturday night. It lies spreadeagled in the dirt. I stare at it, as something's odd, something I can't quite work out. 'So you've noticed,' says our guide. 'Possums have their tackle on upside down.' And damn me if he isn't right. The little critter's got his very neat, matt-black meat and two veg sewn on back to front. Now, whatever induced evolution to think that having your testicles upfront was a comfortable idea? We drag the possum behind the truck through the wiry button grass, laying a scent trail up to a hut on the shore, and there we peg him down.

The far north-west coast of Tasmania is a wild place. They tell you it's a bit like the west of Scotland. It isn't, really. This is in another league. This has a black belt in ruggedness. A coastline with a sinewy, keening abandon. There is precious little land in the world further south than this. Between here and Patagonia, a day away round the globe, the Roaring Forties skim the heaving, heavy sea. The ripping, flailing winds that helter-skelter round the Southern Ocean come to spank this coast with a relentless gusto. The rocky shore is tortured into a macabre and dramatic beauty. The waves stand up on their hind legs and lunge at the land, to be flayed into bone-white shreds by the black rocks. In the late afternoon, the sky is glowing pale gold, dark-mauve clouds are filigreed pink, thousands of mutton birds (sheerwaters) fly low over the silver water, and we hurry back in the teeth of the wind to our hut. Cabins, lean-tos and bothies squat all over the wild places of Tasmania, home-made out of bits and pieces, recycled offcuts, old front doors and driftwood. They have a serial charm. Men here like being out in the dark: they're happiest whittling and fiddling, grilling something they've picked up at the side of the road. This hut is one room with a little bunk room tacked on the back. It has a fireplace and tables and chairs that were chucked out of a post-war kitchen. We sit round the table and eat abalone stew with bread and butter and wait, the room lit only by orange firelight, the wind fretting the windowpane and rattling the latches and hinges. The chimney coos and mutters as we watch the darkness outside, the dead possum strapped out in a pool of moonlight.

Tasmania was discovered for the old north world by the second-greatest dead-reckoning navigator who ever sailed, the Dutchman Abel Tasman. He guessed there must be a great land to the south. He found Tasmania and called it Staten Land because he thought it was attached to Argentina, and sailed on to discover New Zealand and then back up round Australia without apparently noticing it. He gave us the first map of Tassie. Ever since, 'map of Tassie' has been the universal Australian euphemism for a lady's front-bottom area. Its outline resembles a charmingly old-fashioned hirsute pudendum. 'Going down to Tassie' will get you a laugh in any bar on the mainland. Tasmanians are the eternal fall guys of Australian humour. The jokes usually involve incest, stupidity or bestiality.

Outside, there is a skin-puckering scream. We press our faces to the window like characters from a nursery story, watching for the beast. Just beyond the pool of light in the sticky dark, a creature with a head the size of a pit bull terrier's and the body of a delicate black piglet sidles up to the possum. A Tasmanian devil. An old male, his face scarred by fighting, alert and belligerent with blazer-button eyes, a black cork nose and a burst of fine whiskers. He grabs the possum and tugs hard. The gape of his maw is huge, a powerful jaw with murderous teeth. Devils are unique to this island, one of the small band of carnivorous marsupials. They have their pockets on upside down. The females give birth to twenty or thirty tiny young that crawl like blind, bald maggots into their pouches. They only have two pairs of nipples. The four toughest get a grip, and for the rest, life's short race as one of the world's weirdest animals is already run. Devils are being ravaged by cancer. A unique Tasmanian-devilish cancer, of course, that grows root-like tumours on their faces. Nobody knows why and nobody has a cure. The devil has few relatives to mourn him. He behaves like a hyena but genetically is closer to a bandicoot. The cancer seems to be contagious. Forget bird flu: we really don't want infectious face cancer to jump species.

We stare at this strangely engaging little grave robber caught in the reflective firelight, with the roaring sea behind him. He looks up and sniffs the gusting air, listening for his carcinogenic competitors. He has only two natural enemies: a reckless Toyota and every other little devil he ever meets. The Tasmanian state government has been trying to copyright the devil to get back some of the money from Taz, the Warner Bros cartoon character. They resent the cash it makes, and the libel. They tell you that the charm of Tasmania is that it has the look and pace of a time gone by. They'll probably mention 1950s England, a country of villages with corrugated iron instead of thatch. Actually, it's not like that at all. Charm is too small and dainty a word for what Tasmania has. It doesn't allow for a place left out at the edge of the world, or for the strange quality of the silence, as if it's breathing slowly, waiting. It's nothing you can put your finger on. A flicker in the corner of your eye. A secret not so much hidden as unspoken. Bits of it do look very like bits of England, north Wales or the Lake District. But more, it looks like a landscape that had been invented to look like England. You drive down country roads and for a moment they're perfect, but where a tree should be a beech or an oak, it's a gum or a leadwood. The sheep in the meadows are the wrong sort of sheep: big woolly merino. I get out and stand beside a field, thinking how strange it is to travel all this way and arrive at a hyper-real Hampshire during rationing, and then I notice the field is growing poppies. Opium poppies. Half the world's pharmaceutical morphine comes from Tasmania, and it's grown here because they have such a close-knit, well-ordered, law-abiding, scary society. They don't like outsiders knowing they're farming class-A drugs. So it's sort of half Hampshire, half Helmand province.

Tasmania is a land that has been constructed out of memory and homesickness. Just a glance at the map and the names sing like a sad echo. Sheffield, Beaconsfield, Devonport, Ben Lomond, Perth, Swansea, Runnymede, the River Esk, Weymouth, Bridport, Ben Nevis, Melton Mowbray. Fading postcard names of places that the people who pinned them here on the very edge of the habitable world would never see again. They settled and grew apples and made English cheese, wore ties, ate Sunday roasts, made Christmas pudding in the middle of summer. Subsequently called Van Diemen's Land, it was a penal colony, vicious and hopeless, a skip for the rubbish and broken bastards from back home. Finally, they petitioned to change the name to Tasmania, like an island on its own witness-protection programme wanting a new start. Society here was truncated, bitter, guilty, mocked and self-reliant, and ultimately stoically admirable. I sit out in the pearly dawn one day watching the mist curl over a pond in a blind valley where a hamlet of cottages hold each other at arm's length. It was a familiar rural ensemble that summoned old-world literature and lyric couplets. Then, out of the rushes, cutting a smooth V through the still water, where there should have been Ratty or Jemima Puddle-Duck, is a duck-billed platypus. Overhead, a family of yellow-tailed black cockatoos raucously stand in for the lark ascending.

There are places that look like old England and there are places that look like nowhere else on earth. Tasmania has a rainforest that has an elemental, speechless beauty. Rainforests around the rest of the world are smelly, soggy, dank and deeply disappointing. Tasmania's cool, temperate forest is a great buttressed and hammer-beamed cathedral to the green gods, to Gaia and Puck. Everywhere you look, it has composed itself into artful vistas or Titania's boudoir. The canopy is made of huge, slow-growing eucalyptus, blue, red, grey, yellow, white. Some of the tallest trees in the world are here, the celery-top pines, pencil pines, leatherwoods, myrtle beech, sassafras, pepperbush, wattles and tree ferns, and on the ground a velvet carpet of bright lichen and moss. The variety of green stuff beggars the English woodland. This is some of the oldest living landscape in existence. I want to believe this is as close to the primeval forest as we can ever get. If that isn't genetically true, it is spiritually and emotionally. If you travelled here for nothing else, you should see this forest: it's the stillness that's so gorgeous and unnerving. A huge, silent library of greenness. Things do live here, lots of things, but none of them say anything.

In a dappled meadow there's a shuffle of leaf fall and gingerly we pick up an echidna, one of the strangest concept creatures God ever put into limited production. It's curled up into a ball like a hedgehog. It is both spiny and hairy. It has a snout like an anteater and large, mechanical digging hands that appear to have been put on back to front. It has only one relative, the platypus, making them a nuclear family of suckling egg-layers. The Cradle Mountain rainforest is an impressive place to walk. There's a great hike over the spine of Tasmania, where the weather is like Wales but without the Gaelic moments of dry, sunny optimism. It was up here that I discovered the odd truth about wombat dung. No creature has grown so snugly into its name as the wombat, and they have this remarkable poo. It's square. Wombats lay organic dice: they have special bones in their backsides for squeezing and shaping and slicing. The reason for the cubic turd is that wombats like to mark their territory neatly, and they lay their personal Lego as high as possible on logs and rocks so that it doesn't get lost in the grass, and they've made it square so that it won't roll off. Nanny nature thinks of absolutely everything.

Forty per cent of Tasmania's ancient rainforest is now national park, and the rest is going to be protected, but not for seven years. Forestry is the biggest single industry. An old-fashioned, muscly, mannish, moustached, hard-hat and plaid-shirt job. Tasmanians have worked in logging for generations. They're proud of their trees, proud of the little English farms they've carved out of them. The Huon pine is a rare endangered tree, its wood so hard and oily and straight that it never rots in water and was used to make masts and yachts and most of the window frames on the island. The King Billy pine, named after William Lanne, Tasmania's last full-blood Aborigine, has a grain that's so beautiful it's used for panelling and floorboards. The coming moratorium on cutting old-growth forests has spurred a frantic impetus in the loggers. You can't hire a truck or lorry anywhere in the state: they're all being used for lumber. The sound of chainsaws trills over the forest: the ancient trees and their undergrowth are being clear-felled so they can plant a mongrel weed, shining gum, which grows like bamboo; most of it is sent to Japan. The forest is being rubbed out by special pleading, arm-twisting and back-scratching corruption. The rest of Australia looks on with an environmental horror, but Tasmania is used to that: it's always been a place apart.

If what you know is the Northern Hemisphere sky or, more likely, the reflected city lights, then the southern night sky always comes as a surprise. The Southern Cross pointing a compass; the Milky Way closer, brighter. It is a younger sky that doesn't come with classical poetic baggage. I sat next to a hardwood fire on the edge of an open pasture, bright eyes pricking the shadows. Every so often a stuttering log would illuminate a dancing quoll. Quolls are another strange and specific Tasmanian creature, a carnivorous marsupial that comes in two flavours: striped and spotted. These are the small striped ones like stoaty cats. I've seen a spotted one stuck to the road. Craig, the man who made the fire and cooked strange indigenous Outward Bound food, is telling us tall stories about the thylacine, the Tasmanian tiger, the largest of the carnivore marsupials. The last one died in captivity in the 1930s, and there is an old grainy film of it in Hobart Zoo, madly pacing its little cage. A strange, rangy animal. Craig stares into the fire and says quietly that he's seen one, twice. It's out there, wary and rare in the silent forest.

Tasmania's east coast couldn't be more different from the west. Protected from the weather, it's tropical hot, with sand dunes running down to empty, pristine beaches out of which punch humpbacked granite boulders like half-buried Henry Moores, turned a beautiful rusty pink by indigenous lichen. On the shoreline pied oystercatchers dodge sand plovers, Arctic terns, Atlantic gulls and pelicans. Over the scrubby marsh grass where the pademelons graze, wedge-tailed eagles quarter the land. The rolling sea is full of fish and whales. It's as perfect a beach as you will find anywhere in the world. This is the Bay of Fires, given its name after the campfires of the Aborigines who were driven into this corner of the island. Tasmanians don't boast about it: they're modestly reticent when it comes to what they did with their Aborigines. But the English in Tasmania quietly and without international fuss managed one of the very few wholly successful systematic genocides, perhaps the only one, in the world. They bribed, cajoled and bullied the Aborigines to leave their island for a better life on Flinders Island, a barren outcrop of rock off the coast. The natives were killed by pestilence, starvation, the weather, neglect and despair. Six Aboriginal women survived on this rock in the sea like a grotesque inversion of the sirens. They were used as prostitutes by passing whalers. Tasmania has had a hard childhood, an abused infancy. It's built on bones and tears, rage and homesickness, and considering all that, or perhaps because of it, it's grown to be a singular and remarkable place.

On the Legerwood Road, in a little logging and railway community in the north-east, they had a ceremony in 1918 to commemorate the local men who died in the Great War. They planted trees for them along the dusty road. Douglas firs for Alan Andrews and George Peddle. Deodars for William Hyde, John McDougall and John Riseley. A sequoia for Robert Jenkins, and at each end of the line a Weymouth pine for the Anzacs and Gallipoli. By 2000 the trees were old and unsafe and had to be cut down; the community asked Eddie Ross, a chainsaw artist, to turn the stumps into portraits. Here's John Freeman blowing a trumpet; he died burning rubbish on top of an unexploded bomb. George Peddie was a sawmill manager and bushman; he died at Passchendaele. Here he is in his bush coat, with a cross-saw and axe. John McDougall was nineteen when he died in France. He'd been a railway porter. He waves his flag for a train that's always expected. Robert Jenkins was from Cornwall. He was engaged to Miss Trippy Forsyth. He sits in a trench, looking up at her patiently waiting on another branch. They all stand with a coarse and primitive dignity on a quiet road opposite a post office where you can get ice cream.

They're not just an awkwardly moving remembrance of a sacrifice made on behalf of a nation that used this distant, forgettable outpost as a criminal dustbin, but a memorial and metaphor for all Tasmanians. These hard, naive people, shy and silent and capable, growing out of the stumps of their trees

April 2007

Blindness in Africa

Kenya

This is the month of the short rains in Kenya. Tourists watch the sky with expensive resentment; the locals with joyous expectation. At breakfast a woman dressed as a trick-or-treat Karen Blixen tells the waiter, 'It's raining,' as if it were something she hadn't ordered, and please would you bring something brighter. 'Yes,' he replies. 'It's a blessing.' And offers her the sunniest of smiles.

As ever, Nairobi is a city that feels like it's bursting out of its skin, just on the edge of pupating into something unexpected and brilliant. Next year, the year after, sometime. But at the moment it's a wriggling, blind grub, smelling of diesel, sweat and damp. The hawkers dodge the traffic offering sunglasses and watches; a little fist taps the windscreen from under a tree of Stetsons and safari caps, just behind him there's a man selling wrought-iron hat stands. It's the boundless optimism of Africa that never ceases to astonish and humble.

Tarpaulin shanties spread into every gap and crevice like spilt milk around the post-colonial, borrowed-money skyscrapers. There are dozens of medical missions and exclamatory one-off churches, every billboard is for mobile phones, and along the roadside squatters set up entrepreneurial stalls that will sell, mend or copy anything. The papers are full of anti-corruption drives, promised by men so tempered in graft they could pick locks with their tongues. There are five-year plans for everything from prosperity to literacy, based on nothing but wishful thinking and foreign aid. There are grisly murders and a fearsome argument about the economic, moral and public-health implications of buying second-hand underwear. And then, in every roundabout and beside every pavement, there are beautifully planted bright strips of flowers and ornamental shrubs.

The Kikuyu are eternally wedded to their gardens and they bring the rhythm of planting and tending from their desiccated villages into the city.

The Thika School for the Blind is in Nairobi's outskirts. It has very nice strips of garden. The school was started in 1946 for colonial soldiers blinded in the war. It's still run by the Salvation Army and boasts disability, not inability. Today it's a school for blind and sight-impaired children from all over Kenya. African schools have a strangely time-warped feeling: the blackboard worn grey, sloping desks, maps, diagrams and biblical aphorisms on the wall, children in bright uniforms, the noise of sing-song rote learning, rapt attention and perfect manners. They are a nostalgic reprise of the 1950s. In the English class a teacher who has glasses as thick as a pub window is asking the pupils to make sentences using double words, 'I'm awfully, awfully sorry', 'very, very happy'.

A couple of the children look like they're asleep at their books; they're not, they're pressing their eyes against the page to pick out words a letter at a time. Others are using templates and styluses to nimbly prick their answers in Braille. The eyes of the class roll and blink or remain glued shut. Bible black blind. The dinner bell rings. Gingerly, they get up and feel their way to the door.

Outside, in the cloistered walk, gaggles of children hang onto each other for comfort and guidance. Three schoolgirls lead their blind teacher. The blind teach the blind, who lead the blind to lunch. A plump little girl, eyes tight shut, feels for my hand and holds it, telling me her name, asking for mine. Her grasp is soft and damp, intensely needy. I can feel the fingers searching like moles' noses to find kindness and kinship, and a little care. In the garden the jacarandas are in blossom, the most beautiful trees in Africa with their thick, mauve-blue blossoms that smell of dusty sweet shops. They stand out against the deep purple-grey of the thunderous sky. The herbaceous borders are bright with geraniums, and pale-green succulents that sit in the red earth; along the fences garish bougainvillea spills abstractly. The windows and doors of the low brick building are pale blue; there's a yellow stripe painted along the walls. The uniforms are dark blue, the grass is a dun tan, faces are black except for the occasional albino. The pigment of their washed-out eyes is damaged by the sun.

The black and white blind, in their blue uniforms, chatter into a lunch of brown beans and pale-yellow maize, oblivious and excluded from the sight of Africa around them. These children will pass from the junior school to the senior; some will take their Braille cards to university, a few may come back to teach or get work with an NGO. For most, the future doesn't look hopeful; it doesn't look like anything.

Africa is a hard enough place if you have all your faculties, but as the extended family, which has always been the continent's social services net, frays and unravels, these children have fallen through the holes. A few still have the love and security to go home to in the holidays, but most are left here, orphaned by their disability, their families too far away, unwilling or unable to support them. Illness and injury are never simply medical problems in Africa; there is always a metaphysical dimension of witchcraft and spells, the signs of wickedness and evil intent. These children struggle not only with their personal darkness, but with the black sightless superstition of their culture that has them doubly cursed.

The smallest children, merely four or five years old, have their lunch in the kindergarten, and like mice in calico frocks they hold hands and take each other for their nap. Outside, under a mango tree, a class of the blind and subnormal, the brain-damaged, congenitally short-changed, genetically deprived, oxygen-starved, love-starved children sit in the grass peacefully rocking or playing games with their fingers.

The little girl who came up and said hello to me stands up, announces her name and says she wants to sing us a song. 'Lazy Mary it's time to get up, time to get up; Lazy Mary it's half past six in the morning.' I walk through the boys' silent, empty, motherless dormitory. Rickety-iron bunks, blankets worn thin. Every child has a battered tin trunk, but there's nothing else. No chairs or desks or wardrobes, nothing on the walls, no photographs of Mum or Dad or siblings or ponies, no 'miss you' birthday cards, no football boots, no toys, nothing personal, nothing private, nothing individual, nothing that's soft to touch or comfort, nothing to cuddle, no ragged bears from home. Nothing to say that they ever existed in this bright-sighted world at all.

The Kikuyu Hospital in Nairobi is a bats' cave for blindness. The short-sighted, the glazed, the faded-eyed, those caught by sticks and stones, with sores and pustules, with scars and cuts, from all over East Africa, are brought by their daughters, mothers, grandchildren and sisters. By 9 a.m. the queue of fading light is hours long; so much of African life is eked out waiting, sitting on hard places in pain, exhausted, holding down the fear with a God-like stoicism and shy good manners.

Joyce has walked 300 miles from her remote village, led here by her daughter. By African standards she's old: that's to say over here she'd be in her early middle age, her prime. By anyone's standards she's poor and painfully thin, hugging a grubby blanket round her bony shoulders. She lost her left eye years ago to a blow, a thorn, a fall, any of the many accidents of the bush. Now her right eye is clouded by a cataract. The blinds have been drawn down. She's given an injection behind her good eye, a local anaesthetic. Then a rubber ball, a dog's ball, is pressed over the socket with an alice band. This is not high-tech medicine. She's wheeled into an operating theatre, only an operating theatre because it's a room with scalpels.

I take off my shoes, put on a mask and stand beside one of the three tables that have patients with sheets on their heads and a small square cut in the middle where the spot-lit eye stares through, held open by metal clips in an expression of silent horror. It's unnerving to stare back into the bloodshot, liver-yellow, dark, sightless eyes.

The cataract operations are being done by nurses who have been trained to do this particular surgical procedure. With a small scalpel they slice through the top of the iris, with a saline solution and with the tiny knife and tweezers worry out the cataract like extracting a miniature oyster. The nurse holds it up on the tip of his blade so I can see, then he takes a new plastic lens and slips it into Joyce's eye. He picks up a needle with tweezers, and with a thread thinner than a human hair he puts in one stitch. Then he tapes a bandage over her eye, and she's done. Tomorrow she'll see again. See her grinning daughter and the brisk, concerned doctor, and she'll see the 300 miles of road home. What she won't be able to see is the money to pay for her headful of light. The Kikuyu Hospital charges for its treatment. If a patient has a treatable condition but can't pay, they do it anyway and ask you to help. One hundred staff see 80,000 patients a year, and they're always 30 per cent in the red. 'Isn't this miraculous,' a public-relations girl whispers. No it's not. It's medicine. This is no divine intervention, it's very simple. These nurses do up to sixteen cataract operations a day and they're incredibly good at it.

The quality of care here is equivalent to Harley Street or New York; that's not according to me or them, but visiting eye surgeons from Harley Street and New York. And so it should be. What is standard practice in London shouldn't be proof of the mysterious ways of an omnipotent Creator in Nairobi. This is how it works: £17 gives someone back their eyes, gives them their children back, their home, gives them back their work, their usefulness, their dignity.

There are no more instances of cataracts in Africa than in Europe. You just notice them here because you can see more of them, and more of them can't see you. So much goes untreated, so much blindness is either preventable or treatable, and none of it is that complicated or that expensive. Trachoma, for instance, an infection that can affect anyone, but usually children. It comes from getting dirt in your eye and rubbing it. Over time it inverts the eyelid and the eyelashes scrape and score the eyeball until it's useless and opaque. It's said to be one of the most painful conditions imaginable and it's preventable merely with education and hygiene. And it's curable with a dab of ointment or a pill. It doesn't cost a fortune, it doesn't even cost pocket money. River blindness, caused by a parasite from lakes and rivers, was once endemic in West Africa; it's now rare and could be eliminated altogether. Abuja, the new capital of Nigeria, is built on land that was left uninhabited because of river blindness. Now there's a city there, curing and preventing. Curing blindness in Africa is doable and affordable, and it's straightforward. You pay, they see.

The bush on the edge of the Greater Masai Mara game reserve that crosses the border into Tanzania's Serengeti is a crumpled red landscape of akasha, thorns, termite hills and dry ravines. This land is dotted with Masai homesteads, wattle-and-daub huts behind thorn palisades. Water comes from boreholes just under four miles away, women make the journey every two days, the lucky ones have a donkey; either way, there's not a lot left over for washing.

Small, muddy children with snot-caked faces regard us with wariness. The herds of goats and skinny cows are guarded by small boys and rangy dogs. I've been brought here by the local medical taskforce, who are searching for patients.

Many of these people are fearful of Western medicine and hospitals: the grip of superstition, spells and witch doctors on rural Africa is a real medical curse. The nurse who works out here wears thick glasses, he's Masai himself and was once treated for deteriorating eyes, and then became a qualified paramedic. He leads us to a tiny hut. Stooping low, I crawl into the almost pitch-black room full of stinging acrid smoke. Squatting down, I finally make out a pair of figures. An old woman, hopelessly blinded by glaucoma, and her daughter sit together. The girl's life is devoted to leading her mother around the small world. Blindness in Africa invariably makes invalids of two people.

The old lady is led out into the day and stands, eyes wide, gasping for the light. In the thorn trees, white-browed weavers twitter and fluster like hysterical interior decorators; grey louries feed on berries, hornbills saunter, glossy starlings pick at insects in the dung and iridescent lilac-breasted rollers flash past like strobing neon. A straight and beautiful young Masai woman, decorated in beads and wearing a toga, walks through the thorn fence. She smiles and speaks quietly to the paramedic.

Gently, she lifts her child. He's six months old and hungry. Esther has walked nineteen miles because she heard the doctors might be here today. She thinks something's wrong with Nayianoi's eyes. She's noticed he seems to want to follow the light, and as she knows other people who have been treated and seen their recoveries, she trusts the hospital and the nurses to look at him.

A quick examination shows that the lad has a congenital cataract. He's technically blind. But an operation will fix it. Children have to be treated early: if they don't see by the time they're seven, they never will; the brain never develops the ability to decode light, but this one will be fine. He won't end up in a Salvation Army bunk: £17 will do it.

Esther sits under a tree and feeds him, answering my questions. She's twenty-four, this is her third child, the other two are fine thank you. What does she want him to be when he grows up? She grins shyly. A doctor.

November 2006

Ghana

Ghana, in 1974, was the last place in the world to change from driving on the left to driving on the right. Not many people know that, including a worrying number of Ghanaian lorry drivers. The capital, Accra, sits on the Gulf of Guinea, in the great indented bay in which, a month of ages ago, the corresponding lump of Brazil would have fitted. That was before South America drifted off to make a new world. It was from this fetid coast that the fortified trading posts were built by entrepreneurial Europeans to transport slaves to those Americas.

This year, as Liverpool and Bristol and Westminster celebrate the bicentenary of the abolition of the slave trade and Tony Blair, self-proclaimed champion of Africa, is, as I write, lighting up the Dark Continent with his smile of sincere concern, the only people who did find the humility and bravery to say sorry for slavery were, oddly enough, Ghanaians. The chief of the Ashanti, the largest and toughest of the tribes here, apologised to his neighbours for capturing their ancestors and flogging them to the sickly white ghost people for guns, smoke and mirrors.

Ghana isn't celebrating the abolition of the slave trade. Why would it? But it is throwing a bit of a party. The capital is full of banners and flags. There are commemorative baseball caps and T-shirts. Ghana is fifty years old. In 1957, whichever royal was available and expendable put on a white suit and a hat with feathers and pulled down the

Union Jack, while the band of the sweaty Royal Marines played 'God Save the Queen' for the last time and 'God Bless Our Homeland Ghana' for the first. This was the beginning of a self-determined, post-colonial Africa, for better and for worse.

In the last blink of a half-century, Ghana has stumbled, tripped and learnt to walk the walk as a functioning country, not simply by the pitiful standards of Africa but with the qualifications and caveats that apply to all nations. Never forget, it took Britain 900 years to get to the position that Ghana has achieved in fifty.

Ghanaians swapped sides of the road so that they could coincide rather than collide with the driving of their neighbours. You look at them and you realise what a bastion of hope, probity and diligence Ghana is: Togo, the benighted ex-German colony; Burkina Faso, which was once Upper Volta and whose name means 'country of honest men', more a mission statement than a nation; and Côte d'Ivoire, effectively cut in half by a vicious, miserable, circular civil war. Ghana stands as a model country, its tribalism no worse than English, Scotch and Welsh teasing, its corruption manageable. It has gold and diamonds, though not the bloody ones that interest Leonardo DiCaprio and Damien Hirst. Here they are all lucrative and industrial. The climate is hot and humid, the rainfall high and everything you plant grows. Stand too long on a wooden leg and you'll get acorns.

It's also one of the most popular countries of Africa. Ghanaians are famously loud and funny and gregarious. There is none of the cultural cringe or resentment you find in many poorer, badly done-by countries. But, perhaps most importantly, it's a nation of very strong women: matriarchal, imposing of breast and bum, girt in fabulous robes and headdresses. Girls here have a nation of brilliant role models, from the women who sell dried fish in the markets to Cabinet ministers. Ghana is the only African country to have a law specifically to protect women from domestic violence. If anywhere is an advertisement for the benefits of emancipation, Ghana is.

The heat and the humidity also make this one of the most lethal places for humans, an Eden for infectious diseases, microbes, flies, ticks, worms, parasites and fungi. In the eighteenth century it was a certain death sentence for Europeans who stayed too long. Malaria, cholera, meningitis, yellow fever, sleeping sickness, blackwater fever and many more filthy conditions carried their greedy souls away by the armful. The average life expectancy of a white administrator was no more than six months. If they survived that, the quinine probably rotted their livers.

I've come to look at one plight in particular: river blindness, a chronic condition that potentially affects 125 million people. Eighteen million are believed to be infected, mainly in Africa. So we travelled out of Accra into the rural eastern province to trundle down burnt red-dirt roads through the thick bush. Here, in between the jungle trees, there are stands of maize and orange, cassava, yam, plantain, mangoes, palm oil and cocoa bushes. The cultivation and the jungle run into each other, not like the patchwork of European fields, but more like a tie-dye. At the end of a rutted road over a rickety log bridge we stop and walk through the still, dappled forest. There is a bright clearing and a village of rough, wattle-and-daub huts that sprawl with little gardens and corrals for pigs. Goats and their kids chew flip-flops and pant in the shade of thorn trees. Chickens scratch the undergrowth, ducks sit in tin bowls of muddy water, dust-coloured dogs roll in the earth like discarded welcome mats. Overhead, the spectacular acacia flowers are brilliant-red, and the weaver birds conduct their hysterical social lives in the wild fig.

Ghana is one of the world's biggest exporters of cocoa. The village smells deliciously like a warm tin of Quality Street. That and goat. Under the shade of a propitious almond tree the people have gathered to listen to a district health worker, a determined woman on a crutch. She explains to them the treatment for river blindness. They listen with good nature and less-than-rapt attention.

Onchocerciasis is the doctor's name for river blindness; oncho is what the nurses call it. It is a parasitic condition delivered by the tiny black simulium fly that breeds in fast-flowing rivers. The flies feed off blood like the tsetse fly and the malarial mosquito, both of which are in the infectious queue here. They pass on a parasitic worm that grows and grows and then breeds other worms under the skin. Over years, the parasite will spread through the body, ending up in the penthouse of your eyes, where it causes blindness. With an optician's magnifying lens, you can actually see the worms wriggling in the back of the sightless eye.

The blindness is incurable, but it's not the only symptom. The worms itch. They wriggle and wriggle and itch and itch with a relentless, agonising, unscratchable itchiness. They itch all day, they itch every day, they itch for ever and they leave scars and they stunt the growth of children and they facilitate cancer. Oncho has blinded entire communities here. They used to find villages with nobody over the age of thirty who could see. They lived lives in opaque blackness, with children leading them like cattle on the end of sticks, who in turn waited for their light to dim and go out, to be left in the dark with the unbearable scratching and the wriggling worms. Whole areas of country have, in the past, been abandoned. Villages collapsed back into rainforest. The problem was colonially treated by liberal doses of DDT (the only liberal thing about colonialism). This worked, up to a point. But the cure brought as many problems as the disease.

Today the progression of oncho is treatable. There is a tablet. Simple. Mectizan. The fly isn't born with the parasite. It has to catch it from a human. People are the carriers of the disease, not flies, so you treat people. Mectizan prevents the big worms from breeding, so it's a prophylactic. If you have them already it stops them spreading and saves your sight. The parasites live for up to eleven years. Keep taking the tablets, they'll die childless.

River blindness can only be eradicated if you treat everyone in an affected community and you have to treat them for years, which is why the nurses here are telling the village again why this is all so important. Children come up to be measured against a pole. The dose you're given depends on your height. They take sips of water from their mothers and swallow operatically. The village headman and the elders sit and banter on plastic chairs, casting fond, watery eyes over fat, glossy babies. Everybody is going to get their eyes tested. They're going to make a day of it.

There's a rather clever board for those who can't read. The letter E is written the right way, facing left, on its back, and facing down.

The patients just point which way the decreasing-sized characters are facing.

I slide off to look over the rest of the village. The school sits in beds of marigolds, the blackboards have quotes from the Bible and a drawing of a teacher. Everything dozes in the morning sun. There are few places as welcoming and as deeply pleasurable as a well-fed African village that isn't expecting the Janjaweed or a platoon of child soldiers to turn up. Ghana is stable and safe. It has the rarest and most precious commodity in a continent rich and benighted by commodities: a rough optimism. Sitting in the shade, watching the children spin hoops and strip inner tubes for catapults, listening to the doves in the mango trees, is simply bliss. Wherever you're from, it feels like coming home.

Back with the medical officer, I ask if perhaps I could see someone who actually has river blindness. It would help with the story. 'Yes, of course,' she says. They ask the headman. He asks a group of women. They go off and, in a couple of moments, we're taken to see a man sitting outside his house. He's middle-aged, although it's very difficult to tell how old anyone is here. The humidity and the palm oil give them fantastic, smooth and glossy skin. He is almost completely blind. The nurse examines him. One eye, she says, he lost by trauma – he got poked by a stick. The other one is a cataract. Oh dear, that's bad luck. I thank him for his time. He stands up and I notice a pendulous, ungainly swaying in his baggy trousers. He has a really eye-watering case of elephantiasis, which has swollen his scrotum to the size of a Friesian's udder, the unluckiest man in the world. The village, of course, thinks he has been cursed.

A toddler clings to his mother's dress. He has an abnormally large head. The district nurse suspects it's hydrocephalus. He needs to go to the local hospital. It's lucky we came. We could take him or arrange for a truck to come back and pick him up. But the mother shakes her head. No, thank you, that won't be necessary. He's being seen by the local witch doctor, who knows how to fix it. 'Are you sure you wouldn't rather go to hospital? This is serious,' says the nurse. 'No, no,' says the mother, 'really, the witch doctor understands. Someone's put a curse on me. It's something I did.' What'll happen to the child? I ask. 'It'll die,' says the nurse, in a voice she wants to be matter-of-fact.

After a pause she says: 'We found a river-blind person for you.' A lady sits on a porch under a drawing of a boy playing football. The nurse examines her rheumy eyes. It's not river blindness. It might have been once, but she went to the witch doctor first. And what did he do? The traditional treatment. That is, to stick a pin through the front of the eyeball and dislodge the lens. Does that work? 'No.' Could it ever possibly work? 'No.' She didn't go blind, she was blinded. The good news is she wants her daughter to take the tablets.

We go to another village, on the way driving through a market town where every other shop seems to implore God for commercial gain: Power from God's Spare Parts, Good Shepherd Credit Union, God Is One Battery Centre, Only God Can Take Care of Me Café (closed). Ghana is going through a fervent religious revival, both Protestant and Islamic, but intertwined with the religion there is a dark, ancient superstition, a fearful belief in the supernatural, which kills as many Africans as all the conditions that nature makes them suffer. The witchcraft mutilates or murders them and the shamans keep the sick from getting treatment in hospitals. Every medical story I've ever written about Africa has been bedevilled by witchcraft. At best, rarely, it's a placebo. More often, it's agonising and worthless. It blames and punishes victims, usually women: they are accused of causing the sickness of their children and the impotence of their husband.

Finally we find someone with river blindness. An ancient lady sits in the shade of the jungle making brooms from fallen palm leaves. She makes one a day, which will earn her a sixteenth of a pound. She doesn't know how old she is, but she must have been middle-aged when Ghana was born.

The absence of more river-blinded Ghanaians could be seen as something of an anticlimax for a story about river blindness in Ghana. But, you know, it isn't, because I was looking for the wrong story, or at least looking for it in the wrong place. The programme of preventive treatment is succeeding. Public medicine like this should ultimately eradicate the disease, and do you know how rare that is, not just to cure an individual, but to cure the planet of something? And do you have any idea how rare that is in Africa?

The cost of administrating the programme is 12p per person per year. That's for one person for one whole year. And that's nothing. The reason it's so nothing is because the drug itself is made and given for free by Merck, one of the biggest multinational pharmaceutical companies. They've been donating it since 1987. Mectizan was actually invented as a veterinary drug, very efficient at worming cattle. Worming cattle, worming Africans. When they found by accident that they had a cure for an illness that 125 million people might get and not a single one of them could pay, Merck did the right thing: they did what you and I would have done, they did the human thing: took some of the pills off the cows and made the eastern province of Ghana a healthier, happier, brighter, less itchy place to live.

June 2007

Madagascar

The high ground glisters and flashes like a pasha's ransom in the clear, shimmering heat; the sun catches the facets of crystal stones and splinters the light. This is all semi-precious rubble. A pixelated goblins' landscape of treasure, a gravel of uncountable finery. Quartz in all its geometric, prismatic brilliance splashes the day with the colours of a rhinestone trousseau; it's like the scorched end of an ancient rainbow. Outcrops of boulders have been worn by the wind to look like the spines of vast, extinct lizards, twisted and knotted into each other, an ossified orgy. Climbing them is difficult. We stumble and scrabble up the knuckle-slicing boulders with diamonds in the soles of our shoes.

This is an astonishing, comparison-defying place, the teasing imitation of unlimited wealth in a land of flawless eighteen-carat poverty. Tough, wiry men walk up these high ridges carrying axes and jemmies to mine amethysts and crystal eggs to sell for a pittance to hippie shops in the West as side-table whatnots and pendants of calm and luck. This place must have the best damn feng shui on the globe.

Beyond the spines of stone, the landscape stretches away into miles and miles of uncompromising plateau, merging into shuffled peaks and ravines like the frown lines on an ancient face. It's inhospitable and magnificent. I squint across into this clear, sharp sunlight and the steadily steepling morning heat and my thoughts turn naturally to Haywards Heath.

The invisible mesh of connections that lace the world are rarely plain, never simple and invariably surprising. Of all the out-of-the-box, broad-brush ideas that launched the millennium, most lasted no longer than the fireworks, but one quietly ambitious wish turned out to be prophetic and has become symbolic of our belated reborn concerns for the fate of the world.

In 2000, Kew Gardens was given a heritage grant to collect and store 10 per cent of the world's seeds, rising to one-third at some time in the future, if the cash keeps coming. The problem is, they're actually going backwards, discovering more new species than they're collecting. It's shaming that so much of the world we're losing is meeting a nameless extinction – so they built a repository in Haywards Heath.

It looks not unlike a Bond villain's lair, but with a gift shop – concrete and glass Nissen huts made to be act-of-man-and-God-resistant. Inside, in quiet laboratories, diligent scientists and voluntary pensioners sift through seeds and test them for fecundity before they're stored in a chilly, dry fertility clinic, prosaically in jam jars. So, do you go off to rainforests and pick up rare seeds and bring them back here, and pensioners give them a wash and a brush, then you put them in a larder? I ask. 'No,' says Paul Smith, head of the Millennium Seed Bank. 'We can't collect from the rainforests because the seeds are wet, and if they dry out they die.' But you can keep them damp, I say, on blotting paper. 'No,' he replies with a measured politeness. 'Because then they germinate.' Ah, right, of course. Why are we going to Madagascar? 'I think I'll leave that to the seed collectors to explain,' he says, with a thin smile.

A man who knows Madagascar well told me that people who've never been to Africa before are blown away by it, and those who know Africa well are poleaxed by it. 'It's not remotely what you think. Forget everything your experience leads you to expect. It is utterly singular – one of one, and ever more will be so.'

Madagascar is the fourth-biggest island in the world, larger than France, larger than California. It sits off the east coast of Africa the other side of the Mozambique Channel. It is also the world's oldest island; its humpy granite and marble backbone was ancient when the parvenu Himalayas were still speed bumps. Five hundred and fifty million years ago, it was at the centre of the supercontinent Gondwana – you can still see where the bump of Brazil once fitted into the Bight of Benin; where India connected with East Africa, and Australia attached to Antarctica to make one vast land mass before tectonic plates pulled the land apart, leaving Madagascar pristine and isolated in the Indian Ocean, free to develop in its own way. Unique is a word that is only memorable for its ubiquity and its grating qualification, but in the competitive geographical table of one-offs, Madagascar stands alone as a nature-made temple to the singular. It is the unique, bumper Christmas assortment of uniqueness. Around 90 per cent of everything that lives here is endemic – it doesn't live anywhere else. Put into context, Britain has between thirty and forty indigenous trees (none of them endemic); Madagascar has at least 4,200. There are almost 12,000 plant species in Madagascar; it's not just peculiar species, it's whole genera. There are eight endemic plant families, eighty different chameleons – half the species in the world – and most of the planet's orchids. It is the only place where you can see lemurs, the gentler, local-greengrocer pre-monkeys of the arboreal canopy who were made extinct everywhere else by the more aggressive out-of-town-hypermarket, shelf-stacker apes.

Madagascar is what's officially known as a biological hotspot, a self-contained reserve of unparalleled natural diversity, value and potential, and also a site of unrequited loss. There are, though, remarkably few indigenous animals. None of the super-mammals from over the channel – no elephants, lions, giraffes, no big carnivores at all, no dogs, no rats, no ungulates or ruminants, no grazers or browsers, no antelopes or sheep or deer, nothing that's poisonous and, remarkably for Africa, very few things that have thorns. It was a place where the gentle greensward needed no deterrent, was born with the upper hand and grew in a bewildering, clamorous profusion and diversity, unrivalled anywhere else in the world. This was five-star plant heaven, a bosky Elysium of exponential geotropic opportunity.

There are ten separate habitats here – from rainforest to arid, spiny forest by way of humid, semi-humid, damp, occasional showers and sunny intervals. For tens of millions of years, green was the only colour to be seen in Madagascar, until the winds and the currents and curiosity introduced a new, non-indigenous ubiquitous species. Man only arrived here a mere 2,000 years ago and really only began to colonise 1,500 years back, so the world's oldest island is the most recently discovered by humans. Mind you, we've made up for lost time. Almost immediately we extinguished a number of lemurs. There used to be one the size of a gorilla, but most likely it was peaceful and foolishly trusting, and there was the mythical roc, the elephant bird, famous in fairy stories, the largest bird ever to peck the earth. Marco Polo claimed to have seen one called the *Aepyornis*, native to Madagascar but now extinct for hundreds of years. It stood ten feet tall and laid the largest eggs that tested the physics of shells: they were thick enough to support their own glutinous content, but also thin enough to allow the chick to tap its way out.

Bizarrely, the men who came here didn't come from Africa. When Africans colonised everywhere else in the world, they missed out Madagascar. The first humans to set foot came the long way round from South East Asia and Indonesia, which is a bit like finding out that the Isle of Wight was populated by Greeks. Later, Bantu people from southern Africa did settle here, making a roughly homogenous, occasionally fractious mix of two continents. There are still straight-haired and curly-haired people.

The seed-hunting team spreads out across the hard ground. They look like ancient hunter-gatherers, keeping within shouting distance on the uneven rock. There are two teams: seed hunters and a mapping team who are compiling the first exhaustively definitive atlas of Madagascar's flora, minutely extrapolated from satellite images and painstakingly verified on the ground. It is a Domesday Book of the vanishing. This sort of eco-geography is the coolest, most compelling pool of green propaganda at the moment. Most ecological information is a great ball of statistics used diagrammatically like a pie crust over the globe. But this is real-time observed, down-to-earth and irrefutable.

Not much is growing up here. There's a small, pretty, yellow flower with a large, knotty root that looks like an elephant's foot and so is called a *Pachypodium*. There's a little herb that smells strongly of sweet turpentine and liquorice and is a distant relative of rosemary. They find an aloe – one of the hundreds of indigenous aloes. One aloe tends to look very much like another, unless you're an aloe detective, which luckily one of the collectors is. He's the author of the definitive guide to Madagascar's aloes, which I badly wanted to be called *Aloe, Aloe, Aloe*. Collecting seeds sounds easy: in fact, it's a Sisyphean pain.

To begin with, they have to be ripe, and only an expert can tell – happily, we have one of them as well. And you have to be passing at just the right time, and then you have to collect 3,000 of them.

Kew is well aware of its plant-napping history: intrepid, bearded men and hearty, deranged women plundering the virgin flora of the southern world, to fill the dank garden centres of Surrey. So this global seed project is only done in conjunction with indigenous botanical gardens, and they share the seeds: 1,500 each. The right to use them for commercial, medicinal purposes or as jewellery rests solely with the country of origin. This is important. There is no hint of pillage. This is about saving the planet, not exploiting it again; 3,000 seeds isn't too bad if it's an orchid, which has hundreds of seeds in each pod, but it's a rupture if they're coconut. In fact, the largest seed in the world is the coco de mer, the nut that was brought back by sailors as a rude joke because it looks like beautiful genitalia and is now endangered.

Under a stunted tree by a river we come upon a gang of fierce men armed with spears. They've lit cooking fires and stabbed the entrails and tripes of a cow on their blades and are hanging them in the flames. They say they're a posse scouting for a larger group of vigilantes who are following; chasing bandits who have stolen the villagers' cattle. They will trail them through the high passes and across the plains, then fight and kill them. They grin and mime the demise of bandits. We wish them well and move on. Banditry is also endemic in Madagascar. Cattle-thieving is a way of life for some tribes, and cows are the only real wealth. They're eaten sparsely and kept for status. They arrived just after man and altered Madagascar's happy, green reverie.

That night we camp in a village. It's safer than being out in the open because bandits may be after cattle, but they're not averse to a little opportunistic robbery of a *vazaha*, the local term for a white man, who might be buying bulk crystals for health spas in Europe.

In general, Madagascar is pretty safe, the Malagasy are pretty friendly, except, as in so much of Africa, when it isn't and when they're not. The next day we drive across the central plateau of the island. This road is one of the country's main arteries. For 500 miles we travel along what is not much more than a dried-up riverbed traversing mountains, curling and twisting back on itself, as if unsure of its own purpose or destination. In parts, drivers and herdsmen have gone off in search of smoother detours, cutting new roads, so the single track splits into three or four lanes, but will amble back together 100 yards or so further down the trail.

We travel in two Land Rovers full of people and kit. The drive takes fifteen hours and we never get above second gear. We pass only one truck and four lunatic Italians on motorbikes. There are villages of three-storey, brick-built houses with thatched roofs and rhythmically contoured steps of paddy with elaborate aqueducts and little canals. The people are dressed in bright nylon blankets, which seem to have come from car-boot sales. They used to wear woven shawls made from the wild silk of rainforest moths, but I expect Chinese nylon is cheaper. Some of the men sport mother-in-law wedding hats. Never having seen them on a mother-in-law, they think they're rather dashing.

Rice is the staple carbohydrate. The Malagasy have to eat it three times a day: at breakfast as a vile, sloppy porridge with shards of meat or fish, for lunch and dinner as a slightly firmer porridge with soggier lumps of meat or fish and chilli salsa that could remove nail varnish. Their capacity to stow rice is prodigious: they even drink the water it's boiled in. Of all the cuisines I've had to endure in Africa, Malagasy is effortlessly the worst. And this is one of the worst car journeys I've been on. It's not improved by the insistent and constant twanging of Malagasy pop music. The driver seems to need it to stay alert.

But we spine-jar and stutter across the roof of the island that is the most fascinating and huge landscape. It slowly curls past as a long, undulating steppe of grassland, with occasional clumps of imported gum and fir trees that have replaced the hillsides of indigenous forest. In the distance there is always a plume of smoke, the bright flickers of scrub fires.

For all the hours we drove, there was a constant warning plume, or leaning column, of mauve smoke – a malevolent marker of plunder and destruction. And then we passed through quarters that were seared charcoal-grey, the aloe scorched, trees blackened as if the flames had been in too much of a hurry to finish the job. The hot air of the car would be tinged with the sharp smell of fetid smoke. There is never anyone with the fires; there is hardly anyone up here at all. The little flames are like questing, grazing animals, the only inhabitants invading refugees; then suddenly we're in the middle of it, the fire dancing down the road, athletic and furious, searching the scrub for food, hissing and snapping, competitively leaping ahead, grabbing mouthfuls of green, belching and farting smoke and smut. A pack of flames: the leaves and branches twist and turn and shrivel.

This whole, huge landscape, the breadth of England, has been made by fire. There is no indigenous grassland in Madagascar; the soil is thin; it's the herdsmen who constantly immolate the earth, to eke out the grazing for the zebu, the hump-backed, pick-axe-horned cattle that are so intrinsic to Malagasy society that our local botanist couldn't believe they weren't indigenous. It is the zebus that have irrevocably eradicated so much of Madagascar's primordial landscape. But the Malagasy themselves seem to have a particular fascination with fires. They don't always light them for pasture; sometimes it's just to see them burn. There is a pyromaniac in all of them. As it gets dark, we come off the plateau and stop at a neon-lit truckers' café. Every lorry is manned by Chinese. Madagascar has huge resources of minerals and metal under its old skin. Until now the lack of infrastructure and the roads have made it uneconomic to mine. That was until China started eating the earth like a ravenous zebu. Now, ironically, it's the mining concessions that are protecting the forests, preventing the Malagasy from torching it.

We come to the western dry forest at Kirindy. To be frank, you need to be something of a specialist to get excited about arid forests in the dry season. It's a grey mess. A pale, dusty, dense confusion of tinder and, if you didn't know any better, you'd think it was dead. We walked through it and listened to the weebling cry of the male cuckoo roller as he called, plaintively, 'Shag me, shag me' to any available female. And then to a gap in the trees, where a clan of red-necked brown lemurs slip across the path.

The seed team find a hibiscus that they need. One of the tree climbers, an agile chap with knotted legs like strings of garlic in support tights, makes like a lemur and shins up the trunk and shakes it. Seeds fall like grey confetti, and we collect them in the twigs while the sweat bees cover us like Highland midges.

I found a beautiful orchid – white, with a delicate yellow centre. It's wild vanilla, but the seeds are unripe. Orchids are named after testicles. If you have a bollock removed, the operation is an orchidectomy. They're elegant, delicate, but somehow ballsy. That night we walk in the silent silver forest. It's an unnerving place. The paths are mottled with inky shadows, some of which turn out to be mouse lemurs. In the flashlight beam, their tiny pinprick eyes pierce the dark. Fifty feet ahead a pair of larger eyes flash in the torchlight, and instead of running in the opposite direction they begin gingerly to approach us. We stand, breathing in shallow, silent gasps. In the forest a night bird calls a shrieked alarm. The animal is about the size of a dog fox, but more lithe and sinuous, more like a big cat or a mongoose. It comes right up to us, right up to my feet, bold with curiosity. A beautiful, otter-like face with the wide, deep, round eyes of a night hunter, a long body and an unfeasibly elegant long tail that twitches warily. This is the fossa, the only carnivorous mammal in Madagascar, indigenous and rare, a night hunter of lemurs and roosting birds. It sniffs with an epicurean delicacy, prowls around us and then saunters off through the forest, the trees' shadows striping its dark fur. It is an indelibly memorable meeting. Apart from having the most extravagant tail of all predators, the fossa is also said to have proportionately the longest penile bone of any mammal. Inside the pitch-black of my mosquito net, I drift to sleep listening to it hunt through the forest floor.

In a clearing there is a grave. A piece of ground the size of a double bed protected by a carved wooden fence. Although Madagascar is mostly Christian, Catholic and Protestant from French colonists and English missionaries, underneath, spiritually, the Malagasy are united by ancestor worship and the cult of ghosts. There are fearsome obligations to the dead. Many tribes exhume, wash or rewrap the dead at regular intervals. There are stories, perhaps apocryphal or legendary, of villagers having ritualistic sex with the dead, and of post-mortem cannibalism. The dead inform and direct the living. The ghostly world exists in parallel with the living one and then there are *fadys*, loosely translated as 'taboos', but both more or less than that. Some are as mild as superstitions; to transgress others can risk death or expulsion. There are *fadys* about the days of the week, colours and food; it's *fady* to hand an egg to someone. It's *fady* for children to mention parts of their father's body, or even to say his name out loud. It's *fady* to place your dung on top of anyone else's dung, so introducing the Malagasy to toilets was tricky. For some, twins are *fady* – one must be killed. The purpose and the value of the zebu is mostly that you take it with you in death. Funeral feasts can involve thousands of cattle and are a big source of collective protein. Zebu aren't just currency and social status, they're spiritual insurance.

Across two rivers, on terrifyingly insecure ferries, we get to the *tsingy*. In a country that runs superlatives ragged, the *tsingy* is a landscape so extreme, so unlikely, it can really only be described with heavy understatement. Soaring out of the jungle are a series of jagged, saw-toothed limestone pinnacles that look like a Gothic cathedral. The cliffs of sculptured stone form deep ravines and gullies, tunnels and caverns. They are virtually impassable except by death-wish climbers. But a couple of years ago a group of French mountaineers made a trail over and through the *tsingy*, bolting foot- and handholds into the rock, stretching hawsers and precipitous rope bridges over ravines.

If you're relatively fit and have comprehensive insurance, you can spend five hours in the intolerable heat traversing this astounding outward-bound adventure park. Being old and frail, fearful of heights, terrified of enclosed places, hysterically insecure and with no natural sense of balance, never having worked out whether I'm left- or right-footed, I loathed every moment, but I'd pay to do it again like a shot.

Scientifically, the *tsingy* is a rare view of comparative evolution. The gullies and ravines, with their spotlit shafts of sunshine that crawl along the walls, have grown to be pristine individual microhabitats. Within yards you can see two examples of flora that have not been in contact with each other for millennia. I traversed a pinnacle, swearing and pleading, and came upon a spindly tree that was blowing smoke from the end of each branch. Clouds of pollen were being puffed into the air. It was like a magic tree from a fairy story. There was no breeze, the air was still. I asked our man from Kew what it could have been. He said he didn't know. Actually, what he said is what all experts say, that he'd have to go and look it up, he wasn't absolutely sure, and had I been drinking enough water?

And then there are the baobabs. Baobabs are the most . . . here we go again . . . singularly bizarre and mesmerising trees in the world. There are eight varieties worldwide, six indigenous to Madagascar. One is shared with southern Africa and one is in Australia, a keepsake from Gondwana. When they burn the forests, baobabs are the only trees that remain, too big for the flames. The Malagasy call baobabs 'queens of the forest', and there is a *fady* protecting them. They stand lonely and magnificent in the blasted landscape. Nobody is sure how they're pollinated – perhaps it's by bats. There is a famous avenue of baobabs stretching along a dusty road beside a marshy lake full of lilies. It is the march of the baobabs. It's difficult to make something as prosaic as a clump of trees sound exciting, but this is nature's Angkor Wat. This is as impressive, tongue-tying and neck-prickling as any medieval cathedral. There is something melancholy about these great, red sentinels of the rooted world. They stand mute but expressive; they're hollow so nobody knows how old they are. If you need to believe that flora have a spiritual dimension, it's easy to imagine the baobabs have souls. The team from Kew say quietly that they don't find any baobab saplings, they have no children. Baobabs may already be the ghosts of the forest.

Hoarding seeds is one of the oldest instincts of civilisation. In times of fear, seeds are kept as practical talismans, a belief and trust in the future, a prayer that there will be a harvest. If you ask what the seed collection at Haywards Heath is for, they'll tell you airily and a little wistfully that it's insurance. If in the wild a plant fails, becomes critical or ceases to exist, here it is. Its life and fertility are held safe and we can revive them. Except the truth is, we probably can't. If a habitat vanishes with all its innumerable variables and enabling causes, then, with the best will in the world and all the seeds you can fit in your pocket, you can't put it back together. You can't manufacture a rainforest from scratch; the world isn't a herbaceous border. They can replenish and protect, but the seed bank is at best a vegetable catacomb. And it isn't insurance, it's a rebuke, an ark that reminds us of our sins. And although the scientists who run it with such ardour and care talk in the thick, dry Latin of empirical research, that is first and last an emotional endeavour. It is an animistic prayer of hope. A collection of seeds for the future; a hope that this bunker won't be the final harvest. And it isn't the collection that matters so much as the faith of the collectors. The hope against hope that we won't ultimately reap as we have sown.

In nine days in Madagascar, over 2,000 second-gear miles in two Land Rovers, over two rivers, two teams comprising fifteen people collected just seven species of seeds.

November 2007

Return to Haiti

Children's wards in emergency hospitals don't get any easier. Knowing what to expect just makes it worse. But I've learnt not to talk. You just can't trust your voice. And don't let them see you choke. The one thing they really don't need is any more expensively imported Western tears. The tented wards of this make-do hospital are pitched in the courtyard of an old concrete-and-brick one that was untouched by the earthquake, perhaps protected by the little icon of the Virgin Mary. The sick and injured won't go back inside. They're terrified of another shock, of being trapped in their beds under this sorry, suspended, crushing weight. So it hangs empty.

Outside is the Cité Soleil, on the edge of Port-au-Prince, which was, even before the earthquake, the worst place on earth to be a child. This corrugated slum, built of slime and shit, with its open veins of infectious effluent is also, by a fathomless irony, shaken but unshriven by the hand of God. It still sprawls triumphant, in all its malignant, blighted horror.

The maternity tent is a mixed, sweet-and-salt place. Babies are all blessings, tokens of hope, and most mothers lie on their little camp beds, safe for the moment in the bubble of relief and joy that birth brings. But this is no time or place to be an infant or a new mother. Most of these women have lost family, their own mothers, and have no homes to return to. A woman sits, bent and shrouded in misery, on her lap a tiny sprite of a thing, baggy in its own skin. His eyes flutter, head lolls, too heavy for the spindly neck. I've seen this before, this mite, havering in the doorway of life. A doctor whispers that he has hydrocephalus. An hour or so away, in Florida, they'd fit a pipe in his head and drain the liquid. 'But we can't do it here, and, anyway, he'd need regular medical help over years. That isn't available.' His prognosis? The doctor shrugs. The little heart pounds in its chest, the stubborn breath stretches the ribs. Only when it's hopeless, when death waits impatient in the corner for the final count, do you truly comprehend how tenaciously fierce, how brave the imperative mechanics and the vital spark of life are. In the cot next to the dying child is a bright little boy wedged between cushions. He has huge eyes and beams up at me, holding out his arms. 'He likes to be hugged,' says a Belgian logistician. 'He trusts everybody. He was left in a rubbish bin.' A Haitian rubbish bin, a post-apocalyptic cess-skip. He was missing a finger. 'Probably eaten by rats,' which is not as nightmarishly rare as you might think. Rats come in the night and eat toes, fingers, sometimes noses. He is about nine months old.

This isn't a newly unwanted child – not a guilty secret or a family sin. Someone looked after this little lad for as long as they possibly could, and then in the midst of horror, of death and the earth-moving despair, they made him rubbish. He chuckles and stretches his hands out to me, and I know that if I pick him up it will be impossible ever to put him down again. What have you called him, I ask. 'Herod.' Say that again? 'Herod.' You named this child after the man who ordered the murder of the innocents? There is no tragedy so utter that a Belgian, with the best will in the world, can't make worse.

This earthquake was a women's tragedy. It was, of course, a nation's tragedy, but it leant particularly heavily on women. There are no figures, but it seems that more women died than men. It was the time of day, the late afternoon, women were at home cooking, making the children's tea, when the sky fell. In the amputees' wards my rough count finds twice as many women as men, and the hospitals are beginning to see an increase in the number of rape victims. There is a lot of muttered gossip about the vulnerability of girls, their families smashed, orphaned, foisted on neighbours and distant relatives in overcrowded camps, themselves mostly built and maintained by women, who still do all the washing, cleaning and cooking and protect the young. On the benches, women wait to see the doctor. Quiet and serene, they hold each other's hands and mantle wan children with their arms, hard, capable fingers resting in laps, their faces ironed by grief, set with a brutal resolve. There's something else I've seen before that's difficult to explain: there is a terrible, calm beauty in calamity.

I was last in Haiti for its despairing bicentennial in 2004. It was the most frightening place I'd ever been to. I was gassed, shot at, threatened with voodoo zombies; there were bodies in the streets. I watched the army beat up students, and a lad was shot and killed in a gang fight in front of me. The streets were run by trucks of thugs and murderers known as the *chimères*. It's rumoured President Aristide, a one-time Catholic priest, used voodoo practices to hold on to power. The place seethed with fury and lashings of violence. It wasn't anarchy. Anarchy implies a philosophy, a rough purpose. It was a howling chaos. The one belief that united most Haitians was the conviction that the country was, and always had been, cursed. As I left, I thanked God I'd never have to come back to this bleak and benighted place. Be careful what you're grateful for – you may get seconds.

The new airport is a surly chaos of duffel bags and boxes. Most of the people milling helplessly appear to be groups of American fundamentalist Christians. There are a lot of kids on God-sanctioned adventures dressed in African safari gear and T-shirts proclaiming their goodness. They are excited and crass. The other half are Haitians returning home to find family, to pick through rubble, bringing money and blankets and CD players. We were held up on the runway in Miami for three hours; a group of excited Baptists passed huge bags of beef jerky over the heads of the people to whom they were coming to offer holy succour.

The fenced-off airfield is a vast dump of stuff: military tents, warehouses, helicopters and equipment. There are hundreds of charities here, NGOs, international bodies, thousands of workers, volunteers, professionals, some more useful than others. They all need beds, food, water, Western sanitation. The first concern of all these organisations is the health and safety of their members – an enormous amount of the logistics is used to support the purveyors of logistics and the mongers of prayer.

The American Army and the UN police and peacekeepers sit behind their barbed wire, maintaining themselves with a bored, grumpy, fat indolence, occasionally motoring up the road in armoured personnel carriers and mirrored Ray-Bans. They don't go to the plastic and tarpaulin cities if they can help it. And they can help it most of the time.

At first sight, Port-au-Prince looks remarkably as I remember it – even before the disaster it was the crumbliest, most backward and pitiful capital in the Western Hemisphere. As we get into town, I start to notice the collapsed buildings. Tectonic plates are capricious in their choices. Random houses fall in on themselves; their neighbours remain upright. Buildings pushed onto their sides split open to reveal the eerily empty doll's-house rooms of domestic probity. Rubble spews into the street in great emetic mounds. Electric cables swag the traffic, supermarkets, offices, hotels, the presidential palace, cathedrals, all rent and laid low by Haiti's geology. On hillsides, the poorest breeze-block-and-concrete homes have collapsed into forlorn heaps, throwing up pathetically mutilated furniture, ragged, bright clothes, crockery, shoes, shattered ornaments, kitchen utensils, shredded books and fluttering photographs of the dead, all like a bitter harvest of chattels. It looks so insignificant. So undramatic. So bereft of gravitas and dignity – just annoying rubble. The air is hot and heavy with moisture, stiff with the stench of rot and dung, and sometimes you stumble into the sickly-sweet stink that is unforgettably a corpse. The smell of departed souls, the gagging odour of sanctity. Bodies still lie entombed under slabs. Nobody knows how many.

Just to get this straight, lest we forget, this is the greatest, most cataclysmic disaster of the modern era, the worst natural organic event since the demise of Christ. The official death toll is somewhere around 230,000. Local people think it's much higher. If you're into top-ten lists of misery, you might argue that the Asian tsunami was worse, but that was spread over two continents. This happened in the space between London and Brighton in a nation of barely 10 million.

The survivors do their living in the streets. On every piece of flat land there are lean-tos and shacks. The bivouacs of the displaced choke petrol-station forecourts and lay-bys. The parks are like human beehives. Laundry is strung from trees, charcoal fires smoke, pigs and chickens pick through the syrupy rubbish. Ranks of throat-scarring portable loos cling to the outskirts in a vain attempt to stop the shit infecting everything.

As there is no regular or clean water, it has to be brought to the city every day by tanker. Urchins sell small plastic bags of water that tastes of chlorine. This doesn't feel like it's a short flight from Florida, or one half of an island that is a golf-strewn, five-star holiday getaway. Haiti has always seemed more African than Caribbean. It's like Accra or Freetown. Haiti has held on to its slave roots, the dark pride of being the very first black republic. The first black army to defeat a white one since Hannibal. The only non-European army to lay Napoleon low. The French extracted a terrible price for this humiliation. They took Haiti's entire hardwood forest as reparation, which led to the worst soil erosion of any country in the world. Now the main industry is aid, drug- and gun-running and stitching cheap T-shirts.

The first wave of disaster relief has departed, and with it the news crews. I can find only a desk man for AFP diligently trying to rustle up a story a day, and a camera crew from Al Jazeera. Contrarily, and without apparent irony, the preferred story in a natural catastrophe is a good-news one: miraculous rescues and escapes, acts of heroism and bravery, selfless rescue workers from Rotherham, sniffer dogs from Barking, saintly surgeons from Surbiton. As the hope of more wide-eyed victims being plucked from the grave diminishes, as the disaster medics wrap up their kit and go, so too do the twenty-four-hour rolling-news teams. This is very expensive stuff, and nobody has the budget or the audience for the grim, dull depression of resurrection.

The emergency hospitals are no longer dealing with trauma. They have to see to the grind of exacerbated poverty, the infantile diarrhoea, the constant respiratory problems, the infections and sores. In the makeshift hospital run by the Swiss, the most common complaint they're treating is MUPS – medically unexplained physical symptoms. Aka grief. Or the need for a bed. Or the yearning for some attention, or the hope of a pill that might make it all right.

A young doctor, eyes bright with messianic ire, tells me about the initial response to the crisis: 'We are finding people in the shanty slums with the metal armatures, the rods, the broken legs still in place. People holding their medical notes who were treated and dumped.

There is a woman we found living in a plastic-bag tent. She had fourth-stage breast cancer. In the West it would be considered too far gone to operate, but someone flew her to the Dominican Republic, gave her a mastectomy, stitched her with metal staples and somehow brought her back and left her in Port-au-Prince. She has a CD with her medical records. A CD. Her wound is infected – we don't have the equipment to remove the staples. She is still dying. Who could do that? And the people the Americans took away – the ones with crush injuries, the respiratory trauma, who needed breathing tubes. They went to the aircraft carrier. Where is it? Gone. Where are the patients?'

There was so much haphazard, arbitrary emergency medicine, so many children flown around the globe towing film crews. Surgeons and doctors from rich, First World hospitals took pride in giving First World treatment, began long courses of drugs and procedures that nobody can afford, from pharmacies that don't exist. There was an assumption that someone else would arrive in their wake and turn this into a real, functioning country.

There are hundreds and hundreds of amputees. The most common injury among survivors is the guillotining of an arm or a leg, severed by a wall or a ceiling. There are many children without feet or hands. The amputations were done quickly; victims had often been lying for hours or days, crushed. Now that they have to be given prosthetics, the long process of rehabilitation, of exercising atrophied muscles, must start. A lot of stumps were left raw and weak. The victims have to have their legs re-amputated. A woman wails beside a bed, waving her hands, imploring God. Her husband and sons are dead. She is with her daughter, who lost a leg and now must have it cut again. Is there no end to the pain, to the disappointment? She cries hopelessly.

But medicine is no longer the most pressing concern. There is a boiling, unreported problem with logistics. It's getting practical aid to the millions who live under plastic. This is the second wave of the disaster. If they drive a truck full of tents, or buckets, or beans – just about anything – into a refugee camp, there is a riot. The charity workers are bullied and beaten, the goods are fought over, destroyed, stolen, to reappear again on the black market. There is no infrastructure, no order, no way to distribute aid. The government has no power. The NGOs are young volunteers who can't police themselves; the UN and the Americans have no mandate or desire to get physical; and the victims, struggling every day without practical help, grow angrier. They know that huge amounts of money have been given for their relief, they know that third-rate pop stars and reality-show contestants are covering saccharine power ballads for their benefit, that stand-up comedians and over-the-hill soap-opera actors are running marathons on their behalf, but they're not seeing it. What they see are streets jammed with 4×4s in the branded logos of charity, driven by white kids. This is a country that has only ever existed as a kleptocracy – a masterclass in corruption. Everyone knows that the money, the goods must have been stolen by businessmen, by charities, by American Christians, and they're being sold. So people are beginning to take desperate measures – they have started kidnapping white aid workers as a lever to get back what should be theirs. This is also kept unreported.

Médecins Sans Frontières, whom I travelled with, have just had two nurses kidnapped. They were freed after a few days, unharmed. MSF say no ransom was paid – they never pay. The police say someone paid. There are rumours about other NGOs; nobody wants to make this public, but executed bodies have appeared, and it changes the whole shape of the problem – makes everything much, much more fraught, much harder, more cautious, and slower.

The two or three expensive hotels left in the old colonial part of the city are packed. Not with charity workers but born-again baby-nappers and businessmen, here to make an opportunity out of a disaster. There is a good deal of potential – a lot of money to be spent. Sharp-eyed buccaneers sell phone masts and digging equipment. Experts hawk their expertise. T-shirt moguls are in the market for T-shirts.

A half-trashed, ferrety little expat Englishman buttonholes me at a bar. He's selling protection: 'I cover all of Latin America.' He's doing a brisk trade in bodyguards, drivers, kidnap insurance, all the belt-and-braces kit of paranoia. It's expensive, but, he says, charities pay to protect their staff, or, rather, the people who pay charities pay.

It all comes out of the aid budget. He nods at a large and threatening Haitian standing in a corner. 'There's my security. Of course he carries a gun – probably won't need it, but I wouldn't go out after dark without him.' I give the bloke a long look. I wouldn't go out after dark *with* him. 'You should think about it,' he says. 'You're high-profile, work for a rich international company.' Thanks, but I think I'll stick with my tried and tested strategy. 'Oh yeah, what's that?' Hysterical begging and soiling myself.

We drive to the outskirts of the Cité Soleil to deliver tents to a small community. On the way, we pass ghost camps; smart local entrepreneurs put up fake rag towns, like Venus flytraps, to catch unwary charities. There are signs on the road saying simply 'Help'. The distribution has taken days to arrange. The community appointed a leader, a dignified and stalwart woman. There is a list of which families will get tents. The team of MSF workers hold a masterclass in putting them up. The community has spent a couple of days clearing the land; they've organised their own security. It's friendly and jolly, but it's an awful lot of work for a very small distribution. Getting here, we drove up the wrong road and came across a gang from the slum, their faces obscured with scarves and balaclavas. They cut the attitude of hard men the Third World over, and turned us back. They're guarding the city's landfill, a broad plain of smoking detritus, the stuff that has been thrown away a dozen times before it gets here. This is their fiefdom, the last scavengers at the end of a long train of disposable, replaceable Western civilisation, the violent vigilantes of filth. And underneath the smoking, stinking field that is their harvest are bulldozed 100,000 mangled corpses.

Another winning top-ten fact: this is a disaster that, uniquely, cost more than the country is worth. Haiti is technically an insurance write-off. In New York there is a donor conference where they're asking governments, philanthropists and charities to stump up $17 billion. That is 120 per cent of Haiti's value. Bill Clinton said that if the international community put Haiti back to the way it was the day before the earthquake, it would have failed. This is a once-only opportunity to build a whole new country from scratch, perhaps to offer something of the good wishes the new nation should have been given 200 years ago. The big, blue-sky idea is to build a brand-new city. This port is silted up and unusable. For this sort of money they could just abandon Port-au-Prince to the dead, leave its cursed slums to the zombies. But right now, the aid distribution of the tents, the food, the plastic legs is a race against time and the patience of the survivors. The rains are coming. There is the serious threat of mudslides. Nobody knows how the newly fractured geology of the city will behave.

We go to another shanty town built up a precipitous hillside. They call it, with a marvellous irony, Tapis Rouge – the red carpet. In the ruins at the top of the slum, two boys hold a wailing, ecstatic service of mourning in a collapsed house. From up here you can see right across the city to the sea. The main street slaloms away with rills of red, foaming water, like pale blood. The first thunderstorm of the year has just passed. Everything gleams, the streets are full of people, vivid and energetic. Children shout and jump ropes, kick balls and fly tiny tissue kites. Neighbours sit on boxes, chat and listen to radios. 'Hey, *Blanc*,' the girls shout, '*bonjour, Blanc*.' The girls flirt, with hot, teasing energy. They look directly and quizzically deep into your eyes, with a hooded mischief. They flash their teeth and poke the tips of their pink tongues out. The girls, hands on their hips, sashay and shimmy. They do it not for money, nor from desperation, nor really in the expectation of any consummation, but for the quick, intense pleasure of being able to, for the exercise of their power. To feel attractive, not to waste the terrific force of their youth, and for that fleeting thrill that is lifted out of this grief like a little tissue kite. Flirting is sowing a seed of human contact, blowing a kiss to another world, a moment's light optimism, and it's heart-breakingly touching, and funny, and unnerving.

We slip down the hill in *a cappella* clucking of sucked teeth, clicked fingers, skipping songs and laughter. At the side of the muddy track, wet children sell mud cakes, smooth, round biscuits made of water and soil and a little fat, baked in the sun. They are eaten by the starving: fill your mouth with earth, your stomach with the grave. I have never seen these anywhere else in the world. Mud cakes are a Haitian speciality.

We're here to see the slum's headman, to organise the giving of survival packs – a basic starter box of life: a tarpaulin, a bucket, soap, water-purifying pills, sanitary towels, nappies and some food. We find him in a lean-to, sitting behind a desk, flanked by silent muscle and lots of children. There are mobile phones, a telly, a DVD player, a satellite decoder. He is instantly recognisable – it's the black Tony Soprano surrounded by the trappings of his power. He's amused and friendly, with an edge of smiling psycho-menace. With an air of a man who's rarely been told 'no', he tries to make these negotiations for aid sound as if they were organised by him on behalf of his people. The MSF negotiators are firm and poker-faced. He does what bullies do: he pats children and makes light of the things he can't get. His lieutenants look stony. The children weave between their legs like cats. They're all aware that disasters like this only happen once in a millennium. This is an opportunity – they're strung and tense, waiting to catch the wave.

We leave and I ask why they're doing business with the gangs, these malevolent bloodsuckers who've blighted Haiti since the Tonton Macoutes, who make the poor poorer and a lot of them dead. 'At the moment, these are the only people who can guarantee the security of a distribution.' But they'll give it to their cronies, sell it, use it as leverage. 'We hope not. We will do what we can, but it's more important to get this stuff into the community until we can deliver so much it loses its value.' These are the hard truths of charity.

The late-afternoon light is soft and warm. The distant sea shimmers like lamé. The slum could almost be homely, lounging in the silky red earth. On the crowded street a teenage girl bathes from a bucket; naked to the waist, she's skinny as a whip, glossy with bubbles, and gasps with a flashing white smile, her hands held in a simple, supplicant blessing as her mother pours water over her back. It is a small baptism – washing away the cruel earth, the dust of death and grief, the loss, washing away the past, leaving a laughing girl bathed in the shining, golden light.

April 2010

Creation Museum

It's not in the nature of stoic Cincinnatians to boast, which is fortunate, really, for they have meagre pickings to boast about. They could, though, if they were the bragging sort, brag about a quaint old optician's shop that will make you a new pair of spectacles in an hour – by chance I am both short-sighted and had an hour to spare. As the nice lady gave my new lenses a polish, I asked her if she thought the eye was such a complicated and mysterious structure that it could have been created only in one inspired, far-sighted moment by God and not by the blind trial and error of natural selection. 'That kind of makes sense,' she smiled. But then, Galileo invented a refracting telescope and the Church locked him up for pointing out that, as he learnt by observing the rest of the solar system, the earth isn't the centre of the universe. Do you think that glasses might be the work of the devil? She smiled again. 'Would you like a hard or a soft case with that, sir?'

Perhaps the biggest thing the citizens of the 'Queen of the West' have to tell a tall tale about is the Creation Museum. Twenty minutes outside of town, just over the Kentucky border, it was placed here with prayerful care to be accessible and available to the greatest number of American pilgrims coming by road, presumably in surreys with fringes on top. Build it and they will come. November was the 150th anniversary of the publication of Charles Darwin's *On the Origin of Species* – last February the 200th anniversary of the birth of its author – so now seems like a good time to see what the world looks like without the benefit of science. Or spectacles. Although both these anniversaries appeared to pass without ever troubling most Americans – there were precious few commemorations, TV specials, or pop-up books – it's not that they don't care about where they came from; it's that our collective origin is a trip-wire issue, a knuckle-dragging skeleton in the closet. If you want to get through a class, a dinner, a long-haul flight in peace, it's best not to go there. This is one argument that refuses to evolve.

I took Paul Bettany, the actor who plays Charles Darwin in the film *Creation*, along with me to photograph the museum. He has played crazed and murderous apostates in films the devout ban themselves from seeing – in *Legion*, Bettany stars as the archangel Michael, who defies a vengeful God hell-bent on destroying mankind. He once played a Wimbledon champion. Here in Nowheresville, Kentucky, tennis is considered a game for Europeans and other sexual deviants. I can't imagine what they think of English actors.

Just off a motorway, in a barren and uninspiring piece of scrub, the museum is impressively incongruous, a righteously modernist building resting in landscaped gardens filled with dinosaur topiaries. It cost $27 million and was completed in 2007. It answers the famous question about what God could have done if he had had money. This is it. Oddly, it is a conspicuously and emphatically secular construction. There is no religious symbolism. No crosses. No stained glass. No spiral campanile. It has borrowed the empirical vernacular of the enemy to wrap the literal interpretation of Genesis in the façade of a liberal art gallery or library. It is the Lamb dressed in wolf's clothing.

The next things I noticed were the very illiberally accoutred security guards. They are absurdly over-armed, overdressed and overweight. Perhaps the museum is concerned that armed radical atheists, maddened by the voices of reason in their confused heads, will storm in waving the periodic table, screaming, 'I think, therefore I am!'

The Creation Museum isn't really a museum at all. It's an argument. It's not even an argument. It's the ammunition for an argument. It is the Word made into bullets. An armory of righteous revisionism. This whole building is devoted to the literal veracity of the first eleven chapters of Genesis: God created the world in six days, and the whole thing is no more than 6,000 years old. Everything came at once, so *Tyrannosaurus rex* and Noah shared a cabin. That's an awful lot of explaining to do. This place doesn't just take on evolution – it squares off with geology, anthropology, palaeontology, history, chemistry, astronomy, zoology, biology and good taste. It directly and boldly contradicts most -onomies and all -ologies, including most theology.

We start with the creation of the world, and of light. And there you are, immediately – Houston, we have a problem: you get light three days before you get the sun. But that's fine, we've got an answer: the sun is, in fact, what God made to keep the light in. It was an afterthought, a receptacle born out of necessity.

The early bits, it must be said, are rather boring, like walking past a lot of TVs showing nature programmes, with the gravelly voice from trailers for disaster movies: 'In a time before man . . .'. There's a room that has all the stuff God made on each day; the exhibit looks like holiday photographs or the brochure for an eco-safari. Included with the birds of the air are, apparently, the bats, who are mammals and will be annoyed. But we don't have time to nitpick. What is truly awe-inspiring about the museum is the task it sets itself: to rationalise a story, written 3,000 years ago, without allowing for any metaphoric or symbolic wiggle room. There's no poetic licence. This is a no-parable zone. It starts with the definitive answer, and all the questions have to be made to fit under it. That's tough. Science has it a whole lot easier: it can change things. It can expand and hypothesise and tinker. Scientists have all this cool equipment and stuff. They've got all these 'lenses' and things. They can see shit that's invisible. And they stayed on at school past fourteen. Science has given itself millions of years, aeons, to play with, but the righteous have got to get the whole lot in, home and dry, in less than 6,000 years, using just a pitchfork and a loud voice. It's like playing speed chess against a computer and a thousand people with Nobel Prizes.

But we should cut the creationists a little slack, because every new bit of evidence, every discovery, is a nightmare for them. Take the ark. The big-boat business poses all sorts of questions. But, again, they've got answers. There are models and plans and layouts of the vessel. You can walk through a part of the hull. There's biblical carpentry and weather reports. And the dinosaurs are on board. (They were probably small ones, the museum helpfully adds.) But recently scientists found a new giant rat and a fanged frog in Papua, New Guinea, so now some Noah-ists have to redesign the amphibian quarters. The rats probably sort themselves out. OK, so you get everybody aboard, 10 million creatures, times two, without the neighbours noticing. Where did the water come from? You have to flood the whole world. Did they import water from the Scientologists? No: it came from under ground. There is a great reservoir, presumably for flooding purposes, under our feet. I assume that's where it went back to. Why don't we drill for it to water Phoenix? (By the way, the flood is where we get fossils from. That's all the dead stuff, caught in mud.) When the waters abated, the animals got off, stretched and walked around the world eating one another's children. I'm not making this up. Nobody's making this up. This is what happened.

There is a bit of a sniffy disclaimer between the Flood and the Tower of Babel about Cain's having to have sex with his sister. First of all, there's a statute of limitations on this stuff, and it can be excused on some biblical technicality, and we shouldn't be so prurient as to keep asking about it. The dinosaur thing, though, is a problem. Creationists didn't have to bother about it before the nineteenth century, but nosy, faithless scientists – and Michael Crichton – have made them irrefutable. According to the museum, their extinction was caused by men killing them, possibly for sport. I will later learn that this may have happened in the Middle Ages, when dinosaurs breathed fire and were hunted by knights.

It all gets good when the leading man arrives. Adam comes on looking like the Hispanic bass player for a Janis Joplin back-up band, with a lot of hair and a tan. He looks a bit stoned. As well he might be, because he's all on his own in Eden. Nothing can do him any harm, and he's got the whole pharmacopoeia at arm's reach. And then you get to Eve, a demure, foxy little girl who could be Juliet in a Guatemalan school play. Her long hair is meticulously glued to her pert and perky breasts. Adam has his as yet unnecessary organ of generation decorously concealed behind foliage. There is something wincingly salacious about this bearded hippie and his schoolgirl mate. And he has what looks suspiciously like a belly button.

The most compelling evidence for the ineffably mysterious ways of God are the people who've come here to load up with ammunition for the constant and relentless argument with the free world. Here, it's safe to say, no one is going to get flung into the fiery pit for overdosing on vanity, though they may get done in early for overdosing on carbs. There was an astonishing number of women dressed as if they'd come from the little house on the prairie, in long, floral frontier frocks with bonnets and shawls. Their men are in bibs and braces, with straw hats, authentic pudding-bowl haircuts and Abe Lincoln beards. They stare at this Hispanic Adam with a touching reverence and a vengeful fury. This goddamned – and I use the word advisedly – dark-eyed wetback is the reason for all the sin and evil and communism in the world. If it weren't for him, we'd live for ever. On the other hand, if he'd lived for ever, we wouldn't be here. (Just as an aside, a point of order, wasn't it divinely unfair of God to say, 'If you eat the fruit of the tree of knowledge, I will bring death unto you'? Death is a difficult if not impossible concept to explain to an illiterate man who has never seen anything die. And while we're at it, if God planned on everything living for ever, what was the point of heaven?) 'This is the Garden of Eden,' a man with jelly-mould hair said to his little Tom Sawyer son. 'Really?' replied the lad. 'Really,' said the man.

The Garden of Eden is well worth the trip to Petersburg, Kentucky. Seeing as this museum is in the literal-truth business, this must be the literal Garden of Eden. This is exactly what it looked like. This is no simile, no mock-up, no artist's impression. This is it. And it takes your breath away. Sharing the perfect rest stop with Adam is a whole mess of animals. There's a worried-looking sheep, a fox, a chimp, a wallaby, a bear, a llama, a scarlet ibis, a fallow deer, an ibex, a cougar, a dinosaur and a snake. It could be the diorama in a hunting-goods store. The animals aren't doing much, just hanging out, waiting for something to happen. There's nothing to do. No hunting, no mating, no nesting, no getting better, no getting worse. Just the infinite drip, drip, drip of bliss. Things that weren't in the Garden of Eden at its planting but came later as part of the fruit-knowledge-shame-punishment plea bargain – poison weeds, carnivores, carrion eaters, fear and thorns – are of great concern to creationists. A fossil with thorns is proof that it must have been made after the fall from Eden, because Genesis is quite specific about Eden's being un-sharp and blunt, or, you might say, dull and pointless. I spent a lot of time in the Eden picnic area, trying to wrest some sort of spiritual buzz, a sense of the majesty and the mystery, but it's conspicuously absent. Literally beaten to death. This is *Ripley's Believe It or Not!* It is irredeemably kitsch. In fact, it may be the biggest collection of kitsch in God's entire world. This is the profound represented by the banal, a divine irony. (The penchant for kitsch is something that gay men and born-again Christians share.) This tacky, risible and rational tableau defies belief, beggars faith. Compare it to the creation story in Michelangelo's Sistine Chapel, Masaccio's *Expulsion from Eden*, or any of the thousands of flickering images, icons and installations based on faith rather than literalist realism. It truly makes you wonder: is all this righteous ire, all this money, all this Pentecostal flame-throwing the best they can come up with? This cheap county-fair sideshow – this is their best shot? It may be more replete with proof than a Soviet show trial, but this creation is bereft of any soul.

Back in the entrance lobby, where we get our photographs taken in the Garden of Eden with the dinosaur and the ark (through the scientific miracle of lenses, computers and green screen), one of the security guards smiles brightly at me. It's about the first smile I've seen all day, and its warmth makes me smile back. I notice his embossed badge. His name is Adam.

January 2010

Mozambique

The diving guide got stroked by a Portuguese man-of-war. The passively poisonous and potentially fatal jellyfish traced its long, gossamer tail across his face. The pain must have been unspeakable, but he's tough. When he's not spear-fishing, he takes bow-hunting safaris to skewer buffalo, like Robin Hood in shorts. He dragged himself back on board, hoping the adrenaline and the fear would stave off the anaphylactic shock, screaming for his two Mozambican deckhands.

One of the things that can mitigate the agony of oceanic poison is urine. Piss is the palliative, the guide explained to me as we sat in the long, open lounge at Vamizi Island Lodge, while the full moon shattered in the waves and the waiter uncorked another bottle of Cape wine. 'So I had to wee on myself' – and he did a little mime to show me how, crouching and bending over, apparently trying to kiss his bum goodbye.

I was struck by two thoughts. First, how typical of a white South African to do it the hard way, and not work out that the ergonomically most efficient way to wee on your own face is to lie on your back with your legs in the air and let gravity fix it; and second, what a wonderfully funny, sybaritic and blissful place this was; and that I must go fishing. That's three thoughts.

There is a trick to travelling through Africa. It's not kit, or cash, or pills, or planning. It's all in the expectations. Don't carry any. Leave them behind with the weather. Don't expect to get anywhere at any time. Don't expect to get anywhere specific at all, and you'll be perfectly content in this big beef rib of a continent. My mistake was to imagine I could wrest an extra beach day by flying overnight to Nairobi, rather than taking the daytime flight to Dar es Salaam, thereby adding an unnecessary airport and an extra country to the rickety suspension of probability.

We landed on time, but the connection to Dar, to meet the small plane to Mozambique, wasn't there. Possibly had never been there. I like Nairobi airport. I've spent a lot of time in it, listening to the muffled tannoy announce that yesterday's flight to Kigali has been postponed till tomorrow, that the flight to Bujumbura will now depart at midnight and land at Kisangani instead. It's built in a circle, appropriately, the gates radiating off like the spokes of a flat tyre. There are lots of little tourist shops selling kikois and carved rhinos and safari books with photos that are a whole lot better than yours. There's a mosque with a glass wall and a couple of the faithful wrapped in prayer blankets, fast asleep.

There aren't any seats in this place for the hundreds of stranded would-be passengers who sag and expire on the floor: a marvellous mixture of American students do-gooding for God, Germans wanting to shoot and mount things, adventure trekkers with rucksacks bigger than five-year-olds, and grounded African high-flyers clutching their NGO conference bags advertising sleeping sickness, glaucoma, Aids and illiteracy.

All the ills of Africa can be seen in complementary laptop cases and T-shirts in Nairobi airport. And the poorer the passenger, the better-dressed they'll be. Europeans on ten-grand adventures look like khaki washing baskets. The children of subsistence herdsmen wear neat suits and ironed shirts, with their hair combed and plaited. It is a lesson in expectation. I could spend all day watching the Europeans perspiring into their expensive great expectations and dumping their tempers on the faces of Africans, who absorb white fury and moneyed entitlement the way Africa absorbs good intentions and aid without any perceptible improvement in circumstances.

By the time a plane was found with both engines working and a confident pilot, it was already evening in Dar es Salaam, too late for the connection to Mozambique, but just in time for the rush hour. Dar es Salaam is not a memorably beautiful city, but it is a busy one. It's the main port not just for Tanzania, but for a handful of landlocked countries, and it has a road system designed for three donkeys and an Austin-Healey. The roads are like horizontal rock-climbing, and twice a day it all comes to a heaving, belching stop for three hours. The government thought about fixing it, then decided it would be easier simply to move the capital to Dodoma. Nobody knows where that is, so nobody goes there, and the streets are presumably blissfully empty.

Dar's choked pavements are lined with thousands and thousands of workers who wait, with limited expectations, for hours and hours, for the crawling sardine buses to take them to shanty suburbs. Then again, if we hadn't had a forced night in Dar, we would never have discovered the Oyster Bay Hotel: startlingly elegant and comfortable, with sophisticated food, expansive rooms and a pool. The perfect place to stop after travelling through the Serengeti or the Selous before the flight back to Europe.

The next evening, we boarded a Cessna Caravan – the Airbus of Africa – to Mozambique and the island of Vamizi, set in the Quirimbas archipelago, a chain of thirty-two islands that arc into the Indian Ocean. These coral plinths were once home to slavers and smugglers. They just make it to the surface of the deep Indian Ocean. Flying over them, you see the characteristic pale, eau-de-nil sea, like a startled iris dropped into the saturated viridian of the deep water. The Indian Ocean coast of Africa is one of the least exploited and most beautiful stretches of beach in the world.

Vamizi Island is a pearl in a thousand miles of crushed shell. Those who wear rubber and walk backwards in flippers say the archipelago is one of the top-ten diving sites. Personally, I get claustrophobic in a bath cap and only fill the sink halfway. Vamizi Island is as remote as you could wish a beach holiday to be. You can see that as either good or bad. For me, it's perfect. I like the slobby, faux adventure of getting here, and when you arrive, they lay before you the great invisible magic carpet, the oxymoron of the travel brochure: barefoot luxury. This island is a nature reserve, the whole deal is low-impact and pale-greenish. The island has no fresh water, so no mosquitoes, but the local villagers have to import theirs daily by dhow. The hotel desalinates. Everything you eat has to be flown from South Africa, the shopping ordered three months in advance. That there is anything on the table is an African miracle. Lunch is made with panache and occasional brilliance, and there's plenty of fish. But this is not the marble-and-gold-tap opulence of Mauritius.

The things that are here are ideal: the wooden and woven suites of rooms are self-contained and spread so far apart you can't even hear the honeymoon couple. They have what you want – airy verandas, huge beds, generous showers and a fridge – and they don't have the stuff I can happily holiday without: telephones, televisions, Wi-Fi, room service. You're on your own with the sea and the masked weaver-birds, which construct their beautiful nests in the fringe of thatch, like speculative starter homes. They look like wickerwork penises and scrotums. The males fuss and flutter, hanging upside down on the grassy bellends to attract picky females, who will occasionally deign to disappear up a urethra and inspect the mod cons.

Travel writers tend to be snooty about beaches and time spent on them: serious travellers are about more than this mindless meandering, the self-basting and novel-skimming. But I think they miss – or aren't open to – the deep therapeutic mystery of beaches, all of which are in most respects the same, and that is rather their point. This one is made of coral and shell, ground by the sea. It never gets too hot to walk on. The water lolls, cool and clear, flashing shoals of fish. The horizon boils clouds that slowly build to great towering nimbi, which pass on to the north. The pleasure of a beach is in being with yourself, at peace, without expectation. Collecting shells is one of the most underrated and pleasing occupations: the beauty and the engineering, the amazing construction, the profligacy of their manufacture.

It is an antidote to incontinent consumption, collecting these handfuls of ingenuity of such metaphysical worth, but free of any value. Walking on a beach is just engaging enough to prevent you obsessing ahead or behind, mulling troubles and worries – but not demanding enough to stop the serendipity of bubbles from the unconscious and the chaos of free association. There is, in the margin of the land, a particular freedom, a specific contentment, a time out of time at the border of the three great elements of the earth: land, sea and air.

My partner, Nicola, loves fishing. Her dad, a great African, taught her to cast a line, so we took a fisherman and his boat into the blue, set the rods with their gaudy, malingering lures and trolled around a submerged volcano, taking it in turns to grab a screaming line. Everything I caught, you could have won throwing darts at a fair. Everything Nicola hauled in was the size of a fat American ten-year-old. I like catching barracuda: they are psycho killers, too hard and cool to put up a fight, daring you to reel them in, but once on deck they go ripper-mental, chewing chunks out of everything, mad eyes sparkling with terminal malevolence. Then Nicola grabbed a rod that was keening line, and for twenty minutes fought a fish that bent the fibreglass as if it were straw. Finally, she landed a giant trevally, one of the finest, toughest, most energetically determined game fish. It was a once-in-a-lifetime fish, a fish to bore dinner tables and send children to sleep, a screensaver fish. And for one beaming moment she held it, then let it slip back over the side.

For me, for us, any day spent in Africa is worth two anywhere else, and a day on an African beach is worth a week.

February 2011

Auckland

My children asked me if Auckland was named after the Orcs because New Zealand is where *Lord of the Rings* comes from. I told them yes. It's more interesting than saying, 'No, actually it's named for a dull, wet town in County Durham famous for bishops' palaces and where Stan Laurel went to school.' You can only know so much in a lifetime, and what you do know should be as amusing and exciting as possible. So Auckland being the ancient seat of slow-witted but single-minded tough bastards with weird facial hair is acceptable. It's a first-date fact. The sort of fact you say on a first date to induce a high-scoring first impression. Mind you, if you're talking about Auckland on a first date, you've got a lot of ground to make up.

You could believe pretty much anything about New Zealand because it's so damn far away. I know that it's not that far if you live on Norfolk Island, and it's only a couple of hours from Melbourne as the kiwi flies. But for the rest of us, everyone else in the world, it is the edge of the habitable globe. (Globes don't technically have edges, but what's technology got to do with New Zealand?) It's a day ahead and a decade behind. You could if you wished believe that New Zealand was the home of flightless parrots and men who share their breath with strangers.

There is something singularly emotional about New Zealand. That sounds like a tautology. Once you've been there, it also sounds right. It is one of that small confederacy of eccentric islands. Places that are shaped by their geography, and have to look inwards for their entertainment and self-confidence. Whose cultural DNA is limited and, after generations of being passed back and forth, has grown strange and exotic. Who could have imagined that New Zealand's twin obsessions would turn out to be rugby and flat white coffee? That sort of inverted diversity only comes from island people. I've always been fantastically drawn to them, coming from a pretty weird island myself. Auckland is a city that lulls you into a smiley sense of numb normalcy, particularly if you come from the UK. You think you know this place. They drive on the left. The street furniture and the architecture and the general timbre of places are familiar, but you soon understand that the bits that you think you know are merely the net curtains veiling a radical singular truth.

The wonderful thing about New Zealanders is that they're such straight-faced, quietly friendly eccentrics. They look familiar, like black and white Scotsmen from the 1950s, but just behind the moustaches and possum-fur beanies they are a free contemporary ballet of thought associations. I sat in a café with a flat white and watched people walk along a street that has an indigenous name like a Welsh telephone directory and that they just call K Street. The folk looked homely, and just as I'd left them back in Dundee, but there was something wrong and it took me a moment before it leapt out and kicked me between the eyes. One in three people wasn't wearing shoes. Not as in wearing sandals or flip-flops or Japanese toe gloves, but barefoot. Men in suits, girls in peasant frocks, schoolchildren, street sweepers were nude from the ankle down. They weren't making a great deal about it, it wasn't a parade or a demo, it wasn't freedom from bunions day, it was just New Zealanders being themselves. And when I pointed this out to a local journalist, she thought I was making it up to be interesting, and then asked if I'd like to see my hotel's pet wetter. It was one of the great sights of the city. A place of pilgrimage and reflection for native and visitor alike.

The wetter turned out to be a glass box with a sorry fern in it. I made polite tourist noises about not having anything quite like this back home, and she rolled her eyes and opened the little trap door behind which was the *weta*, or as we know it, grasshopper. It was a distressingly large grasshopper, as far as grasshoppers go, which isn't far. As a tourist attraction it was pretty tiny, insignificant even, but seeing as we're here, with the indigenous and naturally endangered *weta*, let me pass on the intriguing fact that they come in a variety of flavours: ground *wetas*, tree *wetas*, and I think a fanged, toothed, tusked or clawed *weta*, and possibly a bed *weta*. (That last one is a first-date fact.)

I asked someone whether there was a museum here (there's always a museum), and they said yes, it doubled as a war memorial. Well, if the *weta* was a surprise, the museum was a sit-down-and-check-your-pulse shock. It's vast. It would have been vast in Paris, or Tokyo. In Auckland, it was like the crash-landed mother ship designed by Edwardians, a huge and dignified building draped with the remembrance of Portland stone, incised with the release of the nation's martial splendour and stoically borne mourning. At its gates stood a life-sized replica of the cenotaph in London. The whole thing sat on a hill. Only a very small island would have built this huge memorial. New Zealand sent more soldiers to the Great War per capita than any other nation. This wasn't built out here to impress anyone else; who else was ever going to see it? This was the ark of who they are. It said, 'We are considerable, and we are memorable, and we don't give up our future to death easily; there aren't that many of us.'

The first Auckland Museum was a converted cottage on the outskirts of town. It exhibited wool and it had 700 visitors in the first month. They came to marvel at the variations of wool. Later, it grew to include Maori artefacts, and Gauguin – Paul Gauguin, that Gauguin – came to visit. This is not a first-date fact, this is a real fact. Gauguin did drawings in the museum and incorporated them into his paintings when he went to live in Tahiti. Gauguin is famous in Tahiti, not for being a painter but for being interested in underage girls and introducing the island to a fatal epidemic of syphilis. He was of course an astonishing painter: the bridge over the tricky gap between impressionism and expressionism. But you can't help wondering how he might have ended up if he'd stayed in New Zealand. The history of art would have been very different. I imagine that he would probably have become a barista, and possibly an amateur surfers' tattooist. He'd have met a Chinese girl from Dunedin, who'd have taken him to a sensible Scots doctor, who'd have had his bits and pieces cauterised.

August 2011

The Rohingya

Nabin Shona comes into the small room carrying an air of worn disappointment. She offers me her hand. It is limp and light and dry, like briefly holding an autumn leaf. She's been waiting for over an hour, but in a refugee camp every wait is merely a twig on a tree of waiting. She sits opposite me on a plastic chair and arranges her headscarf. She is dressed with a sober, threadbare modesty and tells me her name and her age: forty-two. She looks older, her eyes are dark rings; in her nose, the tiniest gold stud.

The room is shabby, a clerk's office made of plaited bamboo and corrugated iron. The air holds its breath and hangs like a hot hand towel waiting for the imminent monsoon. A fan creaks in the ceiling, when the emphysemic generator has the energy. I say what I've said many times today. 'All I want to know is what you want to tell me, your story, what happened.' She speaks in a reedy whisper, the translator leans forward: 'They came in the night, the army. They wanted to steal my goat. I was beaten.' I think beaten may cover a more intimately shaming truth. A lot of the women say 'beaten' as if the word tasted of bitter medicine. 'I was taken to the army camp and my legs were trapped between bits of wood.' She calls them *kinda*, a sort of stocks. 'I was seven months pregnant. I had to leave three small children at home by themselves. My husband had already fled to avoid being used as forced labour by the soldiers.' Her legs still hurt. She shows me the scar. When a bribe was paid she came here to the refugee camp. She was eighteen.

Nabin starts to cry, rubbing away the tears, collecting them between her finger and thumb because she doesn't want to leave them to fall alone in this place. She has been here, waiting, for twenty-four years. They took her twelve-year-old daughter to prison for avoiding repatriation. She's had four more children in the camp. She fades to a halt, sagging under the humiliation of her emotion. I ask if there's anything else she'd like to say. She takes a breath and looks up, fierce in her despair, her voice suddenly clear and brittle: 'Why don't they poison all of us? Or drag us into the sea?'

This isn't an exceptional story. I've chosen it because it is so typical, so ordinary, so banal. Kutupalong is a refugee camp in Bangladesh on the Bay of Bengal, one and a quarter miles from the porous and fractious Burmese border. It has been here for more than twenty years; so have many of its inhabitants. The camp hides off the main road in a landscape of neatly square paddy fields, salt pans and fishponds. Officially there are 12,000 refugees here, and a further 18,000 at another camp, Nayapara, about twenty miles away. Unofficially, there are an additional 200,000 unregistered refugees, many living in makeshift shelters that have mushroomed around the two camps.

These refugees are the Rohingya, a poor rural minority from Burma. According to the UN, they are the most persecuted people in the world. Think of that: how pitiful your lot must be to contend for that fathomlessly miserable accolade. They have been systematically preyed upon by the majority Burmese: beaten, raped, murdered, abducted for slavery, their goods looted, their crops and land stolen, they have been hunted by mobs, excluded from all social and political life in a systematic and prolonged campaign of intimidation and vilification that is not simply ignored by their government but actually sanctioned, encouraged and inflamed. The most widespread and heinous abuses are perpetrated by the military and the judiciary. It is, though, pretty much ignored by the rest of us. Not only is this the worst, it is the least-known and -reported pogrom in the world today. Compared to all the other degrading and murderous bullying on earth, this has one startling and contrary ingredient: the Rohingya are Muslim, the Burmese are Buddhist. The gravest, cruellest, state-sponsored persecution of any people anywhere is being practised by pacifist Buddhists on jihadi-mad, sharia-loving Muslims. It doesn't really fit in with the received wisdom of how the world works. The Burmese say the Rohingya are dogs, filth, less than human, that they are too ugly to be Burmese, that they are a stain, a racial insult and that, anyway, they are Bengali – illegally imported coolie immigrants, colonial flotsam.

In the last census, they were not allowed to call themselves Rohingya; only if they admitted to being Bangladeshi could they register as existing. Burma does recognise more than a hundred other cultural, racial and religious minorities, just not the Rohingya.

The truth is that they have lived peaceably and happily alongside Buddhist peasants for hundreds of years. It is said they derive from early Arab traders who converted the locals to Islam before the Mughals ever got to India. They had their own language, they were a part of the ancient Arakan empire and they are very similar to the Bangladeshis along the border because, under the British, the border between India and Burma didn't exist. The current military government, as if wiping dog shit off the sole of its shoe, decreed the Rohingya were no longer Burmese and they were made stateless. Consider that: what that means. You have no rights, no access to law, to education, no healthcare, no protection from the police, the army, the courts, no passport.

Abu Kassim was beaten by soldiers who took his ID card, confiscated his fields and his house and gave them to a Buddhist. He went to the administrator, the magistrate, and asked for fairness. The judge took him by the neck and threw him to the ground and said: 'Your home is in the clouds.' He cries at the memory.

The stateless have no voice, no civil rights at the tap of the computer key, they were made unpersons – vulnerable, despised and loathed; criminals in the only home they'd ever known. Their children are never safe, their daughters are objects of careless lust, husbands and sons are feral beasts of burden. They can't complain to international law, only God listens. It is a humourless mockery to know that, technically, making people stateless is illegal.

Amir Hamja is seventy-seven, an old man with a long beard, a white skullcap, funereal eyes. He remembers colonial Burma. 'Things were better with the British. There was law. When the Japanese came, we Rohingya fought with the British. The Buddhists wanted independence. They thought the Japanese would get it for them.' Amir was beaten and humiliated. Humiliation is a word that comes up repeatedly. For people who have very little, respect and dignity grow as precious possessions. He too begins to cry: 'They humiliated the imams. They made them lie down and the soldiers walked on them. They stripped them and did their washing on their backs. Men were made naked so they said they would be more like humans.' Still, two decades later, this casual theft of dignity is more than he can bear.

Orafa Begum is nineteen. She was born in the camp. She wears the hijab that covers her face. More and more girls are wearing full veils and long black dresses – it isn't their tradition, but fathers are insisting, frightened of the awful humiliation of a molested or raped child – and they are being made to stay in their tiny, dark hovels.

Orafa pulls down her veil so she can speak face to face. She has a beautiful young face with dark eyes. She helps in the school here. She had a brother who died from an eye infection, another brother has an untreated urinary infection, her mother is deaf, her father – an imam – was beaten and is now mentally handicapped. Orafa supports them all. In her beautiful eye, she has a cataract.

The camp itself is a miserable, collapsing, higgledy-piggledy, stinking sty of a place. The huts are tiny, made of mud and blistering corrugated metal with ripped, rotting, plastic-sheet roofs augmented with leaves. Along each of the little alleys that separate the dark huts are deep gutters of sewage, in which chickens and bulbous, mangy, Muscovy ducks dabble for sustenance. Come the monsoon, it will be an impassable mire of filth that seeps into every room, clings to every foot.

There is a problem here with water: there's nothing like enough. The water table is brackish. The women and children spend hours waiting to fill tin gallon-jars around an emetic pump. I crawl in through the hobbit door of a hut that is Stygian-dark, the only light coming from a tiny, low window and the smouldering wood under a clay stove. There is nothing here: a roll of blankets and the dirt floor, a few rags hung from a string slung between nails.

These two rooms, barely the size of a pair of Portaloos, are each home to a family: one of six, the other of four. As a temporary stop it would be vilely uncomfortable, but the families have lived here for more than a decade.

Khalija Khaeun is sixty-five, her face deeply lined under her hijab. 'I have a beautiful daughter; the soldiers came to rape her. My husband died in the military camp, where he was taken to be a slave. He was beaten to death for being too weak to carry bricks. A few months ago, my nephew was hacked to death in Burma. My son was attacked in a bazaar. In my life there is nothing but sorrow and suffering. Even the birds can make a nest. We have nowhere.'

In the rudimentary medical centre I'm shown the birth room: two iron beds with thin, crumbling foam mattresses and a birthing chair with stirrups that looks like a piece of angry feminist art. A baby is born here almost every day; only those who have enough, and can harbour plans for the future, worry about having too many children. To those with nothing, children are the only hope, their only means of production. The Rohingya are making children at a cataclysmic rate.

The children born in these camps don't count as refugees, they are not registered and therefore no provision is made for them. The nurse tells me they have no anaesthetic, no oxygen, no gas. 'What do you do if someone needs a caesarean section?' I ask. 'Well, we have to phone for an ambulance from Chittagong,' she offers hypothetically. 'That would be two hours away on a good day.'

She smiles and takes me to meet the doctor, past a queue of young mothers with their babies. He is an effusive and ebullient man in a jacket and tie. I ask him what his main medical concerns are: some infant diarrhoea, there is a constant fear of polio, meningitis, cholera, but the biggest problem is respiratory disease, he says. 'You know, smoky huts, lots of asthma, bronchitis.' He smells strongly of cigarettes, and the pack that was on the desk when I came in has been surreptitiously hidden. 'You smoke over the mothers and the children.' It comes out as an accusation rather than a question. He grins sheepishly. 'Well, you have to have a little pleasure.'

There is precious little pleasure here for the inmates. There are no amenities for fun, it's too hot to kick a ball or play cricket. Some lads huddle over a home-made board and play a game which is half shove ha'penny, half pool. In a dark room, women who have been raped or abused or divorced press cakes of carbolic soap. They work in silence.

The smell of cleanliness is overwhelming, as is the finger-wagging parable of their dirty humiliation. In another room, young girls sit sewing sanitary pads and pants. There is no childhood to be had here.

I walk past a hut and can hear rote chanting. It is a mud madrasa. The young imam beckons me to come in. Neat lines of tiny children are repeating pages from the Koran. A little girl, about my daughter's age, is bidden to stand and recite. In a sing-song voice, like an echo of distant bells, the Arabic pours out of her, her eyes gaze at something unseeable: it is both gossamer-fragile and profoundly strong. The stream stops, we clap, she stares at the floor and goes back to sit with her friends. My translator says, 'That was the story of Noah, the flood that washes away the wicked world.' Education means everything here; it is the only value that's convertible into a future.

Before I was allowed in to visit this camp I was summoned to the Bangladeshi Foreign Ministry. I sat in an office for fifteen minutes and watched a civil servant in an elaborate sari and coiffured hair with a monochromatically pale face talk on the phone and tap at her computer. 'Sorry,' she says with exaggerated politeness. 'Let me say that you are the first journalist who has been given a visa to visit the camp. This is a test. What happens in the future depends on what you write. You understand our conditions?' I've been told previously I must never refer to the Rohingya as Bangladeshi, that I must only visit the two official camps and not mention any of the unofficial ones, that I must be accompanied at all times by two government officials who will sit in on all interviews. The two minders never appear, I suspect through incompetence rather than second thoughts. However, I am made aware of secret military policemen who shadow our movements and hang around in the crowd listening. 'They are the ones who smile,' says a refugee helpfully.

Official Bangladeshi policy is that the Rohingya are Burmese and Burma's problem, that they should be encouraged to return. Often they are forced back, which international law says is illegal. The camps are kept basic so as to not attract more refugees and because they are sources of irritation and jealousy for the surrounding Bangladeshis, who are not much better off. I have some sympathy for Bangladesh: this is one of the most crowded, beset countries in Asia, it doesn't need an influx of new mouths who will undercut the already barrel-scraping wages that Bangladesh pays. 'It's all Burma, Burma, Burma now,' says the civil servant. 'Everyone in the West wants to do business there. There's so much money to be made in Burma. No one wants to confront them over the Rohingya.'

Abdulla is sixty-eight. He looks stern and angry. He tells me about his son. The tears roll down his face. Nea was eighteen, he spoke English and translated for the UN aid workers. The Bangladeshi police came to the camp to put down a demonstration against forced repatriation and they brought local villagers in to help them. The villagers looted and beat the refugees. Nea was accused of telling the UN what was really going on. He was dragged out into the street and the local peasants stamped him to death.

The unofficial part of the Kutupalong camp, the one I'm not allowed to see, marches right up to the edge of the official one. There is an invisible border; it is the same but worse. There is no rudimentary medicine, insufficient food, no carbolic soap or sanitary pads. The stink is fouler, there is less water, the huts are meaner and filthier, the alleys between them narrower. Only the people are the same: stone-faced, ragged, veiled, xylophone ribs and pot bellies, exhausted by boredom and disappointment, doubly stateless, unregistered, unrecognised, unconcerned, hopeless. It is not difficult to escape the camp. There are no walls and there are Bangladeshi gangmasters who, for a cut, will take them to labouring work in Chittagong, where they are paid half of what the pathetically paid Bangladeshis get. If they're caught by the police they're pushed back across the border. Other gangs promise to take young men to Malaysia, a Muslim country where they can find work. It is a long journey via Thailand. The Thai Navy used to pick up the boats, take them ashore, feed the refugees, give them water, then tow them back out to sea, saying they had done their humanitarian duty. No one knows how many Rohingya drowned. It is probably thousands. Halle Mustafa is seventeen. 'My brother was arrested in the bazaar. We borrowed money to pay the bribe to get him out of prison. He ran away to Malaysia. We haven't heard from him in two years.' My translator whispers he is definitely dead, thrown overboard at sea. It happens to a lot of the boys. Halle sews intricate beadwork. She is the only earner among four sisters and two brothers and is still paying off the ever-steepling debt for the missing brother's freedom. Rohingya are also used as cross-border mules for a drug called *yaba*, a violent, hallucinogenic amphetamine invented by the Nazis that has been growing in popularity in the East for both work and play.

What they haven't done yet, the Rohingya, is fight back, become terrorist suicide bombers or call for jihad. They pray and they hope and not one of them can tell me why the Burmese turned on them with such implacable violence and hostility.

The Rohingya aren't allowed to travel outside of their villages without permission, making them ghettos; they are forbidden further education, there is a curfew and a ban on groups of more than four people, making worship in mosques impossible; there are restrictions on marriage – they must get permission, which can take years – living together without being married is punishable by imprisonment; there are petty laws on things like the cutting of beards and there is a two-child policy that doesn't apply to the Burmese.

And the rest of the world has the historic repetition of turning its back on the problem that isn't loud or gaudy enough, that doesn't fit the current plot or threaten anything we want and is too small, too distant and too awkward to try and fix. It was after the military coup in 1962 that the violence became systematic: bullies bullied frightened peasants who turned on their neighbours and bullied them as catharsis.

Mustafa Shafial was a photographer for the National League for Democracy, Aung San Suu Kyi's father's party. Many Rohingya supported them. Mustafa's business was burnt by police. In desperation she gave her house to a Buddhist neighbour on the understanding that they would give her back half of it when things got better. Aung San Suu Kyi's silence about the persecution and the plight of the Rohingya who supported her vaunted father is deafening, shaming and telling. 'Aung San Suu Kyi has done nothing for us,' says Mustafa. 'Rohingya died for her party, but she can't even recognise us.' Narul Hakim is fifty-five. He spent thirteen years in a Bangladeshi jail, unable to raise the bribe for enough space to lie down: 'We slept squatting in a line of prisoners.' In Burma he was a village headman and he organised a demonstration in the camp against the forced repatriation. The police falsely accused him of the murder of Rohingya who were shot in the riot. He has yet to face more trials. 'Our lives are over. There is nothing for us now. We only fight for our grandchildren, that they can belong somewhere, have a home.'

He takes a little package out of his pocket and says, through tears, 'Look here,' and unfolds a handkerchief. Inside are worn and tattered cards and passes, official letters with inky stamps. They are the remnants of his identity. 'This is me,' he says, offering me the little slips of card and plastic that accredited his existence: that once connected him to hope, to ambition, to a future, just to belonging. 'When I die,' he says, 'someone will have to write a certificate, they will have to say that I was here, that I lived.' Later, in the cool of the golden afternoon, I see him in the camp holding his grandson, a little boy with huge, solemn brown eyes who was born here. Narul hugs him tight and stares at him with a terrible, intense love.

June 2014

Mexico

Border towns all seem to be looking over their shoulders: they have secrets, places to be. This one squats on a river at the edge of Mexico; the main street runs into the scrub on the bank. There is a mural of a grinning coyote chasing a chicken – a dark joke for people who don't have a lot to laugh at. Coyote is the name given to smugglers; chickens are the people they trade in.

It's early, but already the day is hot. On the riverbank there is a smell of charcoal, frying tacos and sweat. Men in dirty vests and shorts struggle to deposit goods onto makeshift jetties, where rafts of planks lashed to inflated inner tubes strain on skinny ropes. The business here is running cornflakes and motorbike parts, ketchup, tampons, probably a few drugs, a little light armament, information, messages of regret, apologies, threats, promises, despairing love and, of course, people.

They smuggle lots and lots of people here. No questions asked, they'll smuggle anyone: me, for instance. For a handful of pesos, a coyote will take me over the border. I've never actually met a people-smuggler before. Mine's briskly friendly, a plump man, benignly Mexican, with a droopy moustache. He doesn't look like a kidnapper, another favoured local profession, but I've never met a kidnapper either. He has hard, hairy hands and a gondolier's boater. The hat may be ironic.

The river, broad and viscous, shimmies and curdles in clay-coloured swirls of sticks and dead stuff. The little barque is precariously unstable. I squat among the boxes of snack food and sanitary ware as we pole out into the current. My smuggler strains and grunts, punting for the further shore as we spin downstream.

A quarter of a mile on, there is a bridge that is the official border. Guards must be able to see us, but are unconcerned. This is not the

Rio Grande, I'm not being smuggled into the United States; we're at the other end of the country, in the southern state of Chiapas, where Mexico meets Guatemala.

The Guatemalan border town is a mirror of the one I've just left. It is perhaps a little seedier, the wailing music a bit louder, with dozens of shops selling charitably cast-off American clothes. After half an hour, I walk back down to the river and find another coyote to smuggle me back to Mexico, this time with a huddle of giggling Guatemalan women, going for a day's duty-free shopping.

The story about Mexico and migrants, as seen from the US, is all about Trump and his wall and wetbacks; but the truth is that the crisis is down here in the heat, unseen, unnoticed. Last year, an estimated 400,000 people came across this border, fleeing the murderous triangle of Honduras, El Salvador and Guatemala. Mexico is a net recipient of refugees, but few outside this unforgiving place know or care that it receives almost the same number of desperate souls who fled Syria for Europe last year. There is nobody here handing out bottled water and fresh fruit, offering festival tents and Instagram selfies with National Theatre actresses.

Licho is a big man who seems to be folded up in a corner of his own body. He has solemn brown eyes, a downturned mouth; I have to lean in to hear him. He works on the illegal dock humping goods, people. Back home in El Salvador, he was a butcher. 'A gunman came and shot my father in front of me. I picked up a machete and killed him.' Why didn't he shoot you? 'No more bullets.'

Licho was eighteen. He went to jail for seven years. 'I'm pleased,' he whispers. Maybe he means proud. 'I paid for my crime. I had to kill for the memory of my father.' He came to Mexico with his wife to escape the inevitable retribution. He has two children. It's hard, he'd like to go back to see his mother. He'd like to be able to teach his son to be a butcher. Mauritzi, a spindly, handsome boy, spends his day neck-deep in the thick river. A human tug, he pulls the rafts to shore for a few coppers. He, too, would like to go home, but can't. His brother was killed because his cousin was in trouble with the gangs. Then they came for him.

The crisis in these three Central American states has been caused by the carcinogenic spread of gang violence. All of them had systemic problems with corruption and coups in the past; but, contrarily, the gang pandemic was inflicted after the political violence was over. Once the Salvadoran Civil War had come to its exhausted end in early 1992, the US government deemed it a good time to return Salvadoran political refugees and criminals, in particular members of gangs – or *maras* – that had taken over areas of Los Angeles. Two gangs in particular: Mara Salvatrucha, also known as MS-13; and Barrio 18, or M-18. The gangs quickly took root in the three capital cities: San Salvador, Guatemala City and Tegucigalpa, the capital of Honduras. They don't deal in drugs in the way that the Colombian or Mexican cartels do. They may sell a little marijuana or cocaine on the street, but mostly make their living from protection, backed by operatic violence that would beggar the imagination of the Mafia. They are constantly at war with each other.

Carlos Umberto, a carpenter, sits in a dingy concrete room with a mattress on the floor, a lavatory in the corner and ragged clothing hanging from a sagging string across the wall. He is here with his wife, Oldin Michele, and two sons. He looks shocked, his face far older than its thirty-eight years. He paid protection – he calls it rent – of $15 a week. It was a lot. Then the gang demanded $50. He sold his tools to pay it. He borrowed more money to buy more tools, and they stole them because he must be rich. Then they demanded his eldest son. He strokes the lad's head. The boy, no more than nine years old, curls next to his father, who says: 'They said they would kill me. They demanded sex from my wife and told her to smuggle drugs into prison inside her.' He blinks back the tears. 'I ran one night. I got the children and my wife, and we left everything. We have nothing.' The boys cling to him with tight, solemn faces.

The cruelty of the *maras* is so terrifying that anyone running from them has the right to claim asylum in another country. These people are the first in the world that the UN has designated as refugees from gang violence. But once across the border river here, they are not safe or secure. They have to register as refugees at an office a couple of days' walk away, and the road has police checks. If they are caught, they will be locked up as illegal immigrants in detention camps. Husbands will be separated from wives, teenage children from their mothers, and there is no hurry to process paperwork. The detention centres are violent and frightening, so most refugees make their way across country as best they can. Chiapas is rural, it's the mango season and the great plantations of trees are heavy with pendulous fruit, picked by teams of wiry men. The land is sparse and dry, dramatically bleached. Above us there is always a spiral of zopilotes, the black vultures whose carousels mark the thermals and corpses – reminders of the constant presence of unlamented death. Chiapas has had its own troubles: this is the home of the Zapatistas, peasant revolutionaries who are in a permanent stand-off with the government. Many of the people are Mayan; there's a lot of army, a lot of police. Everyone is poor. The refugees make their way through this baked, bitter landscape aiming for the very few charity-run safe houses and the railway. The train north is called the Beast.

José and Juana sit in a little courtyard of a safe-enough house with sixteen members of their family. José's face is taut and pale in deep misery. Children go through the motions of play, but quietly, as a comforting memory, or they just sit and stare. Juana, straight-backed, takes a breath to slip into the terrible depths of her story.

Henry Alberto, her eldest boy, went to school and was brilliant, diligent and good. She has his reports, but she can't read them; she is illiterate. Gangs came and told him to join them. He refused. He wanted to carry on going to school, and then to college. He graduated from school. He had his eighteenth birthday, and then they came back for him and killed him: graduation, birthday and funeral all in the same week. Juana dissolves. She sinks under the weight of her story and drowns in tears; her hands reach to touch someone who isn't there. Gaping, salted grief washes over the room. The others drop their heads, turn against the pain. Henry Alberto will for ever be the best of them, the exception, unsullied by experience. He was killed by his friends, boys he'd known all his life. She gets his graduation photo: Henry Alberto, looking like a million school pictures in his borrowed robes with a rolled certificate, smiling, proud, relieved, hopeful. His mother's breath is sodden with mourning. The gangs have a relentless need for children. The attrition rate in their endless turf wars is trench-terrible. Children hold their own and others' lives in such scant regard: the gangs send kids to kill their friends and neighbours to prove loyalty and mettle. If they refuse, their own families are victims of the next child desperate for peer approval and purpose.

Further up the road, now, in the state of Oaxaca. Here is the railway where the Beast rests. It's just a track with dusty boxcars, the rails strike straight ahead into a vanishing point at the foot of shimmering mountains. Horses graze at the weeds between sleepers. This town is featureless, no one stirs, there is no café, no bar, everything is shuttered, dead. There are people here; I can hear muttering, a tinny radio, but nobody is out in the street.

At the edge of the town, there's a Catholic shelter for refugees; a handful of exhausted Salvadorans sit in the shade of a painting of the suffering Jesus. I knock on the door, the panel opens and, behind the grille, there's a bad-tempered face wearing cobble-thick glasses, saying: 'No one is here. The hostel is closed because there is no water.' The man who runs it finally appears. He talks to me guardedly and says that outside of town is one great unmarked grave. There are countless refugees buried there, who were robbed, raped and held for micro-kidnapping, one of the world's fastest-growing illegal businesses. It is done over mobile phones, demanding a wired ransom, usually no more than $1,000. Killing is the simplest option for non-payment.

In Mexico, almost 95 per cent of crimes go uninvestigated, and you are more likely to be banged to rights for a parking offence than to be found guilty of a murder. No one really knows what happens to many of the 400,000 refugees who come here. We do know that 170,000 Central American migrants were detained in Mexico last year, and 134,000 were stopped at the US border. Yet only 3,423 asylum applications were made in Mexico. The police and army are regarded as corrupt and impossible to challenge. Salvadorans mutter that this hostel is not a good place, things happen here, people have vanished. A disproportionate number of refugees are women and children, but many are also gay or transgender.

Alejandra is in a women's refuge. Her exaggerated, theatrical gestures and expressions show a world-weary but amused sadness. She is transgender, has long, thin hair and a fine-boned face, etched by cigarette smoke and moulded by low expectations. She is also missing a number of teeth. Alejandra had the most humiliatingly dangerous job in the world. As a street prostitute in terrifyingly macho San Salvador, she was threatened, spat upon, beaten, abused, raped and robbed. 'The police locked me up in the dark without food or water for fifteen days.' She was the lowest form of human life, with no one and nothing to turn to. She waves a dramatic hand through her hair and grins, in the manner of someone practised at defusing fearful situations with submission. She is here in a refuge with her niece, Gabriela, who also used to be male. (What are the odds?) Alejandra is forty-one. She says what she really wants is to make a wedding dress, one beautiful, beautiful wedding dress. For herself? 'No, no, it will never be for me.'

Gabriela, now nineteen, dressed as a girl and went to school in an act of amazing bravery. 'They beat me like a *piñata*,' she giggles behind her hands, her eyes filling with tears. 'My brother beat and bullied me constantly. I tried to kill myself, then I ran away, here, with my aunt.' She wants to be a cook. They pose for photographs, damaged and lost, but made incandescently beautiful by their survival and self-belief.

William, a farmer of fifty-eight, has been married for forty-three years. His wife was nearly fourteen when they tied the knot. He stands and declaims about the farm he lost. Caught between two gangs, he took a gun into the night and fired and fired and fired until he ran out of bullets. He chants a litany of the things he used to cultivate: cucumbers, parsley, coriander, berries, hens, turkeys. He fled only because he knew his sons wouldn't leave without him. Then his strong voice shreds: 'I am in hell, I want to go home, I know I will die.'

None of the refugees I spoke to said their goal was to get to the United States. Almost all said they would like to go back home, to be safe. There is a passing assumption that most of these people may be refugees when they arrive at the Mexican border, but they'll be economic migrants by the time they reach Texas; that they are on a long conveyor belt, drawn to the land of the free and the fat. Many have relations in America, and certainly they would be safer there than staying here, but the odyssey, with or without coyotes, is still an Everest of hardship and danger, months fraught with anxiety.

I met boys on the road who had lost limbs under the wheels of the Beast, men sent home after years in US internment camps or prisons, who are trying to get back to the States to be reunited with wives and children they haven't seen in months. And MS-13 and M-18 are spreading across the border like an invasive species. You see their tags graffitied across the walls of hostels and phone boxes. They've come to settle scores, to exact their executions. They circle like the vultures.

There is another tale that is the most extraordinary I think I've ever been told: the story of Romero and Rebeca. Romero is a young man, serious and naive, self-effacing to the point of shyness. He grew up in San Salvador; his father died when he was young. He and his elder brother were brought up by their mother. He looked up to his brother, who looked after him until becoming a local gang leader with M-18.

Romero grew friendly with the woman next door, Rebeca, who was older than him, a political activist from a centre-right party. When he was fifteen they began an illicit affair. It wasn't straightforward: Romero is gay, Rebeca is transgender. She was an activist for LGBT rights.

Then M-18 began social cleansing, killing gay and transgender people. Rebeca's boss was uneasy about her sexuality and told her to bind her chest, stop wearing make-up and dress like a man. She refused; the politician sacked her and arranged for the gang to have her cleansed. A man came to her in the night, a man she knew – it is always a man you know – and shot her twice in the stomach, missing her spine by a fraction. She didn't die, but had forty-five stitches.

As soon as Rebeca could walk, she ran.

She told no one, couldn't tell Romero – to protect him, and because it was too sad and for the best. But Romero's brother came and found him, and said he knew he was queer and nobody in their family could be a deviant. The boy who had been his protector and a surrogate father now held a gun to his head. He must leave for ever, never return, 'never see our mother again'. And then he shot him, shot his young brother through the kneecap.

An hour later, their mother returned to find her son bleeding on the floor. He told her that he was gay and heartbroken, that his love had left without a word, and his brother had shot and banished him. His mother said she knew, had always known; she loved her sons, would always love them, but he needed to leave, to flee the country, as his brother would return as good as his word. Imagine, for a moment, being that woman.

Romero fled into the dark, made his way up the most dangerous road in Latin America, to the Mexican border. He found a coyote who would take him across the river. He headed to the little regional town of Tapachula. He begged in a municipal park, police took whatever money he gleaned, local Mexicans beat him up. He slept on a bench and, one morning, he woke and saw a figure – 'a vision'. He shouted. His exact words were: 'Oh my love, my love it's you!' It was Rebeca. She turned and saw him.

I speak to them in the small room that is paid for by the UNHCR, by you. It is their home. She is still an assertive, dynamic, angry activist; committed, protective. He is quiet and demure. They constantly look at each other, as if to confirm the star-crossed truth of their odds-defying presence. They have a mattress, two chairs, a lot of cosmetics, some elaborate scars – and each other.

'Rebeca is your first love, then?' I ask. 'And my last,' he says gently.

June 2016

THE WORLD ON A PLATE

Food in England

When the editor of *Tatler* asked me if I'd like to join the magazine and write celebrity interviews, I wrinkled my nose and said I'd rather not ask impertinent questions of the meritlessly notorious about their underwear.

She in turn raised her eyebrows and asked, what would I like to write, then? I said I couldn't help but notice *Tatler* didn't have a recipe column. 'Most of our readers have no idea where their kitchens are,' she replied tartly. But they took six articles as a novelty test. That was a quarter of a century ago, and proves that I know more about food than journalism. But that absurd request turned out to be the most fortuitous of my career. I've been writing about what and how we eat ever since.

Back then, no one would have predicted that breakfast, lunch, dinner and tea would become the abiding story of the new century. There is not a day when food, or some aspect of it – production, distribution, fashion, medical attributes – isn't in the news.

In retrospect, I couldn't have chosen a better specialisation. Being interested in food in an aesthetic and cultural sense was a slightly odd hobby, the preserve of gentlemen, usually effete gentlemen, who motored to the South of France to buy olives and wine, and had pâté instead of pots of meat. They opened recherché restaurants called Chez Gilbert or Peregrine. And there was Elizabeth David, who wrote about a Narnia-like southern Europe as a personal therapy to her own unhappiness. And then, as a first, chaste offering of food porn for the new middle class, like my parents, she would coyly tell you the addresses of Soho shops that would sell you garlic in a plain brown paper bag and chemists that offered olive oil that might be used for purposes other than the one for which it was designed and sold – which was, of course, peeling out impacted ear wax.

I was from the generation that was born at the end of rationing and to a national board that was grey, meagre, parsimonious, dull and of poor quality. As a nation, we took a contrary pleasure in the grim utility of food. Caring too much about what was on your plate was unseemly, effeminate, French. Food was fuel, not pleasure. Not caring about what it was, as long as it was hot, had got us through the Blitz and won an empire. George Orwell's observation that prep schools expected children to finish dinner as hungry as when they sat down still pertained in certain quarters. There was a polite rule that said never compliment the food or the paintings in someone else's house, the assumption being that they would both be quite adequate. Adequate being what most British food aspired to be.

One consequence of this was that we have inherited a sparse lexicon of words to describe food and eating. In a language that invents descriptive terms with drunken abandon, all food writers suffer from the meagre cupboard of gastronomic terms. The silence of the lamb. Then the few words that we did have were designated as embarrassingly non-U. And one of my first jobs on *Tatler* was to compile a blacklist of socially risible food words – tasty, sumptuous, moist, delicious, mouth-watering.

So how, and more interestingly why, did we get to the table we're at now? From rationing sugar to having Jamie Oliver call for a punitive tax to stop us eating it. Where London is one of the most sophisticated and inventive cities to eat in, unquestionably – unarguably – preferable to Paris. When, twenty years ago, the most famous chefs in Britain were the Roux brothers and Mosimann, and posh cooking was still something that the French, or the French-ish, did, and TV cooks were practical home-economics women and Fanny Cradock or Keith Floyd, a bibulous, outspoken amateur Peter Langan who was a cross between Peter Hitchens and Terry-Thomas. Or the chip-fat-haired Gary Rhodes.

It was an era when canapés were the height of sophistication – how smart to replace the chipolatas on sticks with quail eggs and pastry boats. Only a handful of restaurants would count as destinations. Langan's was the first one that I ever saw paparazzi outside; at the next table were Mick Jagger and Jerry Hall having quail eggs in pastry cases with David Bailey and Marie Helvin. Down in south London, a new chef was starting a home-grown reimagination of our food. Marco was cooking at Harvey's. Beside him were Christian Delteil and Nico Ladenis. In west London, Simon Hopkinson had a tiny restaurant on the Fulham Road and Antony Worrall Thompson was fantastically fashionable with Ménage à Trois, which sold only starters and puddings to Princess Diana. Terence Conran redesigned the way restaurants should look, transforming posh, ducal dining rooms or theatre sets of Italian or French cafés into smart machines for eating and serving food in.

You could measure the time from the 1990s to now by the rise and fall of fashionable ingredients. Where today is the once ubiquitous filo pastry? The never-ending lamb shank followed by the relentless pork belly? When were you last offered a *filet en croûte*? And why can I never get barley risotto? Once, you couldn't escape it. Or salmon? Or avocado and prawn cocktail? Avocado is, interestingly, one of the few ingredients to have migrated from lunch and dinner to breakfast. I remember the first one I ever saw. My mother brought it home, wrapped in tissue paper. We argued about whether to peel or cut. There was the mystery of the huge stone and then that miraculous texture, like vegetable dripping. Where is the French onion soup? Any soup? Or the sticky toffee pudding, which has been relegated to provincial pubs? Fried goose liver with lentils and Sauternes *jus* has been rendered politically incorrect.

Or you could measure the passing years on fashionable vinegars. There was the malt of our grandfathers, replaced with wine vinegar, red then white. And then the fruit vinegars, mostly raspberry. And then there was cider, which was usurped by balsamic, which in turn was supplanted by Japanese rice vinegar. And somewhere in between all that there was a brief, faint summer of verjuice.

The 1990s were also the moment of the mad social torment of the dinner party. Not simply being asked to share a family supper, but a whole new social nightmare of almost unfathomable hospitable anxiety. There were dinner-party advice columns and cookbooks that included napkin-folding and centrepiece-arranging. Whole snugs and offices and spare bedrooms were turned into dining rooms, and small kitchen shops appeared that weren't also hardware stores or the corners of department-store basements. Steel cutlery that wasn't pretending to be silver.

I managed to get disinvited from all dinner parties very early since writing an intemperate article about sending the food back after estimating the expense of being invited to somebody else's dinner. I haven't been asked to a single dinner party in the intervening two decades. The restaurant and Tinder have thankfully rendered obsolete the middle-class mating hell of dinner parties.

Or you could measure the last twenty-five years in cookery books. From Marco Pierre White's *Heat*, Nigella, Jamie Oliver, Simon Hopkinson's roast chicken, hairy ladies and fat bikers, to Fergus Henderson's *Nose to Tail Eating* – probably the most influential cookbook of the century so far. And now there are the bright and cheerful healthy-eating tomes of half a dozen clear-eyed, shiny-haired teenagers with a strict food orthodoxy and a medical condition. You could also measure the time in diets. I started off by interviewing Montignac, who was a weight-loss guru with his book *Dine Out and Lose Weight*. It was very French and encouraged red meat, chocolates and red wine. He died of prostate cancer. And then there was Atkins and all the little Atkins, and the 5:2 and the cabbage diet and the Paleo Diet, and the regular demonising of ingredients and food groups along with the proselytising of other ingredients and food groups. New superfoods arrived like prophets in the desert – pomegranates and apples, beetroot and quinoa, wheatgrass, yoghurt, sprouting seeds, chai, green tea, blueberries, wild rice, kale.

And then there's the equipment that passed through your kitchen without ever breaking a sweat. How many of you still have a chicken brick lurking in the cupboard? Or an asparagus steamer left over from your wedding list? Or the Alessi Lemon Squeezer, or Singing Bird kettle; a melon baller, a pepper grinder with a torch attached (why?) or an electric bottle opener or carving knife? The olive-wood truffle shaver. The spork. All the insecure variations of whizzers and juicers and pulsers and bullets, and now you're just left with your Spiralizer. A social archaeologist could detect the age of your kitchen, and probably your marriage, from the colour of your Le Creuset cookware.

What I can say is that since I've started writing about what to eat, culinary culture has drunk deeply from the bottle marked 'drink me', and has grown and grown and grown. Our interest in food has gone from enthusiastic to obsessive, from grave necessity to the cause and cure of all ailments. It is political and social, it is neurotic and celebratory, the object of snobbery and community.

There is apparently no end to your interest and appetite. The more cookery books you buy, the less you cook. And Brillat-Savarin's much-misquoted observation that 'if you tell me what you eat, I will tell you who you are' is still as true as it ever was, thank God. And it should keep me busy until I eat my lunch through a straw.

September 2015

Motorways

It's all very well you saying that it's better to travel hopefully than to arrive, but let me tell you, it's better to arrive than to travel back from wherever it was you were going to hopefully in the first place. Why does the journey back from holiday take an hour and a half longer than a journey to a holiday? It's just another example of the common man's coarse theory of relativity: E=M25.

Baps week is over for another year, the Ford breeder wagon piled to the gunwales with piscinely unsullied shrimping nets, bits of smelly ectoskeleton, a plaster Cornish pixie and thirty-odd bags of damply decomposing shorts and T-shirts, and two prickly, pink, squirmy children. We waved goodbye; goodbye house, goodbye sea, goodbye sheep, goodbye garage, goodbye hedge, goodbye telegraph pole. No, we can't go back and say goodbye downstairs toilet. No, it won't mind, the garage will tell it you said goodbye. Yes, I promise. Goodbye everyone, see you next year.

Everybody does it differently, but personally I don't like lying to small children. The truth may be unwelcome, but it's easier to remember. So when we get 100 yards down the lane and the first one says are we nearly there yet, I don't say, yes, just round the corner. I say no, we've got 240 miles to go. No, it's not as far as Africa. No, it's further than to Smith's. Yes, further than Smith's and back. Yes, further than Smith's and back twice, hopping. Look, if you ask again in the next 100 miles I'll make you eat your legs. No, 100 miles isn't as far as Golgotha. They slip into silence, that ominous calm before regurgitation.

I must say children are very matter-of-fact about being sick. There's none of that histrionic glottal groaning, that 'Hugh!' and crying that adults go in for. Flora introduced breakfast to the velour upholstery, the map and the plaster pixie with a decorous sigh, and then just sat there blinking. 'How much fudge did you eat for breakfast? As much as Africa or as much as to Smith's and back?'

It's the hottest day of the year. Welcome to that peculiarly English end-of-the-hols smell: new car, sodden towels and fudge puke. The inside of the breeder wagon has turned into the tropical carnivorous plant house at Kew. Time to stop for lunch.

Now, even the directors of motorway service stations would have to agree that there's rarely much between them. They are generally much of a muchness. We stop for a pee and petrol rather than caprice or gastronomic inquiry. This isn't a criticism, I'm a devotee of service stations. I rather love them. I love their Valium brightness, their anonymity, their timeless placelessness. They're on the way somewhere, but they're not anywhere. Service stations are imbued with an unnatural lethargy. You're not supposed to stop on a motorway. Stopping on a motorway is an act of disobedience. The hum of the grey river keeps calling you back.

I'm also riveted by the people you see here. You never see them anywhere else, but they're always here. They make you wonder, has the world been taken over by Venusians in bad latex masks who have learnt human from watching the shopping channel and listening to local-radio traffic reports? There's always a caucus of the Euthanasia Defence League and a covert meeting of the Secret Serial Killers Support Society. And then there's the shop stocked by bizarre impulse, selling sewing kits, fishing anoraks, dried-flower arrangements, soft-porn novels, rude mugs and eighteen sorts of digestive biscuit. And the arcade games. And six styles of lavatory: men, women, women with wheelchairs, men with wheelchairs, men with children, women in wheelchairs with children, disabled Klingons. This Welcome Break was a twilight zone as normal as any, except that in the vestry entrance there was a large mural of a seventeenth-century battle. Usually the artwork in service stations is restricted to a lot of oily prats in goggles playing Toad in Edwardian cars called things such as Ernesto Bresaola in the Ainsley Painsley Grand Tourer, overtaking Major A.N.C. Jockey-Short in the mighty Frumerty Farnsbarns on the infamous Brighton-to-Hove corniche. Herding the children into the restaurant, I suddenly realised where we were, where we really were. Roll music and establishing shot of crashing waves.

In 1685 the Duke of Monmouth, illegitimate son of Charles II and serious Protestant, landed at Lyme Regis... look, you've got to read this bit, it's good for you. He collected a ragbag of low-Church Cornishmen (the Hedgerow Army), had himself proclaimed king at Taunton – not a good place to decide to be king – and marched east to usurp James II's throne. He made it to this service station on the M5, tired and hungry. The pitchfork country boys found a Churchill and the king's army having breakfast and the battle was all over by lunchtime. Monmouth was beheaded and one of the saddest, most shameful episodes in British history took place, the Bloody Assizes. Hanging Judge Jeffreys toured the West Country, stringing up anyone accused of sedition on less evidence than Michael Howard needs to get foreign visitors taken off the guest list at Heathrow.

The Battle of Sedgemoor happened at about this time of year, on a day very like this one. Battlefields are strange, uncomfortable, desperately sad, reverberating places. So tell me, who puts a cafeteria called the Welcome Break next to a battlefield? The dining room here is decorated with photographs of historical re-enactment groups going through the seventeenth-century motions, waggling their authentic sewing skills at each other. Who are these Sealed Nits and why do they always do battles? Why isn't there a society recreating the Jarrow March or the Black Death on bank holidays? The self-service cafeteria is the usual collection of disconnected ingredients. It's almost impossible to put together a coherent meal in one of these places: it's like a mad foodie quiz game. I ate a breakfast of sorts, the Blonde had a secretary's lunch, while the kids ate tea. The quality of the food is surprisingly fair – lots of do-it-yourself fresh fruit salad and wholemeal bread. The coffee is drinkable. My sausage was abysmal, but the fried egg was carefully cooked by a skinny boy on a self-lubricating machine that just did eggs. He broke the yolk at his first attempt and slid it into the bin provided. He smiled and said sorry, he'd try not to do it again, in a soft West Country accent. Through the fat haze I suddenly saw him standing in a makeshift dock apologising to an ulcer-ridden, vindictive judge for his life and his God.

We sat under a framed photocopy of the gazette of the hanged, a litany of earthy West Country names such as Trevillion, Redruth, Fletcher, Smith. Who hangs an executioner's list as decoration in a Welcome Break next to a battlefield? On the wall opposite, the king's standard was crossed with Monmouth's. A plain banner with the unequivocal statement: 'Fear nothing but God', bold in black and white. On a table beside it was a small plastic sign with an equally unequivocal, equally bold 'Nut allergies: some of our products contain nuts.' Another list of names: frangipane tart, paradise slice, battenberg dip, toffee temptation, dutch almond cookie. I stole the sign, it's on my desk now; a little modern memorial, a reminder of how far we've come from fearing God to fearing nuts.

As we left, I looked out past the banners of the battling AA and RAC, cheaper petrol and friendlier service. On over the farmland, the fields that still roll away as they must have done 300 years ago, dissected by hedgerows where, a mere relative blink away, terrified and wounded, the remnants of Monmouth's routed army hid and recited psalms. Yea, though I walk through the valley of the shadow of death. The Sedgemoor Welcome Break is, without doubt, the most surreally weird place I have ever eaten in and, if you're passing, don't miss it. You need a big appetite for irony and metaphor and you need to understand what's really and truly on your plate.

August 1996

Country Hotel

Leaving London is not something to be undertaken lightly. Most of us moved mountains to get here in the first place. We know that beyond the pale of the M25 stretches a land of dried minestrone in earthenware mugs, a place where the apartheid salad still flourishes, ingredients living separate lives on the same plate, with a hard-boiled egg that's turned watery-pink in the effluvia of pickled beetroot. Out there in the badlands, there are wholefood cafés still plying the druidical tofu heresy of brown-lino lasagne, and villages where to own two grey apples, a Chernobyl cabbage, thirteen sorts of instant coffee and a dozen Taiwanese plastic rayguns makes you a greengrocer. The outlands are not to be braved on a whim – and certainly not without breakfast.

But if you must, then you must. And if you must, then the north-west road to Oxford is as good a way as any to get to the sticky brown. Actually, the road to Oxford contains one of England's greatest marvels, one of our most precious natural treasures. I've never seen it in a guidebook or a British Airways office. I don't know if it has even got a name. But it's a wonder. It's a cutting.

Now, you're probably not fantastically excited at the thought of motorway cuttings per se – and, truth to tell, they're not in my top-ten I-spy list – but this is a very impressive cutting. About half an hour outside London the road slices through a grey hill and then, opening out ahead of you like double doors on to a garden, is England. A perfect vale of fields and farms and steeples and copses that pans out to entrance you with all that Elgar, Betjeman, Falstaff, Jack Hargreaves, briar-pipe lump-in-the-throat stuff.

It's not a real place, of course. It's the fever-induced hallucination you know you'd get if you were dying of something distasteful in a foreign field. And you know that if you actually stopped and tried to walk in it, it would evaporate into a twee jungle of poker-work house names, dwarf conifers, antique shops and Happy Cuppa caffs. It's a vision that only exists from the motorway. Without the road it would be nothing. Which goes to prove something I've thought for ages: the countryside can only really be seen at seventy miles an hour.

Anyway, we motored through the Celia Johnson loveliness and cut off the motorway into the Chilterns: Jilly Cooper country, cruet and cuckolding country. After the interminable nightmare of roundabouts, we got to Broadway. Broadway is the sort of place that makes you think the return of the Black Death might have an upside. Essentially, it's a street of what they inevitably call 'honey-coloured' stone, but what you and I know as taupe: it's the colour of a travelling salesman's summer suit. Every corner is clipped and polished with a self-satisfied, cryogenicised veneration. There ought to be a statue in the middle of Broadway to the unknown smug git: a gent in polished brogues, flat cap and natty windcheater, with a patronising grin and the raised finger of Middle England.

Broadway is choked with meandering tourists, who gawp as if they were being shown a fleeting glimpse of the Bovis show estate for heaven. They each buy a little china stoat playing golf with a magpie in the greengrocer's before being bused back to their grim reality.

I'm fascinated by the gentlemen's outfitters of rural England. There is always one called something like Country Style selling clothes of a hideousness far beyond the wit and imagination of mere mortals. They must be designed and made by malevolent goblins. But the high point of Broadway was not its slacks – it was two women in broad mocha-, pistachio- and blush-striped frocks selling ice cream from an old Napoli cart, in straw hats. If I could have had one wish there and then, it would have been to transport them both lock, stock and Cornetto to downtown Kosovo.

The hotel we were staying at fits very comfortably into all this. It's one of those places that wasn't so much built as found, then endlessly restored. We were met by a nice young man in a tailcoat. 'Can I tell you anything?' Well yes, you can tell me why you bods in country hotels always dress like ushers who've misplaced a wedding. And you can tell me why this place has so many completely pointless walls. And you can tell me why country hotels are built on eggshells. And why rural carpenters have competitions to invent the most complicated door-catches in the world. How do you get out of here? 'It's simple sir. You pull this with this hand. Press this with the thumb of your other hand, and with your next hand just flick.' Hold on, what next hand?

Actually, the place isn't that bad. It's perfectly nice. True, it has hanging baskets and public rooms whose only point is to hold up the hunting prints. And every door has got a title. 'You go through Sir Scurvy Suckbutt, past Lady Scratchmott and you'll find yourself at Lord Dankbender. Don't go in there.' It's the sort of place that makes a personal secretary on a dirty weekend with her boss think he loves her. It's very comfy and quaint and clean and . . . and it's just . . .

Look, what I really hate is what country hotels turn me into. I become a man who jingles his change and has an opinion on pewter mugs. And I eat dozens of weird things. We had tea in the very, very Judith Chalmers garden. I'll have tea and scones with cream and jam and crumpets and scones and fruit cake and fancies and muffins and biscuits. And did I mention scones? It's the same with breakfast. I tick the menu like a *Cosmo* quiz. I'll have kippers and porridge and toast and croissants and scrambled eggs and sausages and bacon and tomato and mushrooms and All Bran and prunes and a rose in a glass.

Who is this bucolic Mr Pickwick person I've become? I didn't even think it strange when I went to my room and found a pair of chambermaids looking like star witnesses from *The Crucible* lurking in a corner. 'Hospitality sherry?' one of them grunted in a thick Worcestershire accent, then ran out, laughing maniacally. 'Don't drink it,' I warned the Blonde. 'You'll give birth to children covered in thick black hair with goat's eyes.'

And in the bath I had bubbles and wore a plastic disposable shower cap and ate a soggy shortbread. The Blonde caught me. 'Why are you wearing a cellophane condom on your head and eating a biscuit in Diana Dors bubbles?' I can't explain it. Everything came over fuchsia pink and I must have passed out. I think I've been taken over by the evil spirit of the country-hotel weekend.

On to the restaurant. Two things are paramount in getting the measure of the restaurant. One: no smoking, so ipso facto this is a bad review. And two: the menu said, 'Dress code: our guests inform us that they enjoy dressing in a smart manner.' Now isn't that just beyond anything? Do you need to know any more than that? Our guests inform us, mind, not tell. And they enjoy dressing smartly. Enjoy it! 'Oh, I do enjoy this little frock.' It has surreal possibilities. Sex code: 'Our guests inform us that they enjoy the missionary position in a smart manner.'

The rest of the menu is pretty low-key after that. It's too long and everything has two ingredients too many. It's a dining room that's trying too hard. This being Sunday lunch, and me now being utterly possessed by a smug-git rule person, it had to be beef. I started with potted salmon on a fennel-root salad with cucumber and hollandaise sauce. Nasty – a fisherman's poultice of thick squidge with added splat.

The pot-roast sirloin of Scottish beef with thyme gravy, rissoles, potatoes, rosemary-glazed vegetables and Yorkshire pudding took longer to read than it did to eat. The beef was very good, slightly underhung, but very nice. If a place like this can't do decent beef, it might as well shut up shop. And, of course, the Yorkshire pudding was like a melted tennis ball. Why anyone still makes these things is completely beyond me. They have nothing to do with Yorkshire or pudding or food. Bread-and-butter pudding with vanilla ice cream afterwards was . . . do you know, I can't remember, so I suppose it wasn't memorable. The menu did boast what has to be a contender for the most comprehensively disgusting dish of the year: chickpea fritters with green beans and tikka sauce. Yum.

All in all, the hotel is everything it sets out to be: the Noël Coward version of Norman Bates's motel. But fair's fair: if you want a dirty weekend you couldn't pick a neater, cleaner, snugglier little place. And that, finally, is what bothers me about country hotels: you just know that on Saturday night everyone's doing it. Because, between you and me, what else is the point of a hotel in Worcestershire?

The place was heaving with Middle-English lust. Except me, that is. The Blonde took one look and said: 'If you think I'm coming anywhere near a weird old geezer in a paisley nightshirt, puce nightcap, furry bedsocks and a Peter Rabbit hot water bottle with a face full of chocolate truffles, think again.'

May 1998

Meat

I learnt to cook because I had a couple of drinking mates who were butchers. No, actually, I learnt to cook because I was signing on and I had a couple of drinking mates who were butchers, and if I was going to get my round in, economies had to be made. As food and rent were my only other expenses, the Chinese takeaways and gynaecological doners were obviously going to have to take a hike. Malt and hops supplied all the nutrients I needed, and if I ever felt that telltale twinge of scurvy, half a lager and lime did the trick. It's a mistake to think that the drinking classes don't look after themselves. I started every day with a double shot of Benylin expectorant and vodka for the sake of my health. (I do recommend it as a cocktail: chilled martini glass, twist of lemon, shaken not stirred. It has to be shaken, of course.)

So I learnt to cook as the cheap option. I'd hang out in the butcher's and pick up whatever they were throwing away: lamb spare ribs – called park railings, and traditionally served as the kitchen lunch in French restaurants – or pig's ears, which are wonderful, but need cleaning first. Pigs have ear wax just like humans.

And then there's the stuff that's next-to-free: tripe, gizzard, trotters, calves' feet, pickled tongue and ox heart, which makes the most sensational roast when stuffed – which, of course, you can't do any more, because the health fascists insist that every one is slashed in the abattoir to check for disease.

Being poor and unemployed is the best way to learn how to cook. You've got time, you're hungry – and nothing makes ingredients more precious than them costing a sizeable proportion of your disposable income. But, more than that, poverty is the true mother of good cooking. The greatest dishes in the world weren't invented in high-tech kitchens by brigades of celebrity chefs. They were made in hovels and huts by anonymous women who had never read a recipe and would cry if they dropped an egg.

So, gingerly, thymely and sagely, I wandered around the extremities and dark crevices of defunct animals with a growing excitement. At the time, sitting in the butcher's drinking Special Brew and telling slurred lies seemed like the most appalling waste. I now realise that it was the best investment I ever made.

One of the things I learnt is that most people who go to butchers (women) think three things. One: they want to get out again as soon as possible. Two: raw meat is intrinsically disgusting and only an unknowable transubstantiation turns it into the divinity of a sausage. And three: every time they set foot on sawdust, their minds are wiped pristinely clean. They've absolutely no idea what they're looking at – they just don't want any of it. So in the space of one held breath, they ask for steak, chops, a chicken and, occasionally, calves' liver. The rest of the corpse is just so much carnage.

Butchers, of course, don't mind if all their skill is reduced to slicing bums and lower spines: these are the most expensive cuts. But when, years after my drinking days, I taught cooking, one of the first lessons was to reveal where meat actually came from. I used to ask one of the students to take off their clothes and get on all fours on the kitchen table. The others then had to play a grown-up version of pin the tail, mignon and osso bucco on the donkey. Using someone else's body to work out which cut of meat is which is the quickest way to learn butchery – and make friends. Most of you aren't that different from pigs; you're just deficient in the nipple department. Remember: the more work a muscle does, the more fibrous and tasty it will be; the closer to the bum, the more soft and bland.

The sorry decline in British butchery skills is mostly down to you only ever eating one-eighth of a beast and getting your recipes from restaurant chefs, who want quick-to-cook cuts that can be portion-controlled. But it's also partly the fault of the Meat Marketing Board – may they all drown in fermenting slurry – who take a tithe on every animal slaughtered to publicise the industry. They are mad proselytisers of French cadaver disposal, sometimes called 'seam butchery'. This is based on muscles, which are delicately prised apart to make small, elegant cuts to which fat is added. This suits French haute and bourgeois cuisine. Traditional English butchery, on the other hand, is skeletal. Animals are jointed, the bone is left in and there's no need for extra fat. This suits our heritage of slow cooking, where portion control means 'Are you full yet?'

I remember the first time I went to Smithfield, early one drunken morning. It was a vision of heaven: the raising of the dead to be born again as dinner. I had no idea that meat could be as varied and wondrous. I'd far rather spend an early morning in Smithfield than at the Chelsea Flower Show.

September 2000

Smithfield

Smithfield was my idea. At five in the morning, it's difficult to remember why I imagined this would be a good place to talk to Heston Blumenthal. It is the oldest food market in London, first used as a cattle market 800 years ago. This place has run with a lot of blood. It's also where they dispatched criminals, dissenters and rebels. Wat Tyler was murdered here by the lord mayor; William Wallace was hanged, drawn and quartered. I haven't been here in the morning since I was a student, when you could a get a drink with breakfast, as the pubs have licences to open for market traders. The bummarees, the porters who wore black tarred hats, have all gone now, but there is still a stern and sticky menace to the place – butchery and blood. In the central cobbled aisle, under the glass roof like a great railway station's, stands the market constable. Not a policeman, nor a noddy security guard, but a Dickensian figure employed by the City of London to oversee markets. He has a portly authority, calling gruff acknowledgements to men pushing tumbrils of meat. 'Someone,' he says, 'some-one' – he hyphenates the word for emphasis – 'has just stolen a pig. Picked up a pig and run off with it.' He shows no inclination to run after it. 'Just wait till he tries to get it on the bus.'

As I'm considering pork with an Oyster card, Heston trots up, sorry for being late. The last time I spent a day with Heston it was also in a market. It was the great food square in Marrakesh, where we meandered between stalls, eating snails with pins. We ended up in a stall eating cold boiled cow's udder, which had a pappish, wobbly texture and a faint, infantile flavour. Heston concentrated, rolling it around his mouth. 'You know what this tastes of?' He searched a virtual larder of memory. 'It's the smell of milk bottles in junior school left by the radiator.' He was absolutely right – that is precisely what cold Moroccan bovine bap tastes of.

We walk through Smithfield, past the gently swaying carcasses. Market traders in the dawn are not full of the milk of human kindness, they are not like the jolly costermongers from *My Fair Lady*. This is repetitive, humping, fatty work for skinny wages. They glower under their white hats and bellow like Cockney bullocks. Heston is expanding. He has two restaurants in Bray, an olde-themed pub that does for the Sunday cardigan trade and the three-starred Fat Duck, where he makes extraordinary food that is sometimes called surreal or experimental, postmodern or edible chemistry. What it is really, is intensively researched deconstruction of the assumptions and conventions of the table. If you care about food, if you eat out a lot, it is utterly brilliant, as satisfying as atonal music, but if you eat what is put in front of you, and only occasionally in restaurants, then it would probably be confusing and infuriating. Now he is opening a new restaurant in the Mandarin Oriental Hotel on Knightsbridge, his first foray into London. So what's it going to be? 'Brasserie food, but English, from reconditioned recipes. There will be a rib of beef and chips. I found a great recipe for mushroom ketchup.'

Expanding a restaurant business is the terrible, double-edged mezzaluna of high-end catering. Blumenthal is a great brand, a world-renowned chef, popular on television. His Bray restaurant turns away thousands of customers who would all love to give him hundreds of pounds, but can't. For any business, that's a weeping waste, but you can't cook in two places at once. What is happening to Gordon Ramsay's international empire of fine dining is a warning. So Heston will oversee his new kitchen, but the chef will be Ashley Palmer-Watts, who has been the chef at the Fat Duck for eleven years. Allowing good cooks to go off and make their own kitchens while not becoming competitors is another imperative of expansion. Even though the cost of dinner at the Duck is memorably expensive, so are three-star overheads. The Bray kitchen has more cooks than customers. The concentration needed to maintain quality at this level is relentless, and the profits are laughable compared with pizza and burgers.

Heston has now set his gimlet eye on researching old English food. He is reconstructing Tudor and seventeenth-century recipes for Knightsbridge: meat apples with parsley custard, a pie made with apple, rose and dill. He is naturally drawn to more elaborate and manipulated dishes, things made for show or to impress, before food came in courses. On one of his TV shows he made meat into a bowl of fruit. A mandarin was, in fact, chicken-liver parfait. We examine sides of purple beef. 'You know the French called us *les rosbifs* not as abuse, but because the English were the best at roasting meat in front of fires. Technically it's a very skilled job and they would send English cooks to France to teach them how it was done.' We talk about a medieval recipe that calls for the plucking of a live chicken, which is then basted and rocked to sleep before being taken to the table between two roast chickens. As they are carved, the naked hen awakes and runs clucking past the startled diners. That's the sort of *coup de théâtre* that Heston loves.

We go to a Smithfield pub for a fried breakfast and a pint of Guinness. The bar smells sour, the news is on the flat-screen telly, there are wide-boy traders here, a couple of shambling drunks and some loud, raddled girls who've yet to find someone to take them home. 'Do you think I could get an Earl Grey tea with skimmed milk?' Heston wonders. I doubt it. 'It has to be skimmed, I can't bear the taste of scorched milk fat.' Who can? An assistant is dispatched to Starbucks for the Earl Grey and Heston prods a sausage with a forensic interest and then notices that the table wobbles. He rocks it, then tries not to rock it, and I can tell it bothers him to distraction, but he doesn't want to mention it. Spending time with Heston is a bit like being out with a cross between Mrs Bridges from *Upstairs, Downstairs* and Sherlock Holmes. He is obsessive about everything he looks at. He wants to know how it works or why it doesn't work, and what would happen if you stuck it in nitrogen and covered it in seaweed. He talks as intensely about refining the online booking system as he does about making ice cream. Heston is even-tempered, smart, cultured in all sorts of unculinary ways, happily married, apparently nice to work for, gentle, reasonable and very good company. He also has nice manners. He is all the things most chefs aren't. But behind the *Tomorrow's World* spectacles and the just-too-trendy jackets there is an enigma. It's as if he were a bowl full of ingredients, each one delicious and surprising, but you can't quite work out what it's going to be when it's cooked. One of the constant themes of his food is to make things that aren't what they seem. I remember eating squares of jelly at the Fat Duck, one yellow, one red. As the waiter put them down, he said: 'This is orange and beetroot.' The red was orange, the orange was beetroot. A golden beet, a blood orange. It was simple and it was smart. It's not some gastro sleight of hand, it's a deeper magic. It's a sense that he is not all that he appears to be. His slightly nerdy, blandly comforting persona masks someone else. Heston smiles and says, 'Well, I'll take that as a compliment,' which is no answer, just another misdirection. He seems to be Holmes, but he could as easily be Moriarty. His expression is inscrutable, but friendly. He looks like butter wouldn't melt in his mouth. And perhaps it doesn't.

November 2010

Chinatown

I remember Chinatown when it was Chinahamlet. The inscrutable, sad and intrepid immigrants from Hong Kong, heads down in the steam and neon light of a gloomy, coal-gas-stinky London. Those hanging chains of dribbling red ducks were the most exotic food things I'd ever seen, as fascinating as Selfridges' Christmas windows. The little restaurants south of Shaftesbury Avenue and north of Leicester Square had a whiff of tong menace about them. Furious little men with dextrous cleavers. They were frequented by other chefs and waiters from the West End, and tweedy Soho intellectuals – skinny, pale men with unmanageable hair and horny glasses, awkwardly chatting up girls in flat shoes with kohl-black eyes and Camus on their laps.

Chinese restaurants were bohemian louche lunches before liaisons, the dinner of mistresses. Chinese was the first ethnic food most of us ever ate: lemon chicken in cornflower-citrus-semen sauce, the glottal assault of sweet and sour porky gristle at a time when pineapple was still a luxury ingredient.

Silently, the Chinese moved into every town and village in the country, opening Pagoda and Lotus takeaways in foul-mouthed, soot-black, angry, stupid, back-to-back streets. Whenever I came across them in the grim North, I wondered at their fortitude, the inner resolve and the flickering comfort of some grand dream that sustained them in these grassless, thankless, vicious places. Putting up with drunken vileness, thick-tongued racism, uncaring slurping, the insistence on chips and forks and ketchup. The tiny margins made on using cuts of pig, lamb and chicken the English didn't deign to bother with. The tedious, relentless jokes about cats and Alsatians. And the grinding, chilly, thankless loneliness of it. There should be a huge statue on the M1, like the Angel of the North; it should be to the Unknown Chinaman, the silent, uncomplaining brigade of foodie missionaries.

I walked through Chinatown last week for the first time in a year or so. It's a tourist feature now, and a multicultural boast, with illuminated Chinese-style gates and pictogram street signs and good-luck dogs. And there are still dozens of restaurants, ruby ducks hanging in the windows and furious men wielding cleavers.

But there are also streams of Chinese schoolchildren, teenagers now, talking with London accents and dressed in baggy ghetto gear. The restaurants are no longer full of adventurous bohemians and exhausted chefs, but the provincial young up for a night's clubbing or ten-quid-a-day tourists in town for *Chitty Chitty Lion King*.

I've never known where to eat in Chinatown. If I ever do stumble on a good meal, I forget where it is, and by the time I go back it's called something else. I phoned other critics to ask for their recommendations. None could give me any.

Chinatown has become pretty much like the rest of the West End: a cheap fuel stop between drink and drugs. It's a shame (but perhaps not for the Chinese). A couple of years ago, when Bloom's, the last Jewish restaurant in the East End, was shut down by the rabbis, there were wails of sorrow: 100 years of history and culture come to an end. But the truth was that the Jewish community had moved on to more salubrious burghs. They got professions in place of jobs. Catering is the business of first-generation immigrants. Cypriots, Maltese, Jews, Bengalis, Lebanese have all hocked everything to sell cheap food so that their kids won't have to.

Perhaps the demise of Chinatown is a credit to the Chinese community that's moving on. On the other hand, it may also be all we deserve. We refuse to see Chinese food as anything more than cheap. In the end, if there's no encouragement, ethnic restaurants will serve what they can get away with.

The popular prejudices about Chinky takeaways make it difficult to improve the quality and sophistication of the dishes, or to charge more. It's far easier to take your Peking Pagoda and turn it into the Bangkok Banyan. Thai food has a chic cachet, a summer-holiday honeymoon romance. So hundreds of Hong Kong Cantonese became

Siamese overnight. Phuket? Why not? Most Indian restaurants are run by Bangladeshis, and most Greek restaurants by Turkish Cypriots, and most sushi outside Japan is made by Koreans.

The immigrant cook didn't come here to improve or educate us, just to make money. And perhaps having to pretend to be someone you're not is all part of the diaspora experience. If we're stupid enough to pay more for a Thai spring roll than a Chinese one, more fool us. But it's still a shame that almost every wave of immigration has been a missed opportunity. We only consider it a success when they're just like us. But what's so great about that? The joy of immigrants is their difference; it's not when they've been bullied, ridiculed and ignored into eating Pop-Tarts, wearing iPods and talking Estuary.

April 2004

Barbecues

Jonathan Swift pointed out that it was a bold man who first ate an oyster. He was almost certainly wrong. The bold man was the first to order a medium-rare steak. Man and our proto-ancestors who lived near the coast and on rivers would have eaten shellfish since before they walked upright. There would never have been a time when men didn't eat oysters. But cooked meat, that was a big ask. Possibly the bravest, boldest leap of idiot hope ever. There were lots of forks in the evolutionary road, many of which were decisive. The first time a hominid stood up and stayed there. The first time a hominid used a stone to crack open a bone. The first time he said, 'Shit, shit, shit' when he whacked his thumb instead of the bone with the stone. The discovery not of the wheel but of the axle. All of these might be considered game-changers on the road to reality television. But few were as decisive or as game-changing as the first barbie.

Swift imagined that oyster-quaffing was bold because almost everything else we eat that is or was sensate is cooked. The natural order of meat, fish and fowl is to be put to the fire. We've been eating cooked food for so long we imagine that it is the natural right way to consume bodies. But raw – or rotten – was the only way to consume meat for far longer than we've been cooking. Imagine the first man who pulled a charred antelope corpse from the smoking plains of East Africa and dared his mate to eat it, and then gingerly put a bit of the semi-cremated stuff in his mouth. A chef, a friend of mine, disagrees. He says the smell of roasting meat is so delicious that early humans must have been fighting over morsels from the wildfire. I think he's romantic but wrong. No smell or taste is intrinsically attractive. We have to learn to associate them with good things. Pre-barbie man is more likely to have thought that the smell of charred flesh was the scent of danger and death. His favourite food smell was faint decomposition and blood.

So apart from a bet or a dare or initiation bullying, why eat cooked meat at all? The question is why do we no longer eat raw meat, and the answer has little to do with gastronomy. Nobody knows exactly when we came to the Promethean discovery of the ability for fire to make kebabs; the most conservative guess is 40,000 years ago, which is 30,000 years before farming. But actually it's more likely to have been 250,000 years ago, and some suggest it may be as far back as 4,000,000 years ago. The huge disparity in times shows that all these dates are only academic guesses. It also shows that early man was far better at tidying up after himself than most modern humans at campsites.

The reason for taking killed or scavenged corpses back to camp and putting them in the fire would have to be very good indeed. Cooked meat would have to be some sort of huge improvement on the raw stuff. And the truth is in our mouths. Our Swiss Army Knife teeth and our little stomachs, as opportunist hunters and gatherers, need to be able to eat everything, unlike, say, the big cats or the vultures that only eat corpse. We don't have heavy-duty equipment in our mouths. We aren't good at ripping. We don't have claws or beaks. Our molars aren't great for cracking and sharing. We can't afford to sleep for twelve hours a day to digest.

The simple reason for cooking is volume. You can eat an awful lot more cooked meat than raw. The burning helps the business of cutting, chewing and digesting. A single food animal goes much further roasted. Bones can be cracked and the baked marrow and brain extracted. These are incredibly high in fat and protein, which is particularly good for gestating and lactating females, but also for the manufacturing of grey matter, big brains.

There has been speculation about which came first for the thinking ape: a large brain or dextrous hands. It's not the devil that finds work for idle hands, it's a questing mind. So did the brain grow to give its fingers something to do, or did the possibility of tool-making inspire more problem-solving capacity? The question is usurped by the interesting hypothesis that they may both have been started by cooking.

Roasted meat is more efficient than raw meat. It can feed more people, therefore making family and clan groups potentially bigger, less vulnerable, braver. So cooking delivers healthier infants and a cleverer, stronger species. When something is that much of an improvement, then it's in our interest to make it also attractive. Cooked meat is not just medicinal but aesthetic. We associate the smells and the tastes of steak with pleasure. The aesthetics serve the best practice of the group.

Our species alone seems to make judgements about the cultural value of our daily food. So your mother may have had the ancient wisdom when she told you that you needed to eat up to be strong. To eat one forkful for mummy, one for daddy, and one for all the poor children not as lucky as you. She wasn't quite as timelessly clever when she told you to eat up your vegetables – apparently ancient man ate very, very few of them. Right up until the evolutionary equivalent of last weekend, we didn't do vegetables much. We weren't lightly cooking the spinach along with the mammoth.

Before you got the side orders, you had to wait for the next huge crossroads in human development. It's almost as important as cooking on fire: it's the invention of the pot. Really. Ceramics, clay thumb pots and coil pots – 12,000 years ago, they meant you could cook with water, and that's a whole other thing. Then we could eat grasses, principally rice and wheat. We could make bread and porridge and congee. When you can do that, you've opened up the possibility of farming, of staying in one place. There really is no point in trying to cook barley a grain at a time in a fire. And when you've got farming, you've got land ownership and the nation state. And it's merely an evolutionary stroll onto musical corkscrews and motion-sensitive air freshener.

January 2012

Eurostar

One of my earliest memories: travelling north by train for summer in Edinburgh and North Berwick; the station, all that noise; steam trains, the power and the glory, the smoke and the steam. They could belch and sigh like a god pouring water on Vulcan's forge. They were terrible, fabulous things to a five-year-old.

I remember the men who ministered to them, the men who tapped the wheels like farriers. The drivers with their black faces and shiny caps on footplates in the clouds. The peaked and polished ticket collectors with emergency-chained racing watches in their porky palms. The bustle and expectation of a journey that took longer than the imagination.

But my strongest memory, stronger than the noise and the smell of sulphurous haste, is damp handkerchiefs. Stations were filthy, the trains were filthy. Everything was mired in grime. I remember my mother and nanny in relays licking their handkerchiefs to wipe my face and hands, an unequal struggle against the fallout of the Industrial Revolution. All down the platform, little tableaux would be performing the same thing on grown-ups, dozens of couples imitating the first scene from *Brief Encounter*, pulling motes from each other's eyes, and beaming.

From those small, cold, gritty summers grew an abiding love of trains. Trains were the most exciting thing that happened to me until the frenetic onset of puberty. It is hardly an exclusive love. Railways are the great British passion. Railways are our great gift to the well-being and happiness of the world, along with Shakespeare and marmalade.

Railway journeys have that magic ability to improve like love affairs in the memory. The bit that improves most is railway dining. Talk to old men about the Pullmans of the Great Western and you would swear they had eaten at the court of the Great Khan. Catered by the man who taught Escoffier everything he knew. The Pullman car, stiff and white with napery, rhythmically tinkling china and glass. The amazing heaviness of the cutlery; the comforting menu; the half-bottles of unfashionable wine; the scalding handles on the teapots; the miniature jars of honey; a kipper as we hurtled through Crewe; and the jolly stewards as finely trained as acrobats, who in my remembrance cheered with my brother and me as we passed the sign saying Scotland. I don't expect the food was actually ever very good. But the memory cannot be faulted.

I mention all this because the memory of great journeys and the love of trains are the most precious asset that Railtrack owns. It overrides all the delays, the cancellations, the leaves on the track and the ghastly Travellers Fare.

Given the romance of a train, can somebody please tell me why, in all their privatised wisdom, they have tried so hard to make the Eurostar Tunnel experience so much like terrestrial flying? Flying is possibly the most barbaric and depressing way of getting from A to B. Flying must come a close second to being dragged barefoot behind a flatulent mule.

I had been told great things about Eurostar. Great and expansive things about the conviviality, comfort and comestibles in the first-class salon. Like Rick and the water in *Casablanca*, I found I had been misinformed. What I did find was an aeroplane with vertigo. I had imagined something like the Orient Express designed by Starck. What I got was Air Maroc club class.

The first big disappointment is that there is no dining car. You are served on uncomfortable foldaway tables in your seat from a hot trolley. Breakfast on the way out was a model of how to put a hot cart before a hungry horse. They have obviously decided that you simply have to serve a traditional English breakfast. In fact, they say so in three languages on the menu: *Engels ontbijt*. Well, not even airlines are stupid enough to imagine they can serve you fried food from a hot trolley. It tasted exactly like *ontbijt* sounds. Disgusting sausages, unspeakably mean, flabby omelette that looked like the sort of thing you see growing on damp beech stumps, tomatoes (the plural was an exaggeration) and mushrooms. Tiny plastic coffee and the corridor blocked with attendants and trolleys for most of the journey.

There was an alternative: a Teutonic cold repast of ham, cheese and hard-boiled egg. In my experience, only Germans can face that first thing. A waitress with a basket full of good brioches and fresh pastries and a proper cup of tea would have been a vast improvement. But then they could not write 'Full English Danish' on the menu.

Fast-forward to the return journey and dinner. The grilled Mediterranean veg mysteriously managed to be both flabby and raw. Fillet of beef a good piece of meat humiliated beyond the dreams of the Marquis de Sade. Or grilled halibut that had to be glutinously prised from the lid of its container. All this followed by a sugared fruit dessert that defies simile or metaphor.

What made all this ten times worse was that we were coming back from a weekend in Paris, still with the taste of the *plat des fruits de mer* on the tips of our tongues, still picking bits of truffled guinea fowl and *tarte tatin* out of our teeth. This was a truly horrible Ealing Comedy joke.

A first-class ticket can cost £100 more than a second-class one. It is a lot to pay for six inches of bottom room and a sticky halibut. I assume there is some fantastically good committee-type reason why they do not have a Pullman car, but if they can do it on the Orient Express, I cannot imagine what it is.

The odd thing, though, is that since my weekend I have been telling everybody that they simply must go on the train. The trip is becoming another great magic railway journey, along with the *Rajasthan Express* and the old *Flèche d'Or*. Three hours to the heart of Paris. I'll never go any other way. But next time, and please God it's soon, I shall go second-class and take a picnic wrapped in the large white handkerchief that my mother still makes me take on train journeys just in case I encounter Celia Johnson.

March 1995

Paris

I love Paris in the spring. Paris is where good Americans go when they die. How are we going to keep them down on the farm after they've seen Paree? We'll always have Paris. No city has been anthologised, crooned at, soliloquised, rhymed and mooned over like Paris. My favourite quote is from Haussmann, the man who designed the place. He said Paris was a sinister Chicago. According to my atlas, there are 10 Parises. One in Ontario, Arkansas, Idaho, Illinois, Kentucky, Missouri, Tennessee, Texas, Kiritimati in the Pacific Ocean and, of course, the one on the bend of the Seine in the flat plain of northern France.

Paris is also a prefix for style. For coquetry, for sweetness, elegance; it's a tease. In fact, there are far more than ten Parises. Everybody who has ever been there carries Paris away in their head. It glitters in reverie. And, more than anywhere else in the world, Paris is also a place that lives in the minds of the people who've never seen it, a capital of the imagination, an international virtual city, where finally we can all let go and perhaps be the person our present circumstances won't allow. You could write that book in Paris, paint that screen, screw the *tatin* off the tart. You could wear velvet and wave your hands. You could sit in a café all afternoon. You could get drunk for breakfast. Paris is the get-out-of-responsibility-and-guilt Never-never land for the put-upon, the buttoned-up and the guiltily diligent and obliged.

No place in the world, with the possible exception of Hiroshima, has had such a comprehensive PR makeover as Paris, because it really wasn't always like this. Before the French Revolution, Paris was famous for being filthy, dark, smelly, dangerous and pestilential. The medieval city huddled over its own disgusting mire, while its denizens slit each other's throats and poxed whores passed on syphilis, widely known as the French disease. Paris was where you ended up if you were too deranged, feckless, dangerous or disgusting to be allowed anywhere else.

The revolution changed everything. What was a proper murderous horror show of random terror to live through was seen as a beacon of reason and hope in places where you could sleep peacefully at night. It is ever thus with liberals. The revolution became trendy. Everyone wanted one and, of course, no one actually wanted to go and live in Paris. So the sort of people who did move in were artists, writers, misfits and ne'er-do-wells, and they in turn grew to be romantic, just as long as you didn't have to live next to or eat opposite them. Revolution had been so successful for Paris it just kept on having them all through the nineteenth century, becoming more and more romantic and ideal as more and more people got shot, locked up and died of cholera.

The artists and writers got better at being ne'er-do-wells, who in the end did well, and the city got a makeover. Haussmann, the chap who thought it was a sinister Chicago, redesigned the city into the grid of reason, an ordered duty. That is the familiar map of today. It's actually an open prison. It wasn't done through order and beauty in long walks thinking lofty thoughts. It was done so that they could put down the annual revolution quickly and efficiently – the boulevards are for moving troops, the wide vistas are fields of fire, the great roundabouts artillery positions. Paris was the only modern city specifically designed to facilitate the economical massacre of its own citizens. Who says the French have no sense of humour?

I first went to Paris in 1969, six months after the last abortive revolution when the students, Peugeot factory workers and couturiers' zip-stitchers had taken to the streets and the theatres. And de Gaulle had lost his nerve and gone to check on the loyalty of the Foreign Legion in Marseilles. It's so typically French that every other revolutionary in the world takes over power and the radio station, but in Paris they storm the theatres. Six months later, when the car workers and seamstresses and the police had all gone home, the students were still there on stage having twenty-four-hour philosophy-athons and passing motions of solidarity with the anti-aircraft gunners of

Hanoi. The paving stones were still ripped up and there were piles of loose cobbles at the side of the streets on the Left Bank. Gangs of CRS (Compagnies Républicaines de Sécurité) riot police lurked in malevolent huddles sucking on Gitanes. I remember seeing Jean-Paul Sartre in the Deux Magots. I'm not sure this isn't communist editing of memory, but I do certainly remember it. At the age of sixteen, Paris hit me with a sucker punch: Sartre and beautiful women with boyish haircuts carrying poodles, policemen in capes, booksellers on the Seine, Courbet and Géricault in the galleries. I'd just read *The Outsider* and *Down and Out in Paris and London* and I was a pushover for Paris and have remained hopelessly besotted ever since.

What actually did it for me was breakfast. My father had installed us in a *pension* in the rue Saint-André des Arts. Every room looked as if it had been decorated by Colette and cleaned by Édith Piaf. Breakfast in the morning was a baguette with butter and jam and milky coffee. Unexceptional, just like breakfast at home. Except that it was utterly exceptional. The bread had an eggshell crust and a soft white centre that smelt of comfort. It wasn't the white, steamed, ready-sliced stuff of home. The butter was as pale as death and had a creamy yellow sweetness that was a thousand taste buds from the sputum-yellow, over-salted Anchor stuff I was used to. The jam was thin and formed pools in the butter and tasted intensely of strawberries, not the thick, livid-red anonymous fruit of England. The coffee came in pottery bowls and tasted of that particular French combination: hot, with milk and chicory. The apparent familiarity was what made the reality so astonishing. If the French had eaten herons' tongues and cancan dancers' sequins for breakfast, I would have been excited but not shocked. I realised that all my life I'd been eating a pale, sad shadow and that the food in England was a horrid charade compared to this. It was perhaps the most important breakfast of my life. It was the beginning of a lifelong fascination with and adoration for food.

It also taught me that the things that surprise you and move you are most often those that are closest to the familiar. And that Paris's great trick was quality. It did the same as everyone else: it just did it in silk and by hand. It was a city that had invented proletarian revolt, yet made its living out of exclusivity – from frocks to soup to whores.

The Paris I saw in 1969 was already disappearing, and when I go now it's almost completely vanished. The cobbles are gone, and the *pissoirs*. The art's all been moved and Les Halles – where I ate onion soup at five in the morning with a restorative eau-de-vie and at lunchtime a dish of chicken stewed with crayfish – has been taken over by pizza, cappuccinos and public mimes.

But there is enough Paris in my head to shroud the reality with a purple existentialism till I die. I will continue to see what I want to, which has always been another of Paris's great tricks. She was an ugly old dame who convinced everyone she was really a beautiful young ingénue. She smelt of sewers and sweat, and we sniffed pastis and violets. She talked ineffable bollocks and we heard charming romance.

Paris is a confidence trick that was invented in the nineteenth and early twentieth centuries by a collective act of wishful thinking. An act of auto-hypnotism made by writers, artists, musicians, poets and plain girls in good hats, who levitated the city to be a demi-utopia of brilliance and arty afternoon humping. Paris was and still is not exactly a lie, but a fantasy, and very little of it has anything to do with the Parisians, who, despite history, culture and cuisine, have managed to remain an earth-bound, grasping, bad-tempered lot of scowling *misérables*. As Hemingway said, Paris is a moveable feast: you take it with you as a picnic in your head. And it's a city that's often best visited from the comfort of your own home.

Date unknown

Benidorm

Where did you go for your hols this year? White-water rafting on Baffin Island? Yawn. Took a timeshare mud hut on a Body Shop reservation in the Brazilian rainforest? Ho hum. Visited every fat pietà between Constantinople and Syracuse in a sedan chair? Boring. Went on a feminist consciousness-raising camping holiday in Riyadh? Dull, dull, dull.

Guess where I've just come back from? Benidorm. I can't tell you the pleasure I've had informing my world-weary friends. It gets a bigger reaction than a whoopie cushion at a coronation. Benidorm! they shriek. Benidorm – how could you? The Birdie Song and mum's paella and chips, wet T-shirt contests and sangria-vomiting competitions. If a good deal of the pleasure in going away is being able to hold court when you come back, then you can't do better than Benidorm. The very name will rivet a dinner table.

Abroad is one of the last areas of life that is still overtly, unashamedly snobbish. There is no meritocracy in abroad. However hard it works, Rimini is never going to be U and, no matter how slovenly, overpriced and rude, Venice is always going to have John Julius Norwich and his ilk fawning over it like antique dealers over a duchess. Benidorm is a loud, brassy, page-three lassie out for a laugh. She's all front and she's my kind of girl.

The best thing about Benidorm is that she has no past. She was never anything other than a giggling teenager. There are no Roman remains, no old fishing port, no municipal museum and art gallery, nothing to put your bifocals on for, nothing to write a guidebook about. The old European aristocracy of tourist cities shamelessly live off history and their ancient conquests, renovating their venerable, sagging faces with conservation plastic surgery like divas showing off their best side to the paparazzi. Benidorm is a teenager born out of cheap package tours, cheap fags, cheap beer, sun and sex in the 1960s. She's no looker, but she's willing and she's anyone's.

Abroad brings out all of our pretensions and our insecurities. Remember the stress involved in trying to order à la carte in Biarritz, or deciding what to wear for drinks on the boat off Abu Simbel? Oh God – have you come all this way and not found the monastery with the saint's gallstones? Forget all that in Benidorm, which, 100 years old this year, has spent millions of pounds on upgrading its image, conveniently enough for the thousands of European wrinklies about to weather a low-cost winter there.

In Benidorm there's nothing to see, and it's certainly no fashion parade. The moment you step onto the promenade you breathe a sigh of relief; whatever you packed, it's going to be fine. This is bri-nylon's spiritual home, a conservation area for cerise tiger skin. Here you don't just physically relax, you culturally free-fall. Along the promenade, the bars all have Hammond organs and a little dance floor. Old show tunes with a syncopated beat bleat into the sunlight, retired taxi drivers in blazers and cravats glide across the parquet with widows in elasticated waistbands, charm bracelets and white peep-toe sandals. After dark, the bars are transformed into discos and the beat becomes deeper and simpler. The stacked sunloungers on the beach shudder and giggle. Joy-driven cars with puce-faced lads hanging out of every window shrieking Esperanto football chants honk past little knots of beautiful Donnas and Marias who stand, like the cigarette girls in *Carmen*, swinging velvet motorcycle helmets and studiously ignoring the boys. Just to underline Benidorm's claim to be entirely beyond the pale of European culture, I should point out that it's the first town that saw the point of Julio Iglesias.

Shopping in Benidorm is like shuffling around a huge, open-air 1960s Woolworths. Precarious piles of shoes on trestle tables bask under signs telling you that, despite appearances, they are all real leather. Racks of cheap belts long enough to support fifteen-pint-a-night guts sway next to rows of sweatshirts proclaiming non-existent

American universities and tiny bum-floss bikinis in the local colours of mauve-and-lime leopardskin. There are amusement arcades with children waiting for their dads, not predatory men. There's a joke shop that sells black soap, rubber dog shit and plastic vomit. (I rather thought plastic sick in Benidorm was a bit coals to Newcastle.) There's a jolly sex shop. 'What you fancy?' asks the salesman, peering over a boggling display of tonguedoms. 'You like black girls with white men? White men with white women? White men with black men?' 'What about that one with the Dutch bint and the Labrador,' says a Brummie accent in a 'Love Me Tender' T-shirt.

Every two or three yards there's a café, some sporting Union Jacks and signs promising that Lorraine and Colin from Lincoln offer a warm welcome and half a chicken with chips. HP sauce bottles stand like sticky sundials on paper tablecloths. A chain of waffle makers called Mannequin Pis have large logos showing a small boy peeing into your crêpe. But most of the cafés are Spanish and make some of the best tapas you'll get in Spain, because most of the tourists who come to Benidorm are in fact home-grown tool operators from Navarra, market gardeners from Aragon, traffic wardens from Galicia with their wives and insomniac children. All come here to eat pigs' balls and squid, to swill Muscatel and sweet almond milk and melt into the plastic beach sunloungers, happily rubbing oily shoulders with their vinegary counterparts from Lancashire, Cheshire and Nottingham, Rotterdam and Essen.

If you want to go and see real Spaniards in real Spain, go to Benidorm. In fact, if you want to see what the EC single-market federalism is actually all about, go to Benidorm. I will bet you five quid to 1,000 pesetas that in 150 years the spiritual descendant of John Julius Norwich will be trying to raise money for the Benidorm in Peril fund. The jerry-built high-rise hotels will have preservation orders on them and the rooms will be full of Channel 4 arts producers and their personal assistants. The good-time girl will have been thrust into a matron's stays, with airs and graces and a guidebook, and it will all be a shame. Benidorm is a European Disneyland that doesn't need a fantasy. It's an affordable fortnight's hangovers, legovers and sunburn for those of us who are employed by the people who sneer, and who vacation in places that look good in a photo album. But, best of all, Benidorm is a holiday away from holidays.

October 1993

El Bulli

There was a slightly panicky moment during dinner when I asked for some hint or indication of how much more there was to come. A great deal of the pleasure in food is expectation, but open-ended expectation is a bit scary. It would be nice to know how much expectation we were expected to expect. The waiter looked at his list and calculated: 'Well, you've had thirty courses. Maybe you're halfway through.'

This is the *Götterdämmerung*, the penultimate dinner at El Bulli, Ferran Adrià's restaurant on the Costa Brava. It is the most mythologised diner in the world, presided over by the most respected and influential chef. It has conjured up more hot opinions than hot dinners. A broadsheet food critic wrote a knowing, dismissive, 1,500-word review of its demise yesterday, mentioning in passing that she had never actually eaten there. No surprise. But no other reviewer would dream of doing that about a play or a painting or a book. Food is so basic and personal, so wrapped in emotion, that we're allowed our untasted prejudices.

'What do you think about that Spanish place that does chemistry-set cooking?' It's one of the top-three questions that all critics get asked. My answer is simple. First, tell me what cooking isn't chemistry. And then: it's brilliant. Bright, intense, exclamatory mouthfuls that surprise and entertain. It's funny and beautiful, elegiac, delicious, disgusting and occasionally speechlessly moving. If you think that's the sort of critic's snobby pretension that makes expensive restaurants such an absurd con and you'd rather have a cheese sandwich, then that's fine and your loss.

Adrià is in his kitchen, where he greets guests before dinner. Behind him are the chefs – dozens and dozens of them. A great chorus line of cooks. This food is as labour-intensive as an epic movie. Adrià is energetic and excited. He is also one of the nicest men you'll find in a kitchen. He speaks halting English that is more semaphore than verbal, but it's better than my Catalan.

'You've lost weight.'

'Yes,' he laughs, and mimes running.

'Are you sad about closing El Bulli?'

His eyebrows shoot up. 'Sad?' he beams. 'No, no, happy happy.' And then adds: 'Of course, a little bit sad. But the next thing is very exciting.' He is setting up an academy, a blue-sky symposium.

'For cooking?'

'For cooking, for architects, for designers,' he raises his hands, 'for thinking, for brilliance, for the top, top, top, best people.'

'Will you still cook?'

'Of course. But also I'll eat.'

'Can I come?'

He laughs: 'Of course, of course.'

Everything about El Bulli is a counter-intuitive tease. The trips, the expectations. First of all, the place itself: it's perfectly nice. The roof fits. It's a holiday home on a grey beach with a few bobbing weekend boats. It's neither exclusively chic nor a spectacular vista. The name El Bulli is inherited from a German couple who were fond of French bulldogs. Their photographs are everywhere. There is nothing in this mise en scène to prepare you or influence your judgement. It is, though, a wonderfully insouciant jest when you consider this was probably the most exclusive restaurant in the world. Each year the booking line opened for only two weeks. The restaurant served just dinner and only from June to December. There were between 2 million and 3 million inquiries for a table and maybe several thousand places available. But the place never made any money. El Bulli lost millions of euros – the brigade of staff easily outnumber the customers – and the prices were not as much as you would pay for a three-star dinner in Paris or London. This might have been the most expensive restaurant in the world. It could have been cloned out to Dubai, Shanghai and the Maldives. It could have cashed in. But it never did.

Adrià once told me: 'I'm a chef. This is where I cook. How can I be in two places at once?' So this penultimate-night audience isn't a crush of glitter and glamour. The atmosphere is easy and relaxed and expectant. The food, too, is counter-intuitive.

We begin with a sort of soft white bun with a green filling. In the mouth it dissolves and miraculously becomes a mojito – sugarcane in a mound of ice, infused with caipirinha. There is a cheese macaroon, a frozen gorgonzola balloon, a book of beautifully pressed flowers that you tear out and eat on their spun-sugar pages. A soup of prawn brains, a perfect pale oblong of veal marrow covered in caviar, foie gras frozen into quinoa and dissolved in consommé like a beach.

The courses come at the rate of ten an hour. We eat for five hours; fifty courses. It's the gastronomic version of a Wagner opera with the best bits of the Cirque du Soleil dropped in.

'This is nostalgia,' said the waiter. 'For the last time we do everything. Everything must take a bow. It is not an ordinary dinner.'

It certainly isn't.

July 2011

Bologna

Italy is Europe's great illusion. How does it do it? How does it float there without visible means of support? All the lights on, the sound of flirtatious laughter and silly pop songs and the wafting scent of tomato and garlic. It dresses so well, eats so well, lives so well on apparently nothing but charm, smiles, lies and expressive hands.

Perhaps Italy isn't really run by technocrats, the Mafia, the Vatican and the EU. Perhaps it's really run by Derren Brown. Everything about this place defies conventional wisdom or social and economic gravity. And perhaps that's why so many northern European slaves to fiscal and ethical rules dream of escaping to Italy with its benevolent corruption, charming sexism, entertaining crime, egalitarian nepotism, inclusive racism and soulful mendacity.

Italy is the triumph of wishful thinking over reality. And every year I take the children for a week there just to see how life might be if we weren't who we are, living in the pragmatic north. This time we started with a weekend in Bologna. I'd never been. It's famous as a great lunching city, in the middle of the richest food region in Italy, Emilia-Romagna. Bologna is famous for the three Ts: towers, tortellini and tits. Actually, they're more explicit about the local sexual expertise: what magistrates used to call acts of gross indecency are the proud speciality of the local ladies.

Bologna's gift to the world, apart from the other thing, is students. This is the home of the first-ever university and it's also famous for breeding communist politicians out of middle-class fat, and for eating. When we got here we found it was closed. Down the road, Florence is stacking the American tourists like café chairs. In Venice you can walk across the Grand Canal on the bodies of drowned Japanese. Tuscany is a traffic jam of Notting Hill TV producers sweating in panama hats and other people's wives, talking too loudly about the dolce bloody vita and very decent local grappa. The Ligurian and Amalfi coasts are thick with yachts, mobile-phone masts and Albanian friends of Berlusconi. August is Italy's big cash cow of tourism – but not for Bologna, apparently.

This is a city you can walk round. It was built for it, with the longest collection of arcades in the world and beautiful terracotta buildings and enormous barns of churches. Bologna didn't go mad for Italian art. Its one favoured painterly son is Morandi, an artist of worthy, relentless, decorative boredom. The city had its mind on lower things – commerce and five courses of lunch. It was run by the mercantile class, the people who really know how to love their stomachs.

The first stop from the airport was Tamburini, a delicatessen where the sweet smell of preserved pig grabs you like a suede balaclava. There is a waft of pecorinos and Parmesans of varying ages. It all smells like heaven. The variety and quality of butchered goods and curdled milk is spectacular. At the back there is a small self-service restaurant, where you can slide a tray past great bowls of tortellini stuffed with pork, and the butcher will give you a board of mixed charcuterie. The tortellini are vibrant and make you wonder how they get that much flavour into this little twisted navel. It is the Tardis of taste. *Tortellini en brodo* – tortellini in clear chicken broth – is the most perfect dish when done well, and one of the most insipidly disappointing otherwise. It either sings like a Verdi aria or it moans like Olly Murs.

Bologna's other speciality is mortadella, the great pale-pink pork meat sausage that has been infantilised by Americans as baloney, taking its name from the city, if not its texture or taste. Mortadella is fragrant and soft with a mild but rich flavour, like eating Tintoretto's angels' bottoms. And there was a marvellous brawn, or head cheese, where snouts and faces and odds and ends of the freshly slaughtered pig were boiled with a lot of pork fat and pressed into a grey, greasy sausage. It was complex and unctuous and, like all the best piggy things, had a round sweetness that was almost flowery: the scent of old tobacco and wilting lilies.

But the restaurant I want to commend to you is La Drogheria della Rossa, an ancient pharmacy that has kept the old jars and accoutrements of Italian hysterical hypochondria and potion worship, but now serves simple local food off a short menu. Although this city is famous for its ingredients and expertise, it has barely a single Michelin-starred restaurant – which goes to remind you what a paucity of taste Michelin has.

The best food here is relaxed, colloquial, unfussy, personal. We started with the inevitable plate of charcuterie and boned sardines with onion. The manager who delivered them said rhetorically, and without the expectation of contradiction, that if everybody ate sardines the world would be a better place. We sat outside on a quiet street. Beside us were local workmen and local working women. The manager walked between the tables chatting in that gravelly voice only Italians seem to cultivate, smoking a cigarette and brandishing a bottle of light white wine he sloshed into glasses as he passed, the bottle and the fags waved in the air as he extolled the fish and damned local politicians. Above us, pigeons cooed in the midday heat.

The twins had fresh spaghetti with *ragù*, an authentic bolognese: chunky and meaty and not even on nodding acquaintances with the runny slop that was the first spaghetti sauce to get to post-war England. And I had ravioli stuffed with potato: an unlikely combination for carb-conscious northern Europeans, but a plate of divine delicacy and gorgeousness. The potato was puréed with a little cheese, butter and thyme to a creamy elegancy and stuffed into pillows of handmade pasta. It was followed by fillet steak in a dank, dark sauce made of ancient balsamic vinegar. Pudding was mascarpone ice cream – I haven't even mentioned the ice cream of Bologna – and a chocolate flan.

But the reason I'm really commending this restaurant was something that was said. The Blonde asked our host if he was the owner of the restaurant. He looked at her, and spread his hands as an offering and in astonishment. 'As long as you sit here,' he rasped, 'it is your restaurant. When I'm here on my own, it's my restaurant.'

Every restaurateur in the world should have that embroidered on their pillows. It's a perfect evocation of hospitality and maybe a little answer as to why Italy defies the laws of common sense. Its hospitality, while we're there, belongs to all of us.

September 2013

Sicily

Everybody has had a go at Sicily. Sicily was the bandy-legged, unibrowed, evil-eyed, midget good time that was had by just about everyone – Greeks, Venetians, Carthaginians, Romans, Saracens, Vandals, Arabs, Spanish, Amalfians, Genoese and Edwardian homosexuals. It even got a seeing-to from legendary people – the last refugees of Troy are supposed to have settled there. The only colonists who didn't get to stir Sicily's polenta were the Brits. How the Royal Navy managed to miss it is a mystery.

And Sicily got the Normans. The Normans were barely house-trained Vikings with big horses – unimaginative, earthy bullies with silly pudding-bowl haircuts and mad, meaty faces. They invaded Sicily one at a time, pretending they were on holiday. Little gangs of Normans on stag nights would wander through Italy getting drunk, singing 'One Magna Carta, there's only one Magna Carta', until they all turned up in Palermo. Then, one night, before you could say 'William, you bastard', they had laid their towels all over the prayer mat and claimed Sicily for Normandy. It was the first successful invasion by tourism and, apparently, the Sicilians were rather pleased. The Normans were atypically light-handed and liberal, and left the running of the island to the Arabs.

The great surprise for me in Sicily was the thumping beauty of Norman culture with a suntan. If what you're used to is the Tower of London and all those surly castles, the cathedrals and palaces of Sicily come as a big shock. The church at Monreale is a revelation. Why didn't our hunting-obsessed, rugger-bugger Normans ever do stuff like this back home? The cathedral glistens and vibrates with the most perfectly complete mosaic interior I have seen. It's a vast hangar, God's Terminal 5.

I've always found mosaic the most dismissible of visual arts – after video, obviously. It subordinates imagination to intellect, replaces intuition with a plan and, in the most fey sense, sacks artistry for craft. As I get older, though, it grows on me – or I grow into it. There is a streak of aesthetic rigour and collectivism about mosaic, the democracy of those hard little tesserae giving themselves to the greater good, no one piece more important than any other. In a parable, mosaic becomes a labour of dedication and endurance.

Sicily's history ought to make it the poster child of multiculturalism. Sicilians should be the most easy-going, inclusive, welcoming and non-judgemental people in the world, but what did multiculturalism give them? The Mafia. Sicily is inverted, mistrustful, secretive and vengeful. It's a great truth that where you come from, what you look like, which way you pray and how you dance count for little compared to how much you get paid. Happily, however, we don't have to think about any of that here. The food is strangely brilliant. Where multiculturalism failed as a sociopolitical template, it makes a very nice dinner plate.

Best sandwich filling of the year? In a little bar on a pretty square, there was a man slicing anonymous lumps and throwing the bits into a vat of bubbling water. I'll have one of whatever you're making, I said in the international language of fast food. He grabbed a ciabatta roll, split it, daubed a thick layer of ricotta, stuffed it with a generous wodge of the boiled meat, added a sprinkle of some other cow's cheese and handed it to me, with a wedge of lemon. I inhaled the first half, as you do with things that are better than gratitude sex with a film star, then tried to make the second half last till teatime. It was the epitome of the defining characteristics of Italian food: the finest, simplest ingredients, arranged with careless panache, coming together to create a whole that is greater than the sum of its parts. We're back to mosaics again. I asked the chap what the meat was and, in the international language of autopsies, he explained it was spleen and lung. Go ask for that in Pret A Manger.

March 2008

Stockholm

Subeditors are strange creatures. There'll be one lurking around here somewhere, making sure my words are smelt correctly and the punctuation and syntax is proper. They're nocturnal and blinky and tend to suffer from logorrhoeic OCD. I once knew a lady reporter who slept with one. She said it was an uncommon experience. His pick-up line had been, 'The deadline approaches. Let's put this one to bed.' They do have a quiet, subversive sense of humour, like wicked voles. They run secret competitions to see who can get the most boring headline printed. Past contenders have included 'Five marinades to put a zing in Australia Day'. 'Colon massage without tears'. 'Matchboxes: a lifelong obsession'. 'Odd numbers – explained'. But the winner, and now something of a legend, is from America, where a newspaper ran a feature headlined 'Canada: gentle giant of the north'. In Europe it would be 'Scandinavia: putting the fun into functional'. Our relationship with our own liberal giant of the north is both envious and pitying. Every government south of the Baltic invariably prefaces any social initiative with the assurance that it has already worked very well in Sweden. Sweden is the litmus test, the guarantee of safety, efficacy and worthiness.

Needless to say, none of us has ever managed to live up to the high standards of selfless earnestness set by Scandinavia. But we aspire. Sweden is the role model we are told to look up to if we are willing to pay 60 per cent tax and have three sorts of recycling and carve butter knives in our spare time. We too would be allowed to take naked saunas with strangely beautiful blonde women. Sweden is the nearest place socialist atheists get to imagining what nirvana would be like, a commune of the quietly contented, the concerned with healthy exercise and state-sponsored consensual sex. And while our heads say, 'Yes, yes, Sweden,' our craven hearts pant, 'Oh, oh Italy, useless land of corruption, crime, lies, laziness and insecurity.' Europe offers up its collective prayer, passed from St Augustine of Hippo: oh God, make me Scandinavian, but not yet.

I have been spending a little time in Stockholm recently, and I think my Swedish time of goodness may have come. Stockholm is one of the most approachable cities in Europe, small enough to be walkable but large enough to have distinctly different areas. It's both historically beautiful and contemporarily workable. You rarely get both these things in the same place. It's made up of a series of bridge-linked islands in an archipelago. In the winter, the sun stealthily creeps above the horizon at about 9 a.m., and then slips along the rooftops like a cat burglar before going somewhere warmer at about 3 p.m. The light is beguiling, slanted and opalescent, bouncing off the ever-present water, falling on the reflections of windows. The city's architecture is principally Nordic baroque and madly romantic. And something that they winningly called *funkis*, a 1930s functional architecture. Shops and restaurants glow with candlelit cosiness. It's a city that puts a brave face on itself.

And then there are the people. The first thing you notice about the people is that there's nothing to notice about them. This would be the worst city in which to be a fashion designer. Everyone's rich but everyone dresses dull. Everybody studiedly and purposefully looks like everyone else. They choose to dress down to a common denominator: a black jacket and a woolly hat. The watchword for Swedes is conformity. They do it to put each other at ease, by never standing out. You couldn't tell how rich anyone here was by looking at them. The idea of ostentation is anathema. It is the outward and visible sign of a society that has the narrowest margin between rich and poor. This is the secret, they say, of a happy, homogenous community. It is also the curse of a very dreary one. But only to look at. Underneath, Swedes are beguiling. They are blessed with a shortened sense of humour and a long streak of introspection, pessimism and solitary depression, which makes conversation wonderfully dark brown, polished with a thoughtful stoicism.

And Swedish history has a remarkable turnaround in it. For most of the 300 years since the Thirty Years War, the Swedes have been constantly bellicose, fighting the Russians, the Poles, the Norwegians, the Latvians, the French and almost anyone else who ever passed by. They kept a vast army and a bigger navy; they built masses of guns. Their reputation in central Europe is for cruelty, efficiency and ruthlessness. German children are frightened by the thought of the Swedes coming in the night. (You can imagine how much it takes to frighten a German.) And then something happened. Sweden saw the light. Or just had enough. It stayed neutral (or neutral-ish) in both world wars. It hid Jews. It looked after refugees. And collectively decided to remain non-aligned and become a liberal, ethically astringent, socially careful paragon of common sense. I don't think any other nation has had such a dramatic temperament makeover.

I was asked here to judge a restaurant award, the A.A. Gill Award for Best Restaurant to Take a Visitor To. So I concentrated on eating local produce in restaurants that you might call home-grown. One of the great things about the current vitality in Nordic food is the limited number of ingredients. Scandinavia has a very short harvest and a very long winter, so an awful lot of produce and its preparation is spent in preserving – salting, brining, pickling, setting in fat, soaking in sugar. The hunt for the perfect ingredient and the most careful husbandry with an obsessive ecological care is the leitmotif of their cuisine. Tastes grow special through their limitations more than their bounties. Swedish hospitality has been marked by years of famine and failed harvests. The menus and the kitchens are immensely generous, because dinner is a poultice and a bath and a blessing. It wraps the dark dissonance of the Nordic soul as much as fills their thickening stomachs. You watch people eat in restaurants and they have a greater reverence for the stuff on the plate than you see elsewhere in the West. They eat with care and a quiet respect. Food is a blessing and a responsibility.

I sat next to an old couple in a smart traditional restaurant in the centre of town. The two of them concentrated on their plates as if they were going to sit and plan, consuming with slow care, each forkful put together with a delicate deliberation, chewed with respect.

They spoke softly and little, in a companionable way, because to chatter and gossip would have been disrespectful to what was given to them: the herring and the dry bread. It was another Swedish lesson in the true value of things.

March 2012

Budapest

Budapest. Great city. Unexpectedly great city. I had low expectations of Hungary. What does Hungary conjure up for you? Exactly? Strangely empty, Hungary. But then I just fell in love. It's my experience that you fall in love with cities within twenty-four hours, or not at all. You don't grow to love them, and Budapest just puts out. It has that thing that great cities all have: the harmony of contradictions. Rough and dapper. Elegant and funny. Secret and hospitable. Broad and narrow. Baroque and Stalinist. Fur and nylon. I was there with Tom the snapper: 'Ooh, ooh, I know this place. We have to have dinner. Really brilliant. I was doing this *Vogue* shoot here, and we all went. It was really brilliant. Really cool. Really brilliant food. It's called, um . . . it's called Gundel.' OK, book it, Danno.

Now, there are three immutable rules for a happy, regret-free life. Never make a pass at an oriental girl whose Adam's apple is bigger than her breasts; don't put anything in your mouth that involves a bet; and never, ever eat at the suggestion of a photographer. Gundel turned out to be the most expensive restaurant in central Europe, and a place that existed solely to give an authentic taste of Magyar cuisine to Japanese tourists. Actually, the food wasn't bad; I had goulash. Which turns out to be soup, not stew. And it's also the name for a Hungarian cowboy, although 'let's play goulash and Indians' doesn't have the winning note to it. (Although, pedantically, out here, it would be 'let's play goulash and Ottomans', which sounds like supper on the sofa.) What it did have was gypsy violinists. Ah, now I remember what Hungary's famous for. The most stressful thing in the entire world is to be shut in a room with a questing gypsy violinist. In terms of naked anxiety, it's way beyond your phone going off during Hamlet's soliloquy, swimming with jellyfish, or getting dressed up in a Formula One bondage costume in the back of a cab between traffic lights. I watched the great white violinist and the midget accordionist saw their way through the tables of tourists. He circled a hapless Korean couple. They shrank in terror and numb incomprehension as his fat, malevolently bland face, with its slick black pate and golden grin, loomed over them. He winked a terrifyingly dull eye that rolled back in his head, and with one fluid movement, too fast to decipher, he was among them with a Liszt Hungarian Rhapsody. It was horrible. Shrieking notes of psychotic dexterity, wringing screaming tremolos and pitiful vibratos from every riff. The air was filled with sentimental death. There is no known defence against an adult male gypsy violinist in an enclosed space: in a Hungarian restaurant, no one can hear you scream.

As quickly as it had begun, it was all over, in a foaming lather of sweat, schmaltz and paprika. The silence hung as mordant and doom-laden as the ear-scything. The Koreans were dead in the water, strudel hanging from their lips. The great predator paused for a moment, regarding them with grim detachment. He was waiting for something – but they didn't know what. The man's jowls wobbled. His wife began to sob. 'Pay him!' we all mouthed. Money, give him money. But it was too late. The hellish bow was again drawn coldly across the fret. I knew what was coming. No, no, make it stop. Not 'The Blue Danube'! He minced the first stanza, and then, with a Paganini-ish dexterity, played pizzicato.

The great bow tapped the Korean breast, and the poor man knew it was a sign. Desperately, he tried to decipher it. Of course! The wallet. Money. He flung the entire contents of his Prada travel purse at the gypsy, his wife hysterically ripping off earrings and a small Rolex. The gypsy pouched his tip, turned, and slowly swam on.

The ham-and-eggs combination of music and food seems to be as old as rhythm and fire, but some people hate it more than the popular sex-and-poetry combo. I must admit that sometimes music in public places is like ethereal chewing gum that sticks mintily to your ear; there's nothing quite as mournful as the echo of easy-listening classics played in empty restaurants to give them some atmosphere, like lavatory spray covering up the fetid stink of loneliness, failure and tinned bisque.

November 2008

Polish Food

Poland has a grim history, cursed by the neighbours from hell, Prussia and Russia, and, occasionally, Sweden. The relentless invasions and laying-waste, the bullying and occupations, have meant that Poland has one of the largest diasporas: 20 million Poles wander the world. That's a lot of toolboxes. And there's a calumny: that Poles are all plumbers and bodgers. There's Copernicus, Chopin and Conrad. You wouldn't have trusted any of them to change a ballcock. And our own Miliband brothers: maternal Poles. They couldn't screw in a light bulb, and Ed is begging to be our first Polack PM.

Before Poles became Europe's U-bend cleaners, three times they saved this continent from the cusp of catastrophe. Without the Poles, we would irrevocably have gone down the plughole. Jan Sobieski, with his heavy cavalry, at the cost of his own nation, vanquished the Ottomans at the gates of Vienna, thereby ensuring that Westminster Abbey was never a mosque. In the Battle of Britain, it was the Polish fighter pilots that made the nip-and-tuck difference. The Polish squadron was the most effective, with the most kills. And then there's the Miracle of the Vistula. In 1919, Lenin, having beaten the White Russians, thought it would be an appropriate moment to export the blessings of communism to the rest of Europe at, as Trotsky put it, the point of a bayonet. The door to the West was Poland. There were to be co-ordinated uprisings in European cities that would begin as Poland capitulated. Its army was beaten back to the gates of Warsaw, then, against all the odds, it stood and held, defeated and then routed the Russians with brilliant *élan* and panache, and a great deal of shouting. The 203rd Uhlans captured a Russian radio post and continuously read Genesis in Polish and Latin to block the airways.

Polish food is, I'm told, chewed-over history. The leftovers of all the armies, traders and immigrants who've moved across its central European farmland. There are ingredients and methods from Germany, Russia, Lithuania, Ukraine, Bohemia and the Jews. Before the recent advent of Polish supermarkets and sausage takeaways, there was one famous Polish café in South Kensington: Daquise, started for homesick Poles during the war. They had a disproportionately romantic reputation in the polyglot, blacked-out city: they had the best uniforms, the best manners, the worst tempers and the best – or worst – sexual appetites.

I used to visit Daquise as a student in the 1970s. It was tired and run-down. The customers tended to be old men with cravats, tobacco-yellow moustaches and sad eyes who would drink lemon tea and shake their heads at each other. The menu was indecipherable: if you asked the tractor-mechanic waitress what any dish was, she would bark that it was 'kibbige mit sassige'. Everything was kibbige, mit or mit-out sassige. This was where Yevgeny Ivanov, the Russian spy and Lothario, would meet Christine Keeler, the femme fatale of the Profumo affair, along with Mandy Rice-Davies, who, in turn, lived with Rachman, the slum landlord, and who retrospectively said that her life had been 'one slow descent into respectability'. She converted to Judaism and boated up the Thames with Libby Purves and a toy Alsatian as an homage to Jerome K. Jerome. You really couldn't make any of that up. Keeler, Rice-Davies, Profumo, Rachman and Ivanov – such a perfect group casting for a flickering *Carry On Blighty*, and Daquise was their shabby, evocative set. In hindsight, they also seem oddly prophetic of characters in London today. The owners of Daquise retired and asked a woman who runs restaurants in Warsaw if she'd like to take it on. She did, and it's been very nicely made over: more stripped-back than done up. I don't expect they had trouble finding builders. The dumb waiter's still here, with its pulleys exposed. It's light and tastefully faded.

I took Jake Walker, top fiddler and specialist bow dealer, and Camilla, the editrix. The menu starts with cold, then warm, and soup. Herring, beetroot and horseradish, mixed-vegetable salad (don't call it Russian), *pierogi*, sweetbreads, and marinated salmon with potato pancakes. A borscht with dumplings, which is not like Soviet borscht, but a clear, spinel-red broth that's both sweetly refined and trollishly earthy. And then there was the sour rye soup: rye that's been left to steep in bacon stock, but comes with boiled egg. Now, I love soup. I think there's nothing like enough soup on menus, or in life. Soup may be the answer to almost everything. Our existences are written in soup. This may be the Rosetta Stone of soup, a grand polonaise of blissful, clever, witty, sympathetic, encouraging and entertaining soup. Not just a great anecdotal soup, but a comforting, attentive soup, with an egg. This is the soup your mother wanted you to marry. If you're not attached to a soup at the moment, or you're just fooling around with hot-and-sour, this soup alone is worth a date at Daquise.

The *pierogi* dumplings are those substantial parcels full of woodland, peasant goodness that are so characteristically *Mitteleuropa*: neither sunny ravioli nor sulky dim sum. They are like the internal organs of Russian dolls. For main course, Camilla had *pulpety* – veal meatballs. *Pulpety* is such a pretty word: you might consider it for your next girl-child, or small dog. It came with mashed potatoes and dill sauce. I had the topside of beef, poached in its own effluvia, with vegetables, served with horseradish. If you ever consider leaving the sour soup for another dish, this is the one: big and meaty, but tender and yielding. You have a dash of the piping power of a Paul Newman, with the sultry nubility of Pola Negri (both Polacks), and it comes with a bonus spoon and a quart of muscly broth.

Puddings were pancakes with cheese, and more *pierogi* with fruit. The maître d' was a sparkly and amusing man, in a suit, but with blue trainers, as if we wouldn't notice. The waiter was an Indian from Maharashtra, who knew the cricket score in Mumbai. The chefs who came up for their lunch were having veal Holstein, with a fried egg and pickle. They held their knives and forks like a monkey wrench and crowbar: tools for a man's job. And for these reasons, and because there are still rheumy-eyed old men wearing cravats and sipping lemon tea, I'm giving Daquise a full five stars, and a kiss on both cheeks. And also because we owe the Poles.

They've done a damn sight more for us than we ever did for them, so it's a token, a thank you, for the gates of Vienna, the Battle of Britain and the Miracle of the Vistula. And fixing my ensuite bidet on a Sunday.

April 2011

Jordan

When you stop and look around, it dawns on you that the things that make Jordan unusual and so special aren't what it is, but what it isn't. First, in case your geography is a little rusty or Asia-centric, remind yourself who Jordan's neighbours are. Go on, have an informed guess. 'Meet the Neighbours' is a very good game for long bus journeys or delayed flights. What countries march with Turkey, for instance? Surprisingly tricky, that one. What country has the most neighbours in the world? That'll be China, with fifteen. How many can you get? A clue – one of them is the country with the second-most neighbours.

Back to Jordan. It shares a border with Syria, Israel, Iraq, Saudi Arabia, a touch of Egypt and it can look into Lebanon's guest bedroom. Even given the tough 'hood, those are the neighbours from hell, and little Jordan sits in the middle of them like a good deed in a remand centre.

What you notice about Amman, the capital, is that it doesn't have megalomaniac architecture of extreme religiosity or obese wealth. There isn't a vast, bulbous mosque with neon towers and surround-sound calls to prayer. Neither is there a Norman Foster glass-and-steel postmodern concert hall or a branded Louvre franchise. Jordan hasn't really fought a war against anyone. It's had an after-hours ruck with Israel, but not enough to indulge in memorials to martyrs or put up huge statues to generals.

But the thing that Jordan really hasn't got a lot of is oil. 'We used to resent the fact that we didn't have oil like the other Arab countries,' a waiter told me. 'But then we saw what they did with it and we're quite pleased now.' Everyone would like to be a bit richer, but who wants to be like Iraq or Bahrain? Jordan does have oil, but it comes in tins from olives. They are the world's seventh-biggest producer of olive oil. Their main export is garden produce, cucumbers. There's a lot for Jordan to worry about: their debt is vast, their income shaky, they don't have any of their own water and their politics could be healthier (though, like New Zealand, they're really, really sentimentally fond of their royal family). The nation is the size of Scotland and immensely proud of itself. Jordanians tend to be better-educated than their neighbours because there is no entitlement to money here, no family business. There are very few free lunches in Jordan. I sat at a table at Hashem, a street café that is something of an institution, and I ruminated on what a general curse unearned wealth is – worse than undeserved poverty. At least with poverty there is a chance you can work your way out of it. But not wealth. No amount of toil will relieve you of the spirit- and character-sapping succubus of inherited cash.

Hashem has just gone into my personal top-fifty restaurants. It takes up an alley off a busy street downtown, so the people-watching is good. Boys come round with trays of sweet mint tea and hot flatbread. There's not much of a menu – not enough to write down. It's hummus and the best light, elegant falafel – not like those great goitres the Israelis scoff – parsley salad and a dish they call fool, which is beans and bread and Moorishly delicious in both senses of the word. It's a café that is confident of the quality and expertise of its perfectly simple offering. There isn't even a loo. You can always run over the busy road to the first-floor café opposite, where old Iraqi gents sit and play one of those games of cards that you only win with the death of all the other players, measuring out the hot days in the flickering, louvred light of this large room. Where the television shows Arab oily wrestling and the radio plays Egyptian pop songs and the waiter does the rounds with a metal box full of hot coals to replenish the hubble-bubbles, and the air is thick with the smell of apple tobacco and mint and hot bread from the baker's downstairs, where there is a long shop that is entirely constructed of bread like a Grimms' fairy-tale house. There is a chute in the roof out of which drops a rain of pittas like the bread of heaven. Into the oven is shovelled flatbread stuffed with cheese and olives, poppy seeds and chilli – completely delicious – and men-in-white wife-beaters with hairy backs shout and laugh at each other and make fancy Day-Glo pastries and honey cakes. It's a scene that is the crusty dream of every

Western organic shopfitter, but a million miles from our precious and self-conscious artisan or sourdough genuflection to wheat intolerance.

Another restaurant – I can't remember the name – on an upper floor is hugger-mugger with tables, which means that you're essentially eating in a canteen decorated with black and white photographs of Jordanian singers and film stars of the 1930s and 40s. It serves grilled meat produced on precariously balanced platters, fabulous *labne*, goat and mutton. It's all dense with smoke and Arab arguments. Pudding comes from a sidewalk seller making sweet farinaceous slop with nuts and honey on paper plates.

An hour's drive out of the capital across the rolling desert there is the Dead Sea. You look across its thick waves to the coast of Israel and lie on baking sun loungers with French backpackers and with Americans who've come for the odd pleasure of wading into the Jordan where, it's said, Christ was baptised by John the Baptist, and then sing 'One More River to Cross' and, after a few beers and a lot of the local raki, grow garrulous and fumblingly homoerotic. When the waiter asks if they'd like a bill, they reply with damp lips that it's 'not I, it's he that comes after me', and the waiters, with their dark, lustrous eyes, smile knowingly as if they've never heard that before, or been so obliquely propositioned. You have to cover yourself with a thick, tarry mud that smells faintly of chemistry lessons and bicycle-repair shops and giggle and then gingerly descend the slippery steps into the sea, where you lower yourself into the warm, flopping brine, not knowing quite what to expect. Is this perhaps a Styx, a truly dead sea that will take you away, or will you be the first man to sink like a stone? No, you bob, and the mud regretfully returns to the deep and you feel like a ham or a soused herring, and get out and find that the water has washed away the sins of the flesh – but only skin-deep. It cured my psoriasis and washed my skin till it was as soft as a liberal's good intentions. In the shade, a man under an umbrella will write your name in a bottle of coloured sand. A name written in the sand on the Dead Sea seems to be such a glowing metaphor, such an obvious parable for something or other, but I can't quite place it.

May 2013

Algiers

Every part of the Mediterranean has its talismanic fish dish. The rascasse bouillabaisse of the South of France, the tuna of southern Italy, octopus of Greece, the great oily mixed fried fish of Spain. In Algiers it's sardines, the most ubiquitous of shoals. Back home they're relegated to the metaphor of a crammed tin, a lonely man's supper, but here, on the hot south coast, sardines come in great glittering migration. In Algiers, they are everywhere – beloved and cheap, elegant and honest. The flavour of a freshly grilled sardine is as good as anything that comes out of the sea, and the citizens never tire of them.

You can forget, or fail to remember, that Algiers is on the Mediterranean. From our side, the north side, it looks like such a European holiday sea, but Algeria owns its longest stretch of coast, and is just across the water from the Balearics and the Spanish costas. The city obliquely stares at Marseilles, which, in so many respects – cultural and historic – is its sister port.

Not many people visit Algiers these days. The country is coming out of a particularly dark and murderous civil war and seems to be suffering from a collective post-traumatic stress disorder. It hadn't welcomed Europeans for some time. We were with Mourad Mazouz, owner of Momo and Sketch and the spectacular Parisian restaurant Derrière. This is his city, and it was once packed with travellers and Europeans. The ferries pass back and forth in the busy port. It is one of the most beautiful places on the Mediterranean, built on a huge bay, with white French colonial colonnades with blue windows and shutters on the boulevards in front of the Ottoman casbah, crumbling and feral.

Because there aren't that many tourists, there aren't that many tourist restaurants, but there are cafés. Hundreds of them. Algiers got the benefit of being colonised by two great café societies, the Turks and the French. Men sit and argue volubly at little tables, play slam-dunk dominoes and greasily slapped cards, and smoke as if it were an endurance sport. As with all cities that tend to live as large families, the best food is eaten at home. Algerian cuisine is particularly polyglot, a stew of Berber, Arab, Jewish, French and southern Spanish. The Algerian fleet sailed round the world as pirates and traders. It is through North Africa that Europe got many of its ingredients: sugar cane and spices and roses and lemons and oranges.

The Algiers fish market is dark and cacophonous and slippery, a warren of traders, of ice-boys, of bandy lads pushing trolleys, balancing baskets; the mongers sit cross-legged, like henna-stained Neptunes, surrounded by their silvery wealth. It is difficult to think that all this came from the same waters as the neat goods in the refined and epicurean markets of Nice.

One of the great surprises are the desert truffles, a distant relative of the French and Italian ones. These are Arab delicacies that are exported to the markets of Riyadh and the Gulf. They are grown in arid, sparse soil and collected by the Berbers, who look for the telltale cracks in the earth. They say that the truffles grow where lightning has struck, an electric gift from the heavens. If there are a lot of storms, with the spring rain, then there will be a good crop of truffles. They're brown, the size of small potatoes, and have a strange, distinguished but fugitive flavour. It is dusty, secret, like the smell of a gardener's pocket. We eat them, cooked in rancid butter, with a stew of lamb that has been hung so high and so long, its flavour ululates. The combination of these competing, turning methods on the truffle is extraordinarily broad and emphatic. Deep, sour, carnal and mordant, it is absolutely the taste of the place. This dish wouldn't travel, no restaurant in Europe would serve it, but here, in the warm night, it is intimate and sensual. And deliciously authentic. After it, I'm offered small apples stuffed with almonds and stewed with mutton bones, again a mouthful that is consistently discordant, uncompromising and foreign, but also beguiling. We have sherbet of lemon, mint and orange-flower water, and a perfect, comforting bread made of spelt.

The great pleasure of dinner here is that you can't just chew and forget. This is not easy eating. Nothing is bland or edited, and it is a reminder of how much of our food is. Here, you need to concentrate; there's nothing passive about dinner. You need to wrestle what's in your mouth, come to terms with it, take your time. And you need to concentrate on who's sitting next to you. We never had a meal that didn't come with an argument. Algerians talk with purpose and varying degrees of force. The opinions are like the mutton, high and gamey. They thump the table, wag fingers, roll their eyes and make gasping, sighing, plosive noises, like car horns, to underline infuriation or ridicule, or just move the argument along. Everybody is bloody furious all the time; it's invigorating.

The best meal was dinner at Mourad's family home. A white couscous, with mutton and chicken and turnips and carrots. My grains were given just the right amount of stock by Mourad's father, who explained with signs that the dish must be eaten not too dry and not too soupy, in the way you might explain to an idiot how to do up his shoelaces. After the sweet cake and mint tea, the men take oranges and peel them with strong craftsmen's fingers. Without drawing breath they pass the segments to small children, clouting the backs of little heads with affection. The dining room is full of the scent of citrus and mint and the fog of guttural voices putting the badly mistaken to rights.

November 2009

Marrakesh

Marrakesh is one of the great cities of the world. Situated a day's travel from the foothills of the High Atlas and the ports of the Mediterranean, it was a caravanserai where the merchants could rest one night in relative safety – for which, *inshallah,* they must have been grateful. The local Barbary tribes made a living preying on the camel trains that brought ivory, spices, gold, salt, slaves and precious stones from the dark interior of Africa. Marrakesh wasn't exactly a piece of altruistic urban planning, more a protection racket: one of the tribes realised they could make a decent living charging the merchants a tithe not to slit their throats.

Now I know some Europeans turn their noses up at Marrakesh. 'My dear, the people. How can you stand being hectored and bothered all the time by chaps trying to sell you stuff non-stop?' a metropolitan friend asked askance. (Seeing as he's a DJ, I thought it was a bit thick: a question of pots and kettles, motes and beams.) But Marrakesh is about as different and exciting a place as you can travel to for a weekend, situated just a day away from the snow-capped High Atlas of Friday and the hectic, stinking port of Monday. I went because the Blonde was shooting a commercial there.

One of the things I love about this city is the food. At sunset in the big market square they set up trestles and charcoal fires. Among the snake charmers, monkey handlers, letter writers, tumblers, fortune tellers, water carriers and men sitting at tables piled high with teeth, whose smiles cheerfully contradict their skill, you can eat fish stew or bean soup, or boiled sheep's heads displayed like happy diners having their brows massaged with thin, oily broth. Every stall is a specialist, selling just boiled eggs, or ox hearts finely chopped into bread parcels, or pungent fish kebabs, or glistening sheets of tripe. There are traders touting dates and almonds, tiny pastries and mint tea, men squeezing the sweetest orange juice, and boys carrying trays of warm sugared doughnuts. There's the smell of charcoal mingled with mint and cumin and jasmine, and all the noises of drumming and thrumming and the insistent wailing of holy men. There are barkers selling carpets and Spanish fly, the small green beetles now renamed Berber Viagra, and the colours of the setting sun in the dusky air: the bright kaftans and children's frocks, the fruit, the dark Berber blue of the turbans and the charcoal-black eyes glimpsed through the turret slit of veiled women.

We sat at a stall where I ate a bowl of snails: not like your French snails – garlic and cow-fat blobs of gristle pushed into a rented shell – but real horned snails, cooked in their homes with cumin, ginger and chilli, and uncurled with a toothpick. The taste is of blind earth and the smell of long-closed cellars. A taste that teeters on the repellent but is endlessly subtle and varied, a shadow of decline and regret. The women at the stall snigger. It is mostly women who eat the snails, for some ancient, secret medicinal quality hidden under their voluminous kaftans.

Every time I go to Morocco, I'm amazed at how venerable the food tastes: the flavours and smells and methods have such ancient lineage. I rarely talk about the archaeology of food – by its nature it is transient and new – but certain dishes and cuisines are a more direct link to the past than any ruin or object in a museum. Morocco's food is biblical, and although we know precious little about what the Romans ate, this diet must be similar: the same raw materials, the same utensils.

The thing that changed European food root and branch was the discovery of America: something like a third of our staple ingredients were unknown before the Elizabethans. Morocco has an essentially pre-Columbus table. There is the occasional potato, a sweet salad made with tomato, but you won't find chocolate here, or the maize mealie meal that colonised sub-Saharan Africa far more effectively than any European army. This really is an ancient, mysterious and polished cuisine.

But enough of all that. It is time for us to wave goodbye to sunny

Marrakesh, city of a thousand bedsit carpets and slippers that smell like a picnic hamper containing last year's tuna sandwiches – until next time, *inshallah*.

June 1999

Cape Town

When you think about it, we don't eat much really. Well, of course, we eat loads – vast loads. But we don't eat much. If God made the world and everything in it for our delectation, then we've been parsimoniously finicky about what we put in our mouths. Worldwide, most of our consumption is commercially limited to about seven types of grass, five makes of animal, about a score of fruit and the same of roots and veg. We do better with fish – a hundred or so varieties – but we only really eat one bird: a solitary, stupid, Indian jungle fowl.

And it's getting less. Or fewer. Granted, there are people in dark corners and up alleys who partake of guinea pig, laver bread and puffin, but you're not going to find any of these included in a limited-edition McMuffin lunch option or a club-class, long-haul dinner. And yet, despite this, we consider ourselves to be a daring and epicurean species. Just look at the number of cookery books published every year. You'd think we were eating galaxies. The truth, however, is that it's all just variations on a theme. Ingredients are like keys on a piano – the possibilities for harmony and melody seem endless – but there's a whole orchestra we never touch. You've probably slept with more people than you've eaten different species.

So why do we consume so conservatively? Mostly, it's to do with farming. When we were hunter-gatherers we tried everything at least once: dinner was the algorithm of opportunity over necessity. But static farming is all about making choices. You can't grow everything, so you grow what grows well and learn to love it. You can herd sheep, but you can't herd antelope. Sheep flock, antelope fuck off. As farming gets ever more intensive, we grow fewer things. It's only by endless exotic renaming that we're led to believe our stomachs are sophisticated world travellers.

Thinking of all this was partly why I ate zebra in Chiswick last week. It's not bad, zebra. If I'd been asked to guess how I thought it tasted, I'd have said it would be like a positively discriminated free-range donkey. Actually, it's more like beef, with a fine, soft texture and a flavour that starts big and meaty, then just cuts out. It has no depth or roundness – but then, if you've seen lions' table manners, why would you bother?

The other reason I ate zebra is that I've just returned from South Africa. As farming is closer to its roots there, people still eat a bewildebeesting and beguiling range of ingredients, including a lot of insects. (Insects are terribly underrated here: four legs good, six legs better.)

I was particularly keen to find some Cape Malay food. I hadn't been to Cape Town before. It's a bit like a cross between Sydney and San Francisco, with a hinterland of vineyards and that attractive atmosphere that you always seem to get next to the sea. Table Mountain laid with its cloth of cloud is as extraordinary a focal point as the Golden Gate Bridge or the Opera House.

Cape Town could well be the cheapest place in the world (or, at least, the cheapest place where there's actually something you want to buy), and it's having a bit of a foodie turn – again, rather like Sydney, though with more mixed results. At worst, it's like 1970s nouvelle cuisine cooked by David Attenborough and makes you realise that, though apartheid is horrible when applied to people, it's sometimes quite sensible on a plate. At best, it's an inventive and confident mix of ingredients and traditions – and it's just such a joy to be offered fish and vegetables that haven't been boring you to death on tables back home.

But indigenous Cape Malay was hard to find. The original Dutch settlers brought skilled Malayan slaves to the Cape and for 300 years they fiercely kept their Muslim identity and their unique table. We were finally directed up through the brightly coloured Malay quarter on Signal Hill to a little lean-to café where an ancient grandmother cooked what she felt like: samosa and mutton curry, a wonderfully farinaceous bean curry, a chicken that remembered Cecil Rhodes, and melktert – a sort of custard tart, but poorer. The view across the city and the mountains was spectacular. The food, served on ancient and exhausted tableware, had that authentic solidity and savour that tells you it has been places and seen things. It's food that means something.

I've been saying for nearly a decade that South African cuisine is the coming thing and have been consistently wrong. So all I'll say now is this: it really ought to be. If you want a taste of what I mean, there's a place in Chiswick.

This is possibly the worst-designed restaurant in London, set in two rooms, neither of which is a kitchen, as if, in a very South African way, they've been unable to decide where to relocate the kitchen so they've put it in both, making the space awkward, lumpy and smoky. It's decorated with the only boring photographs ever to come out of Africa. But forget all that. The menu has seventeen dishes, all of which you can eat either as starter or main – and almost all of them contain ingredients that, unless you're South African or a vulture, you've probably only seen on the Discovery Channel. Kudu, blesbok, impala, springbok, wildebeest – now how much more exciting than beef, lamb or pork is that?

Kudu is probably the most like beef, and wildebeest the most gamily original. There's kingklip, a big fish, and Cape sole, which isn't a sole. There's pap (mealie meal – or as they always call it, 'African polenta'), rooseveldt potatoes, morogo, a sort of spinachy stuff, and those particular South African squashes that send the Blonde into paroxysms of reverie – she's from Durban – but which I think taste like warm-water-flavoured Artex, only nastier. There's monkey gland, which is a sauce, and Amarula Dom Pedro, an alcoholic milk shake (kids grow up fast in Africa).

Any one of these things is worth the trek to Chiswick, and the kitchen combines them with a hearty verve and rough, home-made skill. I particularly want to commend to you bobotie, a Cape Malay dish that I failed to find in South Africa. When it's well made, it's a marvellously cunning mixture of the exotic and familiar, an authentically African shepherd's pie, and here they do the second-best in London – the Blonde's mother being in pole position. I wish someone would take this menu and this kitchen and stick it behind a decent room, somewhere that didn't feel it ought to have Michael Caine defending it.

November 2002

Desert

Do you know the difference between a duck and a goose (apart from one being 'get your head down' and the other 'get your bottom felt up')? It's that ducks have penises and geese don't. Now you see, there's a thing. You could have gone through life just thinking geese were the big ones and ducks the wee fellas, when actually it's quite the reverse. I discovered this because I've been lurking in southern Africa, where enthusiastic men in enthusiastic shorts tell you stuff like that. I'm also in a position to pass on the fact that there are only four birds in all creation that boast penises: ducks, pigeons, ostriches and, damn, I've forgotten the last one. Widow Twanky, maybe.

Stranger than all that, however, is the red-billed buffalo weaver, a sociable bird that constructs large communal nests. Beneath its apparently conservative black suit it hides a dirty secret. Buffalo weavers have prosthetic penises; a dildo bone. Males and females engage in elaborate public matings that end in what can only be termed orgasmic feathered frenzy – and at least one of them is faking it.

Now, what on earth is a small bird doing with a strap-on? What was God or Darwin (whichever came first) thinking of? The more I rub up against nature, the more convinced I am that it's not some born-again hippie dame with a grand plan and membership of a donkey sanctuary, but a weird, delinquent kid. Nature is the toy-box of a bored adolescent, brilliant but psychopathic. There's no plan, no balance; just caprice and cruel spectacle.

One of the grandest things that sets us apart from all this is the way we eat. We sleep, defecate, work, play and have sex in much the same way as everything else (except buffalo weavers, of course), but nothing comes close to eating like *Homo sapiens*. No other animal has constructed such an elaborate edifice of behaviour around food. From farming to Frappuccinos, we're out on our own. We're the only animal that craves variety. Everything else is happy to eat the same thing day after day.

Occasionally, it's interesting to take a look at how the other half of creation eats, and in the Kalahari I went to one really memorable dinner. I can't remember what proportion of Africa's biomass is made up of termites, but it's a lot. Once a year, when the conditions are just right, they take to the air for the first and last time in their lives. Nobody knows how they know when to go or how they tell each other, but for weeks before they've been secretly growing wings. When the breeze is just so, millions and millions of them take off, and the thunderous desert air is alive. In the afternoon sunlight they look like hot snowflakes, or animated dandelion down.

The defining thing with deserts is that if you want to survive, you need to be a specialist. There isn't much to eat or drink. There's no such thing as a free lunch. Except today. The white ants take to the wing, and it's manna from heaven; the January sales. And the place goes open-mouthed, peristaltic-gulleted, tongue-lolling bulimic. Chats hover with beaks agape; jackals nip and snap at the air; the strange and nocturnal aardwolf, an ant-eating hyena with peg-like teeth and a huge, furry tail, blinks in the sunlight, gulping; and from out of the earth come hundreds of bullfrogs and thousands of scorpions to feast.

The ground squirms with gluttony and looks like a Brueghelian vision of Discovery hell. The bullfrogs eat the ants with their sticky tongues, then the scorpions with their bony teeth, then, finally, each other, choking on cannibalistic mouthfuls that are bigger than their heads. Perhaps one in a million ants makes it to a new nest and attracts some mates to begin the process over. Their collective leap is such an act of hope, such a huge vote for life and fecundity, such a force of nature. And, next day, it's a desert again. The cupboard is bare. A gabar goshawk hovers beadily, and the sand glitters like mica. The desert is blanketed in gossamer fairy wings.

I mention this only because it was a feast more exotically decadent and rapaciously amoral than any that could be organised by a louche caterer or barmy emperor. And it was a reminder of the real raw power of lunch. Though our elaborate relationship with food marks us as most human, the bit of our brains that deals with appetite and taste, that lump right at the back, is the oldest part, the part we share with the bullfrogs.

January 2004

Hot Dogs

Every Fourth of July, Nathan's sponsors the World Hot Dog Eating Contest at Coney Island, a strange and rather malevolently dystopian funfair. It has freak shows and one of America's first roller-coasters, the Cyclone, which is made of wood, makes a noise like the end of the world. Last time I was there, there was an abandoned lot on which household furniture had been dumped – along with a black man wearing a football helmet. Drunk white men in teamster T-shirts rented paintball guns to shoot him.

Coney Island, with its milky Atlantic light and clacking boardwalk, is a parable of an older, archaic America. And it's most celebrated for Nathan's Famous, the original New York dog. The competition is ten minutes long, billed as a celebration of the nation and all it stands for, which appears to be gluttony, tastelessness, waste, mindless spectacle and competitive consumption.

It's televised, and a large crowd chanting 'USA! USA!' comes to see the semi-professional scoffers. It is one of the most disgustingly distressing sights known to mankind and should be taken off the internet, because it's a recruitment video for eating disorders. The contestants fist sausages into their yawning maws and soak buns in water to squirm them down their gullets. They gag like hysterical, corpulent cormorants. If they're sick, they get disqualified. It's called a 'reversal of fortune'.

The hot-dog competition transgresses 2,000 years of respect, manners, hospitality, decency and appetite for food, without even touching on the symbolism of deeply unattractive men deep-throating penile wieners without pleasure or respect. The sight of it is fundamentally wrong on so many levels, with a meaningless glottal disregard for everything I cherish and find most elevating in civilisation. In fact,

Nathan's Hot Dog Eating Contest is a gourmand's ultimate horror movie. And because of that, I rather love it.

It's run by IFOCE – the International Federation of Competitive Eating. I'm not making it up. And they have stars, such as Joey Chestnut, the world-record holder, who consumed sixty-nine – yes, sixty-nine, I'm not making that up either – hot dogs in ten minutes. To offer some context of this achievement, in 1980 the winner ate nine and a half.

IFOCE runs lots of eating contests: hamburgers, of course, bratwurst, jalapeño peppers, buffalo wings. And I wondered what the best – or least worst – food to eat competitively would be. I settled on elvers: baby eels. The Blonde said oysters, which is one of the many reasons I love her. I had a ring round the office. Clare, from the *Magazine*, who's Irish, said she could neck pancakes, or potatoes. Sarah, the editor, went for watermelon. A clever choice. But we couldn't agree on whether to spit or swallow the seed. Camilla Long's first suggestion was impractical, unmeasurable and unprintable, so she settled for vodka and tonic. India Knight chose gherkins, adding that she'd down the brine as well. Jeremy Clarkson didn't even have to think. 'McVitie's dark-chocolate biscuits,' he bellowed, implying that he's been in training.

And I asked Giles Coren, over the way on *The Times*. He wanted caviar, naturally. I asked him to suggest what would be the worst thing to put in your mouth competitively. 'Oh, without a doubt, a tasting menu,' he said with feeling, adding: 'Gordon Ramsay's tasting menu.'

Personally, I think there are few worse things than hot dogs – I'd rather eat witchetty grubs. Actually, I wouldn't mind a witchetty grub right now; then the fugu fish, the potentially lethal Japanese pufferfish, or ortolans. Though a globe-artichoke-eating competition might be rather elegant.

The hot dog is the cheapest of American foods. A German-Jewish beef sausage brought over by immigrants, it was street-and-stadium food for the masses. It's what the poorest feed their children. But now it's been tarted up, dressed up and given a restaurant in Soho, of course. These are gourmet hot dogs, they say, topped with 'inventive and health-oriented ingredients, in a hip, tri-level space'. The addition of 'hot dog' to that sentence immediately turns it into a record contender for the most oxymorons. Hot dogs aren't supposed to be healthy or inventive or gourmet or hip.

The interior of this place is leaden with over-branding. Every surface is logoed or decorated with self-promotion, the general theme being Marlon Brando and Jimmy Dean's motorbike café. Only a team of bright-eyed, wet-nosed PRs could tell you why.

We asked for, and unfortunately got, a kimchi dog, a plain Jane dog, a pulled-pork-and-slaw dog and a Soho dog. And we were told to sit down with an electronic tag. The waiter would trace us with Google Maps or a drone or something.

The room is noisy and bright and half full of kids not eating very much, but flicking through potential hook-ups on their phones. This would be a good Tinder rendezvous: if what you'd ordered turned out to be a plain Jane dog, a Soho dog or even a plain old dog, you could just make your excuses and leave.

The food comes on disposable plates, and what they promise is brioche buns. They didn't have much evidence of being enriched with egg and butter – it was just soft bread that wasn't ergonomically up to being a container for the sludge and sausage. The first thing is that the hot dog doesn't work as hand-held food. And then, for all their exclamatory, self-congratulatory hype, the variations on a theme all tasted pretty much the same. And that wasn't very nice, with varying volumes of sour, hot, wet and fatty.

Nothing is identifiable by its constituent parts. I couldn't pick out kimchi from coleslaw. It was just large, brown mouthfuls of stuff that wasn't very well made and didn't taste very good – a bit like eating a fat man's reversal of fortune. The fact that it was ethically and carefully grown and conceived really didn't mitigate the effect. The chilli 'n' cheese fries were a particularly noisome compost.

This is plainly the opening salvo in a regurgitative chain. Twice as much effort has been put into the looks, style and decor of the room than into the actual food. And anyway, hot dogs belong on carts and at football games and at the seaside. They're street dogs; they're not house-trained to come indoors and sit at a table, being gussied up in falderals and fandangles. It's cruel and redundant; it's not an improvement – just a reminder of their mongrel limitations. In twenty minutes, I'm afraid I failed to finish a single one.

July 2015

Kuala Lumpur

In Kuala Lumpur, the taxis have the word 'taxi' written on their illuminated signs. It's a loanword, born for life on the other side of the world. So it's spelt phonetically to fit comfortably into the Malay mouth: 'teksi'. Every time I see one, it makes me smile because it's an imitation of how an old-fashioned, upper-class Englishwoman would call a taxi. No one draws more effortless humour from mispronunciations and innocent slips of the tongue than the native English. A teksi is exactly what an upper-class clipped vowel would demand for the privileged waiting to be taken somewhere else. Well, having stopped this teksi, I have nowhere else to go with it – it's just a small, unattached, inconsequential jettison from the great rolling slide of human communication. Personally, I have an amateur bore's fascination with etymology, which I treat like entomology, sticking words on pins and putting them in cases as curiosities, rather than a scientific inquiry.

I'd never been to KL before, and I wondered if everybody used the abbreviation 'KL' because 'Kuala Lumpur' sounds like the king of the Oompa Loompas. We only had one night, so we went to a food district where there were stalls and street cafés. Of all the myriad concoctions and confections and conceits of how hospitality offers up a hot meal, no one has ever arrived at a more exciting and compelling and invigorating version than the compendium of an Asian food market. The eliding smells, noises, character and the light, the pageant of people, the whole tapestry of egalitarian comestible experience folded together with anticipation.

After crisp-fried ray and sticky chicken wings and fish-ball soup, and a fat, cold, flabby slub of inedible duck on a tepid salmonella reserve of boiled rice, I noticed the sign that offered – no, promised – frog porridge. Frog porridge. Who could resist frog porridge? Is there a questing mouth that doesn't lick its lips at the dinner gong of frog porridge, with its welcoming resonance of nanny, jimjams and breakfast Beatrix Potter? The stall had a string of lights, a small preparation area that was crowded around a couple of gas burners and some desperately exhausted and overworked pots. A slightly larger area contained a skinny manageress overlooking a series of rubbly, frotted, curling ledgers and the wooden till bulging with sticky notes in half a dozen currencies. She had the look of her own star attraction, a woman who had been dealing with frogs so long she was unconsciously channelling amphibians. Her eyes had the sheen of insouciance that is the characteristic of both frogs and stall owners. Her mouth was a thin line that might have been set into a humorous knowing smile or pursed irritation. Her throat bulged and wattled as if accommodating an indigestible moth. She sat with an immovable ownership on the lily pad of her domain. 'Are the frogs fresh?' I asked. Her eyes widened for a moment and blinked sideways; the moth was confined to its digestive state. 'Show him frogs,' she croaked to another, less formidable woman, with a mottled, shiny skin that was pulled tight across her bony face. She produced a bucket of slushy ice water and, with a long-fingered hand, rummaged, pulling out a handful of strong, alabaster legs stuck between her fingers.

Only the bottom half of a frog is of interest to the chef; the top, with its wisdom and its humorous bravado and its mythic nursery power, is thrown back into the dark pond. This was a bowl of bisected half frogs, shucked of their green skin. They looked like the elegant legs of an elfin chorus line. The collective noun for edible frogs should be a cancan. 'Very fresh,' the new frog woman said, showing a mouth entirely bereft of teeth with a fat, grey-purple tongue and just a hard pink gum for masticating locusts. I sat on the plastic stool at the wooden table next to a man in a deckchair who appeared to be the frog lady's groom. You'd imagine that if she kissed him with her long, purple-grey tongue, he might miraculously be changed back into a blustering, balletic, baritone frog. But he had to sit here, cursed to being a man.

The porridge came: rice congee, thick and opalescent, blondly munificent, a viscous, soft-grained bed for the more urgent and pungent ingredients. And with it, in a small bowl, blowing steam like a panting pug on a cold day, was frog stew. Hot, seasoned, garishly accoutred frog bottoms, as madly cacophonous as a bowl of hot frogs could aspire to be. This was frog Valhalla, frog nirvana. I scooped them into the downy creaminess of their congee bed and they swam down to its sticky depths, leaving ochre streaks and swirls. Oh, the utter perfection of this final coming-together of the bland and braggadocio! It was as euphonious as a frog porridge could be. A dish of earthy honesty and mysterious sophistication, the evocation of paddy and the inhabitants that shared the water with the rice together again, a transforming apotheosis in a china bowl. It was one of those little moments at the table when you realise that you have the universe on a plate. A great soup of meaning and understanding, of feelings and thoughts that don't have words – just taste and smell and sensation. And it was still just rice and stew in the humid heat at the end of the monsoon. 'Frog porridge, really? Really, you ate frog porridge?' a white man in shorts asked me. 'Frog porridge?'

'Well, put it this way,' I said. 'Would you sup of *risotto aux grenouilles*?' 'That doesn't sound too bad,' he said. 'I've got an appetite for that.' Yes, wonderful stuff, words. It's the way you say it that leaves a new taste in your mouth.

December 2015

Bombay

It bears repeating that, if you're planning on visiting only one foreign country in this life, you should probably make it India. Unless, of course, you are reading this in India; then you might like to consider New Zealand. Bombay is a phenomenal city. You can see in it all those nineteenth-century descriptions of New York and London. It is the whirlpool of commerce and expectation, sucking in great shoals of people equally desperate and hopeful. All the contradictions of metropolises are here: the unfairness of a nation sloughing off its past to become something new. Bombay is like a slice through an ancient tree – all the rings of life are visible at once. You can see things that look medieval, you can trace empires and invasions. Its problems are all the corollary of metamorphosis; the traffic continues to be absurdly frustrating and suicidally rude, but the road signs warning against drink or unprotected sex are curiously polite. The streets can be deep in filth, yet the people picking their way through them are pristinely clean. Bombay is crass and calm, tasteless and civilised. The buildings are crumbling as the skyscrapers spring up behind them. Bombay is the most sophisticated chaos.

One of the nicest things about being there is that it's not here: it's not Europe. Its concerns are not European concerns. India doesn't have the heart-clutching fear that is the leitmotif of the old West at the moment. Instead, it has to cope with too much self-belief, an overdose of optimism. It has a can-do motivation in a can't-do country. A lot of people point out that India is a twenty-first-century aspiration driven by thirteenth-century infrastructure. The basic mechanics of getting through life, from the disposal of sewage to the delivery of babies, are terrifyingly ad hoc. You could make a list of all the things that India does on one hand, and a list of all the things it doesn't do on the other, and they would pretty much cancel each other out. This is a country where visitors rarely go to the country. The vast rural heart of India is too poor and difficult to lend itself to casual sightseeing. If the engine of India is still agriculture, its direction is decided by the middle class, a lot of it by the urban middle class. Much is made of India's middle-classness. In the West there is a self-justifying belief in the innate goodness of the suburbs, and that the real agent of betterment in this world is a growing middle-class family. The bigger your bourgeoisie, the better they work for all the things that make modern life comfortable. The middle class want education and car parks and policemen and international culture, but they also want to go to bed early and they are essentially law-abiding, but most usefully they have a ravenous appetite for stuff. The middle classes consume with an envious alacrity. Commentators in the West assume that 'middle class' means the same thing in Maharashtra as it does in Vermont. An Indian economist told me that anyone who has bought a white good – a fridge, a washing machine, a TV – counts as middle-class here, but what they do share with the West is debt. The difference is that India is still for the most part a handmade country, a crafted place where the cheapest ingredient in any project is likely to be labour. The middle class is more like an entrepreneur class – it's ducking and it's diving, rather than diligently plodding. Everyone has a card and a project. It's an interesting high-wire act being practised by hundreds of thousands of people every morning. Soon it'll be millions.

I was asked to come here to talk to my old friend Camellia Panjabi about food in India. Nowhere is as instantly recognisable on a plate as the subcontinent; the smells and the flavours of masala, the textures and the intensity and the heat. But food here is rooted in home and region. Indians are as passionate as Italians about the grub of their villages and their childhoods, but they are also newly aspirational. The urban class want Western food, or at least a sort of Westernised food.

There is a dividing line here between the traditional Indian and the modern, and it's olive oil. There is a fad, a fashion, an unquenchable demand for the oil of olives which is totally foreign to this continent and the food that goes with it. India cooks with ghee, the clarified butter that is sacred and a blessing, the anointing of India. The BBC, along with a local publisher, has just produced an Indian version of their entertaining magazine. Its proud editor showed me the first issue. There was a chocolate cake on the cover. Few things could be as un-Indian, as anti-Indian as a chocolate cake, but the new India has exactly the same impulses to eat foreign food and wear imported clothes and listen to international pop music as everyone else. But one of the truths of travelling, and one of the traps that travel writers must strive to avoid, is to value the fragility and the pristine nature of other people's cultures above their own. No one's life is any more valuable than or intrinsically superior to anyone else's, and we should stifle the snobbish wince when an Indian insists on a pizza.

Camellia took me out for dinner and said she had a surprise. We sat in a car for forty minutes, and got out on a stretch of urban highway. I looked around for the delicious little street stall or doorway of some regional diner, and instead saw the dreadfully familiar yellow arches of a McDonald's. 'Really, Camellia. I understand the irony, the joke, but I didn't come all this way to eat a Big Mac. I wouldn't eat one five minutes from my own home.' She led me inside and gave me a lecture. 'People want to share in the things they see from abroad. They want what's new and Western.' So how does a company that sells hamburgers work in India, where if you killed a cow they'd burn Ronald McDonald in the street?

Here there are vegetarian burgers, chicken wraps, paneer and a local version of Coca-Cola. People come because it's clean, fast and authentically Western. It's also cheap, very cheap. The best-seller is an aloo tikki burger, a patty made of potato and peas with a hot sauce in a bun, and I must say it was pretty good, in the sense that it was a lot better than any Big Mac I've ever eaten in the West. It is wholly Indian in invention, an adaptation of a street food. India took the look and made the content its own. If there is one thing India can't abide it's blandness in anything – in clothes, in films or in food. They want everything to be vivid, spicy, and when you are here, it's difficult to resist.

February 2012

Hong Kong

Hong Kong is an Anglo-eared approximation of the Chinese for 'sweet harbour', named after the number of incense factories on its shores. The original English occupiers called it Aberdeen. They could possibly have thought: 'Ah yes, that smell evokes the fishy, foggy, dreich granite city.' Homesickness plays cruel tricks with the senses. I went for the weekend to Hong Kong, not Aberdeen, and its literary festival, where a million Chinese visit and buy up books as if they are an endangered natural resource, which I suppose they are.

Hong Kong is one of the great cities to eat in. The food is brilliant: sophisticated, pungent and dextrous, and familiar in a simpler, flatter, blander version from the Chinese takeaways that have colonised every town and village in Britain. The first meal I remember eating in a restaurant was Chinese – lemon chicken gloopy with arrowroot, fried rice polka-dotted with Kerry-green peas, and toffee apples with 1950s eggless, creamless, vanilla-free ice cream. One of the things that particularly fascinates me about food is how and why it migrates, what people take with them and what they leave behind. We know all about the restaurant fusions of Japanese and Latin American food popularised by Nobu, the rim food from Australia and California that mixes Asian and European, the Tex and the Mex, and everything and anything has been squeezed into Spanish tapas. But these are all commercially arranged culinary marriages. More profound and touching are the combinations of remembrance, distance and uprooted habit.

Hong Kong has a ghostly, colonial cuisine that lingers at the edges of this hugely robust and exponentially expanding place like forget-me-nots in paddy fields. The great Anglo-Chinese fusion that is David Tang asked if I'd like to go out for breakfast to a *dai pai dong*, the outdoor caffs that are being assiduously cleaned up by the local government to stop people eating in the street. We bowed into a steaming little shop with its short-order kitchen bubbling outside. It was neon-bright and loud, with sticky little tables and cramped stools, and it was full of people bent over bowls, stoking up for the graft of pushing the enormous economic miracle – pretty girls on the way to luxury-brand shops and wiry workmen going to hump hods or climb ladders.

We started with *yuanyang*, a combination of strong black tea and strong coffee amalgamated with condensed milk, which sounds like a disgusting mistake. In fact it was surprisingly good, the caffeine and tannin smokily winding around each other as a metaphor of Occident and Orient. Then there were thick slices of processed white toast with a smear of more condensed milk, a sweetly ersatz version of French toast or sops. Condensed milk is one of the great uniting tastes of empire – nobody who was given it didn't love it more than the people who had given it to them. Only we back in England are too snobbish and neurotic still to eat it. Then there was a dish of thin broth with macaroni, a fried egg and packet ham, a strangely beguiling bastard of East and West; the egg and ham adrift and drowning in the soup, the macaroni a noodle sent west to be re-educated. And then congee, the rice porridge that is usually lumpy, slimy and noisome to the Western mouth, but here, simmered in vats for four or five hours so it becomes smooth and farinaceous, a subtly silky bolster, the best I've had. You can add all sorts of stuff. I went for cow's blood jelly – not everyone's first choice.

My favourite fusion of the weekend was a restaurant, Amigo, that is an old Hong Kong Italian where the white-gloved waiters serve approximations of French food to the Chinese in a room that looks like a mad Tyrolean tavern with a Mexican mariachi band who sing Abba hits. I found turtle soup on the menu. I haven't had turtle soup since I was a child; it is one of the great extinct flavours. I inquired after the turtle. It might be a case of mistaken identity: the Americans call terrapins turtles, orientals sometimes translate tortoise as turtle, and the Chinese farm a soft-shelled turtle that is, in fact, a pointy-nosed terrapin. This one, I was assured, was from the South China Sea, which probably makes it a green turtle or possibly a hawksbill. It was a Proustian moment of reverie, a wonderful, enigmatic, fugitive taste; little strips of oddly rubbery meat. I know that turtle soup will make a lot of you very, very upset. I am aware, I am sympathetic. Turtles are endangered, so you need to hurry if you want to eat one.

August 2011

Sydney

Sydney is like some long-dreaded blind date. Your mates say: 'I've got to set you up with Sydney. You'll just love it. Really. Right up your one-way street.'

Well, I don't know. What's it like? 'Oh, sooo you. Big. Not wobbly thighs big. Buxom big. Big and physical. Loud and plain-spoken. You know, calls a didgeridoo a practice date. And it looks great in a bikini. Come on, live a little. Sydney's gagging to meet you. Loves food. And here's the best bit: it's Australian. Sydney's anybody's. Knees under the table for breakfast, guaranteed.'

Oh my God, is that the time? Got to dash. Clean the dado rail. Organise the cutlery drawer.

You see, that's the thing about Sydney. The more they rave about it, the more you naturally resist. I mean, God didn't put it all the way over there for no reason. But in the end, good things come to you, whether you want them or not. Seeing as I was spending the Christmas period in the Far East – or what the inhabitants of the Far East call 'Here' – when Sydney found out that I was literally next door and screamed 'Cooee!', it was impossible to refuse.

And so, after a heavenly couple of weeks being frotted by the elegant, ethereal and delicate joys of Thailand, Bali and Singapore, I told the Blonde to brace herself and we headed down under. This, after all, is the land where they think a man in a bath cap with whitewash on his nose is the height of valiant masculine lubricity.

No place on earth could be less like a Sydney than Sydney. It's strange that, considering the Australian habit of shortening every moniker to its pithiest syllable, nobody calls it Syd. And even stranger that, if they were going to name it after a famous colonial, they didn't go with James.

Well, I resisted for as long as possible. But after all of twenty minutes, I had my knees under the table and was moaning 'Show us your yabbies!' Sydney really is anyone's (and, despite my best airs and graces, I am nearly anyone). As cities go, this city really knows how to go-go. It's proof that, as much as anything, weather forges character. For all its much-proclaimed multiculturalism, it's a very Anglo city. You'll feel instantly at home, but whereas back in damp Blighty we sit indoors and think nasty thoughts, they get out in the sun and do dirty deeds. Everything in Sydney happens outside.

One of the reasons I'd resisted Syd in the past is because it's the unholy nest that spawned rim tucker: jabberwocky food, that ghastly excuse for stream-of-consciousness cooking and *objet trouvé* dinners that have infested London with their liver and mango in pineapple fish broth, and crouching tiger prawn, hidden dragon fruit. Like the Spanish dinner inquisition, I was really looking forward to putting this heresy to the auto-da-fé, after telling it what I thought about it: 'Barbie this, heathen!'

But again, pathetically like Oliver, what I actually said was: 'More, please.' This is as good a city to eat in as anywhere on earth. The line between triumph and disaster is very fine. And what is disastrous in London is triumphant in Syd. The new Australian cooking is firstly based on incredible raw ingredients, particularly fruit and fish. We spent an early morning in the vast Sydney fish market. It was like a *Star Wars* think-tank. What on earth are those? And that? And, my God, which way up does that swim? Whereas I'm wary about ordering fish in London, there it's the safest bet on the menu; morgue-slab fresh and prepared with care. And while, in London, the jabberwocky flavours come as a screaming Babel, over there they are as clean, clear and complementary as a string quartet. And it's not just grand restaurant food. We ate marvellous fish and chips on the beach at Manly. The cafés on Bondi do huge, all-day English fried breakfasts and milkshakes served in their frosted metal mixers.

Here, briefly, is a cut-out-and-keep list of places you must go, if you are passing (although the last person who was just passing was Scott of the Antarctic). There are Pier and Catalina on Rose Bay, both with wonderful views of the harbour and excellent fish; Bel Mondo, where we ate amazing abalone; Salt, a truly world-class restaurant; Otto's, a bubbling, trendy billabong, where the local waiters charmingly pretend to be Italian ('Bella signora, ciao mate'); the extraordinarily *soigné* Tetsuya's, which is booked up two months in advance, where there's no menu but plenty of bill, where dinner is a performance that can take four hours, and which serves a unique and sometimes combative Japanese take on haute cuisine; and Yoshii, the best sushi restaurant I've eaten in for a long time, where we had an inspired steamed egg yolk, cooked in its shell, with fish broth and Tasmanian sea urchin.

Well, on our return to the dank old widow that is London, you can imagine that the Blonde and I felt like the jilted pair of a *ménage à trois*, and I said: 'Why don't we give rainy rim tucker one more go? Maybe, like holding a shell to your ear, there will be the echo of Syd.'

I should have known better. The place we chose is a local restaurant, but even living next door wouldn't be reason enough to eat here. Inside, it's a fug of frying oil and do-it-yourself decoration. I asked for a crab and ginger ravioli. As Julia Roberts once memorably put it, 'Mistake. Big mistake. Huge mistake.' What arrived was a package the size and texture of a sodden Cornish pasty that tasted like minke-whale haemorrhoids. Don't ask how I know. And it was all down under from there. I avoided the rare kangaroo fillet. There's nothing rare about kangaroos, and I never saw one on an Australian menu – it would be like eating vermin roadkill. Instead, I had the red-throated emperor with baby fennel. The emperor must have had a red throat because he wasn't very well, and the baby fennel was like trying to chew through the Jolly Green Giant's umbilical cord.

Pudding was mango and coconut black sticky-rice spring roll. The rice was raw, like attempting to chew the bottom of a chocolate goldfish bowl. Altogether, a hopelessly shoddy, misbegotten waste of unloved ingredients. And, more infuriatingly, my appetite. The memory of what this could be made it that much worse.

What brought home to me how far from its roots this restaurant really was were the pair of little Battersea trollops on the next table, who both had streaming colds and did competitive sneezing – mostly into their mobile phones, so that the rest of the pleurisy ward could join in. As I said, the difference between triumph and disaster is very fine. And despite what Mr Kipling says, a critic shouldn't treat them just the same.

I think the reason that jabberwocky food rarely works here is not just the second-rate frozen and air-freighted ingredients; it has to do with a style and philosophy of cooking. European food is made with big, warm, round tastes and textures. It's expansive and grandly harmonious. Southern Hemisphere food is neat and precise and stridently atonal. When cooks in the north try to imitate it, what they get is fuzzy, unfocused, ham-fisted and cacophonous.

Despite all that, it's nice-ish to be back. No worries, mate.

January 2001

Farewell to Australia

For more than a decade, A. A. Gill wrote a monthly column for Australian Gourmet Traveller *magazine, usually filing his copy at night, over the phone, from half a world away. Several of those pieces are included in this book. This was his final article for them, published after his death.*

I should be there, down there with you. I should be writing this on my annual sojourn to Australia, down to file your Christmas copy, sitting on a veranda smelling eucalyptus, listening to parrots and feeling that light, cocky, amused, insouciant naughtiness which is Australia's natural aftershave. By rights I should be checking my wardrobe, thinking about getting a lift to Vanya Cullen's winery for a singular, long alfresco lunch among the grapes and the bees.

Or perhaps it's early and I can go to the beach caff, which always has an enormous number of brown legs in it, and then walk the dunes with Jock Zonfrillo. He'll tug at succulent twigs, mentioning that they are a bit like Vegemite with a hint of urine, and were used by indigenous people to soothe swollen knees and to encourage the annual spawning of dabs. Jock owes me a boomerang.

Or maybe I've stopped in Sydney, and I'm going to meet my editors Anthea and Pat for lunch in a new but not trendy place that's really interesting because of the quality of its sumac, or the phenomenal thing that it does with injera.

But I'm not there because I'm here, in Cawdor, on the coast of Scotland on the edge of the peaty-brown Findhorn River. The heather is taupe-coloured, the rowan are red, like blood-splatters against leaves of tannin-yellow. It all smells of corruption here, tilth and fungus. It's not a bad place. It's a place I love as dearly as I can love the blood-bitter peat, the mushrooms and mud and the bath salts of wet dog.

I'm here because I can't be there because I can barely be anywhere. I have, late in life, unexpectedly become a destination. This is a conversation I might've had sitting down with Pat and Anthea in the smart but not hipster place that has the killer ramen: I have cancer.

There are other ways of putting this. You can cough gently and say, 'My health isn't what it was. I've got a touch of the euphemisms.' But let's be clear: it's cancer, not coyness. And quite a lot of cancer. Not a misshapen canapé. Not a dusting or a dash, not a rumour. I'm a patchwork quilt, a smorgasbord, a litany of malformed cells. A destination for the halt, the gimpy, the wall-eyed malcontents of cell life.

It happens. It happens to half of us. And it happened to me. So I'm here, not there.

One of the consequences of the cancer is cancer treatment, which is far more shouty and intrusive, awkward, rude and bombastic than the stuff itself. Chemotherapy bellows like a sergeant-major, and it's no good whining that you're not feeling so good – could he keep his voice down? It howls. Chemotherapy likes to unleash hell, loves the smell of carcinogens in the morning.

So I can't travel. I'm banned and barred, forbidden from all mass-transit – buses, planes, trains, boats. So I can't see you. I've spent the last decade writing to you once a month about the places I have been and the stuff I have seen and the prophetic business of going; as for most Australians, travel has always been a practice – something that we do, that I did. Now it's not.

Now travel is passive. I wait. I am the sought-out object of scrutiny. I am the day trip, the destination. And I'm not entirely sure where that leaves a travel writer. Could I sit on a bench and wait for a story, a garrulous journeyer who will tell me a tale? Should I be the Diogenes of trippers, the view from the bottom of the barrel?

That is not so far from the truth, actually. I recline for hours, Sergeant Chemo yelling imperatives into my veins, and the world slips back to see me. Places, people, smells, life becomes vivid, and I realise I can make quite detailed and complicated journeys in my head back to places I haven't considered for years.

I just walked down the main street of Ammassalik, a small fishing town on the east coast of Greenland. I haven't been there for over a decade. There's a dog on a chain eating a seal head; the pale locals grin. My head is full of Pokemons and the vivid reality of everywhere I've been.

It's a surprisingly moving and proud realisation that, just when I could do with it most, the world has decided that now is a good time to return the visit. I always said, 'If you're ever in the neighbourhood, pop round. Don't be strangers,' and here it is. Still, I'm not sure where that leaves the travel writer.

I know what Pat and Anthea would've wanted for this issue. Christmas around the world, something warm, sensual, spicy.

There has been one particular dish in my Christmas, one thing we always have. I have to make it. It isn't cultural or regional; it's personal. It's for my daughter. Flora insists on it. For her it is the seal on the year, the promise of the next.

I boil a ham, and with the stock I make potato soup with earthy, farinaceous potatoes, some bland onions, a little sweet carrot, bay, thyme, nutmeg. And then I take three French goose livers and sauté them in redcurrants and port, and press them into a terrine that sits in a ceramic sarcophagus for two days. On Boxing Day the soup is warmed, the foie is carefully sliced, and great unctuous, generous marbled slabs are leeched into the soup, like calving meatbergs.

The warmth and the honest fundamentals of the potato and the ham lap around the cold, recherché and smoothly elitist liver, which softens and becomes garrulous. It is the mouthful of the propitiousness of the year, and hope for the new. And it's a bit like visiting Australia.

I've been thinking a great deal about food and dishes and the movement of appetite and hunger. And that food in its particular and emotional value is primarily there for the transmission of memory and remembrance, the déjà vu of our mouths. Only food does this. All appetite is a remembrance.

I might write about that.

December 2016

Credits

Highlands	*The Sunday Times*
Hyde Park	*The Sunday Times*
The Guinea Pig Club	*The Sunday Times*
St Paul's Cathedral	*The Sunday Times*
Fishing	*The Sunday Times*
Shelter	*The Sunday Times*
Frieze Art Fair	*Vanity Fair*
Goodwood	*Vanity Fair*
The Shipping Forecast	*Australian Gourmet Traveller*
Humberside	*The Sunday Times*
Bethlehem	*The Sunday Times*
St Tropez	*The Sunday Times*
Mykonos	*The Sunday Times*
Moscow	*The Sunday Times*
Sicilian Mummies	*National Geographic*
Puglia	*The Sunday Times*
Canal du Midi	*The Sunday Times*
Beirut	*Australian Gourmet Traveller*
Syrian Refugees	*The Sunday Times*
Ethiopia	*The Sunday Times*
Japan	*The Sunday Times*
Islamabad	*GQ*
Kalahari Bushmen	*The Sunday Times*
Vietnam	*The Sunday Times*
Las Vegas	*Vanity Fair*
Sudan	*The Sunday Times*
Gold Mine	*The Sunday Times*
Tasmania	*The Sunday Times*
Blindness in Africa	*The Sunday Times*

Madagascar	*The Sunday Times*
Return to Haiti	*The Sunday Times*
Creation Museum	*Vanity Fair*
Mozambique	*The Sunday Times*
Auckland	*Australian Gourmet Traveller*
The Rohingya	*The Sunday Times*
Mexico	*The Sunday Times*
Food in England	*The Sunday Times*
Motorways	*The Sunday Times*
Country Hotel	*The Sunday Times*
Meat	*The Sunday Times*
Smithfield	*The Sunday Times*
Chinatown	*The Sunday Times*
Barbecues	*Australian Gourmet Traveller*
Eurostar	*The Sunday Times*
Paris	*Australian Gourmet Traveller*
Benidorm	*The Sunday Times*
El Bulli	*The Sunday Times*
Bologna	*The Sunday Times*
Sicily	*The Sunday Times*
Stockholm	*Australian Gourmet Traveller*
Budapest	*The Sunday Times*
Polish Food	*The Sunday Times*
Jordan	*Australian Gourmet Traveller*
Algiers	*The Sunday Times*
Marrakesh	*The Sunday Times*
Cape Town	*The Sunday Times*
Desert	*The Sunday Times*
Hot Dogs	*The Sunday Times*
Kuala Lumpur	*Australian Gourmet Traveller*
Bombay	*Australian Gourmet Traveller*
Hong Kong	*The Sunday Times*
Sydney	*The Sunday Times*
Farewell to Australia	*Australian Gourmet Traveller*